HINE SIGHT

BLACKS IN THE DIASPORA

Darlene Clark Hine
John McCluskey, Jr.
David Barry Gaspar

General Editors

HINE SIGHT

BLACK WOMEN AND THE RE-CONSTRUCTION OF AMERICAN HISTORY

DARLENE CLARK HINE

Foreword by John Hope Franklin

INDIANA UNIVERSITY PRESS
Bloomington & Indianapolis

Originally published 1994 by Carlson Publishing

The paper used in this publication meets the minimum
requirements of American National Standard for Information
Sciences—Permanence of Paper for Printed Library Materials,
ANSI Z39.48-1984.

Manufactured in the United States of America

Library of Congress Cataloging-in-Publication Data

Hine, Darlene Clark.
    Hine sight : Black women and the re-construction of American history /
Darlene Clark Hine ; foreword by John Hope Franklin.
        p.   cm. — (Blacks in the diaspora)
    Originally published: Brooklyn, N.Y. : Carlson Pub., 1994.
    Includes bibliographical references and index.
    ISBN 0-253-21124-7 (alk. paper)
    1. Afro-American women—History. 2. Afro-Americans—Study and
teaching. 3. Afro-Americans—Historiography. I. Title. II. Series.
E185.86.H67   1997
305.48'896073—dc21   96-37996

1 2 3 4 5 02 01 00 99 98 97

To

Shirley Herd and Virtea Downey

for helping me to see.

Contents

Foreword by John Hope Franklin ix
Preface xi
Acknowledgments xv
Introduction xvii

PART **1**

Lifting the Veil, Shattering the Silence: Black Women's History in Slavery and Freedom 3
Female Slave Resistance: The Economics of Sex 27
Rape and the Inner Lives of Black Women: Thoughts on the Culture of Dissemblance 37
Black Women's History, White Women's History: The Juncture of Race and Class 49

PART **2**

Black Women in the Middle West: The Michigan Experience 59
Black Migration to the Urban Midwest: The Gender Dimension, 1915-1945 87
"We Specialize in the Wholly Impossible": The Philanthropic Work of Black Women 109
The Housewives' League of Detroit: Black Women and Economic Nationalism 129

PART **3**

Co-Laborers in the Work of the Lord: Nineteenth-Century Black Women Physicians 147
"They Shall Mount Up with Wings as Eagles": Historical Images of Black Nurses, 1890-1950 163
Mabel K. Staupers and the Integration of Black Nurses into the Armed Forces during World War II 183

PART **4**

Carter G. Woodson: White Philanthropy and Negro Historiography 203
Black Studies: An Overview for the Ford Foundation 223
The Black Studies Movement: Afrocentric-Traditionalist-Feminist Paradigms for the Next Stage 235

A STATEMENT

Stop the Global Holocaust 249

Notes 251
Index 281

Foreword

The history of African-American women has become an important topic in the intellectual life of this country in the last fifteen years, and Darlene Clark Hine has been one of those most responsible for bringing that subject to its current level of importance. Her admission in the introductory essay in this work that she did not begin to think seriously about women's history until 1980 is a reminder of how relatively new the field is. Already, by that time, I was the subject of critical comments by women who insisted that I gave inadequate attention to women in my general history of African-Americans. As I made every effort to address the alleged imbalance, it is somewhat comforting to realize that even as I was struggling to overcome my own deficiencies, one of today's premier historians of African-American women was just beginning her own very significant work in the field!

While Darlene Clark Hine did not turn her attention to African-American women's history until 1980, her earlier prodigious labors did much to prepare her for the work in which she has been engaged for the past decade and a half. Her experiences both as a student and observer during the turbulent seventies and her work on the white primary in Texas provided knowledge, experience, and insight that would assist her in understanding the problems she was about to explore. Furthermore, she was most certainly influenced by the burgeoning studies in women's history, especially since many of the courses, monographs, and conferences in the field gave little or no attention to the existence of African-American women. Meanwhile, she was doubt-less impressed by pioneer works in African-American women's history in the seventies by Gerda Lerner, Rosalyn Terborg-Penn, and Sharon Harley. The energy and gusto that Hine brought to the subject in 1980 give one the impression that the momentum was already build-ing up to the point that when she finally began to pursue the subject, she "hit the ground running."

Hine's background and her earlier work made her quite aware of the fact that there was more than women's history out there. That awareness would save her from the myopic and self-serving approaches that characterized some of the earlier works in women's history. In-deed, the context of the larger picture would give her own work the texture, substance, and significance that one-dimensional works in this or any other field can never have. Thus, the very conception as well as the execution of works like those on African-American women in Indiana and more especially the monumental *Black Women in America: An Historical Encyclopedia* reflect the breadth and depth of her under-standing of the subject with which she is dealing.

The fourteen essays in this volume, written over the past fourteen years, are representative of the conceptual framework in which Hine works, as well as the broad canvas on which she paints the exciting picture of African-American women's history. They are both diverse and as full of insights as her ample talents allow. Nowhere does her understanding of the larger picture become so apparent as in the fascinating and important essay on Carter G. Woodson's relations with white philanthropists. For the uninitiated these essays provide a welcome introduction to the subject of African-American women's history. To those with some prior knowledge of the subject they are a validation of the viability of the field and an affirmation of Darlene Clark Hine's high standing in the historical profession.

John Hope Franklin
James B. Duke Professor Emeritus of History
Duke University

Preface

The impetus for publishing a selection of my essays on Black women's history grew out of several conversations I had with historian David Barry Gaspar of Duke University during fall 1993. Earlier conversations with historian Elsa Barkley Brown of the University of Michigan in 1989 had planted the idea. Half the essays included were written since our conversation. I am grateful to Barry not only for encouraging me to do this project but also for reading all of the essays and offering perceptive comments about the theoretical and social policy implications of my work.

Two special friends read each essay and offered insightful comments: Anne Boylan of the University of Delaware suggested an organizational structure around themes rather than chronology and Susan Reverby of Wellesley College identified a dozen themes that run through the essays and with her usual grace and elegant commitment helped me to situate my work within the context of feminist scholarship and American social history. My friend William C. Hine of South Carolina State University made invaluable comments and suggestions on the introduction and several of the essays. Betty Brandon and Howard Mahan of the University of South Alabama offered helpful advice and sustaining friendship throughout the publishing process. James D. Anderson of the University of Illinois at Urbana, Jimmie L. Franklin of Vanderbilt University and Arvarh Strickland of the University of Missouri deserve special praise for sharing their uncommon wisdom and wit through the past two decades. I have eagerly awaited this moment to acknowledge all of their invaluable intellectual assistance, moral support, and generosity of spirit.

Community is essential to survival and success in the academy. Once fortified with a strong community of friends, colleagues, and family, seemingly impossible things are more easily accomplished and with much greater pleasure. Four individuals who had played major roles in the production of the *Black Women in America: An Historical Encyclopedia* again aided in the execution of this volume. With unfailing good cheer and support my talented and wise assistant Linda Werbish typed the entire manuscript, including several drafts of the introduction. She provided splendid editing suggestions and (along with Peggy Jeffrey) bolstered my spirits when my enthusiasm and energy waned. Ralph Carlson, as any publisher should, urged the project along. He made the important recommendation that I include the policy essays in the fourth part, and he applauded the inclusion of the stop the violence statement I wrote when my teenage nephews Jammie and Charles Waters were shot and had to come live with me. I am forever indebted to Mary Wyer for her astute and brilliant editing of the entire manuscript. And to Ann Harakawa who designed the book and cover I offer heartfelt thanks for her talent and inspiration.

Members of my special community of dear friends and close colleagues who read essays, engaged with me in endless discussions concerning, among other things, the title, and made insightful comments on individual essays and/or the introduction include Joe Trotter of Carnegie-Mellon University, Linda Reed of University of Houston, David Bailey, Gordon Stewart and Wilma King of Michigan State University, Aldon D. Morris of Northwestern University, Earl Lewis and Robin D. G. Kelley of the University of Michigan, John Bracey, Jr., of University of Massachusetts at Amherst, Richard Blackett of Indiana University, Robert L. Harris of Cornell University, Kenneth Hamilton of Southern Methodist University, Albert Broussard of Texas A&M University, and Joan Catapano of Indiana University Press. A special thanks is due to Michigan State University colleague William B. Hixson who has read and critiqued virtually everything I have written since I joined the history department and to colleague Justin Kesenbaum for his photographic talents.

William C. Hine has been especially supportive for the past twenty-five years. Most of the essays indicate his contribution to my evolution as a historian. I also would like to thank the other members of the Hine clan, John (now deceased), Jeanne, Carol, Tom, and Peter and Diane, and Richard (Ace) Taylor of the Pennsylvania State University for their assistance, caring, and encouragement.

Moreover, I have been extremely fortunate to have a cadre of outstanding graduate students and research assistants. I offer heartfelt appreciation to Earnestine Jenkins, Pamela Smoot, Jacqueline McLeod, Felix Armfield, Eleanor Shelton, John Reid, Carmen Harris, Heran Sereke Brhan, Mary Hess, Randal Jelks, LaTrese Adkins, Kenneth Marshall, and Hilary Jones.

I am grateful to all of the editors of the anthologies in which my essays appeared. I thank them for including my work, and for the helpful comments and critiques that strengthened the essays: Filomina Chioma Steady, Anne Hudson Jones, Kathleen McCarthy, Ruth Abrams, Sandra Harding, Nancy Hewitt, Suzanne Lebsock, Betty Brandon, Elizabeth Fox-Genovese, Virginia Bernhardt, Theda Perdue, Joe Trotter, August Meier, and John Hope Franklin.

As always my family remains my anchor and my salvation. No acknowledgement of my debt to my community would be complete without words of tribute and praise to the women and men who brought me over: Grandmother Fannie Venerable Thompson; Aunts Maplean King, Fannie Perry, Cherrie Mae Foster, and Clotine Mason; Uncles Robert L. Thompson, Herbert King, Dennis Perry of Northwestern University Medical School, John Mason, Robert Foster, Don L. Thompson, and Levester Thompson; Sisters Barbara Ann Clark and Alma Jean Mitchell, and brother-in-law Sylvester Clark, Jr. My precious daughter Robbie Davine makes it all worthwhile.

The questions raised and issues addressed in the scholarship and conversations of a vital and vibrant community of Black women intellectuals enrich my own thinking in immeasurable ways. I owe a great debt to the spoken words and writings of Nellie McKay, Mary F. Berry, Delores Aldridge, Elsa Barkley Brown, Evelyn Brooks Higginbotham, Nell Irvin Painter, Barbara J. Fields, Karen Fields, Paula Giddings, Val Littlefield, Thavolia Glymph, Tera Hunter,

Deborah Gray White, Wanda Hendricks, Gwendolyn Keita Robinson, Robin Kilson, Genna Rae McNeil, Evelynn Hammonds, Jacqueline Rouse, Janet Sims-Wood, Janice Sumler-Edmond, Sylvia Jacobs, Stephanie Shaw, Juliet E. K. Walker, Tiffany Patterson, Lillian Williams, June Patton, Elizabeth Clark-Lewis, Margaret Wilkerson, and Vanessa Northington Gamble. The pioneering works of Sharon Harley, Rosalyn Terborg-Penn, and of Gerda Lerner launched the academic study of Black women and were critical to my intellectual development. I would like to take this opportunity to thank all the members and officers of the Association of Black Women Historians and the Association for the Study of Afro-American Life and History for making a space for Black women's history to flourish. I thank two of our intellectual foremothers Helen Edmonds and Dorothy Porter Wesley, and the great John Hope Franklin, Benjamin Quarles, and the late Nathan Huggins for showing so many of us how to be scholars.

Finally, I am grateful to the Department of History and to Michigan State University for the generous resources made available to me through the John A. Hannah Distinguished Professorship.

Acknowledgments

The essays in this collection, all revised, some considerably more so than others, were originally published as:

"Lifting the Veil, Shattering the Silence: Black Women's History in Slavery and Freedom," in *The State of Afro-American History: Past, Present, and Future*, ed. Darlene Clark Hine (Baton Rouge: Louisiana State University Press, 1986), 224-49.

"Female Slave Resistance: The Economics of Sex," in *Western Journal of Black Studies* 3 (Summer 1979), 123-27; with Kate Wittenstein, reprinted in *The Black Woman Cross-Culturally*, ed. Filomina Steady (Boston: Schenkman, 1981).

"Rape and the Inner Lives of Black Women in the Middle West: Thoughts on the Culture of Dissemblance," in *Unequal Sisters*, ed. Ellen Carol DuBois and Vicki L. Ruiz (New York and London: Routledge, 1990), 292-97. Reprinted from *Signs* 14 (Summer 1989).

"Black Women's History, White Women's History: The Juncture of Race and Class," *Journal of Women's History* 4, No. 2 (Fall 1992), 125-33.

"Black Women in the Middle West: The Michigan Experience," 1988 Burton Lecture, Michigan Historical Society, Ann Arbor, MI. Published as a monograph by the Historical Society of Michigan, 1990.

"Black Migration to the Urban Midwest: The Gender Dimension, 1915-1945," in *The Great Migration in Historical Perspectives*, ed. Joe W. Trotter (Bloomington: Indiana University Press, 1991), 127-46.

" 'We Specialize in the Wholly Impossible': The Philanthropic Work of Black Women," in *Lady Bountiful Revisited: Women, Philanthropy, and Power*, ed. Kathleen D. McCarthy (New Brunswick, N.J.: Rutgers University Press, 1990), 70-93.

"The Housewives' League of Detroit: Black Women and Economic Nationalism," in *Visible Women: New Essays on American Activism*, ed. Nancy Hewitt and Suzanne Lebsock (Urbana: University of Illinois Press, 1993), 223-41.

"Co-Laborers in the Work of the Lord: Nineteenth-Century Black Women Physicians," in *"Send Us a Lady Physician": Women Doctors in America, 1835-1930*, ed. Ruth G. Abrams (New York: W. W. Norton, 1985). Reprinted in *The "Racial" Economy of Science: Toward a Democratic Future*, ed. Sandra Harding (Bloomington: Indiana University Press, 1993), 210-27.

" 'They Shall Mount Up with Wings as Eagles': Historical Images of Black Nurses, 1890-1950," in *Images of Nurses: Perspectives from History, Art, and Literature*, ed. Anne Hudson Jones (Philadelphia: University of Pennsylvania Press, 1988), 177-96.

"Mabel Keaton Staupers: The Integration of Black Nurses into the Armed Forces, World War II," in *Black Leaders of the Twentieth Century*, ed. John Hope Franklin and August Meier (Urbana: University of Illinois Press, 1982), 241-57; reprinted in *Women and Health in America: Historical Readings*, ed. Judith Leavitt (Madison: University of Wisconsin Press, 1984), 241-57. This essay became the basis for Chapter 8 in my *Black Women in White: Racial Conflict and Cooperation in the Nursing Profession, 1890-1950* (Bloomington: Indiana University Press, 1989).

"Carter G. Woodson, White Philanthropy and the Rise of Negro Historiography," *The History Teacher* 19 (Spring 1986), 406-25.

"Black Studies: An Overview," in *Three Essays: Black Studies in the United States* (New York: Ford Foundation, 1987), 15-25.

"The Black Studies Movement: Afrocentric-Traditionalist-Feminist Paradigms for the Next Stage," *The Black Scholar* 22, No. 3 (Summer 1992), 11-18.

"Stop the Global Holocaust," *Chicago Sun-Times* (9 November 1992), 28.

Introduction

These fourteen essays, published over the course of fourteen years, reflect the evolution of my thinking about Black women: as historical subjects and as members of the academic community. When I decided to become a historian, the last group I intended to study was Black women. During the 1960s, Black history included race but not gender. By the time *Black Women in America: An Historical Encyclopedia* was published, almost thirty years later, I had reached a critical juncture in my intellectual migration. For almost two decades I traveled along two winding paths, Black history and women's history, searching for the intersections where race and gender met, in order to construct a history of Black women. Today I stand at crossroads, looking back at choices made, companions encountered, and profitable detours taken.

This introductory essay charts the progression of my modest attempts to contribute to the engendering and transforming of African American history. The process of reflecting on the nature of this intellectual journey is yet another step in an on-going effort to make American history more inclusive. In contemplating my future of studying the past, there are two inviting possibilities. Do I proceed with as yet unasked questions in Black women's history or do I return to the project of writing on the history of Black Americans in the learned professions, a project launched over a decade ago? Whatever my decision, in Hine sight one thing is certain. Unlike my first book *Black Victory: The Rise and Fall of the White Primary in Texas* (1979), I will never again write a history that excludes or marginalizes Black women or fails to consider their work as makers of community. The essays that form this volume are the results of the building, excavating, re-routing, and boundary-crossing essential to centering Black women in American history. Yet, the path I took did not necessarily lead to my current position.

I elected to become a historian during my junior year of undergraduate study at Roosevelt University in Chicago. By 1965 Congress had enacted the Voting Rights Act, signalling the successful conclusion of an important phase of the Civil Rights Movement. The increase in the number of Black elected officials gave every indication that the rifts between Black and white Americans would soon close. But who could have predicted the election of Richard Nixon, the resurgence of white opposition to civil rights, and the white backlash against Black advancement?

Not unlike many of the current generation of Black scholars, during my undergraduate years I joined Black students in demands for more Black professors and for a transformed curriculum that incorporated Black history. To its credit Roosevelt University had a number of Black professors on its faculty and a vocal cadre of graduate students. I enrolled in courses taught by historian Hollis Lynch and by linguist Lorenzo Dow Turner, and I attended the lectures of political scientist Charles H. Hamilton, and the sociologist St. Clair Drake, all of whom expanded my intellectual horizons. As an undergraduate I was impressed and moved by the guest lectures of John Hope Franklin, William Appleman Williams, and Lerone Bennett about the lives and experiences of marginalized and obscured Americans. It was within this fertile environment that I came to appreciate the importance of knowing history.

By the late 1960s I was very much caught up in the Black Arts and Consciousness, and Black Power movements, and was acutely aware that the gap between Black and white Americans seemed to be growing. The decision to become a historian was driven not only by a desire to understand the origins of racism but also by a growing curiosity about the causes of white fear and Black rage. The past can never be recovered in all its vastness, but I came to recognize that historians determine what and whom the larger society would remember, celebrate, and deem important. Even as a would-be historian I was fascinated by the acquisition of power and it appeared that historians possessed inordinate intellectual power. Inasmuch as I could not fully grasp why Black and white Americans were at such deadly odds, I decided to make it my life's work to try to figure out how to improve race relations. Precisely how or why I became convinced that the work of historians could provide answers to these troubling concerns now eludes me.

In hindsight, I am struck by how consumed I was with questions of race and race relations throughout both my undergraduate career at Roosevelt University and my subsequent graduate career at Kent State University where I studied with the historian August Meier. In fact, questions of race dominated virtually all academic conversations. Questions of sex and class were rarely if ever articulated. I distinctly remember engaging in misguided discussions about the absence of a class structure within Black America. There were denunciations of the Black bourgeoisie, deemed to be hopelessly irrelevant. There were no conversations about Black women. They were neither objects nor subjects of history. They seemed important only in conjunction with a man, an organization, or an institution. The historian Evelyn Brooks Higginbotham persuasively argues that the metalanguage of race silences all other discourses.[1] This was certainly true of my intellectual experience in the late 1960s.

Still, I wanted to do history. I explained to my skeptical family that history was indeed a way to earn a living while making a contribution to the ongoing Black Struggle against racism. My parents (Levester and Lottie Mae Clark) humored me, smiled, looked dismayed and probably wondered if I had just decided to stay in school because I enjoyed all the "talking that went on there." Regardless of whether they accepted my explanations, I had convinced myself that as soon as the pages of history contained accurate information about Black Americans then it would be a simple matter to educate people sufficiently so that racial harmony and social justice would prevail. Was I naive?

By the time I arrived at Kent State University in 1968, my resolve to unleash the power of history had been challenged by the riots that affected large sections of the West side of Chicago after Martin Luther King, Jr., was assassinated. The brutality of the Chicago police against the anti-war demonstrators during the Democratic National Convention in August disconcerted me. The escalation of attacks against the Chicago Black Panther Party and the murder of Fred Hampton and Mark Clark (no relation) gave me further pause. Indeed, was the study of the past an effective way to understand the present? Could history actually provide a useful foundation for progressive public policy in the future? And then in 1970, the May 4th killings of Kent State University students by the Ohio National Guardsmen happened. More than any other events, the deaths at Kent State and the killings of students at Jackson State dislodged race as my signal theoretical framework. What was wrong in American society went beyond race, and understanding these problems would require the development of a complex of analytical categories and constructs.

Indeed, the extraordinary events of the late 1960s and early 1970s were an awakening that demonstrated that not only were Black Americans generally omitted from history surveys but also the majority of Americans were not included. When I referred to "Blacks," it was in the generic sense of the term, for I still had no consciousness of Black women. Women were outside of history. To this day, I must confess that I remain perplexed as to how I could have studied American history for so long and with such feverish intensity without being aware of the absence of Black women. Hindsight, the looking back on events and assigning new meaning, is part of the historian's job. The essays in *Hine Sight,* however should force us to look ahead and think more critically about the centrality of Black women to the history of America.

In 1980 I woke up. To be sure, I had begun thinking about Black women in the late 1970s and even published an essay on their experiences under slavery. But Shirley Herd most deserves the credit for ringing the bell that fully awakened my interest and motivated me, waking a hidden need to become more committed. The feminism of the 1970s had not reached me as I was so completely absorbed in reading and writing Black history. Since 1980, however, and the fateful day that an Indianapolis public school teacher named Shirley Herd called and insisted that I write a history of Black women in Indiana, I have published dozens of articles and two monographs on Black women. Moreover, I have helped to edit diverse reference materials including resource guides, anthologies, encyclopedias, and a sixteen volume series on Black Women in United States History with Carlson Publishing. Within this body of work I, as well as other scholars, have analyzed Black women's resistance to slavery, probed the motivations behind their migrations after emancipation, recorded their contributions as institution and community builders, and explored their struggles to gain membership in the medical and nursing professions. I also helped to develop a project to create a Black women's history archive. Through it all I have maintained a specific regional focus, paying particular attention to the history of Black women in the Middle West. It is not only possible but also essential to use both traditional and nontraditional historical methodologies in the social constructions of race, gender, class, sex, age, and region and in defining their interconnections as analytic categories to arrive at an understanding of the meanings of Black women's lives and experiences within the broader context of American history.

Black women's history compels the individual to come to grips more completely with all of the components of identity. Through the study of Black women it becomes increasingly obvious how historians shape, make, or construct history, and why we omit, ignore, and sometimes distort the lives of people on the margins. Taking cues from the life and work of Carter G. Woodson, the father of Black History (my essay on him is in Part 4 of this collection), who tried to fit Black people into American history, my mission concerns the transformation of American history. At the very least an attempt should be made to construct a history that is accurate and representative of the majority of all Americans.

Today, there are impressive shifts underway in American history, especially in the wake of the triumphs of the new social history, and the growth and maturation of Black history and women's history. This is an opportune moment to collect and assess an assortment of previously published essays on the subject. Publishing an accessible collection of these Black women's history essays, most frequently written at the invitation of editors of various women's history anthologies, and preparing this introduction affords me a chance to reiterate how important it is to integrate questions of gender, race, sexuality, and class into all of our historical works. Asking the right questions is often more important and revealing than the answers we discover.

The challenge of selecting which essays to include in this volume provided ample opportunity to ponder some of the important themes that flow through Black women's history. That history has moved toward an increasingly complex theoretical framework on which to organize new knowledge. One of the central projects of this work has been the illumination of the ways in which Black women have worked to "make community." "Making community" means the processes of creating religious, educational, health-care, philanthropic, political, and familial institutions and professional organizations that enabled our people to survive. In the early eighteenth and nineteenth centuries, Black women "made community" through the building and shaping of slave culture. Later the process of "making community" was repeated in post-emancipation agricultural areas and then in urban industrial societies. Black women created essential new communities and erected vast female networks during the transitions from slavery to freedom, and from farm to city. It was through "making community" that Black women were able to redefine themselves, project sexual respectability, reshape morality, and define a new aesthetic.

In sum, Black women came to subjecthood and acquired agency through the creation of community. Although the ideologies of self-help and racial solidarity have long been associated with great men, for example, Booker T. Washington and Marcus Garvey, it is clear that the "race women" in local Black communities were even more critical to the actual conceptualization and implementation of social welfare programs, the nurturance of oppositional consciousness, and the support of essential institutions. Their instrumental contributions in struggles against racism and sexism have only recently attracted the sustained historical attention they deserve.

The subtitle *Black Women and the Re-Construction of American History*, in its dramatic claim of entitlement, suggests the deplorable and exclusionary nature of most written histories of our country's past. To promote more discussion about and movement toward the development of a new, inclusive, and nuanced construction of America's past is one of the motivations for this volume. But as the subtitle implies, the relationship between Black women's history and this larger project is necessarily transformative. A re-construction of American history that does not challenge our assumptions—about the people, power, places, and politics of importance—has failed. If all previously excluded and marginalized groups are to find space on history's center stage, until recently a small proscenium occupied by privileged white men, then our intellectual repertoire must grow. Black women's history by its very nature seeks to empower and make visible the lives and deeds of ordinary folk. On the one hand, the intent is to enable every Black woman in America to view herself as a worthy historical agent and subject. On the other hand, the histories of Black women are centered in, and center, the at once common and uncommon in American life. These histories, and those of all ignored and unknown people and groups, dramatically advance our understanding of the past and of the nature and complexity of American society.

My entry into Black women's history was serendipitous. In the preface to *Black Women in America: An Historical Encyclopedia*, I recount the story of exactly how Shirley Herd, who (in addition to teaching in the local school system was also president of the Indianapolis chapter of the National Council of Negro Women) successfully provoked me into changing my research and writing focus. Although I dedicate this volume to her and to her best friend, fellow club woman, and retired primary school teacher, Virtea Downey, I still blush at the irony of how I went to graduate school to become a historian in order to contribute to the Black Struggle for social justice and yet met her request to write a history of Black women in Indiana with condescension. I had never even thought about Black women as historical subjects with their own relations to a state's history, and I thought her invitation and phone call extraordinarily intrusive. Only later did I concede how straightforward and reasonable had been her request to redress a historical omission. Black women were conspicuous by their absence. None of the social studies texts or state histories that Herd and Downey had used to teach their students made mention of the contributions of Black women. Since historians had left them out, she reasoned, only a "real" historian could put them in, and since I was the only tenured Black woman historian in the state of Indiana at that time, the task was mine.

Herd rejected my reservations and completely ignored my admonitions that she could not call up a historian and order a book the way you drive up to Wendy's and order a hamburger. In spite of my assertions of ignorance about the history of Black women in Indiana and my confession of having never studied the subject in any history course, or examined any manuscript sources pertaining to their lives, Herd persevered. Black women, as historical subjects and agents, were as invisible to me as they had been to school textbook writers.

A less determined Black woman would have relented, but not Shirley Herd. Undaunted by my response, she demanded, thankfully without perfect symmetry, that I connect my biology and autobiography, my race and gender, my being a Black woman, to my skill as a historian, and write for her and for the local chapter members of the National Council a history of Black women in Indiana. In the face of such determination I relented and wrote the book as requested, *When the Truth Is Told: Black Women's Culture and Community in Indiana, 1875-1950* (1981). In the process, I was both humbled and astounded by the array of rich primary source materials Herd, Downey, and the other club women had spent two years collecting. There were diaries, club notes, church souvenir booklets, photographs, club minutes, birth, death, and marriage certificates, letters, and hand written county and local histories. Collectively this material revealed a universe I never knew existed in spite of having lived with Black women all of my life . . . and being one myself. Or perhaps more accurately, I knew a universe of Black women existed. I simply had not envisioned its historic meaning.

As I reviewed and organized the primary source materials the club women had so painstakingly collected, I experienced the beginning of my transformation into a historian of Black women, a true historian of the margin. Following the completion of *When the Truth Is Told*, I, with the help of historian Patrick Bidelman, along with Herd and Downey, launched the Black Women in the Middle West Project (BWMW) for the sole purpose of making a Black women's history archive. With funds from a National Endowment for the Humanities grant and the help of 1,200 community Black women and others, we collected primary source materials from Black women and their families throughout Indiana and Illinois and deposited the bulk of them at the Chicago Historical Society and at the Indiana Historical Bureau.[2]

An unforeseen but invaluable benefit of the BWMW archive project was the rare opportunity it afforded to talk with hundreds of ordinary community Black women about their experiences, deeds, misfortunes, beliefs, and values. Gradually the meaning of history and who made it changed. As I studied the dusty records, frayed diaries, yellowed club minutes, faded photographs, typed autobiographies, brittle newspaper clippings and scores of obituaries, as I listened to oral interviews, and as I engaged in countless discussions with long-time residents of Middle West communities, the sheer force of these everyday narratives and the urgency with which their authors spoke overwhelmed and left me reflecting on what it all meant.

The accounts and the rich resources possessed by these women compelled a reexamination of the cherished values and beliefs internalized in graduate school concerning the nature of the historical enterprise, and a reevaluation of the profession's notions of historical merit and worthiness. When Herd first called me, the fact that traditional accounts of the region's history and the histories of individual states had ignored and excluded Black women seemed unproblematic to me. Clearly, even so-called traditional historians knew that the construction of history reflected the existing system of power relations. Social historians, women historians, and Black scholars recognized that as long as privileged white males held the authority and power to define the nature and content of history, all others would never secure more than a token hearing or representation before the academic canon. Yet I had never extended that analysis specifically to include Black women.

By the 1980s the field of African American history had acquired legitimacy and respect. In 1983 the American Historical Association sponsored a major conference at Purdue University on the research and teaching of Black history. I chaired the committee that organized the conference and edited the resultant volume, *The State of Afro-American History: Past, Present, and Future* (1986). All of the major themes and topics covered were subsumed under three categories: slavery, emancipation, and the urban experience. After the conference the committee recommended that I write an essay to cover the one major theme that had been omitted or that remained inadequately addressed in the other essays. More to the point, as we assessed the state of Black history it became patently clear that the history of Black women was its least developed area and had the least amount of scholarship. If Black history was to be fully representative and accurate then it was essential that Black women be included.

Again, in hindsight it is easy to explain why Black women were omitted from both Black and women's history. Actually, as members of two subordinate groups in American society, Black women fell between the cracks of Black history and women's history. A facile assumption held that whatever was said about Black men applied to Black women and that the history of white women covered Black women. Thus, with a few noteworthy exceptions such as historians Gerda Lerner and Jacqueline Jones, it was only Black women scholars who insisted that Black women's experiences, precisely because of their race, gender, and class, were often different and distinct in fundamental ways from those of Black men and white women. Black women historians argued that historians of Black America and of women had never in fact included Black women or paid adequate attention to questions of difference.[3]

What connects the essays in part one of this collection is a challenge to historians of the Black experience and historians of women to pay attention to African American women and not simply assume that "Blacks" or "slaves" refers only to men or that "physicians" or "nurses" refers only to whites. Although Booker T. Washington, W.E.B. Du Bois, and Marcus Garvey have long been staple figures in Black history, attention has seldom, if ever, focused on Olivia Davidson Washington, Amy Jacques Garvey, or Shirley Graham Du Bois. While many have heeded the call, even today a few historians of women and of African Americans continue to dismiss or question the importance of Black women's history.

The excuses and rationalizations for this persistent devaluation and oversight of Black women in history usually blame the inaccessible nature of records and documents or the absence of scholarly secondary sources. In 1983 this often repeated rationale rang true for me. Thus, the essay in *The State of Afro-American History*, entitled "Lifting the Veil, Shattering the Silence: Black Women's History in

Slavery and Freedom," as one of the first overviews of the topic, noted the lack of abundant primary sources, and is based largely upon the few available secondary sources, unpublished dissertations, and the rare manuscript collections. Actually, that essay was written with several purposes in mind. Certainly, raising awareness of an oversight or neglect was uppermost, but an equally important task was to indicate the themes and topics in need of further investigation. From the perspective of nearly two decades, it is encouraging that in recent years many historians and graduate students have, in fact, taken up the challenges expressed in these early essays.

The history of Black women in slavery was one of the most glaring voids in Black history. At the time the essay synthesizing the state of scholarship in Black women's history appeared there was no book length study of Black women in slavery. In 1979, a piece in the *Western Journal of Black Studies* indicated some preliminary, or exploratory, thoughts about this subject. The primary contribution of "Black Female Slave Resistance: The Economics of Sex" proposed that Black women slaves resisted the peculiar institution in ways that were consistent with their bodies. That is, they attempted to exercise some control over the coerced reproduction of the entire slave labor force by resorting to abortion, infanticide, and sexual abstinence.

Clearly, some slave women saw their bodies and reproductive capacities as their prerogatives. While not all thought and behaved in this manner, those who did attempt to control reproduction engaged in a kind of resistance that struck at the very heart of the slave system and was by its nature exceedingly disruptive and costly, and probably radical. The slave woman's resistance to sexual and therefore economic exploitation posed a potentially severe threat to paternalism itself, for implicit in such action was the refusal of some slave women to accept their designated responsibilities within the slave system as legitimate. This acceptance of mutual responsibility on the part of both the slaves and the masters was, as Eugene Genovese points out, at the heart of the maintenance of the paternalistic worldview.[4] The female slave, through her sexual resistance, attacked the base assumptions upon which the slave order was constructed and maintained.

The "Female Slave Resistance" essay urged the development of a gendered history at the height of the revisionist movement in slavery studies that witnessed the publication of important works by John Blassingame, Leslie Owens, Eugene Genovese, and Herbert Gutman.[5] Black women, as women, occupied rather shadowy space in these celebrated studies in part, perhaps, because Black history and Black Studies had not developed a vocabulary with which to speak or write about gender. This essay implores future historians of slavery studies to ask questions about gender. If I were to write the essay today, I would complicate the analysis by pointing out that there was no such person as a generic slave woman.

While speculating in "Female Slave Resistance" that central concerns of slave women would revolve around survival and resistance, and how to exercise control over their bodies, Deborah Gray White, in the first book on slave women, focused more on the culture, life cycles, and female networks that they developed.[6] Her pathbreaking work, and that of Brenda Stevenson, Paula Giddings, Jacqueline Jones, Wilma King, and Stephanie Shaw bring valuable insights and perspectives to slavery and Black women's studies.[7]

Questions about the relationships between gender and forms of resistance loom large in this collection and the theme of resistance is repeatedly revisited from various perspectives. In particular, the theme of resistance is considered through an examination of the "culture of dissemblance" that Black women created. Dissemblance means the behavior and attitudes of Black women that created the appearance of openness and disclosure but actually shielded the truth of their inner lives and selves from their oppressors, and often from Black men and Black children. They practiced dissemblance in response to rape, the threat of rape, and domestic violence. Not surprisingly, given the prevalence of negative and stereotypical images in the larger society, the facet of Black women's interior lives most shrouded from scrutiny has been their sexuality.

In the essay, "Rape and the Inner Lives of Black Women: Thoughts on the Culture of Dissemblance," I grapple with two issues simultaneously. By attempting to balance the lynching metaphor of oppression with that of rape, I suggest that rape, the threat of rape, and domestic violence were forms of the terrorism that southern white men, and some Black men, used against Black women. Concomitantly, this historicization of rape opens up new lines of investigation into the power relationships among Black women, white men, white women, and Black men across time and region. Clearly, Black women were ahead of white women in the fight against rape; rape was never merely a question of uncontrolled male lust. It was about both racial and sexual domination. Were I to rewrite this essay, I would probe deeper into the sexism and sexual violence that affect Black women in their own communities today. Moreover, I would pay even more attention to Black homophobia. Only by carefully illuminating these ills can we arrive at solutions for their redress.

While similar in many ways, the "Female Slave Resistance" and the "Culture of Dissemblance" essays nevertheless represent two distinct perspectives on resistance. The earlier essay was more about use of the body for resistance and the latter explores the interior meaning of that resistance and the culture it created. The first essay alludes to the political economy of the slave woman's body and the second probes the postbellum culture of the Black woman's body.

There is a need to decipher and to critique the relationship between white women's experiences of their sexuality and Black women's constructions of identity. In fact, the last essay in Part 1, "Black Women's History, White Women's History: The Juncture of Race and Class" complicates matters by urging that Black and white women historians engage in "crossover history" as a first step in coming to understand each other and thus to see with greater clarity the points of intersection. The history of women as a group is shaped as much by differences of racial categorization and class location as by any common femaleness. The underlying social agenda of this essay lies in its appeal to all historians of women to engage in such "crossover history" as a meaningful step in the war against racism, sexism, and class oppression.[8] Any barriers that impede an understanding of the past, and interfere with the commitment towards an inclusive future free of patriarchical domination require elimination.

The essays that make up Part 2 reflect on other forms and manifestations of Black women's resistance. In "Black Migration to the Urban Midwest: The Gender Dimension, 1915-1945," rape is once again the focus. Rape, the threat of rape, and domestic violence motivated thousands of Black women to flee the South, and fueled the proliferation of a nationwide network of women's clubs. Many Black women quit the South out of a desire to achieve personal autonomy and to escape from sexual oppression and abuse both within and outside of their families and communities. Young Black domestic workers were especially vulnerable to sexual assault and harassment at their work sites. The combined influence of domestic violence and economic exploitation is key to understanding the hidden motivation informing Black women's participation in major social protest and migratory movements in African American history.

Migration is not only an apt metaphor for my intellectual evolution as a Black woman historian, it is also central to the organization of all of these essays. Arguably, mobility is one of the most important dimensions of Black women's lives and as such it warrants much greater attention than it has received. Both during and after slavery Black women dared to flee situations that dehumanized them. Many of the early free Black women inhabitants of the Middle West, for example, were escaped slaves or daughters of women who had risked their lives to secure freedom for them. After emancipation, Black women, in numbers that increased with each passing decade, left their rural southern homes for urban ones in diverse regions. The consequence of their relentless movement from farms to cities, south to north, has been profound.

The plight of poor, migrating Black women who landed on the inhospitable streets of Detroit, Cleveland, Chicago, Philadelphia, New York and other northern and middle western cities motivated settled Black matrons to open working girls' homes, training schools in domestic arts, and other group-help agencies to rescue them from sexual exploitation, prostitution, and poverty. The processes of migration and urbanization required that Black women redouble efforts to create and sustain the separate parallel institutional infrastructure of schools, health care clinics, churches, and women's clubs that they had established in the south in the decades following emancipation and the entrenchment of segregation.

As the essay " 'We Specialize in the Wholly Impossible': The Philanthropic Work of Black Women" demonstrates, Black women brought much more with them on their trek to the Middle West than just themselves. They brought the knowledge of how to organize and to build a community. Indeed, in many communities Black women's service and sacrifice, visions and dreams, proved essential to group survival and racial progress. Either through the agency of their clubs or as the bedrock of the Black church, Black women were able to redress the often harsh consequences of migration by operating nurseries and kindergartens for the children of working mothers, or by maintaining job registries to help young single women find domestic service positions. Through countless philanthropic endeavors Black women helped members of their communities to improve their lot, and to adjust, or to change the conditions that prevented economic mobility. As the essay demonstrates, Black women were often just as concerned with helping and educating Black boys as they were with the girls. These women played pivotal roles in erecting an infrastructure of social welfare agencies, community institutions such as penny saving banks and credit unions, as well as political organizations and cultural programs. Although largely ignored in earlier histories of Black civil rights organizations, the work of the club women was just as important as that of the National Association for the Advancement of Colored People, and of the National Urban League in helping to ease the transition from farm to factory, from rural to urban.

The essay " 'We Specialize in the Wholly Impossible' " focuses heavily on the leadership and philanthropic work of Jane Edna Hunter of Cleveland while the adjoining essay "The Housewives' League of Detroit: Black Women and Economic Nationalism," concentrates on the mobilization work of a unique group of women. However, the "Housewives' League" essay emphasizes the importance of female friendships and networks, and it sheds light on gender role conventions within Black communities. The essay illustrates how Detroit Black women were able to utilize the skills they had perfected as club leaders and organizers to mobilize tens of thousands of Black women for collective action. A national network of housewives' leagues saved thousands of jobs for the Black community during the height of the Great Depression. Indeed, all of the essays on Black women in the Middle West underscore their roles as institution-builders and community bulwarks, and all highlight the consequences of their community activism.

Essentially, the Housewives' League combined what I have labeled "communal womanist consciousness" and economic nationalism to convince local merchants and professionals to hire Black workers, display and sell Black products, and to invest some of the money back into the community or risk the loss of patronage. To disarm potential male critics of their activism, the Housewives' League drafted an artfully worded constitution that declared, "We recognize the place of the church and allied organizations among us for the advancement of our group . . . but (we) are not a religious organization." They also cautioned, "We are mindful of achieving political solidarity among us, increasing our opportunity of representation in bodies that control the activities in our city, state, and nation—but we are not a political organization." In short, their dissemblance avoided antagonizing male political and religious leaders and simultaneously demonstrated a facet of successful communal womanism.

Scholarship on, and the assessment of, communal womanism is still evolving. Although I prefer to use the term feminism, I employ both womanism and feminism in my writings, sometimes interchangeably. Both terms are useful and loaded with political meaning. Feminism has a powerful history that Black women helped to create, and I am unwilling to abandon or to diminish that work.

In historian Elsa Barkley Brown's subtle analysis of the connection between theory (or consciousness) and activism, she warns against assuming that theory "is found only in carefully articulated position statements." Brown posits that the clearest articulation of Richmond, Virginia, Black leader Maggie Lena Walker's theoretical perspectives on the power of Black women lay not in her public statements but in her activities, especially the organization and institution (St. Luke Penny Savings Bank) she helped to create. "Her theory and her action are not distinct and separable parts of some whole: they are often synonymous and it is only through her actions that we clearly hear her theory." Brown concludes, "The same is true for the lives of many other black women who had limited time and resources and maintained a holistic view of life and struggle."[9] Still, it is important to remember that there were severe limits to the power of Black women who continuously operated within racial and gender systems in which whites and men had, and continue to have, most of the resources.

The sketch of the Housewives' League of Detroit raises complex questions about power and the intersections of race, gender, and ideology in the Black community. Similar questions link the essays that comprise Part 3. Black nursing history is ideal for studying the social construction of gender and race in America. The essays on health, medicine, and nursing illustrate how professional Black women were able to "make community" within the context of racism, sexism, and economic deprivation. The essays also dissect how Black women nurses and physicians created new images of themselves as subjects, fought for integration into the mainstream of medicine, for greater access to educational opportunities, and for career advancements, all while working to meet the dire health care needs of their communities. Distinct from their white colleagues, they were ever mindful that as Black women professionals their first obligation was to be an advocate for the Black community's health care. There were reasons for this ingrained sense of obligation and advocacy.

The essays in Part 3 underscore that without the institution-building initiative of Black leaders and the material and moral support of the Black community, the trained Black nurse would not have existed. The Black nurse belonged to the community and was by and large a product of the community. The Black community saw in nurses those health-care professionals most responsive and sympathetic to its needs. It often regarded nurses more favorably than it did male physicians. In some places the nurse's rank was equaled only by the minister's. Regardless of the high esteem they enjoyed within their communities as competent professionals, Black nurses frequently confronted unconcealed contempt from white nurses and from Black and white physicians. Thus, in addition to their advocacy roles, Black nurses had to create an intra-professional culture that allowed them the space to forge positive images of themselves as women and as nurses. It is within this context that the formation of the National Association of Colored Graduate Nurses is so important.

The struggles of Black nurses mirror, to a great degree, the historic battles that nurses as a group have fought for autonomy and job control with the white male medical profession. But the conflicts of Black nurses are complicated because of the combination of racism and sexism. In short, there existed no sorority of consciousness among the members of this female profession. White nurses fought autonomy battles against forces outside the nursing profession, but Black women fought against an exhausting combination of internal and external forces. White nurses, as Rockefeller Foundation nurse investigator Ethel Johns revealed, could be just as oppressive to their Black colleagues as male physicians and hospital supervisors were to them. Moreover, white nurse leaders heralded nursing as ideal work for middle-class women at a time when poor Black women were searching for any avenue out of domestic service. Conflicting visions meant that white leaders showed little interest in the needs or desires of Black women nurses, or for that matter, of white working-class women.

These essays, especially "Mabel K. Staupers and the Integration of Black Nurses into the Armed Forces," demonstrate most forcefully how Black women first "made community" among themselves and then marshalled the political power of their professional community to destroy Jim Crow practices in the Armed Forces and within the larger nursing profession. Admittedly written in a mode of unabashed celebration of the strength and resourcefulness of Black women nurses and physicians, the three essays in Part 3 reveal how Black women perceived their professional fates and the fortunes of the communities they served as inseparable.

The final section of the book includes essays on Black studies and Black historiography. They are important to me because they offer ways to think about the place of Black feminist scholarship in the still-evolving intellectual community. To include these essays makes them more accessible to those who create and implement policies, allocate resources, evaluate scholarship, and judge the intellectual work and worth of Black women historians and scholars throughout the academy. The Black Studies overview essay was prepared at the request of the Ford Foundation. It was published in a pamphlet along with essays by Professor Robert Harris of Cornell University and Professor Nellie McKay of the University of Wisconsin and distributed largely to the Black Studies community. One of the most pressing needs is for greater commitment and attention to the production of Black academic professionals in the humanities and social sciences. The second essay on Afrocentric, traditional, and feminist research and teaching paradigms represents an effort to provide a map of the contemporary intellectual conversations concerning future directions of Black studies scholarship and the impact of Afrocentricity.

This volume is published with an explicit underlying political and social agenda. One of the most urgent concerns is addressed in the statement retitled by *Chicago Sun-Times,* "Stop the Global Holocaust." The original title was "Stop the Killing of Black Women's Children," and concerns the rampant violence that is decimating young Black men. We are all affected by this devastation. Moreover, there is a negative picture that is less developed in these essays—the grim conditions of Black health and the absence of adequate health-care delivery sites in inner city Black communities. The status of Black health in the last decade of the twentieth century is not far different from what it was at the dawn of the Black hospital and nursing school movement. A hundred years ago the overall age-adjusted mortality rate for African Americans was one-and-a-half times that for whites; life expectancy at birth for the nation's Black population is only now at the level achieved by whites over 30 years ago. Several factors exacerbate the situation of Black health today: the shortage of nurses and other health care professionals, the alarming and disproportionate rate at which acquired immunodeficiency syndrome (AIDS) is ravaging the Black community, especially Black women, the rise in drug use, and finally, massive unemployment of both men and women.

It is my hope that this book will serve some useful purpose to those concerned about and struggling to achieve social justice. We need to form coalitions and networks grounded in greater awareness of the gender, racial, and class systems that perpetuate inequalities and that divide us unnecessarily. I recognize that history's greatest capacity is to explain why things are. This is what I, in all my intellectual wanderings, have endeavored to do. Having reached this crossroad, I arrive where I began over two decades ago. I believe that it is up to each and every reader of these historical essays to do something useful to make life better, safer, and more worthwhile for all Americans in all our tomorrows.

HINE SIGHT

PART 1

Lifting the Veil, Shattering the Silence

Black Women's History in Slavery and Freedom

Present and future investigations of Afro-American women's past should increase our understanding of the complex interrelationships of gender, class, and race. For three and a half centuries Afro-American women have carried special burdens. They have responded in dichotomous ways: by protesting racial and sexual discrimination or by somehow avoiding it; by rationalizing the psychological impact of racism and sexism or by transcending their victimization. These multiple dichotomies are most graphically revealed through an examination of black women's institutional and organizational lives and their work, and also in their cultural contributions and aesthetic expressions. Black women's history is just beginning to emerge as a vital area within women's and Afro-American history, and much work remains to be done. In this essay I will trace the contours of the field and assess its prospects by synthesizing much of the current literature. Specifically, I will examine the following themes: sex roles and female networks, the black family, work, religion, social reform, and creative expressions.

Before the Civil War the vast majority of black women were slaves. Emancipation required finding ways to give meaning to freedom within a society devoted to circumscribing all attempts of black people to, in fact, be free. Subsequently, industrialization and urbanization not only altered the location but influenced the transformation of the lives and work experiences of the majority of black women. Even more profound were the social upheavals and proliferation of racial and sexual stereotypes of the late nineteenth- and the early twentieth-centuries which affected how black women defined themselves in relationship to each other and to the larger society. Whether slave or free, black women occupied key familial roles as mothers, daughters, wives, and sisters.

Although recent works in Afro-American history have devoted a great deal of attention to the structure, function, and stability of black families under slavery, with few exceptions these works, in attempting to establish the vital importance of the male figure, have tended to deemphasize the role of black women within the family.[1] It is, of course, important and necessary to provide a more balanced portrayal of the actual male/female roles in the black family in slavery and freedom in order to obliterate the myth of the ubiquitous black matriarch. Nevertheless, it is critical that the black woman remain visible in the family. Scholarly revisions must not obscure the indisputable fact that the black woman bore primary responsibility for reproducing the slave labor force and for ensuring the continuation of the black race during and after the demise of the Peculiar Institution.

As wives and mothers, black women nurtured the sick, performed all of the domestic chores, provided primary socialization of slave children, wet-nursed white children, fulfilled the conjugal needs of their men, and all too often endured the forced passion of slave masters and the vengeful brutality of plantation mistresses. Perhaps the most challenging task confronting black women under slavery was how to maintain a relatively healthy opinion of themselves as sexual beings. To the slave masters they were remunerative slave breeders and vulnerable sexual objects. Although instances abound in the literature about black male slaves who fought and died, the men were, on the whole, unable to offer much protection for the sexual integrity of their wives, daughters, and sisters. Indeed, the abused black woman often had to convince her mate that the test of his masculinity was self-restraint, not some action that would deprive her of a husband or her children of a father.

White plantation mistresses were equally powerless in the face of their husbands' brutality, but they often displayed considerable hostility toward the abused slave woman. In fact, they frequently blamed the victim for the sexual transgressions of their husbands and sons. As a result, black women, beginning in slavery, were compelled to construct a sexual self, based on the foundation of self-reliance.[2] Given the fact that many slave marriages possessed virtually no legal sanction and were seldom recognized in the larger society, future scholars would do well to explore how black women, in fact, viewed marriage. How did their view of marriage differ from or resemble those views held by men and white women?

Gender relationships between black slaves were problematic even without the sexual intrusions of white men. Although scholars have devoted scant attention to the social relationship between husband and wife, some writers have suggested that black women shared a greater degree of equality with black male slaves than was the case between white men and women. If such was the case, this equality of status certainly derived, in part, from the fact that black women performed many of the same tasks on slave plantations as did the men. They engaged in hard physical labor, chopped and picked cotton, felled trees, mended fences, cared for livestock, and cultivated food crops. Yet it must be pointed out that similar economic or work responsibilities do not necessarily reflect equal social relations. There was still a sexual division of labor on the plantations. Black women also had to perform socially and biologically determined sex-role stereotyped work. In reality, then, the division of labor on most plantations was decidedly unequal. While all slaves worked hard, the black women slaves were burdened with extra jobs performed only by members of their sex. In the absence of further research, one can only speculate about the tensions this inequitable distribution of work assignments must have engendered in many of the slave cabins.[3]

Performing sex-differentiated work did, however, afford black women the opportunity to develop a separate world of informal female networks that reinforced their reliance on one another. These networks usually evolved through organized group activities such as spinning, weaving, quilting, cooking, and attending each other in childbirth and providing health care. These female slave networks allowed the women to forge a common consciousness concerning their oppression as women while devising strategies for survival. Through their women-centered networks they were able to communicate their feelings, share experiences and world views, and assist each other in the development of positive self-images and self-esteem in spite of the slave-owning society's best efforts to define them to the contrary.[4]

Consequently, their interactions engendered an even stronger sense of community among slaves.

In addition to midwifing, doctoring, and other domestic chores, group activities such as quilting facilitated woman-bonding and cooperation between female slaves and contained significantly larger social implications. Black women, as slaves and freedwomen, converted quilt-making into a social and community affair. Former slave Mary Wright, of Kentucky, reminiscing about quilting offered, "Den wemns [women] quilt awhile, den a big dinner war spread out, den after dinner we'd quilt in de evening, den supper and a big dance dat night, wid de banjie a humming 'n us niggers a dancing."[5] Deserving added emphasis is the fact that the quilt, thus created, represented the individual and collective expression of the voice, vision, structure, and substance of the creators' personal and spiritual lives.

One of the most famous black women quilters was former slave Harriet Powers (1837-1911) of Athens, Georgia. One of her two "Bible Quilts" (1898) now adorns the walls of the Smithsonian Institution in Washington, D.C. The quilt is divided into rectangular panels, each devoted to a particular biblical scene. The panels are filled with appliqued silhouettes of human figures, geometric motifs, and other design combinations that resemble the styles found among the people of ancient Dahomey in West Africa.[6] In much the same way that we can examine the quilts, scholars of the black female experience must analyze other cultural contributions and expressions including hymns, spirituals, blues, lullabyes, poems, novels, sermons, household implements, toys, folktales, and slave narratives.[7]

To be sure, families and female networks were important institutions shaping black women's lives and experiences. Yet, any discussion of the institutional history of black women would be seriously flawed without a simultaneous examination of their involvement in and relationship to the black church and black religion. By the first half of the nineteenth century, religion had become the center of the spiritual and community lives of most women, and of black women in particular. Women, regardless of race and status, played a prominent role within the congregations, organizing voluntary missionary societies, teaching Sunday schools, and raising funds. Representative black women such as Sarah Woodson Early, born on November 15, 1825, in Chillicothe, Ohio, offer illuminating testimony of their work in the church. Woodson married African Methodist Episcopal (AME) Church minister Jordon Winston early in 1868 and shared with him the tasks of religious leadership. She described her work and that of other black church women: "We assisted in superintending the Sabbath-schools when near enough to reach them; always attending and often leading in prayer meetings; and [we] took an active part in visiting the sick and administering to the wants of the poor and needy, and in raising money to defray the expenses of the Church and served most heartily in its educational work."[8]

At some fundamental level all black churches espoused a theology of liberation, self-determination, and black autonomy. Northern black churches were especially active in and supportive of the abolition movement. The promises embodied in Christian scriptures permeated all of Afro-American culture and possessed special meaning for black women's psychic survival and transcendence. The black church became the training arena that enabled free black women prior to the Civil War to acquire leadership and organizing skills and an increased commitment to winning freedom for the slaves and more control over their own lives. For black slave women religious faith nourished hope for release from their earthly oppression and degradation. The body could be tortured and abused while the soul remained pure and untouched. In the latter decades of the nineteenth century, black women enlarged their already considerable influence within the church and extended its sacred horizons to encompass pressing secular concerns. In short, the black church ultimately served as an institutional base, giving moral sanction to black women's quest for freedom and the advancement of the race.

One important aspect of black religious life remained unchanged after the Civil War. The hierarchy, ministers, and theologians of most religions and congregations remained male. Not all black women were satisfied with their significant but nevertheless subordinate and relatively invisible roles within black churches. Denied official positions of leadership, a few extraordinary, free black women found religious audiences of their own. One such woman was Jarena Lee, born free at Cape May, New Jersey, in 1783. She was a protégée of the Reverend Richard Allen, founder and leader of the AME Church.

Allen was not averse to Lee's leading prayer meetings, but he at first drew the conservative theological line against female preaching. Later, Allen relented and endorsed her desire to preach. In the single year 1827 alone, Lee traveled 2,325 miles unaccompanied and delivered 178 sermons, a remarkable feat for any woman during this period in American history. In her autobiography, Lee defended her right to preach:

> O how careful ought we to be, lest through our bylaws of church government and discipline, we bring into disrepute even the word of life. For as unseemingly as it may appear now-a-days for a woman to preach, it should be remembered that nothing is impossible with God. And why should it be thought impossible, heterodox, or improper for a woman to preach? Seeing the Savior died for the woman as well as for the man.[9]

Perhaps the best-known itinerant preacher in the antebellum period was the legendary Sojourner Truth, who combined her mission of serving her people and espousing the rights of women with a mission to spread the news of a God of love. For Sojourner Truth, the abolitionist and women's rights movements were but the secular counterparts of spiritual salvation. At one gathering she declared, "Then that little man in black there, he says women can't have as much rights as men, because Christ wasn't a woman! Where did your Christ come from? From God and a woman! Man had nothing to do with Him."[10]

Like Lee and Truth, Rebecca Cox Jackson was also an itinerant preacher and religious visionary. Born a free black in 1795 near Philadelphia, Jackson experienced a profound spiritual awakening at age thirty-five and felt compelled to preach. Unable to overcome the strong opposition of her family and friends, Jackson severed relations with the Bethel AME Church in Philadelphia and joined the Watervliet Shaker Community near Albany. Four years later, in 1857, she left the community and was granted the right to found a predominantly black Shaker sisterhood in Philadelphia. In 1878 eight black women, three black children, and three white women lived in the Shaker commune, members of Jackson's spiritual family. She died in 1881.[11]

Amanda Berry Smith, born at Long Green, Maryland, in 1837, like her AME predecessors, grew disillusioned by the restrictions on women and ventured forth to become an itinerant preacher (without ordination) and a missionary. She traveled extensively in foreign lands: England in 1878, India in 1880-1881, and Liberia for eight years. Throughout her traveling Smith observed and commented on the common universal exploitation and oppression of women.[12]

Religion, though significant, was not the sole outlet for the talented, intelligent, and spirited free black woman. Many free black women played instrumental and catalytic roles in the reform and humanitarian movements of the early nineteenth century. They were active in founding mutual aid societies and antislavery, suffrage, and temperance organizations. As we shall see, black women were the ones to raise the question of women's rights within black organizations and issues of racism within white women's organizations. Maria Stewart, born free in 1803 and raised in Hartford, Connecticut, is heralded as the first woman to break with convention and speak in public to a mixed audience of men and women on behalf of black rights and advancement. In an 1832 address before the newly formed Afric-American Female Intelligence Society of Boston, she declared: "Me thinks I heard a spiritual interrogation—'Who shall go forward, and take off the reproach that is cast upon the people of color? Shall it be a woman?' And my hart made this reply—'If it is thy will, be it even so, Lord Jesus!'" Stewart cursed the institution of slavery and urged black women to "awake, arise: no longer sleep nor slumber, but distinguish yourselves."[13]

For free black women the line between involvement in religious institutions and in the women's suffrage movement was a permeable one. Because their religious orientation was toward spiritual liberation and personal autonomy, suffrage for black women became the political expression of their persistent yearnings to be free. Prominent antebellum free black women such as Sarah Mapps Douglass, a teacher in the Institute for Colored Youth, and the three Forten sisters of Philadelphia—Sarah, Margaretta, and Harriet—attended, in 1833, the opening meetings of the Female Anti-Slavery Society of Philadelphia. Margaretta Forten later became the recording secretary of the society. Likewise, Susan Paul was present at the organizational meeting of the Boston Female Anti-Slavery Society and later served as one of its vice-presidents and as treasurer.[14] Here as in other aspects of their lives, black antislavery activists contributed to the abolitionist cause in spite of the racial discrimination and prejudice of their white female colleagues.

The experiences of Sara Mapps Douglass are a revealing commentary on the racism that existed among white women in the antislavery movement. When Douglass attempted to attend the national meeting of the Female Anti-Slavery Convention in New York City in 1837, she learned that "colored members were unwelcome." An astonished white activist from South Carolina, Angelina Grimké, noted that, in the New York society, "no colored sister has ever been on the Board and they have hardly any colored members even and will not admit any to the working S[ociety]." Only the timely intercession and persuasive powers of Grimké reversed the bar against black women delegates attending the convention. When Douglass at one point wavered in her resolve to attend the convention, Grimké implored her to reconsider:

> You my dear Sisters have a work to do in rooting out this wicked feeling as well as we. You must be willing to come in among us tho' it may be your feelings may be wounded by "the putting forth of the finger," the avoidance of a seat by you, or the glancing of the eye. . . . I earnestly desire that you may be willing to bear these mortifications. . . . They will tend to your growth in grace, and will help your sisters more than anything else to overcome their own sinful feelings. Come, then, I would say, for we need your help.[15]

At Grimké's insistence Sarah Douglass and Sarah Forten attended the meeting. Across the ocean another black woman abolitionist, Sarah Parker Remond, appealed to English women to fight against the enslavement of darker members of their sex. When lecturing in London in 1859, Remond focused on the exploitation of black women slaves. She declared, "If English women and English wives knew the unspeakable horrors to which their sex were exposed on southern plantations, they would freight every westward gale with the voices of moral indignation and demand for the black woman the protection and rights enjoyed by the white."[16]

From the 1830s to the turn of the century black women encountered similar white hostility when endeavoring to attend suffrage and women's rights meetings. Even Sojourner Truth, that ardent defender of black people's and women's rights was subjected to repeated indignities when attending early women's rights conventions. One male heckler, at the 1851 Woman's Rights Convention in Akron, Ohio, challenged her to prove that she was a woman and some white women activists objected to her being allowed to speak, fearing that too close an association "with abolition and niggers" would damage their cause. It was amidst this climate of racist and sexist hostility that Truth is purported to have delivered the often quoted, "Ain't I a Woman" speech.

> Well, children, war dar is so much racket dar must be someting out o'kilter. I think dat 'twixt de niggers of de Souf and de women at the Norf all talkin 'bout rights de white men will be in a fix pretty soon. But what's all diss here talkin 'bout? Dat man ober dar say dat women needs to be helped into carriages, and lifted ober ditches and to have da best places . . . and ain't I a woman? Look at me! Look at my arm! . . . I have plowed, and planted and gathered into barns, and no man could head me— and ain't I a woman? I could eat as much as any man (when I could get it), and bear de lash as well—and ain't I a woman? I have borne five children and I see 'em mos all sold off into slavery, and when I cried out with a mother's grief, none but Jesus here—and ain't I a woman?[17]

Sojourner Truth was a paradigm to women's rights advocates because her personal experiences proved that women could raise children, do heavy labor, survive persecution, endure physical and sexual abuse, and still emerge triumphant and transcendent. At an 1867 Equal Rights Association convention the indomitable Sojourner Truth warned, "There is a great stir about colored men getting their rights, but not a word about the colored women; and if colored men get their rights, and not colored women theirs, you see the colored men will be masters over the women, and it will be just as bad as it was before."[18]

In the wake of the death of slavery, black women continued their struggle for race advancement and sexual elevation. Black slaves, for the most part, entered freedom with little more than the rags on their backs. Merely staying alive became a struggle. Witnessing the suffering and deprivation, black women like Elizabeth Keckley, a personal servant of Mary Todd Lincoln, swung into action. In 1862 Keckley organized the Contraband Relief Association, composed of approximately forty members. The association collected money, clothing, and food to distribute to the thousands of freedmen and freedwomen who flocked to the nation's capital.[19]

The tradition of female slave networks and the free black women's improvement associations and their work in antislavery organizations and voluntary associations provided the foundations upon which black women forged powerful national organizations. Characterized by a special brand of black female militancy, national women's networks flourished in the late 1890s and the early twentieth century. In 1892 Fannie Barrier Williams, a prominent member of Chicago's black elite, lamented that "Afro-American women of the United States have never had the benefit of a discriminating judgment concerning their worth as women." Williams, a native of Brockport, New York, attended the New England Conservatory of Music in Boston and the School of Fine Arts in Washington, D.C., and taught school in the South before moving to Chicago. During the 1890s Williams gained international fame for her outspoken defense of black women. Responding to repeated allegations of the immorality of black women and the inferiority of the black race, the embattled Williams declared, "I think it but just to say that we must look at American slavery as the source of every imperfection that mars the character of the colored American."[20]

In the late nineteenth century, America moved inexorably toward a society best characterized as "biracial dualism." While white Americans, north and south, accepted black subordination as representing the Darwinian natural order, black leaders of the race focused almost completely on winning educational, political, and economic rights. Black women, on the other hand, focused on eradicating negative images of their sexuality. Thus, by the late 1890s there developed a major division of emphasis within the black protest tradition. Black men attacked racial discrimination as it operated in the public corridors of power. Black women, whose center of influence had always existed primarily in the family, in the church, and in their female associations, believed that part of the overall struggle for true racial advancement depended upon the extent to which they obliterated all negative sexual images of themselves. In an 1893 speech Williams proclaimed, "This moral regeneration of a whole race of women is no idle sentiment—it is a serious business; and everywhere there is witnessed a feverish anxiety to be free from the mean suspicions that have so long underestimated the character strength of our women."[21] Historian Linda Perkins has perceptively observed that "throughout the nineteenth century, the threads that held together the organizational as well as the individual pursuits of black women were those of 'duty' and 'obligation' to the race. The concept of racial obligation was intimately linked with the concept of racial 'uplift' and 'elevation.' "[22]

Black women leaders such as Josephine St. Pierre Ruffin of Boston, Mary Church Terrell of Washington, D.C., and Mary Margaret Washington of Tuskegee, Alabama, heeding Williams' exhortations, launched, in the mid-1890s, a movement to mobilize black women from all walks of life and to engage them in the battle for racial and sexual equality. Ruffin, born in Boston in 1842 and educated in Salem's public schools, founded, in 1894, the Woman's Era Club and edited its newspaper, the *Woman's Era*. She was a founder of the Association for the Promotion of Child Training in the South and the League of Women for Community Service. Mary Church Terrell was the third black woman college graduate in the country (Oberlin College, 1884) and the first black woman appointed to the board of education in the District of Columbia. Mary Margaret Washington, an 1889 graduate of Fisk University in Nashville, Tennessee, served as director of girls' industries and dean of women at Tuskegee Institute.[23]

In 1895 this national mobilization movement of black women received increased impetus from an unexpected source when James W. Jack, then president of the Missouri Press Association, wrote a letter to Florence Belgarnie, secretary of the Anti-Slavery Society in England, declaring that "the Negroes of this country are wholly devoid of morality" and that "the women were prostitutes and all were natural thieves and liars." Ruffin, upon learning of the comment, immediately transformed it into a weapon to persuade black women of the critical need for organization. She wrote to hundreds of black women insisting that "the letter of Mr. Jack's . . . is only used to show how pressing is the need of our banning together if only for our protection." Ruffin, in subsequent correspondence, stressed the broad ramifications of negative sexual images. Even white southern women, she pointed out, objected to the formation of interracial women's organizations because of the alleged immorality of black women. She declared, "Too long have we been silent under unjust and unholy charges." Ruffin aroused black women and informed them that it was their "'bounded duty' to stand forth and declare ourselves and principles [and] to teach an ignorant and suspicious world that our aims and interests are identical with those of all good aspiring women."[24]

Ruffin and the black women whom she contacted had just cause to be alarmed by Jack's characterization of all black women as prostitutes. Arrest statistics of black women on charges of illegal solicitation in Nashville and Atlanta underscore the broader social ramifications of this stereotype. In a typical one-year period in Nashville ending October, 1881, there were 136 arrests of white females on charges of streetwalking as compared with 791 arrests of black women. In 1890 Atlanta listed 380 females among its 5,601 arrested whites as compared with 1,715 of the 7,236 arrested blacks. Clearly, the actions of law enforcement officials reflected a shared belief in the stereotype that depicted all black women as natural prostitutes. It is highly unlikely that women became prostitutes because they were immoral. Certainly more work on this matter is needed, especially on economic factors.[25]

By 1896 black women leaders had mobilized sufficiently to create the National Association of Colored Women (NACW). The NACW merged the resources and energies of scores of local and regional clubs into one strong organization in order to attack the prevailing negative image of black womanhood. Throughout the following decades the NACW grew at a phenomenal rate. By 1914 it had a membership of 50,000 and had become the strong, unwavering voice championing the defense of black women in a society that viewed them with contempt.

Terrell was elected first president of the NACW and occupied the position until 1901. In her initial presidential address she declared that there were objectives of the black women's struggle that could only be accomplished "by the mothers, wives, daughters, and sisters of this race." She proclaimed, "We wish to set in motion influences that shall stop the ravages made by practices that sap our strength, and preclude the possibility of advancement." To elaborate, Terrell noted that while black people, in general, and women in particular, were subordinate in this society, neither the efforts of the black males nor the concerns of white women would lead them to address the twin ills of racism and sexism endured solely by black women. Terrell then went to the heart of a black woman's dilemma. Like Williams and Ruffin before her, she spoke from a Victorian worldview that insisted on measuring a race's progress by the status of its women. She boldly announced, "We proclaim to the world that the women of our race have become partners in the great firm of progress and reform. . . . We refer to the fact that this is an association of colored women, because our peculiar status in this country . . . seems to demand that we stand by ourselves."[26] Her speech again underscored the importance of black women's self-reliance. Under slavery they had to protect their sexual being and during freedom they had to defend their sexual image.

Although considerable scholarly attention has been devoted to the club women's movement, there still remains a great deal to be done in the area of black women's involvement in voluntary and self-help associations. In virtually every city and rural community in twentieth-century America there existed an organized grouping of black women, often led by a cadre of elite educated black middle-class matrons. These clubs and organizations gradually added to their primary concern of upgrading sexual images a concern for women's suffrage and progressive social reform. Almost every black women's club, regardless of who founded it or the ostensible reason for its establishment, focused to some extent on alleviating one or more of the many social problems afflicting an increasingly urban, impoverished, politically powerless, and segregated black population.

Before the emergence of the modern welfare state, black Americans had to rely on their own initiative in order to provide adequate educational institutions, suitable health care programs, and settlement houses. They slowly and unrelentingly erected a nationwide network of institutions and organizations welding together the entire black population. Ida Wells-Barnett of Chicago, Jane Edna Hunter of Cleveland, and Sallie Wyatt Stewart of Evansville, Indiana, are but three examples of midwestern black women who established black settlement or community houses during the era of progressive reform. Moreover, throughout the twenties black women mobilized support for the establishment of black branches of the Young Women's Christian Association, and their institution-building activities reflect the same spirit of volunteerism seen among white women in American society during the Progressive Era.

No accurate social or cultural history of black America is possible without a detailed examination of the institutions crafted by still unrecognized local black women. The creation of educational, health care, and recreational institutions spearheaded by diverse black women's clubs and voluntary associations followed no standard pattern. Rather, women launched new projects or worked to transform existing institutions into structures more adequately designed to address the needs of their respective constituencies. Recurring concerns were for education for the young, food, shelter, and clothing for the aged, medical and nursing care for the sick.

While considerably more work needs to be done in the area, two examples will illustrate this all too frequently ignored dimension of black institution building and internal cultural development. In the South, the black women of New Orleans organized and founded in 1896 the Phillis Wheatley Sanitarium and Nursing Training School, which eventually became, in the 1930s, the Flint-Goodridge Hospital and School of Nursing of Dillard University. Their counterparts in the midwest, black women in Indianapolis, Indiana, founded in the 1870s and continue to the present to support the Alpha Home for Colored Aged.[27]

The pressing need of the black population, and black women in particular, for education motivated several black women, most notably Mary McLeod Bethune, to launch new institutions for their sex. Bethune, born on July 10, 1875, near Mayesville, South Carolina, graduated from Scotia Seminary in 1894 and entered Dwight Moody's Institute for Home and Foreign Missions in Chicago. After teaching in a number of mission schools, she settled in Daytona, Florida, where she founded the Daytona Educational and Industrial Institute for Training Negro Girls. Reflecting on her work years later, Bethune recalled, "The school expanded fast. In less than two years I had 250 pupils. . . . I concentrated more and more on girls, as I felt that they especially were hampered by lack of educational opportunities." Eventually, however, she agreed to merge with Cookman Institute, an educational facility for Negro boys under the auspices of the Methodist Church. Thus, in 1923 the now co-ed institution was renamed the Bethune-Cookman College. Bethune was an active participant in the black women's club movement, serving as president of the National Association of Colored Women (1924-1928). She helped to create the women's section of the Commission on Interracial Cooperation. Most important, in 1935 she founded the National Council of Negro Women. Throughout her later years she played a major role in the nation's political affairs, becoming the first black woman to hold a federal post as administrator of the Office of Minority Affairs within the National Youth Administration during Franklin Delano Roosevelt's presidency.

Bethune is a pivotal figure in twentieth-century black women's history. Her life and work is unarguably one of the major links connecting the social reform efforts of post-Reconstruction black women to the political protest activities of the generation emerging after World War II. All of the various strands of black women's struggle for education, political rights, racial pride, sexual autonomy, and liberation are united in the writings, speeches, and organizational work of Bethune. A good biography of this vital figure is sorely needed.[28]

The turn of the century witnessed many black women engaged in creating educational and social welfare institutions within their communities. Yet, as involved as these women were in the work of institution building, they never lost sight of the major problem confronting black men in America. Indeed, for the young Ida B. Wells (1862-1931) overcoming racism and halting the violent murder of black men remained a central mission among her wide-ranging struggles for justice and human dignity. As a young woman, Wells cofounded in 1889 the militant newspaper *Free Speech* in Memphis, Tennessee. Her scathing editorials denouncing local whites for the lynching of black men on the pretext of protecting the sanctity of white womanhood provoked a mob to burn her press and threaten death should she show her face in the city.[29]

Exiled north, Wells without pause launched a veritable one-woman international crusade against lynching. When the National

Association for the Advancement of Colored People (NAACP) was formed in 1910, Wells insisted that the leadership take an unwavering stand against lynching. Years later Wells withdrew from the NAACP when the organization's leaders failed to adopt the more militant race-conscious posture she advocated. Wells proved equally unsuccessful in persuading leaders in the women's suffrage movement to speak out against racism and to denounce the atrocity of lynching. The young white leaders of the National American Women's Suffrage Association early declared that the organization had only one objective—woman suffrage. These women, especially southern members, feared that too close an association with black issues would jeopardize their cause. It would not be until 1930, the year before Wells' death, that black and white women joined forces to launch the Association of Southern Women for the Prevention of Lynching.[30]

Neither the Great Migration to southern and northern cities nor the ratification of the Nineteenth Amendment to the United States Constitution granting women the right to vote altered the political status and material conditions of the lives of the majority of black women. Like their male counterparts, hundreds of thousands of black women had quit the rural South before and during the World War I years and ventured to northern cities in search of the "promised land." Many single young black women trekked to cities seeking better jobs, decent housing, equal education, freedom from terrorism, adventure, and intellectual stimulation. They left behind, or so they dreamed, racial discrimination, grueling poverty, second-class citizenship, and sexual exploitation. While the war raged and the economy boomed, jobs in industries and factories appeared both abundant and accessible. When the war ended black women and men fortunate enough to have secured employment were quickly dismissed, as employers preferred to give their jobs to returning white veterans. For black women the migration experience only confirmed that the promised land was littered with all but identical racial and sexual ills as had plagued their southern odyssey.[31]

Black women's work experiences were repeated during the Second World War. Traditionally, wartime crises led to improvement in the status of women, as many scholars have argued. The male labor shortage encouraged employers to seek women to work on assembly lines in defense plants and in other occupations that are normally closed to their sex when a full contingent of male workers is available. For black women, however, the status of being the last hired and the first fired remained true throughout the World War II years and after. As historian Karen Tucker Anderson has demonstrated, "both during and after the war, black women entered the urban female labor force in large numbers only to occupy its lowest rungs. Largely excluded from clerical sales work, the growth sectors of the female work force, black women found work primarily in service jobs outside the household and in unskilled blue-collar categories." As late as 1950, 40 percent of the black female labor force remained mired in domestic service. The remaining numbers were involved in unskilled blue-collar labor and in agriculture. Only a small percentage of black women belonged to the white collar professions, concentrating in teaching, nursing, and social work. By 1974 women made up 46 percent of the total black professionals. On the one hand they constituted only 7 percent of the black engineers, 14 percent of the black lawyers, 24 percent of the black physicians and black dentists, and 25 percent of the black life and physical scientists. On the other hand, black women represented 97 percent of the black librarians, 97 percent of black nurses, and 78 percent of the noncollege black teachers. There is little evidence to suggest that these percentages have changed significantly in the past decade.[32] Again, more work needs to be done comparing the economic development of black women with that of their white female counterparts.

In the face of continuing economic subordination, some black women sought relief and escape, as well as symbolic empowerment, through involvement in radical protest movements. During the 1920s black women had formed a woman's arm of Marcus Garvey's Universal Negro Improvement Association (UNIA). Amy Jacques Garvey headed the division and edited the women's department of the UNIA's official organ, *Negro World*. In numerous speeches and essays Amy Garvey reminded Afro-American women that they were the "burden bearers of their race" and as such had the responsibility to assume leadership in the struggle for black liberation both at home and abroad.[33] Here, too, is an area in need of much work, for the role black women played in the UNIA has received scant scholarly attention.

Black women supported A. Philip Randolph's March on Washington Movement, which was initiated in 1941 to end discrimination in defense industries with government contracts. They remained steadfast in their support of the National Association for the Advancement of Colored People (NAACP) and the National Urban League, the more traditional black civil rights organizations. During the course of the war black women did achieve one victory. From 1942 to the end of the war black women rallied behind the leadership of nurses Estelle Massey Riddle and Mabel K. Staupers and the National Association of Colored Graduate Nurses (NACGN) to win integration of black nurses into the United States Armed Forces Nurses Corps.[34]

In addition to cooperating with male leaders of protests and black rights groups and supporting the efforts of women's professional societies in the ongoing quest for integration and first-class citizenship, black women created their own national political organization. In 1935, Mary Church Terrell joined Mary McLeod Bethune in signing the charter of the first council of organizations in the history of organized black womanhood—the National Council of Negro Women (NCNW). The local leadership of the NCNW represented a cross section of black women from all walks of life, though the national officers were all well-educated, middle-class professional women. The unity of women engaged in the struggle is demonstrated by the cooperation whereby Estelle Massey Riddle, president of the NACGN, was elected second vice-president of the NCNW, while Terrell served as first vice-president and Bethune became the president.[35]

The NCNW declared as its purpose the collecting, interpreting, and disseminating of information concerning the activities of black women. Moreover, the NCNW leaders desired "to develop competent and courageous leadership among Negro women and effect their integration and that of all Negro people into the political, economic, educational, cultural and social life of their communities and the nation." To achieve these and other objectives, NCNW leaders founded an official organ, the *Aframerican Woman's Journal,* and dedicated it to achieving "the outlawing of the Poll Tax, the development of a Public Health Program, an Anti-lynching Bill, the end of discrimination in the Armed Forces, Defense Plants, Government Housing Plants, and finally that Negro History be taught in the Public Schools of the country."[36]

This increased organizing activity evidenced during the Great Depression and World War II era reflected black women's growing determination to overthrow a tripartite system of racial and sexual oppression, economic exploitation, and political powerlessness. Undoubtedly, millions of black women had acquired deeper understanding of their entrapment in the prison of white supremacy through membership in such clubs and organizations. Club membership and associations encouraged in black women the forging of a certain mental attitude and a readiness to work and die, if need be, for the liberation of their people. These organized and aware black women became one of the major, albeit invisible and unrecognized, foundations upon which was based the modern Civil Rights Movement of the 1950s and 1960s.

The as yet undiminished proliferation of studies of the Civil Rights Movement will remain incomplete as long as scant attention is paid the roles played by black women such as Rosa Parks, Ella Baker, and Fannie Lou Hamer. What is now required is a full-scale, detailed treatment and scholarly analysis of the Civil Rights Movement written from the perspective of black women participants. Biographies and autobiographies of key female leaders and activists in the movement, similar to Anne Moody's *Coming of Age in Mississippi* (1967) or Daisy Bates' *The Long Shadow of Little Rock: A Memoir* (1962), will shed new light on the origins and evolution of the largest mass movement of black Americans for social change in the country's history.[37] Even a brief examination of the lives of Rosa Parks and Ella Baker suggests new directions to be taken in future scholarship. The work of sociologist Aldon D. Morris is a welcome contribution to civil rights studies in that the author takes pains to elaborate and interpret the roles of black women in the struggle.[38]

Traditional accounts of the history of the Civil Rights Movement portray Rosa Parks as a quiet, dignified older lady who spontaneously refused to yield her bus seat to a white man because she was tired, her feet hurt, and she quite simply had had enough. Actually, Parks, a longtime member of black women's organizations and of the NAACP, was deeply rooted in the black protest tradition and had refused several times previously, as far back as the 1940s, to comply with segregation rules on buses. Morris has astutely observed that Parks' arrest triggered the Civil Rights Movement because "she was an integral member of those organizational forces capable of mobilizing a social movement." It is equally as important to note that Parks was firmly anchored in the church community in Montgomery, where she served as a stewardess in the St. Paul AME Church.[39]

The difference between Parks' previous protests and arrests and the December 1, 1955, incident was that members of the Women's Political Council (WPC), organized by professional black women of Montgomery in 1949 for the purpose of registering black women to vote, swung into action. Since its inception, the WPC had been a major political force within Montgomery. The members consistently challenged the segregation practices and laws before meetings of the city commission. They had demanded the hiring of black policemen and protested the inadequacies of parks and playgrounds in the black community. Some of their demands were met, others ignored. The morning after Parks' arrest, however, leader Jo Ann Robinson, an English teacher at Alabama State College, announced to students and colleagues that the WPC would launch a bus boycott to end segregation forever. She wrote the leaflet describing the Parks incident and rallied the community for action.[40] The women of the WPC were not alone. Similar groups and individuals across the South were ready and eager to heed the call for social action. Black women had been organizing for over a hundred years and their infrastructure of secular clubs and sacred associations was already firmly in place.

Of the many black women participants in the Civil Rights Movement, Ella Baker deserves special recognition and study. Baker was the central figure in the Southern Christian Leadership Conference's (SCLC) Atlanta office during the 1950s. Her determined opposition to assigning black women subservient roles in the hierarchical structure of social-change movements aroused the ire of her male colleagues. Baker was born in 1903, in Virginia, and raised in North Carolina. In 1927 she quit the South and migrated to New York, where she eventually worked in developing the Young Negro Cooperative League. From 1941 to 1942 Baker served as the national field secretary for the NAACP, a position requiring her to travel throughout the South conducting membership campaigns and developing NAACP branches. Baker, when promoted to director of branches for the NAACP, attended 157 meetings and traveled 10,244 miles, all within a twelve-month period.[41]

By the time Baker joined SCLC as its first associate director, she had accumulated considerable organizational experience and had cultivated an invaluable network of community contacts throughout the South. Initially Baker performed routine chores in the central office, her interpersonal and organizational skills ignored and untapped by the male ministerial leadership. Soon there was considerable friction within SCLC, occasioned in part because of Baker's belief in women's equality and her refusal automatically to defer to men. Moreover, Baker insisted that the effectiveness of a people's movement depended upon the careful cultivation of local leadership among the masses.

In particular, Baker objected that the Civil Rights Movement was structured around Martin Luther King, Jr., to such a degree as to block the development of skills among women, young people, and other members of the black community. She advocated a "group-centered leadership" approach which would allow the movement to become more democratic and would minimize internal struggle for personal advantage. Baker and the older male leaders clashed over the types of organizational structure that should be established at SCLC headquarters. She emphasized the SCLC should have clearly defined personnel assignments and obligations. Not surprisingly, Baker's recommendations were seldom taken seriously and rarely implemented by the SCLC leadership. In his study on the origins of the Civil Rights Movement, Morris concludes that "it appears that sexism and Baker's non-clergy status minimized her impact on the SCLC" in the late 1950s. Yet, of all the early civil rights leaders Baker was the one to grasp the significance of the student sit-ins begun in Greensboro, North Carolina, on February 1, 1960. She persuaded the SCLC to underwrite a conference, pulling together more than three hundred students from across the South. Out of this meeting emerged the Student Nonviolent Coordinating Committee (SNCC).[42]

Another heroine of the Civil Rights Movement was Fannie Lou Hamer (1917-1977). Born in Montgomery County, Mississippi, Hamer spent most of her adult life working as a sharecropper and timekeeper on a plantation four miles east of Ruleville, Mississippi. In 1962, she was fired for attempting to vote. Thereafter threats on her life and severe physical abuse plagued her existence. Undaunted, Hamer became involved in SNCC and from 1963 to 1967 served in the capacity of field secretary. On April 26, 1964, when the Mississippi Democratic party refused to permit black participation in the state convention, Hamer and others founded the Mississippi Freedom Democratic Party (MFDP). She became vice-chairman. Later in the summer of 1964 Hamer led a delegation of Mississippi citizens to the Democratic National Convention in Atlantic City. There the MFDP challenged the seats of the all-white Mississippi delegation. The result of the challenge was an unprecedented pledge from the national Democratic party not to seat delegations that excluded black Americans at the 1968 national convention.[43]

The voice and moral vision of black women in the Civil Rights Movement and later in the Women's Liberation Movement may have been muted and unheeded, but the silence was irrevocably shattered during the decades of the 1970s and 1980s. New images of black women emerged in the wake of the Civil Rights Movement. These new images were unveiled to the American public through the creative expression of over a dozen outstanding black women novelists, poets, artists, and musicians. Even today American society—black and white, male and female—knows not what to make of this new array of images so forcefully unleashed by a galaxy of creators, or indeed, what it portends for the future. Some would contend that black women hold the key to the country's future. There is no universal New Black Woman, but what is new is the fact that we are beginning to listen and to see ourselves on our own terms and in our own right.

In 1859 Harriet Wilson, a domestic servant, wrote the first black novel, the semi-autobiographical *Our Nig*. Frances Ellen Harper later in the century published her novel, *Iola Leroy*, in which she chronicled the struggle of a black woman to maintain her pride, dignity, and racial commitment during the years of slavery and Reconstruction. The 1920s witnessed the birth of the Harlem Renaissance. It was an era rich in black creativity. Although numerous black women writers, artists, musicians, and performers participated in and enhanced the cultural richness and ethos of the period, their work, until quite recently, remained neglected and unexamined.[44] Only since the appearance and critical acclaim accorded Alice Walker's *The Color Purple* (1983), Toni Morrison's *Tar Baby* (1982), and Gloria Naylor's *The Women of Brewster Place* (1982), among others, have Americans begun to recognize the literary achievements and contributions of black women.

Although twentieth-century black women's writing in its great diversity defies easy characterization, there are common threads. Harlem Renaissance novelists Jessie Redmond Fauset, Nella Larson, and Zora Neale Hurston and the post-World War II writers Margaret Walker, Ann Petry, Gwendolyn Brooks, Alice Childress, and Lorraine Hansberry, along with more recent authors Gayle Jones, Toni Cade Bambara, Maya Angelou, Ntozake Shange, and Paule Marshall, all reveal a strong sense of race and class consciousness and political engagement. There are important generational differences, to be sure. The more contemporary authors write increasingly and boldly of the sexual conflict between black women and men. Their tone is distinctively more feminist, or "womanist" as Alice Walker would describe it, and their works are much more stylistically unconventional than their predecessors. They stress women's oppression as well as black oppression under capitalism and often offer radical visions of family, sexual, and community relations in ways that repudiate repressive white cultural norms.[45] While recently published biographies of Zora Neale Hurston, blues singer Ma Rainey, and the diaries and letters of Alice Dunbar Nelson are a step in the right direction, we need similar studies of such cultural luminaries as blues singer Billie Holiday, playwright and pan-Africanist Lorraine Hansberry, painter Elizabeth Catlett, and gospel singer Mahalia Jackson.[46]

No complete study and understanding of black women's history is possible without a simultaneous examination of the shape and contours of their creative outpourings. Scholars, historians, and literary critics have only recently begun to scale the rocky and complex terrain of the minds and works of creative black women. When the stories of black women are told in all their complexity, pain, and beauty, then and only then will we be in a position to comprehend fully the meaning of black lives at the end of the rainbow and by extension the entire American experience. There is much work ahead of us.

Female Slave Resistance

The Economics of Sex

The question of the extent and nature of black resistance to slavery has been the subject of a number of recent historical studies.[1] These works, concentrating as they do on the examination of black male resistance to the slave system, have demonstrated that such resistance was carried on both overtly in the form of slave rebellions and covertly in indirect attacks on the system, through resistance to the whip, feigning of illness, conscious laziness, and other means of avoiding work and impeding production. None of these studies, however, has considered in depth the forms of black female resistance to slavery, although they have suggested a methodology for attempting such an investigation. This paper is concerned with uncovering the means through which female slaves expressed their political and economic opposition to the slave system. What behavior patterns did enslaved black women adopt to protect themselves and their children and to undermine the system which oppressed and exploited them?

Unlike male slaves, female slaves suffered a dual form of oppression. In addition to the economic exploitation which they experienced along with black males, females under slavery were oppressed sexually as well. Sexual oppression and exploitation refer not only to the obvious and well-documented fact of forced sexual intercourse with white masters but also to those forms of exploitation resulting from the very fact of her female biological system. For example, the female slave in the role of the mammy was regularly required to nurse white babies in addition to and often instead of her own children. In his *Roll, Jordon, Roll: The World the Slaves Made,* Eugene Genovese acknowledges the uniquely difficult position in which this practice placed the mammy:

> More than any other slave, she had absorbed the paternalist ethos and accepted her place in a system of reciprocal obligations defined from above. In so doing, she developed pride, resourcefulness, and a high sense of responsibility to white and Black people alike. . . . She did not reject her people in order to identify with stronger whites, but she did place herself in a relationship to her own people that reinforced the paternalist order.[2]

While Genovese gives evidence of the mammy's manipulation of her favored position, the pivotal question of how it must have felt to be forced to nurse and raise her future oppressors remains unexamined.

Another major aspect of the sexual oppression of black women under slavery took the form of the white master's consciously constructed view of black female sexuality. This construct, which was designed to justify his own sexual passion toward her, also blamed the female slave for the sexual exploitation that she experienced at the hands of her master. Winthrop Jordan comments in his *White Over Black: American Attitudes toward the Negro, 1550-1812,* that white men,

> by calling the Negro woman passionate . . . were offering the best possible justifications for their own passions. Not only did the Negro woman's warmth constitute a logical explanation for the white man's infidelity, but, much more important, it helped shift responsibility from himself to her. If she was *that* lascivious—well, a man could scarcely be blamed for succumbing against overwhelming odds.[3]

It is clear from several slave narratives that the female slave was well aware of the image of her sexuality that was fostered among the white male population. In her narrative, *Incidents in the Life of a Slave Girl,* Linda Brent offers a revealing observation on the effect of this image on the female slave: "If God has bestowed beauty upon her, it will prove her greatest curse. That which commands admiration in the white woman only hastens the degradation of the female slave."[4] In his article "New Orleans: The Mistress of the Trade," Frederic

Bancroft documents Brent's observation and shows how this image of black female sexuality gave rise to a section of the slave trade specifically designed to profit from the sale of attractive black women, or, as they were known at the time, "fancy girls."[5] Bancroft points out that slave traders frequently prided themselves on the numbers of such women they had for sale and on the high prices commanded by their physical appearance. Often these women sold for prices that far exceeded those which planters were willing to pay for a field laborer. In 1857, for example, the *Memphis Eagle and Enquirer* ran an editorial in which it was observed that "a slave woman is advertised to be sold in St. Louis who is so surpassingly beautiful that $5,000 has already been offered for her, at private sale, and refused."[6]

How, then, did a female slave resist both the economic and sexual oppressions which were a part of her daily life? Three intimately related forms of resistance peculiar to female slaves emerge from the narratives. The first method can be called sexual abstinence. This method ranged from refusing or attempting to avoid sexual intercourse with the white master to a strong wish to delay marriage to a male slave while hope remained that marriage and childbirth could occur in a free state. Elizabeth Keckley, who toward the end of her life became a seamstress for Mrs. Abraham Lincoln, discusses this form of resistance in her narrative, *Behind the Scenes: Thirty Years a Slave and Four Years in the White House.* Her story is typical in outlining the extent and duration of her attempt to avoid the designs of her licentious master. She recalls that she was "regarded as fair-looking for one of my race,"[7] and that as a result of her appearance her master pursued her for four years:

> I do not care to dwell upon this subject, for it is fraught with pain. Suffice it to say, that he persecuted me for four years, and I— I— became a mother. The child of which he was the father was the only child I ever brought into the world. If my poor boy ever suffered any humiliating pangs on account of birth, he could not blame his mother, for God knows that she did not wish to give him life; he must blame the edicts of that society which deemed it no crime to undermine the virtue of girls in my then position.[8]

Presumably, Mrs. Keckley found this experience so upsetting that she could not bring herself to have another child—not even after she had gained her freedom.

Similarly, Linda Brent described her prolonged attempts to avoid sexual relations with her master, Dr. Flint. She recalls that she was able to use the presence of her grandmother on the plantation to avoid her master's advances because "though she had been a slave, Dr. Flint was afraid of her. He dreaded her scorching rebukes. Moreover, she was known and patronized by many people; and he did not wish to have his villainy made public."[9]

Ellen Craft along with her future husband, William, escaped slavery in a most ingenious fashion. Mrs. Craft was so reluctant to have children while she remained in slavery that she and William agreed to delay their marriage until they reached the North. In their narrative, "Running a Thousand Miles for Freedom," William Craft perceptively explains his wife's motivations:

> My wife was torn from her mother's embrace in childhood, and taken to a distant part of the country. She had seen so many other children separated from their parents in this cruel manner, that the mere thought of her ever becoming a mother of a child, to linger out a miserable existence under the wretched system of American slavery, appeared to fill her very soul with horror; and as she had taken what I felt to be an important view of her condition, I did not, at first, press the marriage, but agreed to assist her in trying to devise some plan by which we might escape from our unhappy condition, and then be married.[10]

A second method of female resistance to slavery in general and to sexual exploitation in particular took the form of abortion. Because abortion appears to have been less common than sexual abstinence, it seems fair to assume that destruction of the fetus extracted a higher psychological toll that did abstinence. In a recent study of the black family, Herbert Gutman observes that the conscious decision on the part of a slave woman to terminate her pregnancy was one act that was totally beyond the control of the master of the plantation. Gutman offers evidence of several southern physicians who commented upon abortion and the use of contraceptive methods among the slave population:

> The Hancock County, Georgia, physician E. M. Pendleton reported in 1849 that among his patients "abortion and miscarriage" occurred more frequently among slave than white free women. The cause was either "slave labor (exposure, violent exercise, etc.)" or "as the planters believe, that the Blacks are possessed of a secret by which they destroy the fetus at an early stage of gestation." All county practitioners, he added, "are aware of the frequent complaints of planters about the unnatural tendency in the African female population to destroy her offspring. Whole families of women . . . fail to have any children."[11]

Gutman also recounts a situation in which a planter had kept between four and six slave women "of the proper age to breed" for twenty-five years and that "only two children had been born on the place at full term." It was later discovered that the slaves had concocted a medicine with which they were able to terminate their unwanted pregnancies.[12] Gutman found evidence as well of a master who claimed that an older female slave had discovered a remedy for pregnancies and had been "instrumental in all . . . the abortions on his place."[13]

This last instance suggests that even those women who did not resist slavery through actually having an abortion themselves resisted even more covertly by aiding those who desired them. It is therefore possible that a sort of female conspiracy existed on the Southern plantation. This requires further study. In an interesting twist to the apparently chronic problem of unwanted and forced pregnancies, there is evidence that female slaves, recognizing the importance of their role in the maintenance of the slave systems, often feigned pregnancy as a method of receiving lighter work loads. The success, however limited, of this kind of ploy would also require the aid of other female slaves on the plantation—a midwife, for example, who might testify to the master that one of his female slaves was indeed pregnant.

In their illuminating article, "Day to Day Resistance to Slavery," Raymond and Alice Bauer note that "pretending to be pregnant was a type of escape in a class by itself, since the fraud must inevitably have been discovered."[14] To illustrate, they include the following report in their article:

I will tell you of a most comical account Mr. —— has given of the prolonged and still protracted pseudo-pregnancy of a woman called Markie, who for many more months than are generally required for the process of continuing the human species, pretended to be what the Germans pathetically and poetically call "in good hope" and continued to reap increased rations as the reward of her expectation, till she finally had to disappoint the estate and receive a flogging.[15]

Apparently, the increased allotment of food and the possibility of lighter work were enough inducement for this woman to risk the punishment which she must have known would follow. In this case the slave woman was perceptive enough of the importance of her procreative function for the maintenance of the slave system to manipulate to her own advantage the precise function for which she was most valued by the master.

Possibly the most psychologically devastating means which the slave parent had for undermining the slave system was infanticide. The frequency with which this occurred is by no means clear. Several historians have contended that infanticide was quite rare, and Genovese writes that "slave abortions, much less infanticide, did not become a major problem for the slave holders or an ordinary form of 'resistance' for the slaves. Infanticide occurred, but so far as the detected cases reveal anything, only in some special circumstances."[16] The subject of infanticide under slavery is clearly in need of further study. For our purposes it is important to note that the relatively small number of documented cases is not as significant as the fact that it occurred at all. Raymond and Alice Bauer reveal how both infanticide and suicide were combined in the following account:

> Not only were slaves known to take the lives of their masters or overseers, but they were now and then charged with the murder of their own children, sometimes to prevent them growing up in bondage. In Covington, a father and mother, shut up in a slave baracoon and doomed to the southern market, "when there was no eye to pity them and no arm to save," did by mutual agreement "send the souls of their children to heaven rather than have them descend to the hell of slavery," then both parents committed suicide.[17]

Genovese notes one instance in which "the white citizens of Virginia petitioned in 1822 to spare a slave condemned to death for killing her infant. The child's father was a respectable white man, and the woman insisted that she would not have killed a child of her own color."[18] There are numerous instances in which a slave woman simply preferred to end her child's life rather than allow the child to grow up enslaved. Genovese writes that "for the most part, however, the slaves recognized infanticide as murder. They loved their children too much to do away with them; courageously, they resolved to raise them as best they could, and entrusted their fate to God."[19] He does not appear to be acknowledging the motivations for infanticide offered repeatedly by the slave parents themselves. Far from viewing such actions as murder, and therefore indicating these as lack of love, slave parents who took their children's lives may have done so out of a higher form of love and a clearer understanding of the living death that awaited their children under slavery. Since this explanation is the one offered most frequently in the narratives, and since there does not seem to be any evidence at this time that contradicts the slaves' statements, they should be accepted as reflective of their true motivations.

It is also possible that there were other motivations behind infanticide. It may have occurred as a response to rape or forced pregnancy and it was an act which, along with sexual abstinence and abortion, had economic implications as well. The narratives reveal that slave children were sometimes used as pawns in a power struggle between plantation owners and their slaves. Owners used the sale or the threat of sale of slave children as a means of manipulating their recalcitrant or troublesome slaves, and the slaves in turn used their children to manipulate the behavior of their masters. There is one documented instance, for example, in which a particularly rebellious female slave, Fannie, is told that she must be sold following an incident in which she physically attacked her mistress. To increase the harshness of the punishment she is informed by her master that her infant will remain on the plantation. One of her older daughters recalls her mother's response:

> At this, ma took the baby by its feet, a foot in each hand, and with the baby's head swinging downward, she vowed to smash its brains out before she'd leave it. Tears were streaming down

her face. It was seldom that ma cried and everyone knew that she meant every word. Ma took her baby with her.[20]

In this instance the threat of infanticide on the part of the slave mother was transformed into an effective means for gaining power over the planter and control over at least part of her life. Thus, it seems that there were complex motivations involved in both infanticide and the threat of infanticide.

In attempting to evaluate the consequences for the slave system of these acts of resistance, Genovese's definition of paternalism is most helpful. He writes that, "Paternalism in any historical setting defines relations of superordination and subordination. Its strength as a prevailing ethos increases as the members of the community accept—or feel compelled to accept—these relations as legitimate."[21] As was pointed out earlier, slave women were expected to serve a dual function in this system and therefore suffered a dual oppression. They constituted an important and necessary part of the work force and they were, through their child-bearing function, the one group most responsible for the size and indeed the maintenance of the slave labor pool. Therefore, when they resisted sexual exploitation through such means as sexual abstention, abortion, and infanticide, they were, at the same time, rejecting their vital economic function as breeders. This resistance, of course, became especially important after 1808, when it was no longer legal to import slaves into the United States from Africa.

The slave woman's resistance to sexual and therefore to economic exploitation posed a potentially severe threat to paternalism itself, for implicit in such action was the slave woman's refusal to accept her designated responsibilities within the slave system as legitimate. This acceptance of mutual responsibility on the part of both the slaves and the masters was, as Genovese points out, at the heart of the maintenance of the paternalistic worldview. The female slave, through her sexual resistance, attacked the very assumptions upon which the slave order was constructed and maintained.

Resistance to sexual exploitation therefore had major political and economic implications. A woman who elected not to have children, or, to put it another way, engaged in sexual abstinence, abortion, or infanticide negated through individual or group action her role in the maintenance of the slave pool. To the extent that in so doing she redefined her role in the system, she introduced a unit of psychological heterogeneity into a worldview which depended, for its survival, on homogeneity, at least with respect to the assumptions of its ideology.

The examples quoted above strongly indicate that the slave woman's decision to participate in these particular forms of resistance was made consciously and with full awareness of the potential political and economic ramifications involved. In rejecting her role in the economic advancement of the slave system, she could reduce the numbers of slaves available for the slave trade and undermine her master's effort to profit from exploiting her sexually. The planters were the only beneficiaries of the increase in the numbers of slaves: $1,500 for a good, strong buck; $1,200 for a hardworking, childbearing wench, with no large scale investment necessary to insure future profit. The master could presumably simply sit back and wait for the children to be born. If there was no black male available, he could engage in the procreative process himself. The result was the same, made conveniently so, by laws that stipulated that the child inherited the condition of the mother.

In his *Once a Slave: The Slaves' View of Slavery*, Stanley Feldstein notes that Frederick Douglass makes explicit the importance of breeding slaves, even for the less wealthy planters:

> Frederick Douglass told of the case of a master who was financially able to purchase only one slave. Therefore, he bought her as a "breeder," and then hired a married man to live with her for one year. Every night he would place the man and woman together in a room, at the end of the year, the woman gave birth to twins. The children were regarded by the master as an important addition to his wealth, and his joy was such that the breeder was kept in the finest material comfort in the hope that she would continue providing good fortune to the master and his family.[22]

Perhaps the most revealing example of the female slave's awareness of the sexual/economic nexus inherent in her dual role in the slave system is offered by Jane Blake in her narrative, *Memoirs of Margaret Jane Blake*. She commented that many slave women resisted pregnancy because they did not want their children to grow up in a state of bondage; she continued that if "all the bond women had been of the same mind, how soon the institution could have vanished from the face of the earth, and all the misery belonging to it, been lifted from the hearts of the holders of slaves."[23]

One of the more striking aspects of the subject of female slave resistance is its complex nature. The decision to resist in the three ways that have been outlined involved sexual, emotional, economic, and political concerns. The examination of the strategies that were developed by the female slave to resist sexual and economic exploitation represents a legitimate and necessary area of inquiry if we are to understand slave resistance in general. In connection with this area, we need to know much more about the role that male slaves played in helping slave women resist both sexual and economic exploitation. The dynamics of female slave behavior cannot be fully understood if examined in a vacuum.

Instances of sexual abstinence, abortion, and of infanticide are important for the same reasons that historians study the three major slave rebellions of the nineteenth century. As with the rebellions, the important point with respect to these modes of female resistance is not the infrequency with which they occurred, if indeed they were infrequent, but the fact that these methods were used at all. Through a closer examination of the responses of black women to slavery, we can gain further insight into the interaction of males and females of both races on the southern plantation.

Rape and the Inner
Lives of Black Women
Thoughts on the Culture of Dissemblance

One of the most remarked upon but least analyzed themes in the history of southern black women deals with black women's sexual vulnerability and powerlessness as victims of rape and domestic violence. Author Hazel Carby put it baldly when she declared:

> The institutionalized rape of black women has never been as powerful a symbol of black oppression as the spectacle of lynching. Rape has always involved patriarchal notions of women being, at best, not entirely unwilling accomplices, if not outwardly inviting sexual attack. The links between black women and illicit sexuality consolidated during the antebellum years had powerful ideological consequences for the next hundred and fifty years.[1]

I suggest that rape and the threat of rape influenced the development of a culture of dissemblance among southern black women. By dissemblance I mean the behavior and attitudes of black women that created the appearance of openness and disclosure but actually shielded the truth of their inner lives and selves from their oppressors.

In a poignant and insightful compilation of oral histories of southern black domestics and their white employers, editor Susan Tucker asserts, "The culture of women in general, which includes that of both black and white, has been hidden within our dreams, deemed not worthy of consideration in a male-dominated society, and obscured even to women themselves."[2] While dissemblance may very well be an integral feature of general southern women's culture, it exists in an even more complex fashion among black women who endured the combination of race, gender, and class oppression.

Most women in American society whether two hundred years ago or today, have a fear of rape. Yet black and white women have dealt with this fear in radically different ways, ones which reinforced the silences between them and obscured their vision of each other. Southern white women, as Susan Tucker argues, were taught from childhood that "black men were their potential rapists and that only in aligning themselves with white men could they be spared." These early teachings, added to their fear and economic dependence on white males, made it virtually impossible for southern white women to believe or admit that white men were capable or guilty of raping black women. Thus southern white women attributed the presence of mulattoes in their communities to the lax moral standards of black women.[3]

Now, only recently, are black women beginning to break the silence surrounding the long history of their rape and economic exploitation. Themes of rape and sexual vulnerability have received considerable attention in the recent literary outpourings of black women novelists. Of the last six novels I have read and reread, for example, five contained a rape scene or a graphic description of domestic violence.[4] Moreover, this is not a recent phenomenon in black women's literary and autobiographical writing.

Virtually every known nineteenth-century female slave narrative contains a reference to, at some juncture, the ever-present threat and reality of rape. Two works come immediately to mind: Harriet Jacobs' *Incidents in the Life of a Slave Girl* (1861) and Elizabeth Keckley's *Behind the Scenes: Thirty Years a Slave and Four Years in the White House* (1868). Yet there is another thread running throughout these slave narratives, one that concerns these captive women's efforts to resist the misappropriation of and to maintain the integrity of their own sexuality. The combined influence of rape (or the threat of rape), domestic violence, and a desire to escape economic oppression born of racism and sexism is the key to understanding the hidden motivations of major social protest and migratory movements in African-American history. Historian David Katzman declared in his study of domestic service that, "Although the mark of caste would follow them north, conditions there were different enough to promote a steady migration of young Southern black women northward between the Civil War and the Great Depression of the 1930s."[5]

Second only to black women's fear of sexual violation is the pervasive theme of the frustration attendant to finding suitable employment. Oral histories and autobiographical accounts of twentieth-century southern black women who moved north are replete with themes about work. Scholars of black urban history and black labor history agree that migrating black women faced greater economic discrimination and had fewer employment opportunities than did black men. Black women's work was the most undesirable and least remunerative of all work available to migrants.

As late as 1930 a little over three thousand black women, or 15 percent of the black female labor force in Chicago, were unskilled and semiskilled factory operatives. Thus, over 80 percent of all employed black women continued to work as personal servants and domestics. Historian Allan H. Spear noted,

> Negro women were particularly limited in their search for desirable positions. Clerical work was practically closed to them and only a few could qualify as school teachers. Negro domestics often received less than white women for the same work, and they could rarely rise to the position of head servant in large households—a place traditionally held by a Swedish woman.[6]

Given that many southern black women migrants were doomed to work in the same kinds of domestic service jobs they held in the South, one wonders why they bothered to move in the first place. There were some significant differences that help explain this phenomenon.

A maid earning seven dollars a week in Cleveland perceived herself to be, and probably was, much better off than a counterpart receiving two dollars and fifty cents a week in Mobile, Alabama. A factory worker, even one whose work was dirty and low-paying, could and did imagine herself better off than domestic servants who endured the unrelenting scrutiny, interference, and complaints of household mistresses and the untoward advances of male family members. But one black woman migrant to New Jersey from a small town in North Carolina actually favored performing domestic service work in the

South. She explained, "You'd go about workin'—when I was down home—at eight o'clock; you was workin' till about two- or two-thirty. Then you was goin' home. And it wasn't as hard as jobs in the North, not as hard as here." In spite of the difference and her obvious love of the South, still she admitted that not all was rosy, adding, "When I was there the colored wasn't allowed to ride in the bus with white people."[7]

I believe that in order to understand this historical migratory trend we need to understand the non-economic motives propelling black female migration. I believe that many black women quit the South out of a desire to achieve personal autonomy and to escape both from sexual exploitation inside and outside of their families and from the rape and threat of rape by white as well as black males. To focus on the sexual and the personal impetus for black women's migration in the first several decades of the twentieth century is not to dismiss or diminish the significance of economic motives. Rather, as historian Lawrence W. Levine cautioned, "As indisputably important as the economic motive was, it is possible to overstress it so that the black migration is converted into an inexorable force and Negroes are seen once again not as actors capable of affecting at least some part of their destinies, but primarily as beings who are acted upon—southern leaves blown North by the winds of destitution." It is reasonable to assume that some black women were indeed "southern leaves blown North," and that there were many others who were self-propelled actresses seeking respect, control over their own sexuality, and access to better paying jobs. In *Children of Strangers*, Kathryn L. Morgan recounts the story of how her female ancestors migrated to Philadelphia from Lynchburg, Virginia, and passed for white during the day in order to secure decent paying jobs in downtown restaurants.[8]

My own research on the history of black women in the Middle West has led me to questions about how, when, and under what circumstances the majority of them settled in the region. These questions have led to others concerning the process of black women's migration across time, from the flights of runaway slaves in the antebellum period to the great migrations of the first half of the twentieth century. The most common, and certainly the most compelling, motive for running, fleeing, or migrating was a desire to retain or claim some control of their own sexual beings and the children they bore. In the antebellum period hundreds of slave women risked their lives and those of their loved ones to run away to the ostensibly free states of the Northwest Territory, in quest of an elusive sexual freedom for themselves and freedom from slavery for their children.

Two things became immediately apparent as I proceeded with researching the history and reading the autobiographies of late nineteenth and early twentieth-century migrating, or fleeing, black women. First, that these women were sexual hostages and domestic violence victims in the South (or in other regions of the country) did not reduce their determination to acquire power to protect themselves and to become agents of social change once they settled in midwestern communities. Second, the fundamental tensions between black women and the rest of the society—especially white men, white women, and to a lesser extent, black men—involved a multifaceted struggle to determine who would control black women's productive and reproductive capacities and their sexuality. At stake for black women caught up in this ever evolving, constantly shifting, but relentless war was the acquisition of personal autonomy and economic liberation. Their quest for autonomy, dignity, and access to opportunity to earn an adequate living was (and still is) complicated and frustrated by the antagonisms of race, class, and gender conflict, and by differences in regional economies. At heart, though, the relationship between black women and the larger society has always been, and continues to be, adversarial.

Because of the interplay of racial animosity, class tensions, gender role differentiation, and regional economic variations, black women as a rule developed a politics of silence, and adhered to a cult of secrecy, a culture of dissemblance, to protect the sanctity of the inner aspects of their lives. The dynamics of dissemblance involved creating the appearance of disclosure, or openness about themselves and their feelings, while actually remaining enigmatic. Only with secrecy, thus achieving a self-imposed invisibility, could ordinary black women acquire the psychic space and gather the resources needed to hold their own in their often one-sided and mismatched struggle to resist oppression.

The honing of dissemblance skills was perfected during black women's work as domestic servants. Young Florence Grier, for example, left Oklahoma for California in 1942 and later recalled the sexual politics of domestic service. In a scene that probably resonates in the memories of thousands of black domestics, Grier described her encounter with a white female employer:

> When I said, "I'm not getting a half day, and this is what you promised me when I took this job," she said, "Well, you're just a bit too smart! For your smartness . . . you're just gonna get a dollar, ninety-five cents!" And I said, "if that nickel will do any good, you keep it! But I'm gonna be sure to tell every other negro maid in the town the kind of person you are."

Grier admitted that she was afraid to have been so outspoken. She explained, "To hit back or to do too much talking you could get murdered. You just don't look a white woman in the face and tell her that she was doing you wrong!" On many occasions Grier had to fight the untoward advances of white men in the homes. She declared with wisdom born of resistance that "a man is a man. And I really haven't found any difference in 'em. Only that the white man will want an undercover situation. It's not to be talked about or anything." She elaborated on the variety of approaches or overtures made, such as, "If you're nice to me—you're getting, say you're getting a dollar an hour— wouldn't you like to make your check a little bit bigger?"[9]

The inclination of the larger society to ignore them as elements considered "marginal" actually enabled subordinate black women to fashion the veil of secrecy, or "invisibility," but paradoxically contributed to their failure to realize equal opportunity or to receive respect in the larger society. There would be no room on the pedestal for the southern black lady, nor could she join her white sisters in the prison of "true womanhood." In other words, stereotypes, negative images, and debilitating assumptions filled the space left empty due to inadequate and erroneous information about the true contributions, capabilities, and identities of black women.

This line of analysis is not without problems. To suggest that black women deliberately developed a culture of dissemblance implies that they endeavored to create, and were not simply reacting to, widespread misrepresentations of themselves in white minds. Clearly, black women did not possess the power to eradicate negative social and sexual images of their womanhood. Rather, what I propose is that in the face of the pervasive stereotypes and negative estimations of the sexuality of black women, it was imperative that they collectively create alternative self-images and shield from scrutiny these private empowering definitions of self. I would argue that a secret, undisclosed *persona* allowed the individual black woman to function, to work effectively as a domestic in white households, to bear and rear children, endure the domestic violence of frequently under- or unemployed mates, to support churches, found institutions, and engage in social service activities—all while living within a clearly hostile white, patriarchal, middle-class America.

The problem that this penchant for secrecy presents to the historian is readily apparent. Deborah Gray White has commented about the difficulty of finding primary source material for the personal aspects of black female life:

> Black women have also been reluctant to donate their papers to manuscript repositories. That is in part a manifestation of the black woman's perennial concern with image, a justifiable concern born of centuries of vilification. Black women's reluctance to donate personal papers also stems from the adversarial nature of the relationship that countless black women have had with many public institutions, and the resultant suspicion of anyone seeking private information.[10]

White's allusion to "resultant suspicion" speaks implicitly to one important reason why so much of the inner life of black women remains hidden. Indeed, the concepts of "secrets" and "dissemblance" as I employ them hint at those issues that late nineteenth- and early twentieth-century black women believed better left unknown, unwritten, and unspoken except in whispered tones. Their alarm, their fear, or their Victorian sense of modesty implies that those who broke the silence provided grist for detractors' mills, and, even more ominously, tore the protective cloaks from their inner selves. Undoubtedly, these fears and suspicions contribute to the absence of sophisticated historical discussion of the impact of rape (or the threat of rape) and incidences of domestic violence on the shape of black women's experiences.

However, the self-imposed secrecy and the culture of dissemblance, coupled with the larger society's unwillingness to discard tired and worn stereotypes, have also led to ironically misplaced emphases. Until quite recently, for example, when historians talked about the rape of slave women they often bemoaned the damage that this act did to the black male's sense of esteem and self-respect. He was powerless to protect his woman from white rapists. Few scholars probed the effect that rape, the threat of rape, and domestic violence had on the psychic development of the female victims. In the late nineteenth- and twentieth-centuries, as Carby has indicated, lynching, not rape, became the most powerful and compelling symbol of black oppression. Lynching, it came to be understood, was one of the major non-economic reasons why southern black men migrated North.

The culture of dissemblance assumed its most institutional-ized form in the founding, in 1896, of the National Association of Colored Women (NACW). This association of black women's clubs quickly became the largest and most enduring protest organization in the history of African Americans. Its size alone should have warranted the same degree of scholarly attention paid to Marcus Garvey's Uni-versal Negro Improvement Association. By 1914 the NACW had a membership of 50,000, far surpassing the membership of every other protest organization of the time, including the National Association for the Advancement of Colored People and the National Urban League. By 1945, for example, the Detroit Association of Colored Women's Clubs, federated in 1921, boasted seventy-three member clubs with nearly three thousand individual members.[11] Not surpris-ingly, the primary targets of NACW attack were the derogatory images and negative stereotypes of black women's sexuality.

Mary Church Terrell, the first president of the NACW, de-clared in her initial presidential address that there were objectives of the black women's struggle that could only be accomplished by the mothers, wives, daughters, and sisters of this race. She proclaimed, "We wish to set in motion influences that shall stop the ravages made by practices that sap our strength, and preclude the possibility of advancement." She boldly announced, "We proclaim to the world that the women of our race have become partners in the great firm of progress and reform. . . . We refer to the fact that this is an association of colored women, because our peculiar status in this country . . . seems to demand that we stand by ourselves."[12]

At the core of essentially every activity of NACW's individual members was a concern with creating positive images of black women's sexuality. To counter negative stereotypes many black women felt compelled to downplay, even deny, sexual expression. The twin obsessions with naming and combating sexual exploitation tinted and shaped black women's support even of the woman's suffrage movement. Nannie H. Burroughs, famed religious leader and founder of the National Training School for Women and Girls at Washington, D.C., cajoled her sisters to fight for the ballot. She asserted that with the ballot black women could ensure the passage of legislation to win legal protection against rapists. Calling the ballot a "weapon of moral defense" she exploded, "when she [a black woman] appears in court in defense of her virtue, she is looked upon with amused contempt. She needs the ballot to reckon with men who place no value upon her virtue."[13]

Likewise, determination to save young unskilled and unemployed black women from having to bargain sex in exchange for food and shelter motivated some NACW members to establish boarding houses and domestic service training centers, such as the Phillis Wheatley Homes and Burroughs' National Training School. Their efforts to provide black women with protection from sexual exploitation and with dignified work inspired other club members in local communities around the country to support or to found hospitals and nursing training schools.

At least one plausible consequence of this heightened mobilization of black women was a decline in black urban birth rates. As black women became more economically self-sufficient, better educated, and more involved in self-improvement efforts, including participation in the flourishing black women's club movement in southern and in midwestern communities, they had greater access to birth control information. As the institutional infrastructure of black women's clubs, sororities, church-based women's groups, and charity organizations sank roots into black communities, it encouraged its members to embrace those values, behaviors, and attitudes traditionally associated with the middle-classes. To urban black middle-class aspirants, the social stigma of having many children did, perhaps, inhibit reproduction. To be sure, over time the gradually evolving male-female demographic imbalance meant that increasingly significant numbers of black women, especially those employed in the professions in urban midwestern communities, would never marry. The point stressed here, however, is that not having children was, perhaps for the very first time, a choice enjoyed by large numbers of black women.

There were additional burdens placed upon and awards granted to the small cadre of single, educated, professional black women who chose not to marry or bear children. The more educated they were, the greater was their sense of being responsible for the advancement of the race and for the elevation of black womanhood. They held these expectations of themselves and found a sense of racial obligation reinforced by the demands of the black community and its institutions. In return for their "sacrifice of sexual expression," the community gave them respect and recognition. Moreover, this freedom and autonomy represented a socially sanctioned, meaningful alternative to the uncertainties of marriage and the demands of raising children. The increased employment opportunities, whether real or imagined, and the culture of dissemblance enabled many migrating black women to become financially independent and simultaneously to fashion socially useful and autonomous lives, while reclaiming control over their own sexuality and reproductive capacities.

This is not to say that black women, once settled into midwestern communities, never engaged in sex for pay or occasional prostitution. Sara Brooks, a black domestic servant from Alabama who migrated to Cleveland, Ohio, in the 1930s, could not disguise her contempt for women who bartered their bodies. As she declared, while commenting on her own struggle to pay the mortgage on her house, "Some women woulda had a man to come and live in the house and had an outside boyfriend, too, in order to get the house paid for and the bills." She scornfully added, "They meet a man and if he promises em four or five dollars to go to bed, they'd grab it. That's called sellin your own body, and I wasn't raised like that."[14] What escaped Brooks in this moralizing moment was that her poor and powerless black female neighbors were extracting value from the only thing the society now allowed them to sell. As long as they occupied an enforced subordinate position within American society this "sellin your own body," as Sara Brooks put it, was rape.

At some fundamental level all black women historians are engaged in the process of historical reclamation, but it is not enough simply to uncover the hidden facts, the obscure names of black foremothers. Merely to reclaim and to narrate their past deeds and contributions risks rendering a skewed history focused primarily upon the articulate, relatively well-positioned members of the aspiring black middle-class. In synchrony with the reclaiming and narrating must be the development of an array of analytical frameworks that allow us to understand why black women of all classes behave in certain ways and how they acquired agency. The culture of dissemblance is one such framework.

The migration of hundreds of thousands of black women out of the South between 1915 and 1945, the formation of thousands of black women's clubs, and the activities of the NACW are actions that enabled these women to formulate and put into place infrastructures of protest and resistance: one of these was a culture of dissemblance. This culture born of rape and fears of rape shaped the course of black women's history. It was this culture, grounded on the twin prongs of protest and resistance, that enabled the creation of positive alternative images of black women's sexual selves and facilitated their mental and physical survival in a hostile world.

Black Women's History, White Women's History

The Juncture of Race and Class

The black women's history project is well underway and yet I am troubled and concerned for reasons I shall soon explain. But first the good news. Little did I suspect in 1979, when I wrote my first essay in black women's history entitled "Female Slave Resistance: The Economics of Sex," that within a decade there would exist over a dozen monographs and anthologies, a sixteen-volume series of articles and other writings, and scores of master's theses and dissertations, not to mention a wide assortment of special reclamation projects including the Black Women in the Middle West project, the Black Women's Oral History project of the Schlesinger Library, and the Black Women Physicians project of the Women's Medical College Archives in Philadelphia. In addition, *SAGE: A Scholarly Journal on Black Women* is published twice a year, and research centers at Spelman College in Atlanta, Georgia, and at Memphis State University in Memphis, Tennessee, concentrate on the lives and experiences of black and other women of color. During the past decade, sessions on black women's history have become almost commonplace at major historical conventions. Moreover, historical journals with increasing frequency have begun to publish articles on black women. Whereas I once lamented that the historical experiences of black women had been neglected, obscured, distorted, or relegated to the back pages of our collective consciousness, such is not the case today.

Black women historians have enriched our theoretical discourse and at the same time have reclaimed and made more visible the deeds of their and our forebears. Contemporary analyses of the inter-sections of race, class, and gender, of womanist consciousness, and of the culture or art of dissimulation or dissemblance have challenged both black and women's historians in profound ways. Furthermore, the continuing search for new and more effective strategies to present, and metaphors to illuminate the new knowledges thus far created has inspired many to question and to review how we teach and understand both the politics and poetics of difference. In subtle and nuanced ways with neither fanfare nor declaration, black women historians have put into motion a quiet intellectual transformation. A passage from Thomas S. Kuhn's *The Structure of Scientific Revolutions* has resonance. He writes,

> during revolutions scientists see new and different things when looking with familiar instruments in places they have looked before. It is rather as if the professional community had been suddenly transported to another planet where familiar objects are seen in a different light and are joined by unfamiliar ones as well. . . . In so far as their only recourse to that world is through what they see and do, we may want to say that after a revolu-tion scientists are responding to a different world.[1]

Since black women entered the scholarly record, black and white women's historians have been responding to a different intellectual world. Where this transformation, or indeed its precise contours, will lead us remains yet to be discovered. I am neither sanguine nor naive about the significance or impact of black women's history. Actually I have reason for disquiet.

The reasons for my disquiet are varied but the two solutions are 1) that we all begin to do crossover history, and 2) that we look at class. Allow me to explain. In my survey courses I usually divide Modern African American History into four broad overlapping and interconnected themes in order to clarify the major political and eco-nomic developments, to explain the rise of competing ideologies, and to delineate the roles of representative individuals. The four broad themes are: the Civil War and Emancipation, the Great Migrations, the Civil Rights Movement, and the Changing Status of Black Women.

The first three themes have and continue to command the attention of the vast majority of African American historians of the post-slavery period. The fourth theme has been problematic. Explorations into the status of black women over time, however, fosters the need to do intersectional analysis because for the most part this particular group of Americans has always occupied the bottom rung of any racial, sexual, and class hierarchy: as slaves they cost less than male counterparts; as free workers they were undervalued and negatively stereotyped. Thus few scholars deemed this segment of the population worthy of intellectual inquiry. What lessons could the lives and experiences of shadow women possibly convey about the relations between men and women or black and white Americans that were not already known and documented? Also on a more superficial level, even some black women scholars desired to eschew what they labeled the victimization of black women and instead chose to focus on positive, creative contributions of superachieving or transcendent black women as a means to empower themselves, their students, and their communities.

The scholars of black women's history have wrought well. We now know that black women played essential roles in ensuring the survival of black people under slavery and of black communities in freedom. We know that oppressed people are able to develop, as revealed in the life and writing of the antebellum free black woman, Maria Stewart, a political agenda for black liberation that pivoted on the emancipation and heightened consciousness of black women. Even slave women such as Harriet Tubman and Harriet Jacobs resisted the imposition of beliefs that held them to be little more than mindless sex objects and mules of labor. They too devised simple and complex strategies to challenge white and black patriarchal domination. Slave women such as Sojourner Truth performed labor across the sexual divide and proved the lie of feminine weakness. And as Melton A. McLaurin documents in *Celia, A Slave*, slave women fought and died in defense of their sexual beings.[2]

We now know that black women's angle of vision enabled them collectively and individually to fashion a worldview, to assemble an arsenal of womanist strategies ranging from the culture of dissemblance and a deep spiritualism to the adoption of middle-class values and aspirations designed to shatter demeaning stereotypes of their humanity and of their sexualities. We know that the process of re-imaging themselves was a serious, unrelenting battle that continues to this day. Through the myriad voluntary associations and club activities in the late nineteenth and early twentieth centuries, black women created and sustained innumerable churches, hospitals, schools, clinics, day-care centers, neighborhood improvement projects, and protest organizations. Black women working in tandem with black men founded migration clubs and relocated themselves and their families in western towns and northern cities. They too labored to create and sustain the separate parallel institutional infrastructures that made black survival possible in the age of Jim Crow. And throughout these survival struggles they played instrumental roles—although too often unheralded—in laying the groundwork for the modern civil rights revolution.

Given these accomplishments, why the disquiet? Here is one site of my disquiet. Too little attention has been devoted to the working-class status of black women. The fact is that the vast majority of black women have lived in overwhelming poverty, and a lack of attention to that fact has helped to foster erroneous impressions in the larger society of the mythical, heroic, transcendent black woman able to do the impossible, to make a way out of no way. Accordingly, actual poor black women, especially those on welfare and who are single heads of households, are not only inadequately understood but are also increasingly vilified in contemporary media coverage. They are depicted as one of the causes of our national economic woes and ironically are held responsible by some for the growing economic, political, and social impotence of working-poor black men.

Discussions of racial and sexual oppression without intense grounding in the complexities and realities of class exploitation and inequalities have led to misplaced emphases. Such skewed perceptions of the realities of black women's lives leave room for all kinds of political and intellectual mischief. Black women historians need to readjust some of their attention to relating the history of black women to the tremendous concentration of power, wealth, information, and social resources that remain in the hands of a fiercely intransigent and militantly reactionary white male elite. In short, if we truly intend to do intersectional analyses then class must occupy as much attention as race and sex.

This of course brings me to the second major source of disquiet. Black women historians must begin to research and write histories of white women. Why? Because we need to know more about them. We need to break down these intellectual and professional boundaries in order to develop and refine our methodologies for comparative and intersectional analysis. Some black women historians such as Nell Painter and Wilma King have already completed editing projects of papers of southern white women. Recently I wrote an introduction to the new edition of Katharine Du Pre Lumpkin's autobiography, *The Making of a Southerner*.[3]

I suspect that many already over-burdened and over-extended black women historians will chaff at this exhortation to cross the racial lines in their scholarship. I hear their questions. Won't writing about white women undermine and/or impede progress on the black women's history project? There are so few of us doing this work as it is, why should we dilute our energies? Will researching and writing about white women enhance our understanding of the lives and experiences of black women, of white men, of black men? But perhaps more pointedly, will black women historians achieve or receive authorial recognition within a stratified profession that has tended to categorize black scholars as being in charge of black history? Do black historians who venture into "crossover history" risk more than they gain? I can offer no answers sufficient to allay these qualms. I can only suggest that the efforts extended to study others strengthen the understanding of that which is closest.

For instance, I encountered the autobiography of an aristocratic, southern white woman whose intellectual journey made me want to know more about her. Katharine Du Pre Lumpkin's carefully constructed, wincingly honest autobiography chronicles her own intellectual transformation and conversion to the cause of racial equality and social justice. Given the nature of her intellectual and emotional heritage, the circumstances of her early upbringing, and the depth of the southern commitment to racial hierarchy and gender stratification, Lumpkin's rejection of the ideology of white supremacy and questioning of the status of women were downright radical. Lumpkin's observations about the lives of white southern women anticipated by a generation the historical works of Anne Firor Scott, Jean Friedman, Jacqueline Dowd Hall, and Elizabeth Fox-Genovese.

Katharine Du Pre Lumpkin was born in Macon, Georgia, on December 22, 1897. She received her bachelor's degree from a small college in Georgia, proceeded to earn her master's degree at Columbia University, and in 1928 earned her doctorate in economics at the University of Wisconsin. She taught economics and sociology at a number of women's colleges, including Mount Holyoke and Smith College. In addition to *The Making of a Southerner* (1947) and *The Emancipation of Angelina Grimké* (1974), Lumpkin published, with Dorothy W. Douglas, *Child Workers in America* (1937) and *The South in Progress* (1940).[4]

The first half of her book, *The Making of a Southerner*, lays out in graphic detail what it meant to be southern, white, female, and privileged in the opening decades of the twentieth century. In the final sections Lumpkin recalls the process of her transformation into a liberal democrat, fully aware of the economic inequities, racial proscriptions, and sexual restrictions suffered by those other southerners who were poor white, black, and/or female. To be sure, Lumpkin's voice is atypical but that is why her book is so arresting. Lumpkin painstakingly unravels the old tapestry of myths, distortions, and stereotypes that had blinded her to the existence of white poverty and black oppression. Epiphanies abound. After years of study and soul searching she exhibits a fully awakened racial consciousness and is aware of the social construction of and intersections of race, gender, and class: "What struck me now was the circumstantial convenience of a belief in inferiority to the existence of a slave institution and the perpetuation of its aftermath."[5]

It is imperative to underscore the strategy Lumpkin employs in this autobiography. From the vantage point of someone who has rejected the rationalizations of racism, she recaptures the intellectual world that taught them to her. Thus her treatment of slavery, of reconstruction, and of redemption is essentially the version of reality that conditioned her childhood. They are tales told by her father. Such stories include descriptions of the birth of the Ku Klux Klan. She wrote:

> This much is certain. To my people, as to me in my childhood,

who was reared in their history of those fateful months, no "two sides" to what happened was conceivable. To them there was but one side, made up of true Southerners engaged, they verily believed, in a struggle for existence, for this is what "white supremacy" was to them.[6]

Years of conditioning in the atmosphere of an ostensibly inviolate way of southern life affected young Lumpkin and her brothers and sisters, though not as deeply perhaps as her parents would have wished. Still she recalled:

It was inconceivable, however, that any change could be allowed that altered the very present fact of the relation of superior white to inferior Negro. This we came to understand remained for us as it had been for our fathers, the very cornerstone of the South.[7]

Yet it was inevitable that cracks would appear in the intellectual edifice so elaborately constructed to subordinate black people and maintain white hegemony. For young Katharine Du Pre Lumpkin it began perhaps with a chance observation as her father brutally beat the family cook for committing the dreaded offense of "impudence." The incident produced the first tremors of doubt and misgivings:

Our little Black cook, a woman small in stature though full grown, was receiving a severe thrashing. I could see her writhing under the blows of a descending stick wielded by the white master of the house. I could see her face distorted with fear and agony and his with stern rage.[8]

Note that Lumpkin does not refer to her father but to "the white master," perhaps reflecting unconscious distancing (or maybe she was simply speaking metaphorically). Nevertheless, having witnessed this scene, Lumpkin became blindingly aware that she was white: "I began to be self-conscious about the many signs and symbols of my race position that had been battering against my consciousness since virtual infancy."[9]

Lumpkin was too perceptive and too intelligent to remain imprisoned by fabrications designed to buttress the institutions of white supremacy and the fantasies of the old order. The latter half of the autobiography is largely a tale of personal reconstruction, of her remaking of herself into a southerner free from old biases and lies. It is radically different from the first part. In the latter chapters Lumpkin finds her own voice. She rejects the stories of her father and demonstrates the fruits of years of research and scholarship. In *The South in Progress* Lumpkin explained: "I am mindful of how greatly we need to study our history. Southern problems cannot be understood fully except in the light of an extensive examination of our historical background."[10] The problems explored in the last part include the desperate lives of croppers and farm laborers, workers in mill villages and cities, black peonage, the subjugation of women, the oppressive nature of southern religion, and the hypocrisy of northerners concerning the treatment of African Americans.

But it was the world of the "lower class" whites that enthralled her just as it is the world of working-poor black women that enthralls me. Lumpkin comments on every aspect of their desperate lives from the religious revivals to the inadequate schooling, the "immoral" liaisons, the violence, and the alcoholism. I am concerned about the desperate lives of black women who cannot find jobs, secure education and training, obtain adequate access to health care for themselves and their children, who are devastated by AIDS, drugs, and violence at every turn, and who are held responsible for all the ills confronting everybody in this society—a society that despairs of their very existence. Meanwhile, Lumpkin declared:

> In the Sand Hills for the first time in my experience I had been set down to live day after day in close companionship with deep poverty suffered by whites, a poverty to which I had not hitherto been imperceptibly hardened. . . . I saw more than I otherwise would have.[11]

By the 1920s Lumpkin's search for a deeper understanding of the South and its people unveiled the "rigors of Southern destitution" of the white "lower classes." She concluded, after stints of working in the mills and factories where she observed more poverty and hopelessness, that "the mass of whites in a purely economic sense also had their 'place,' in which they too seemed meant to stay."[12] The autobiography ends with a resounding condemnation of assumptions that working-class white and black southerners were kept separate because of "innate" and "inevitable" differences. Her critique of the economic forces that consigned the majority of its people to poverty led her to declare that "wage-earning whites and Negroes were, functionally speaking, not so unlike after all."[13]

Why should a black woman historian concentrate on the autobiography of an upper-class white southern lady? The reasons are numerous. First, Katharine Du Pre Lumpkin's book is as effective an examination of what it takes to make one kind of white southerner as Benjamin Mays' *Born to Rebel*, Richard Wright's *Black Boy*, Anne Moody's *Coming of Age in Mississippi*, and Pauli Murray's *Proud Shoes* are descriptions of what went into the making of black southerners. In many guises these autobiographies reveal the layered depth of different perceptions and experiences shaped by gender, race, and social status.

Second, Lumpkin's autobiography opens a window onto the past attitudes and values that prevented elite whites from seeing the harsh realities and often demeaning lives led by black Americans, poor whites, and many women and their own roles in creating these lives. Lumpkin was exceptional in many ways but most especially in her ability to see beyond form and structure to essence. As is true of the autobiographical writings of several other atypical white southern women, including Lillian Smith and Virginia Durr, Lumpkin has written an illuminating and powerful book. She penetrates the contradictions, myths, and ironies so deeply embedded in southern culture—in its religion, its economy, its race relations, and its gender conventions. Hers is the poignant testimony of a woman steeped in traditions peculiar to her class and region who through education and will removed the cataracts of racism, curing herself of the blindness that hid pervasive and unrelenting white poverty and the grinding exploitation of agricultural, factory, and mill workers.

Implicit in this discussion is the encouragement of white and black women historians to pay more attention to the historical experiences of economically distressed and exploited black women. This is an appeal for all historians of women also to engage in more "crossover history." When we are all doing each other's history then we will register meaningful progress in the war against racism, sexism, and class oppression. All barriers impeding our understanding of the past and interfering with our present and future struggle against patriarchy must be destroyed.

Lumpkin moved from her discovery of class exploitation to a deeper understanding of racism. I have moved from race and gender oppression to class exploitation. In short, I meet Lumpkin at the juncture of class, race, and gender. This means I have to stretch my understandings. Let me assure you that I seek no escape from the struggle to research, write, teach, and promote black women's history. I believe that at this particular historical conjuncture it is imperative that some black women historians treat white women as a means to enrich understanding of African American women. Likewise white women scholars need to study black women and other women of color to a far greater extent than has been the case. In any event the time for cussing is past, now let's get busy.

PART 2

Black Women in the Middle West

The Michigan Experience

The historical experiences of Michigan black women, from the territorial phase to the post-World War II era, provide a window onto the construction of gender roles and the evolution of black communities in the state and throughout the midwestern region. This essay seeks, as a minimum objective, to answer two questions—when and by what process did black women come to settle in Michigan and what did they do once they arrived? The history of black women is perhaps best understood if organized into three periods: (1) the pioneer phase, (2) the era of domestic feminism, and (3) the period of self-determination.

The pioneer phase lasted throughout the nineteenth century and was characterized by the migration and settlement of black men and women into rural and, later, urban communities. Both in the antebellum years and in the post-Civil War decades, Michigan women helped to create a racially autonomous institutional infrastructure of churches, schools, clubs, mutual benefit societies, and businesses. They created separate institutions to ensure black survival but this never represented acceptance of their second-class economic and political status within the larger society. Leading women of the black elite in Detroit founded clubs and organizations that shaped and defined an intricate structure of social and economic connections and divisions within the race.[1]

The "domestic feminism" phase of black women's history in Michigan spans from 1900 to the 1920s. This period witnessed a frenzy of activity, as virtually every community of black women across the state organized clubs and founded special homes to ameliorate the sufferings of the aged, the poor, the infirm, the orphaned, and to provide protection and assistance to young and vulnerable women adrift. On a scale unsurpassed, educated black matrons, heeding the demands of social responsibility and adhering to prescriptions of virtuous womanhood, aggressively reached out to the black poor. In the absence of state welfare these black matrons assisted recent female migrants and other black men and women through the organization of local and regional networks of self-help agencies, voluntary associations, and racial uplift projects. Furthermore, during the post-World War I years, black women organized a number of overtly political clubs and encouraged their sisters to vote. Through their private and civic work, black club women blurred many of the distinctions demarcating male and female spheres of influence.[2]

The self-determination, or third, phase of Michigan black women's history began in the 1930s and is symbolized by the formation of the Housewives' League of Detroit. At the height of the Great Depression black women across the state played a much more assertive and militant role in the economic and political affairs of their communities. They capitalized on their positions as family planners and engaged in a practice of economic nationalism. Black women spearheaded the movement to encourage members of their communities to support black professionals and race-owned businesses. Thus black women played an important role in the movement to secure and strengthen the economic position of the state's black population.

In spite of repeated assertions of, and allusions to, Booker T. Washington's conservative philosophy of race relations, the activities of the Housewives' League of Detroit reflected a grass-roots, "lets-keep-our-money-in-our-own-communities" nationalist approach more reminiscent of Marcus Garvey. The cooperation between black women and black business and professional leaders enabled black consumers in Michigan to establish an impressive place for themselves in the state's economy. During the 1930s, Detroit, for example, could boast that it had "a greater per-capita volume of business controlled and patronized by Negroes than any other city in the United States."[3]

The contradictions and contrasts of black life and the process by which black men and women constructed and defined gender roles in Michigan beg analysis. The threads of black women's historical experiences in Michigan are tightly interlaced with those of black men. However, by examining the distinct, female strands of Michigan experiences we are better able to understand the myriad ways in which black women aided the creation and survival of families, and religious, social, educational, and economic institutions within their communities.

The Pioneer Period

The much heralded Northwest Ordinance of 1787 expressly prohibited slavery in the region that subsequently yielded the states of Illinois, Indiana, Michigan, Ohio, and Wisconsin. Despite official prohibition, slavery—in various forms and guises ranging from outright life-time indenture, to long-term apprenticeships—existed in the middle west states into the 1850s. Even in Michigan, some interpreted the Northwest Ordinance ban against slavery as prohibiting new imports while permitting those already held in bondage to remain enslaved. One of the earliest cases of a slave fighting for freedom in the Northwest Territory involved a black woman and preceded the Dred Scott decision by several decades. Elizabeth Denison was a slave to Catherine Tucker when the Ordinance of 1787 was passed. She sued for her freedom but lost the case when Judge Augustus B. Woodward, chief justice of the territorial supreme court, ruled that the Ordinance applied to new slaves, not existing ones, because property rights of those previously living in the area (now Wayne County) were not abridged by the extension of U.S. jurisdiction. Lisette, as she was sometimes called, and her brother Scipio eventually escaped into Canada with the aid of white friends. As late as 1810 there numbered some three hundred slaves in the Detroit area.[4]

Slavery subterfuges and race restrictive legislation such as the 1827 Michigan Black Code, a thinly veiled attempt to exclude black settlement, made it difficult for many of the early, ostensibly free, black men and women settlers in the region to distinguish their actual political and social status from that of their fettered brothers and sisters remaining in the South. Michigan whites voted 32,000 to 12,000 against an amendment to the 1850 Constitution which would have given black residents the right to vote.[5] Black children were forced to attend segregated schools. Black adults could neither serve on juries nor hold political office in middle west states. However, black migrants to Michigan and to Wisconsin tended to encounter less overt personal and institutionalized violence from their white neighbors than those who initially settled in Illinois, Indiana, and southern Ohio.

Actually, the Michigan Black Codes were infrequently enforced. Few black settlers ever posted the mandated $500 bond guaranteeing good behavior or registered with county clerks upon entering Michigan. The point here is that while customary discrimination existed, it was in fact less severe than in the law.[6]

Prior to the Civil War there were essentially four means, in addition to natural increase, by which Michigan's black female population grew. First of all, some black women were resettled in the state as members of manumitted slave families from North Carolina, Virginia, Kentucky, and Tennessee. Second, prior to the Civil War, a few black women achieved freedom by accompanying whites into the region as domestic servants, indentured or otherwise bound, and were set free upon fulfilling the terms of their contracts. Third, some free black women living in southern or border states voluntarily migrated into Michigan. Fourth, a sizeable number were fugitive slaves who escaped via the loosely linked network referred to as the "Underground Railroad." The Society of Friends, or Quakers, was responsible for resettling thousands of ex-slaves in Ohio, Indiana, and Michigan. The Underground Railroad proved especially effective in assisting runaways from Missouri, Tennessee, and Kentucky.

Laura S. Haviland, a white woman conductor in Michigan, recounted how she aided Sarah in her escape from slavery. "Sarah was to be sold away from her little boy of three years for a fancy girl, as she was a beautiful octoroon and attractive in person. She knew full well the fate that awaited her, and succeeded in escaping."[7]

Often ex-slaves remained in southern counties in Illinois, Indiana, and Ohio for a period of time, perhaps even as long as ten to twenty years, before moving northward to Wisconsin, Michigan and eventually to Canada. Black migration to Michigan from more hostile neighboring states did increase after the passage of the 1850 fugitive slave law.[8] Overall the black population in Michigan increased gradually during the decades prior to statehood. By 1840 there were 707 blacks in the state. Tremendous growth occurred during the 1840s when the population multiplied three-fold to 2,583.[9]

Throughout the antebellum period, the black population in Michigan remained small compared to that of other midwestern states. In 1840, Illinois had 3,929 black residents, Indiana had approximately 7,000, Ohio led with 17,384, while Wisconsin trailed with only 196 blacks. The relatively small proportion of black residents shaped for a while the nature and complexity of race relations in Michigan, especially in Detroit, the urban area registering the largest percentage of black residents in antebellum Michigan. Many scholars have commented that there appeared to be greater racial integration in housing and in education in Michigan. Others have noted that a very distinct light-skinned African American middle-class took shape in this period and that black men and women made much of the color differences among themselves. Other cleavages, in addition to those based on class and skin color, depended upon whether one was free before the Civil War or was a recent migrant "shot free."[10]

It need not be elaborated that black men and women in Michigan shared with free blacks throughout the region a commitment to the antislavery cause and that black women played a major role in this struggle. Black women never quietly acquiesced to the larger society's definition of "woman's place" as being behind the man, nor did black Michigan women subscribe to the belief that it was their duty to be "seen but not heard." By far one of the most outstanding and outspoken black women of this era was Isabella Baumfree, who took the name Sojourner Truth in the mid-1840s. She lectured across the country on behalf of black freedom and women's rights. She moved to Battle Creek, Michigan, in 1856. In 1878 she spoke before audiences in thirty-six Michigan towns and attended that year's Women's Rights Convention in Rochester, New York. Truth died in 1883 and was buried in Battle Creek's Oakhill Cemetery. In the last decades of her life, Truth was especially concerned about women acquiring the right to vote. In New York City in 1867 she spoke eloquently on behalf of black women:

There is a great stir about colored men getting their rights, but not a word about the colored women; and if colored men get their rights, and not colored women theirs, you see the colored men will be masters over the women, and it will be just as bad as it was before. So I am for keeping the thing going while things are stirring.[11]

Although lesser known than Truth, Mary Clark Cyrus' contribution to the black liberation struggle was certainly significant. Cyrus served as one of the principal agents in the Underground Railroad in the Detroit area. Born to free parents in Kentucky in 1824, she migrated to Detroit with her husband in 1844, where she lived until her death at the age of 84. She was one of many who participated in organized resistance. During the 1830s black men and women had formed hundreds of antislavery societies, and beginning in the 1840s the Negro Convention Movement flourished. In Detroit, leading black and white citizens organized the Detroit Anti-Slavery Society in 1837, thus giving institutional shape to a long-standing hostility to the "peculiar institution."

To be sure, whites' abhorrence of slavery, even in Michigan, rarely gave way to an open acceptance of black men and women on levels approaching equality. In 1836 a group of former slaves organized the Second Baptist Church of Detroit in order to focus more closely on the problems unique to their status and not addressed by the white members of the First Baptist Church with whom they had worshiped for years. Second Baptist did not receive its articles of incorporation until 1839. In the interim the members held regular assemblies in individual homes and in a school building on East Fort Street.[12]

As the numbers of black residents in Michigan increased, and various communities acquired greater stability coupled with increased financial security, a class hierarchy evolved. Often, one of the earliest indications of their middle-class aspirations was manifested in the appearance of local women's clubs and a concern for social uplift on the part of black communities. Desire for upward mobility was not, of course, the only motivation fueling the establishment of antebellum black women's clubs. As early as 1787 black men and women had found it necessary to organize benevolent societies to attend to their physical and spiritual needs and to provide support for those unable to care for themselves.

Still, black women desired to form organizations that performed dual functions. Their clubs articulated philanthropic or social service missions but were also designed to elevate mental and moral status and improve public images of black women. The social and racial uplift work of these pioneer women's clubs included founding and supporting schools and libraries, sponsoring lectures on scientific and literary subjects, and organizing and hosting musical performances.[13] In 1843 a group of black women in Detroit established the Colored Ladies Benevolent Society. The women engaged in a number of fund-raising activities and on the first anniversary of its formation, they met in the Colored Methodist Church (now Bethel African Methodist Episcopal Church) and reported a treasury balance of $126.56. This sum was reduced by half when the women purchased groceries to distribute among the poor black families of the city.[14]

These black benevolent women were part of a larger sweep of women activists in local communities who worked to ameliorate the suffering of the poor, aged, orphaned, and sick, and in the process they acquired a voice in public discourse. To be sure, beneficent action had the added bonus of underscoring the moral and spiritual righteousness of African American women. This was of no small import for black women who as a group were maligned as moral and sexual wantons.[15]

Not all antebellum middle western black women's efforts were directed explicitly towards racial ends. Some of the Michigan black women pioneers were also active in the early movement to abolish the use and sale of alcohol. A leading temperance advocate, Frances E. Preston was the child of a free father and a slave mother. In 1855 her mother was somehow able to move to Detroit where Frances attended school and took courses at the Detroit Training School of Elocution, graduating in 1882 at the head of her class. By the 1870s the crusade for total abstinence was largely a "woman's war," institutionalized in 1874 with the formation of the Women's Temperance Union. Unlike many reform organizations the Women's Temperance Union from the outset was integrated. Indeed the leaders welcomed the participation of black women. Preston was appointed a lecturer and an organizer of the national Women's Christian Temperance Union (WCTU). In addition to her temperance work Preston devoted some of her considerable organizing talents to leading the Michigan Federation of Colored Women's Clubs.[16]

Perhaps the most prominent black woman temperance activist was Lucy Smith Thurman. She was the daughter of Nehemiah Henry and Catherine Smith and was born October 22, 1849, at Oshawa, Ontario, Canada. After completing her education in Canadian schools, Thurman taught in Maryland where she became acquainted with other leading black antislavery leaders, including Frederick Douglass. In 1875 she entered temperance work and for years served as one of the most successful lecturers on behalf of the Women's Christian Temperance Union. Most of her early work was confined to Indiana, Illinois, and Michigan and according to one source was "wholly among white people." This emphasis changed, however, in 1893 when during a WCTU convention she was elected superintendent of temperance work among black people, the first person to occupy such a position.

Like Preston, Thurman became a mainstay of the Michigan black club women's movement. In 1900 she and several other women organized the Michigan State Association of Colored Women's Clubs and served as its first president. Later, in 1907, Thurman was elected president of the National Association of Colored Women's clubs. Mrs. Thurman was twice married, the first marriage taking place at Cleveland, Ohio, in 1847. In 1883 she was married in Detroit, Michigan, to Frank Thurman. She died at Jackson, Michigan, on March 29, 1918.[17]

A few noteworthy black women occupied positions of some importance and prestige in post-Civil War Detroit. Throughout the nineteenth century black women school teachers especially were held in high esteem. They were among the first female professionals in both rural and urban communities, and they often worked for racial advancement on a variety of fronts. In 1869 a statement by the Detroit Board of Education listed three black schools and one under construction. Fannie Richards became the first black teacher employed by the board. Richards was born in Fredericksburg, Virginia, on October 1, 1841, and migrated in 1851 with her widowed mother and siblings to Detroit. Following early training in the public schools she went to Toronto to continue her education. She later returned to Detroit to attend the Teachers Training School.

Once she completed her formal training Richards opened a private school for black children in 1863. Two years later she assumed responsibility for "Colored School Number 2." A friend recounted Richards' description of how she came to occupy the headship of the school:

> Going to her private school one morning, she saw a carpenter repairing a building. Upon inquiry she learned that it was to be opened as Colored School Number 2. She went immediately to William D. Wilkins, a member of the board of education, who, impressed with the personality of the young woman, escorted her to the office of superintendent of schools, Duane Dotty. After some discussion of the matter Miss Richards filed an application, assured that she would be notified to take the next examination. At the appointed time she presented herself along with several other applicants who hoped to obtain the position. Miss Richards ranked highest and was notified to report for duty the following September. Early one morning she proceeded to her private school in time to inform her forty pupils of the desirable change and conducted them in a body to their new home.[18]

The young teacher attracted considerable attention when she joined with John Bagley (a wealthy tobacco manufacturer who from 1873 to 1876 would serve as Michigan's fifteenth governor) and several liberal-minded citizens, along with the members of the Second Baptist Church, to raise money to finance a lawsuit against school segregation in Detroit. On May 12, 1869, the Michigan Supreme Court ruled in the case of *Joseph Workman v. The Board of Education of Detroit* that under the strictures of the Fourteenth Amendment to the United States Constitution black children could not be legally segregated from whites in the public schools.

According to a later account of black education in Detroit,

> There are two district colored public schools in the city, as well as several private ones. . . . The primary school is located on Riopelle Street, near Macomb, and is under the charge of a

young but able colored lady, Miss Fannie Richards. . . . There are 80 seats and the value of the property belonging to the Board is not more than 300 dollars, consisting simply of the furniture and the lease. The number of pupils is 80, thus completely filling the school, and average attendance is no less than 77. . . . Miss Richards' salary is 400 dollars.

Assisting Fannie Richards in her duties was a young woman, Delia Pelham. The salaries of white teachers in the white schools averaged $415.[19]

The salary discrepancy apparently meant nothing to Richards. Rather, in the years following the integration of public schools in Detroit and her transfer to the Everett School, she proudly asserted that she had taught more white than black students. She is reported to have confided a few years prior to her retirement in 1915 that, "I have never been made to feel in any way that my race has been a handicap to me. Neither my pupils nor the teachers have ever shown prejudice; I do not doubt that it exists; I shall be in heaven long before it has all disappeared, but I say it is with a colored teacher as it is with a White one. Her work is the only thing that counts."[20]

In addition to teaching in the Detroit public school system for forty-four years, Richards maintained close contact with the black community by teaching Sunday School at Second Baptist Church. Moreover, Fannie Richards joined with Mary McCoy, a prominent club woman activist, to found the Phillis Wheatley Home in 1898, which provided room and board for destitute elderly black men and women. Richards served as the home's first president. She died in Detroit in 1922.[21]

Mary Delaney McCoy was perhaps the archetype of the pioneer black club woman organizer and the self-trained social reform worker. She was born at Lawrenceburg, Indiana, on January 7, 1846, as her parents, Jacob C. and Eliza Ann Delaney, were making their way out of slavery on the Underground Railroad. On February 25, 1873, she married the noted inventor Elijah McCoy.[22] McCoy's important work in the club movement earned her the appellation "Mother of Clubs." In addition to the Phillis Wheatley Home, she founded the McCoy Home for Colored Children.[23] In 1895, she was instrumental in founding the "In as Much Circle of King's Daughters and Sons

Club" in Detroit. She was also listed on the rosters of the Lydian Association of Detroit, the Guiding Star Chapter Order of the Eastern Star, and the Willing Workers. The Lydian Association was one of the strongest charitable organizations in the state. In return for their dues, members could expect to receive, when necessary, sick benefits and burial fund assistance. Finally, McCoy was the only black charter member of the Twentieth Century Club.[24]

The point here is that Preston, Richards, Thurmond, and McCoy were black women leaders who, at the dawn of the century, ushered in a new phase of Michigan's black women's history. They were the bridge across which a new generation of black Michigan women would travel, leaving the pioneer era and entering into a period of substantial club formation for the purpose of self-preservation, racial uplift, and progressive reform.

Black Club Women and Domestic Feminism

In 1895 white women organized the Michigan State Federation of Women's Clubs. Sixty-four clubs were represented at the organizational meeting in Lansing. (By 1953 the number of clubs comprising the State Federation stood at approximately 500.) At the initial meeting one of the speakers spoke admiringly of the work of Chicago club women "in caring for 60,000 needy women and children, and of possible future work in educational and industrial lines." At a subsequent convention in 1897 the legislative committee issued a report which discussed the major concerns and public actions of the women. The report concluded with a recommendation that "women be appointed on the Boards of Asylums for the Insane, on the State Board of Education and on the State Board of Corrections and Charities, and women physicians be employed in all public institutions where women are inmates."[25]

Michigan black women followed a similar pattern of club organization and gradual involvement in social reform work. In part, black women were motivated to establish separate organizations because of the exclusion practiced by white women. Yet, they also believed there were special problems affecting them as black women that could be more effectively addressed in separate forums. In July 1895, Josephine

St. Pierre Ruffin of Boston presided over the first National Conference of Colored Women in America. Out of this meeting arose in 1896 the National Association of Colored Women's clubs (NACW). NACW was incorporated in 1904, its preamble to the constitution ratified in 1926. The preamble conveyed the purpose of the organization. "We the Colored Women of the United States of America feeling the need of united and systematic effort, and hoping to furnish evidence of moral, mental, and material progress made by our people, do hereby unite in a National Association." Around the country, but especially in urban areas, club formation proliferated as middle-class black women sought to extend into the public arena their collective concerns for social reform and the problems confronted by poor, uneducated, infirm, aged, and unemployed black people.

It is significant that, according to the NACW constitution, each state federation of clubs was required to form four basic departments: Mother, Home and Child, Negro Women in Industry, and a State Association of Girls. One of the major contributions coming out of the middle west that shaped the structure of NACW was the initiation, in 1929, of the Phillis Wheatley Department, under the aegis of Jane Edna Hunter of Cleveland, Ohio. Hunter's Phillis Wheatley Home opened in 1911 for single working women. By 1934 the following cities had similar homes: Denver, Atlanta, Seattle, Boston, Detroit, Chicago, Greenville, Winston-Salem, Toledo, and Minneapolis.[26]

From the outset, although there were many similarities, the concerns of black women—as revealed through the structure and nature of the clubs they formed—deviated in at least one significant way from those of white club women, namely on the racial front. Domestic feminism among black club women was a mix of strong racial uplift commitments and the desire to improve the image and status of black women. Undoubtedly their domestic feminism fed on the prevalent spirit of the Progressive Era which encouraged the voluntary effort to solve social ills.[27]

In 1900 attorney D. Augustus Straker, the political leader of black Detroit, addressed the first convention of the Michigan State Association of Colored Women's clubs organized by Lucy Smith Thurman. Voicing approval of the political implications of black women's organizing Straker challenged the group to "Agitate! Agitate!! Agitate!!" He declared, "I hope before you close your labors you will establish a committee in every city of the State to get employment for our young women and thus protect them against the evil results of idle hands." He continued, "What you need to do is to create American sentiment for equal opportunity for women in the development of true womanhood. Open the stores and the factories, and the millineries, and the school houses, and the counting houses for our young women, as well as the kitchen, the washtub, the nursery and the scrub room."[28] Straker's remarks emphasized what most black women in Michigan knew already, that is, they needed somehow to persuade businesses to hire black women.

Actually, Straker's advice echoed the philosophy of women leaders but he described activities in which black women were already engaged on a voluntary, if not paid, basis. A brief overview of some of the early Michigan clubs illuminates the breadth of social consciousness and the range of community activities in which they engaged between 1900 and 1920. In Ann Arbor four of the six black women's clubs founded between 1900 and 1920 focused on visiting the sick and providing enrichment programs for poor mothers and children. In 1900 a small group of women in Ann Arbor formed the Women's Federation of Clubs with the motto, "Uplift our race morally, spiritually and physically." During the first two years of existence the women made 300 visits to sick persons and raised money for Christmas gifts for poor children.

A few years later, in 1915, another group of Ann Arbor women expressed their concern for children by organizing Mother's Star of Hope club. They concentrated on helping and teaching mothers, declaring that "the object is to awaken in mothers their responsibility as mothers and encourage them to do those things which will assist the child to develop mentally, morally and physically to its fullest extent." The club women achieved their objective by inviting physicians and nurses to lecture to groups of mothers. They arranged picnics for children and held annual Mother's Day celebrations. They gave baby showers and gift baskets to expectant mothers. In Battle Creek, several women formed the Dardenella Art Club in 1920. For a period of two years the club members cared for a mother and her eight children.

They provided school clothing for other needy black children in the community.[29] For the black club women in Michigan, providing support for mothers and children was fundamental to advancing the race.

The largest number of clubs was in Detroit, reflecting perhaps the swelling influx of southern black migrants in search of economic advancement. Indeed, the black population of Michigan increased at a phenomenal rate during the opening decades of the twentieth century. Between 1920 and 1930 the city's total population rose from slightly under a million to more than a million-and-a-half. Eighty thousand African Americans lived in Detroit in 1925, five years later the number stood at 120,000.[30]

Many of these migrants were vulnerable young women. Historian Joanne J. Meyerowitz refers to them as "women adrift," often bereft of family support and impoverished. It was precisely this concern for black girls that motivated the members of the Christian Industrial Club founded in 1940. According to one touching account,

> In the early part of the life of the home a girl came to our city and missed her train, went to the white Y.W.C.A. and asked to stay there. They refused. She begged them to let her sleep in a chair in the hall for the night as she knew nobody, but they refused her even that privilege. She had to go in the park and sit on a bench. She sat in this park for two days and nights until someone came by that knew of this home and took her there. The girl stayed in the home until she married.[31]

In 1917, during the presidency of Catherine Page, the members of the Christian Industrial Club renamed the Home, the Francis Harper Inn in honor of the prominent nineteenth century antislavery advocate, poet and novelist, Francis Ellen Watkins Harper. Their involvement in social uplift work sometimes aroused the ire of white neighbors and in more than one instance black club women found it necessary to persevere even in the face of violence. According to one such account of the fortunes of the Harper Inn, included in *Lifting as They Climb*, "it was quite a hardship in establishing this home as the white neighbors tore down the sign and painted three K's on the house; but by the perseverance of ten faithful members and the help of the Lord they struggled thorough all of this."[32] The mortgage was burned in April 1930.

One of the more elite clubs founded by black women in Detroit was the Woman's City Council, organized in 1921, under the leadership of Eva Radden Jackson. These club women engaged in every form of social and racial uplift work. "The ladies visited the schools and helped get proper clothing for needy children. For a period of time they patrolled the school grounds to keep the men from molesting the girls." The group developed a sophisticated organizational structure. Within the first year the club organized seven branches, each branch responsible for helping children in its vicinity.[33]

The Woman's City Council boasted of being the only club in the state to sponsor summer camps for poor children and mothers. In 1925 the group reported that it operated a camp "for three weeks and during that time 42 children and seven mothers were cared for and they were served 1402 meals during the 24 days of the camp." They cared for a poor mother with two children for six months, and on July 15, 1928, opened a second camp during which they provided care for 85 children and 12 mothers over a five-week period.[34]

The existence of a flourishing black club women's movement in Detroit motivated Veronica Lucas in 1920 to propose the formation of the Detroit Association of Colored Women's Clubs. The Detroit association was federated in 1921 and incorporated twenty years later. Under the strong leadership of president Rosa L. Slade Gragg during the World War II years, the Detroit association flourished. Gragg was born in Hampton, Georgia, the eldest of seven children of Reverend and Mrs. Willis O. Slade, and received her bachelor's degree from Morris Brown College in Atlanta, Georgia. She married James Robert Gragg, a Detroit businessman and became active in the club movement in 1926 when she joined the Current Topic Study Club.[35]

Due primarily to Gragg's indomitable spirit and untiring effort, the Detroit association peaked by 1945 with a membership of seventy-three clubs and approximately three thousand individual members. Gragg enjoyed a significant public service career. In 1941 President Franklin D. Roosevelt appointed her to the volunteers participation committee in the Office of Civil Defense. In 1948 Mayor Eugene I. Van Antwerp appointed her president of the Detroit Welfare Commission with 1,947 employees and an operating budget of $20 million. Gragg is perhaps best known as the founder of the Slade Gragg Academy of Practical Arts, often referred to as the "Tuskegee" of the North. Gragg Academy offered courses in tailoring, upholstering, sign painting, millinery, food production and service, and waitress training. Never one to neglect her duties as a club woman, Gragg was elected in 1958 as president of the National Association of Colored Women.[36]

A variety of other clubs throughout the state, including the Ladies Home Circle in Jackson and the Palm Leaf Club in Ypsilanti, organized initially to pay off church mortgages and then moved into social service, charity, and uplift work. The Dorcas Study Club of Kalamazoo (organized in 1913), the Thursday Afternoon Club in Flint (organized in 1919), and both the Grand Rapids Study Club (organized in 1904) and the Pilierian Study Club of the same city (organized in 1929) combined literary, artistic, and social welfare pursuits with charity and community improvement efforts.

Two clubs stand out for their overt emphasis on political action. The Mother's Club of Kalamazoo, founded in 1917, provided invaluable assistance to poor mothers and needy children by sponsoring clinics, dispensing food, and making surveys of living conditions. It was most important to them, however, to "take interest in civic affairs by getting mothers to register and vote." In 1920 black women in Lansing led by Sarah Thompson organized the Women's Republican Research Club. The club spearheaded the drive "to get the women out to register and vote and attend everything that is worthwhile."[37]

The path from self-development to involvement in political affairs proved more circuitous for the majority of black women's clubs. Lillian E. Johnson, a pioneer member of the Detroit Study Club provides rare glimpses into the inner workings of a Michigan black women's club. In 1938, at its fortieth anniversary, Johnson recalled:

> This Club was organized March 2, 1898, as the Browning Study Club, the name being changed to Detroit Study Club several years later. The founder was Mrs. Gay Lewis Pelham. . . . She organized the club at her home on Alfred Street with the six following women: Miss J. Pauline Smith, who became the first president; Miss Sara Warsaw, Mrs. Tomlinson, Miss Fannie Anderson and Mrs. Will Anderson.[38]

Johnson quoted her earlier reminiscence, at the thirtieth anniversary, to explain why the women banded together.

You must remember at that time, Detroit was in the small city class with less than 10,000 inhabitants. Our women were not in industry and professions as these of later days, with their clubs and many activities, but moved in a very limited sphere, so no matter how bright a scholar they might be before graduating from High School or college before marrying and settling down, as was the custom, except those who elected to become teachers, they were apt to become so dull by the cobwebs collecting in their brain and not able to keep pace with the march of time, being so engrossed in the care and comfort of their families, as there were few good lectures and meetings of an educational nature. Hence a literary club of this sort for study and research served a two fold purpose, being not only a means for further self culture, but also for entertainment. It was an oasis in the weekly routine of duties, eagerly looked forward to by its members. True, there were a few church literary societies, but these annually flourished for a few months and then were no more until reorganized or a new one started.[39]

Through the friendships, rituals, and social reform and race uplift work, the clubs became the institutional anchors from which the women could attack secular ills while simultaneously cultivating self-worth and enhancing their dignity. Within a decade of its founding the Detroit Study Club had been transformed from "just a self culture club and branched out into the broader field of Philanthropy and civil social work in our own city, even though nearly all the individual members already belonged to charitable and welfare organizations."[40] Johnson later elaborated:

The club was established as a purely literary club, the members soon realized the need of sharing the social welfare work in the city, so a department of philanthropy was established sometime during the first ten years. The club contributes liberally to the many charities, civic organizations and educational movements in the city, and cooperates with the National, State and City Association of Colored Women.[41]

The minutes and records of the Grand Rapids Study Club (GRSC) reveal a similar pattern of contributions and involvement in social welfare work. Members regularly taxed themselves to raise special funds to distribute Christmas baskets, clothes, and toys for poor school children. During the Great Depression these Grand Rapids women established a relief fund to provide food for those in need. Women also watched over the playgrounds especially to keep little girls from harm. They raised money for scholarship funds and additional sums to help pay off mortgages of local churches.[42] There remained few, if any, dimensions of black life untouched by the women in these study clubs.

Perhaps to offset charges of exclusivity from within the black community, each year the Detroit Study Club hosted a series of open meetings "to which members might invite their friends, so as to have a fair audience for special programs." Johnson described these open meetings as "enjoyable and beneficial to other women." In 1915-16, the Detroit Study Club's year-long program was devoted to an examination of "Noted Women in Philanthropy and Performance, in Science, the Dramas, Art, Religion, Music, Education, in Industry, Professions, and Politics."[43]

Allegations of exclusivity were not too far off the mark. Membership in the clubs was restricted to hand-picked women who shared the same middle class values, belonged to reputable families, were married to professionals in the communities, or were themselves relatively well educated and positioned. The Detroit Study Club's membership increased from six members at its founding to 13 members a month later. By 1955 the club has grown to 35 members, with a long waiting list. Members met on alternate Fridays at 5:00 P.M., from October through May, usually at the Lucy Thurman YWCA.[44]

The Grand Rapids Study Club began in the home of Louisa Gaines on November 10, 1904. Prospective members had to be recommended by a current member, whereupon a committee investigated the nominee's background. Each woman had a ballot and voted for or against the nominee. A single "no" vote ended all consideration. Lucille Skinner explained, "if the members didn't feel the new woman felt strong enough about the club's goals, they said no." Membership never exceeded thirty.[45]

Until the Grand Rapids Study Club secured, in 1935, a permanent clubhouse all meetings were held in the homes of the members. The hostess was usually allocated fifty cents to pay for refreshments. The purpose of the club was "to unite all efforts toward individual,

home, and community betterment through study and civic cooperation in all things, which portends for the advancement of all groups."
Like the Detroit Study Club and the white women's literary clubs,
GRSC meetings were scheduled from October to May. Significantly,
however, the GRSC meetings were held at 2:30 P.M. on Thursday
afternoons, the traditional maid's day off.[46]

Although much remains to be researched and written about
the domestic feminism of black Michigan women, it is fair to say that
the organizing and club formation work of the opening decades of the
twentieth century accomplished several things. A close examination of
their work underscores the extent to which black women engaged in
institution building and left a distinguished record of self-help. Clearly,
black women fully embraced community-prescribed moral and social
responsibility for the elevation of the race and their sex. They approached this responsibility by focusing, as did their white counterparts,
on protecting the most vulnerable members of the group—young
women adrift, abandoned mothers and impoverished children, recent
migrants, illiterates, the aged, and those who suffered from illnesses.
In the process they developed greater self-pride and self-confidence in
their ability to become agents of social change. This heightened consciousness led, quite naturally, to an expansion of their sphere.

Though well grounded in a social welfare-oriented, club-work
tradition, Michigan black women evidenced a greater appreciation of,
and desire for, public power and a willingness to engage in overt
political activity. They recognized that social work alone would not
overcome economic and educational barriers to their advancement.
Two overarching goals, meaningful protection of the vulnerable and
elevation of their race, dictated that black women acquire and exercise
political and economic power, that they found trade schools, launch
businesses, enter the professions, and agitate for greater employment
opportunities for themselves and their children.

Black Women and Self-Determination

During the 1930s black women in Michigan, but especially in Detroit,
discovered a unique way to gain and wield political and economic
power. They experimented with new strategies to serve their people,
families, and to enhance their status as women. The Housewives'

League of Detroit proved to be the most effective weapon yet devised by any group of Michigan black women in their struggle for racial advance.

On June 10, 1930, a group of 50 black women responded to a call issued by Fannie B. Peck, wife of the Reverend William H. Peck (1878-1944), pastor of the 2,000 member Bethel AME Church and president of the Booker T. Washington Trade Association. Out of this initial meeting emerged the Detroit Housewives' League. Fannie Peck had conceived the idea of creating a housewives' organization following a lecture by M.A.L. Holsey, secretary of the national Negro Business League. Holsey had described the successful efforts of black housewives in Harlem to consolidate and exert their considerable economic power. Peck was convinced that if such an organization worked in New York, it was worth duplicating in Detroit.[47]

Fannie B. Peck was born August 15, 1879, in Huntsville, Missouri, to Thomas and Leanna Campbell. She married William H. Peck in 1899 and the couple moved to Detroit in June 1928. At the time of their arrival the Pecks noted that black women and men had already experienced economic setbacks and severe losses in jobs and businesses. As the Great Depression settled in on African Americans, certainly the most vulnerable segment of the general population, black mothers and homemakers felt the need to stretch their meager resources. While some despaired in the face of bleak economic prospects and limited educational and employment opportunities for themselves and their children, Peck sought to empower black women. As her successor extolled, Peck "had focused the attention of women on the most essential, yet most unfamiliar factor in the building of homes, communities, and nations, namely—The Spending Power of Women."[48]

One of the major challenges to black homemakers and mothers during the economic crisis of the 1930s was finding suitable jobs for themselves and their children. In the wake of World War I, black women found themselves on the bottom rung of the economic ladder, with only a tenuous grip on poor paying, low status domestic service jobs. Not until the post-World War II years would many of the automobile plants and department stores deign to hire even a minimum number of black women. Peck observed in 1942, that "at this time, because of world conditions, women find doors of opportunity for participation opened to them that the most aggressive feminist a few years ago would have never even imagined."[49] The journey, however, from 1930 to 1942 was for black women in Detroit characterized by considerable consciousness-raising and assertive activity as they tested and toasted the combined effectiveness of economic nationalism and feminism.

As Fannie Peck exhorted, black women were not without real economic power. It simply had to be harnessed. In the records of the Housewives' League of Detroit, there are several untitled and unsigned speeches. One speech suggested that black women should participate in the Housewives' League's programs in order to win the respect of white women. "If we are to be respected by other women, if we are to walk side by side with them, we cannot continue to spend thoughtlessly and buy the things we want and beg for the things we need."[50]

Peck recounted some of the early thinking that underlay the founding of the Housewives' League. She declared, "It has been in the minds of our women that they, their husbands and children were the victims of a vicious economic system. They were denied employment in many places where they spend their money, and that even when employed no opportunities for advancement were given." The growth of the league was phenomenal. From the 50 members who attended the first meeting, its membership grew to 10,000 by 1934. In explaining the "marvelous growth" Peck argued it was "due to the realization on the part of Negro women of the fact that she has been travelling through a blind alley, making sacrifices to educate her children with no thought as to their obtaining employment after leaving school."[51]

Essentially, the Housewives' League combined domestic feminism and economic nationalism to help black families and businesses survive the depression. The only requirement for membership was a pledge to support black businesses, buy black products, patronize black professionals, and keep the money in the community. As one leader of the league argued, black women were the most strategically positioned group to preserve and expand the black internal economy. They heard frequent exhortations that: "It is our duty as women controlling 85% of the family budget to unlock through concentrated spending closed doors that Negro youth may have the opportunity to develop and establish businesses in the fields closest to them." The league promised its members that in exchange for their involvement and efforts they would instruct and inform the members of "prices of merchandise, family budget, food values, and all things pertaining to the management of the home."[52]

The Housewives' League members took great pains defining their objectives and assuring potential critics and competitors that they intended to confine their activity to matters relating to the home, family, and community. "We see the great need of our social education, religious and economic improvement, and we have selected the economical as the field of endeavor. The great loss of employment upon the part of our people has reduced us to the place where we have not the sustenance for our bodies, clothes to wear, homes to live in, books to read, and none of the many things which are not any longer luxuries, but are prime necessities to the home life of modern standards."[53] The League adopted the slogan, "Find a job, or Make one and make your dollar do Triple duty." A dollar doing triple duty would "get *you* what *you* need. Give the Race what it needs—*Employment*, and Bring what all investments should bring—*Dividends*."[54]

Interestingly, its constitution contained several artfully crafted declarations of independence emphasizing differences from traditional advancement agencies and structures within the black community. These reflected their awareness of the broad-ranging needs of the race. Yet these somewhat muted statements hint at a deeper understanding of gender politics in the black community. Women did not occupy visible leadership roles within the churches, nor did any at this period hold political office. Section 7 of the Housewives' League constitution reads: "We recognize the place of the church and allied organizations among us for the advancement of our group. We are in full sympathy with their purposes, but are not a religious organization and shall not permit any discrimination for or against to in any way enter our thought or determine our action on any question of policy in our organization." Section 8 offered, "We are mindful of achieving political solidarity among us, increasing our opportunity of representation in bodies that control the activities in our city, state, and nation—but we are not a political organization."[55]

In short, the women carefully let it be known that they were not in competition with other organized black advancement groups. But this did not prevent Gertrude J. West, secretary of the Housewives' League, from sounding like Booker T. Washington when she proclaimed: "This is a challenge to Negro women, who control largely the finance that comes into the home. It offers an opportunity to make Christianity a reality by letting down your bucket where you are, knowing that you must first set your house in order before going out to help your neighbor."[56] Each neighborhood had its own Housewives' League. The leaders attended meetings of the executive board, usually held on the second Tuesday of each month. Any woman who pledged to "help build bigger and better Negro businesses and to create and increase opportunities for employment" was welcomed to membership. One card declared, "A belief in the future of Negro Business and a desire to assist in every way by patronizing and encouraging the same is all that is necessary to become a member."[57]

Becoming a member was the easy part. Keeping up with the League activities required considerable effort. Members canvassed neighborhood merchants demanding that they sell black products and employ black children as clerks or stockboys. They mounted campaigns to persuade black consumers to patronize certain businesses with black owners or employees. Leaders organized lectures, planned exhibits at state fairs, discussed picketing and boycott strategies, and disseminated information concerning the economic self-help struggles of black men and women across the country. The head of the research committee gathered data and made recommendations as to the types of businesses needed in various communities, and reported the results of "directed spending."[58]

By 1946 the members of the Housewives' Leagues no longer had to maintain the pretense of being apolitical. The leaders informed their members that it was wise to employ the ballot in the war for racial advance. "It has become necessary for other racial groups to become more and more concerned about entering politics as candidates for public office, and as organized groups, to see that the masses are educated to their responsibility as voters. Certainly the Negro woman whose home must suffer most, ought become concerned and join hands with other women who realize what happens in party politics effects homes as directly as what happens in her block . . . housing, economic equality, education opportunity for children and security are all affected by government."[59]

It is impossible to calculate the full impact the Housewives' League of Detroit had on the city's economic life. Certainly the League made a significant difference for the women who attended the meetings and became more confident confronting neighborhood businessmen and demanding their interest and needs be met. In assessing the performance of the League, one member wrote, "its greatest accomplishments have been the vision of self-help it has given the Negro woman, the confidence it has inspired in Negro business and professional men and women, the courage it has imparted to our young people to continue their education."[60]

Conclusion

The paucity of manuscript collections documenting the work and contributions of the small numbers of Michigan black women in the antebellum period has serious consequences. The scarcity of detailed data may give rise to unsupported generalizations and speculations about the daily lives of ordinary women or, more likely, lead to disproportionate emphasis on the few known black women activists whose deeds were chronicled in local newspapers and county histories. Rural women often receive short shrift while sustained attention is paid to more resourceful and privileged urban middle class residents. There is an urgent need to discover and collect more primary source materials pertaining to the lives and experiences of ordinary middle western black women in both rural and urban communities.

It is reasonable to assume that black settler women living in the numerous small villages and towns performed many of the same kinds of sex-role specific tasks as required of their white counterparts on the frontier. Like most women they bore the primary responsibility for creating and sustaining family systems. This included giving birth, socializing the young, raising gardens, preparation of food, clothing, household goods, and keeping contact with family members, reciprocating friendships and sustaining harmonious community or neighborhood relations.[61]

Knitting together kinship ties and maintaining complex family systems of varied household configurations, however, comprised one of two essential clusters of the responsibilities, obligations and expectations held of antebellum Michigan black women. The other was largely public. That is to say, black women functioned as stabilizing agents within the often fragile institutional infra-structure that gradually emerged throughout the many diverse small black communities. The church, the school house and the race uplift organizations and societies depended heavily upon the labors, commitment, and support of black women, even when males occupied all visible positions of leadership.

I suspect that gender lines within the black midwestern rural communities were frequently blurred throughout the nineteenth century, particularly within the laboring class. Not surprisingly, aspiring, upwardly mobile middle-class black women throughout the antebellum period played instrumental roles creating and connecting both private spheres of the home and the public arena of economics, social policy and politics, while emphasizing their moral superiority as females. After all, black women, regardless of their status, lived in a hostile society which deprecated and derided their sexuality. Their own emotional well-being and physical survival and the future advancement of the race required continuous vigilance. Michigan black women had to overcome negative stereotypes by cultivating alternative public images of themselves as moral, respectable, upstanding women.

Although men may have been less involved in the day-to-day management of the household, they certainly played major roles in the physical construction of churches, schools, and other dwellings. Moreover, in spite of the absence of formal political power—specifically the ballot—in the years before the Civil War black men assumed responsibility for doubly taxing themselves to pay teachers for their children when local schools barred them. They fought in the courts to have segregation ordinances lifted. In the face of entrenched racial discrimination black communities could ill-afford to adhere to rigid sphere restrictions at a time when the very survival of the group depended upon mutual cooperation. Throughout the antebellum period any black person could be stolen or claimed as a slave by slave catchers. Indeed a couple of the more infamous riots in Detroit's early history occurred when irate citizens, both black and white, violently opposed the recapture of runaways.[62] The point is that black male/female cooperation rather than division or conflict was essential.

Time and space do not permit even a cursory discussion of many themes and individual personalities significant in the history of Michigan's black women. Appropriate questions concerning conflict and cooperation between black and white women, and their personal attitudes towards and the treatment of one another, still need formulation. In this brief format I could only comment on—but not examine fully—the class and color differences between Michigan black women, for instance. Nor was I able to probe into their inner lives as black women, or discuss their relations with black men. Other scholars will have to take up these issues. Indeed, perhaps the best way to close is to indicate the ways in which a fuller history of black women in Michigan may be developed.

A fruitful and illuminating study could be written on the processes by which black Michigan women cultivated a unique black women's culture. Given the prevalence of makeup and hair parlors, the frequency of fashion shows and beauty contests in post–World War II Michigan, especially in Detroit, such a study would necessarily examine black women's changing definitions of physical beauty, and explore the rise of the black middle-class, as well as female entrepreneurship. Moreover, there is a pressing need for more research and writing on the experiences of black women creative artists—painters, musicians, singers, writers, and performers—who struggled to transcend combined sexual and racial barriers to contribute significantly to the cultural life not only of the black community but the entire state of Michigan. Along these lines, studies of black women in the professions are sorely needed. As educators, nurses, social workers, physicians and lawyers, black women made noteworthy contributions to the struggles of their people throughout the state.

Preliminary investigations have convinced me that more work needs to be done on the role black women played in the recent civil rights movement and in the historical struggles to overcome black political subordination and economic inequality on state and local levels. This discussion of the Housewives' League suggests future lines of inquiry. Most especially, it is critical that scholars begin to integrate analyses of black women's efforts as leaders and activists into account of the history of major organizations such as the NAACP, CORE, and the National Urban League.

Although much has been written on the institutional life of black midwesterners—the African American church, the development of private schools, hospitals, businesses, and labor organizations—too little attention has been devoted to the critical involvement of black women. Thus, in spite of the scholarly progress that has been made in the past few years, black women still remain too marginal or tangential, too obscured and silent in studies of black institution building and the black voluntary traditions. I am optimistic, however, that the work I have outlined here will be done. When scholars and writers fully explore the rich complexities of Michigan black woman's experiences the whole study of African American women in the larger middle west will move forward. And, in the process, a basis for a more inclusive reconstruction of both the black and American pasts will be established.

Black Migration to the Urban Midwest

The Gender Dimension, 1915-1945

The significance of temporal and spatial movement to a people, defined by and oppressed because of the color of their skin, among other things, defies exaggeration. Commencing with forced journeys from the interior of Africa to the waiting ships on the coast, over eleven million Africans began the trek to New World slave plantations that would, centuries later, land their descendants at the gates of the so-called "promised lands" of New York, Philadelphia, Chicago, Cleveland, Detroit, Milwaukee, and Indianapolis. The opening page of a privately published memoir of a black woman resident of Anderson, Indiana, captures well this sense of ceaseless movement on the part of her ancestors. D. J. Steans observed that the "the backward trail of relatives spread from Indiana to Mississippi, crisscrossing diagonally through several adjoining states. Whether the descendants came ashore directly from Africa to South Carolina or were detoured by way of islands off the coast of Florida is unknown."[1]

For half a millennium black people in the New World have been, so it seems, in continuous motion, much of it forced, some of it voluntary and self-propelled. Determined to end their tenure in the "peculiar institution," or die trying, thousands of black slaves fled during the antebellum decades, as the legendary exploits of Harriet Tubman and Frederick Douglass testify. Large numbers of them challenged, with their feet, the boundaries of freedom in the aftermath of the Civil War. Many moved west to establish new black towns and settlements in Kansas and Oklahoma in the closing decades of the nineteenth century. Others attempted to return to Africa.² To understand both the processes of black migration and the motivations of the individuals, men and women, who comprised this human tide is to approach a more illuminating portrait of American history and society. Central to all of this black movement was the compelling quest for that ever so elusive, but distinctly American property: freedom and equality of opportunity.

Long a riveting topic, studies of the Great Migration abound. Indeed, recent histories of black urbanization, especially those focused on key midwestern cities and towns—Chicago, Cleveland, Detroit, Milwaukee, and Evansville, Indiana—pay considerable attention to the demographic transformation of the black population, a transformation which began in earnest in 1915 and continued through the World War II crisis.³ As enlightening and pathbreaking as most of these studies are, there remains an egregious void concerning the experiences of black women migrants. This brief essay is primarily concerned with the gender dimension of black migration to the urban Midwest. It raises, without providing a comprehensive answer, the question, How is our understanding of black migration and urbanization refined by focusing on the experiences (similar to men in many ways, yet often unique) of the thousands of southern black women who migrated to the Midwest between the two world wars? As a corollary, what was the nature of the relations between those black women who migrated out of the lower Mississippi Valley states and those who stayed? How might we understand the relationships among the phenomenon of intraregional migration, for there was considerable movement of women between the midwestern cities and towns, the general migration to the Midwest, and women's relations with one another?

By 1920 almost 40 percent of Afro-Americans residing in the North were concentrated in eight cities, five of them in the Midwest: Chicago, Detroit, Cleveland, Cincinnati, and Columbus, Ohio. The three eastern cities with high percentages of black citizens were New York, Philadelphia, and Pittsburgh. These eight cities contained only 20 percent of the total northern population. Two peaks characterized the first phase of the Great Black Migration: 1916-1919 and 1924-1925. These dates correspond to the passage of stringent anti-immigration laws, and the years in which the majority of the approximately 500,000 black southerners relocated northward.[4]

Clearly the diverse economic opportunities in the midwestern cities drew black workers, resulting in a dramatic increase in the black population between 1910 and 1920. Detroit's black population rose an astounding 611.3 percent. More specifically, the number of Afro-Americans attracted by the jobs available at the Ford, Dodge, Chrysler, Chevrolet, and Packard automobile plants in Detroit increased from 5,741 in 1910 to 120,066 in 1930. Home of the northern terminus of the Illinois Central Railroad, the *Chicago Defender*, meat packing, and mail order enterprises, Chicago was not outdone. The Windy City's black population, which in 1910 numbered 44,103, jumped to 233,903 in 1930.[5] Drawn to midwestern jobs, throughout the First World War era, the number of black males far exceeded female migrants. Thus the black population of midwestern cities, unlike in most eastern and southern cities, did not reflect a majority of females.

A perusal of the major studies of black urbanization reveals considerable scholarly consensus on several gender-related themes. Scholars generally acknowledge that gender did make a difference in terms of the reasons expressed for quitting the South and affected the means by which men and women arrived at their northern destinations. Likewise, scholars concur that men and women encountered radically divergent socioeconomic and political opportunities in midwestern cities. Gender and race stereotyping in jobs proved quite beyond their control and was intransigent in the face of protest.

Scholars agree that black women faced greater economic discrimination and had fewer employment opportunities than black men. Their work was the most undesirable and least remunerative of all migrants. Considering that their economic condition or status scarcely improved or changed, for many women migrants were doomed to work in the same kinds of domestic service jobs they had held in the South, one wonders why they bothered to move in the first place. Of course there were significant differences. A maid earning $7 a week in Cleveland perceived herself to be much better off than a counterpart receiving $2.50 a week in Mobile, Alabama. A factory worker, though the work was dirty and low status, could and did imagine herself better off than domestic servants who endured the unrelenting scrutiny, interference, and complaints of household mistresses.[6]

It is clear that more attention needs to be directed toward the non-economic motives propelling black female migration. Many black women quit the South out of a desire to achieve personal autonomy and to escape from sexual exploitation both within and outside of their families and from sexual abuse at the hands of southern white as well as black men. The combined influence of domestic violence and economic oppression is key to understanding the hidden motivation informing major social protest and migratory movements in Afro-American history.[7]

That black women were very much concerned with negative images of their sexuality is graphically and most forcefully echoed in numerous speeches of the early leaders of the national organization of black women's clubs. Rosetta Sprague, the daughter of Frederick Douglass, declared in an address to the Federation of Afro-American Women in 1896:

> We are weary of the false impressions sent broadcast over the land about the colored woman's inferiority, her lack of noble womanhood. We wish to make it clear in the minds of your fellow country men and women that there are no essential elements of character that they deem worthy of cultivating that we do not desire to emulate [so] that the sterling qualities of purity, virtue, benevolence and charity are not more dormant in the breast of the black women than in the white woman.[8]

Sociologist Lynda F. Dickson cautions that "recognition of the major problem—the need to elevate the image of black womanhood—may or may not have led to a large scale club movement both nationally and locally."[9] It cannot be denied, however, that "the most important function of the club affiliation was to provide a support system that could continually reinforce the belief that the task at hand—uplifting the race, and improving the image of black womanhood—was possible.[10] A study of the history of the early twentieth-century black women's club movement is essential to the understanding of black women's migration to the middle western towns and cities and the critical roles they played in creating and sustaining new black social, religious, political, and economic institutions. These clubs were as important as the National Urban League and the NAACP in transforming black peasants into the urban proletariat.[11]

This focus on the sexual and the personal impetus for black women's migration neither dismisses nor diminishes the importance of economic motives, a discussion of which I will return to later. Rather, I am persuaded by historian Lawrence Levine's reservations. He cautions, "As indisputably important as the economic motive was, it is possible to overstress it so that the black migration is converted into an inexorable force and Negroes are seen once again not as actors capable of affecting at least some part of their destinies, but primarily as beings who are acted upon—southern leaves blown North by the winds of destitution."[12] It is reasonable to assume that many were indeed "southern leaves blown North," and that others were more likely self-propelled actors seeking respect, space in which to live, and a means by which to earn an adequate living.

Black men and women migrated into the Midwest in distinctive patterns. Single men, for example, usually worked their way North, leaving farms for southern cities, doing odd jobs, and sometimes staying in one location for a few years before proceeding to the next stop. This pattern has been dubbed "secondary migration." Single black women, on the other hand, as a rule, traveled the entire distance in one trip. They usually had a specific relative—or fictive kin—waiting for them at their destination, someone who may have advanced them the fare and who assisted with temporary lodging and advice on securing a job.[13] Amanda Jones-Watson, a fifty-year-old resident of Grand Rapids, Michigan, and three-time president of the still-functioning Grand Rapids Study Club, founded in 1904, migrated from Tennessee in 1936 in her thirties. She recalls asking her uncle, who had just moved to Grand Rapids, to send her a ticket. She exclaimed, "I cried when it came. I was kidding. My sister said, 'Amanda, what are you worried about? You can always come back if you don't like it.'" Jones-Watson was fortunate. Her uncle was headwaiter at the Pantlind Hotel. She continued, "I got a job as a maid and was written up in a local furniture magazine for making the best bed at the Pantlind."[14]

For Sara Brooks, a domestic, the idea that she should leave Alabama and relocate in Cleveland in 1940 originated with her brother. He implored his sister, "Why don't you come up here? You could make more here." Brooks demurred, "Well, I hadn't heard anything about the North because I never known nobody to come no further than Birmingham, Alabama, and that was my sister-in-law June, my husband's sister." A single mother of three sons and a daughter, Brooks eventually yielded to her brother's entreaties, leaving her sons with her aging parents. She recalled, "But my brother wanted me to come up here to Cleveland with him, so I started to try to save up what little money I had. . . . But I saved what I could, and when my sister-in-law came down for me, I had only eighteen dollars to my name, and that was maybe a few dollars over enough to come up here. If I'm not mistaken it was about a dollar and fifteen cent over."[15]

The influence and pressure of family members played a substantial role in convincing many ambivalent young women to migrate. A not-so-young sixty-eight-year-old Melinda left her home in depression-ridden rural Alabama to assist her granddaughter in childrearing in Anderson, Indiana. Even when expressing her plans to return home once her granddaughter was up and about, somehow Melinda knew that the visit would be permanent. In retelling Melinda's story, D.J. Steans declared that Melinda had labored hard at sharecropping, besides taking in washing and ironing. Even after her sixty-second birthday, she was still going strong. Many weeks she earned less that 50 cents, but she saved a few pennies a day in order to satisfy a burning desire to travel north to visit her great-grandchildren.[16]

Some women simply seized the opportunity to accompany friends traveling north. Fired from her nursing job at Hampton Institute, in Hampton, Virginia, Jane Edna Hunter packed her bags determined to head for Florida. She never made it. According to Hunter, "en route, I stopped at Richmond, Virginia, to visit with Mr. and Mrs. William Coleman, friends of Uncle Parris. They were at church when I arrived; so I sat on the doorstep to await their return. After these good friends had greeted me, Mrs. Coleman said, 'Our bags are packed to go to Cleveland, Jane. We are going to take you with us.'" Jane needed little persuasion. She exclaimed, "I was swept off my feet by the cheerful determination of the Colemans. My trunk, not yet removed from the station, was rechecked to Cleveland."[17] Hunter arrived in the city on May 10, 1905, with $1.75 in her pockets, slightly more than Sara Brooks brought with her thirty-five years later.

The different migratory patterns of black males and females reflected gender conventions in the larger society. A woman traveling alone was surely at greater risk than a man. After all, a man could and did, with less approbation and threat of bodily harm, spend nights outdoors. More important, men were better suited to defend themselves against attackers. However, given the low esteem in which the general society held black women, even the courts and law officials would have ridiculed and dismissed assault complaints from a black female traveling alone, regardless of her social status. Yes, it was wise to make the trip all at once, and better still to have company.

Although greater emphasis has been placed on men who left families behind, black women, too—many of whom were divorced, separated, or widowed—left love ones, usually children, in the South when they migrated. Like married men, unattached or single black mothers sent for their families after periods of time ranging from a month to several years. A great number of women who migrated into the Midwest may have left children, the products of early marriages or romantic teenage liaisons, with parents, friends, and other relatives in the South; but it would be exceedingly difficult, if not impossible to develop any statistical information on this phenomenon. Nevertheless, the oral history of Elizabeth Burch of Fort Wayne, Indiana, offers poignant testimony of a child left behind:

> I was born [December 20, 1926, in Chester, Georgia] out of wedlock to Arlena Burch and John Halt. My mother went north and that's where they—all of it began in a little town called Albion, Michigan and she went back south to have me. . . . Aunt Clyde that's my mother's sister, she was the baby and that was a little town called Albion, Michigan. That's where I was conceived at. That's where my mother went when she left Georgia. My mother decided well she go back up north. She married just to get away from home to go back north and this guy was working as a sharecropper and he had made enough money that year that he was willing to marry my mother and take her back up north. . . . So they left me with Miss Burch— Miss Mattie Elizabeth Burch, namesake which was my grandmother and that's where I grew up and years passed and

years went through I was just on the farm with my grandparents.[18]

The difficulty of putting aside enough money to send for their children placed a tremendous strain on many a domestic salary. It took Sara Brooks almost fifteen years to reconstitute her family, to retrieve her three sons left behind in Orchard, Alabama. With obvious pride in her accomplishment, Brooks explained, "The first one to come home was Jerome. . . . Then Miles had to come because my father didn't wanna keep him down there no more because he wouldn't mind him. . . . Then Benjamin was the last to come." Brooks summed up her success, "So I come up to Cleveland with Vivian [her daughter], and after I came up, the rest of my kids came up here. I was glad—I was VERY glad because I had wanted em with me all the time, but I just wasn't able to support em, and then I didn't have no place for them, either, when I left and come to Cleveland cause I came here to my brother."[19]

On the one hand, inasmuch as so many midwestern black women were absentee mothers—that is, their children remained in the South—their actual acculturation into an urban life style became a long, drawn out, and often incomplete, process. On the other hand, as historians Peter Gottlieb and Jacqueline Jones persuasively maintain, black women served as critical links in the "migration chain."[20] They proved most instrumental in convincing family members and friends to move north. This concept of women as "links in a migration chain" begs elaboration. I suspect that it is precisely because women left children behind in the care of parents and other relatives that they contributed so much to the endurance and tenacity of the migration chain. Their attachment to the South was more than sentimental or cultural. They had left part of themselves behind.

Family obligations encouraged many black women migrants to return south for periodic visits. Burch recalled that "My mother would come maybe once a year—maybe Christmas to visit" her in Georgia from Ft. Wayne.[21] Still other midwestern women returned to participate in community celebrations, family reunions, and to attend religious revivals. Of course, such periodic excursions southward also permitted display of new clothes and other accoutrements of success. Before she made the journey to Cleveland, Sara Brooks admitted delight in her sister-in-law's return visits. "I noticed she had some nice-lookin little clothes when she come back to Orchard to visit. She had little nice dresses and brassieres and things, which I didn't have. . . . I didn't even have a brassiere, and she'd lend me hers and I'd wear it to church."[22] Indeed, Brooks' recollections raise a complex question—To what extent and how does a woman migrant's relation to the South change over the course of her life? When do migrants move from being southerners in the North to southern northerners?

Unable, or unwilling, to sever ties to or abandon irrevocably the South, black women's assimilation to urban life remained fragmented and incomplete. It was the very incompleteness of the assimilation, however, which facilitated the southernization of the Midwest. Vestiges of southern black culture were transplanted and continuously renewed and reinforced by these women in motion. The resiliency of this cultural transference is reflected in food preferences and preparation styles, reliance on folk remedies and superstitions, religious practices, speech patterns, games, family structures, social networks, and music, most notably, the blues.[23] The southernization of urban midwestern culture was but one likely consequence of the migration chain women forged. In short, although unattached black women migrants may have traveled the initial distance to Chicago, Cleveland, Detroit, or Cincinnati, in one trip, as long as offspring, relatives, and friends remained in the South, psychological and emotional relocation was much more convoluted and, perhaps, more complicated than heretofore assumed.

Discussions of the marital status and family obligations—specifically whether the women migrants had children remaining in the South—are indirectly, perhaps, related to a more controversial topic of current interest to historians of nineteenth-century black migration and urbanization. In his study of violence and crime in post-Civil War Philadelphia, Roger Lane suggests that there was a marked decline in black birthrates in the city near the turn of the century. He attributes the decline in part to the rising incidence of syphilis which left many black women infertile. He notes that, "In Philadelphia in 1890 the black-white ratio was .815 to 1,000, meaning that black women had nearly 20 percent fewer children than whites, a figure that in 1900 dropped to .716 to 1,000, or nearly 30 percent fewer." Lane concludes, "All told, perhaps a quarter of Philadelphia's black women who reached the end of their childbearing years had at some time had exposure to the diseases and habits associated with prostitution. This figure would account almost precisely for the difference between black and white fertility in the city."[24]

Without reliance on the kinds of statistical data Lane employs in his analysis, the oral histories and autobiographies of midwestern black women migrants suggest an alternate explanation, though often overlooked, in discussions of black birthrate decline. Sara Brooks, mother of five children, was still in her childbearing years when she embraced celibacy. She declared, "See, after Vivian was born I didn't have no boyfriend or nothin, and I went to Mobile, I didn't still have no boyfriend in a long time. Vivian was nine years old when Eric come. ... But after Eric came along, I didn't have no boyfriend. I didn't want one because what I wanted, I worked for it, and that was that home." Brooks had realized her dream in 1957 with the purchase of her home and the reuniting of all of her children under one roof.[25]

For women, ignorant of effective birth control or unable to afford the cost of raising additional children alone, sexual abstinence was a rational choice. It should be pointed out that a range of concerns—deeply held religious convictions, disillusionment with black men, a history of unhappy and abusive marriages, adherence to Victorian ideals of morality, a desire to refute prevalent sexual stereotypes and negative images of black women as a whole, or experience with an earlier unplanned pregnancy—may have informed many a decision to practice sexual abstinence among adult black women. Only latent acceptance of the myths concerning the alleged unbridled passions and animalistic sexuality of black women prevents serious consideration of the reality and extent of self-determined celibacy. Meanwhile, until we know more about the internal lives of black women, the suggestion of abstinence or celibacy as a factor limiting births should not be dismissed.

The fact that women who migrated north produced fewer children than their southern counterparts warrants further investigation. It is not enough to argue that prostitution, venereal disease, and infanticide account for declining black births in urban settings. Many other factors, in addition to abstinence, offer fruitful and suggestive lines of inquiry. Some scholars have asserted that children in urban as opposed to rural settings had rather insignificant economic roles and therefore their labor was not as important to family survival.[26]

As black women became more economically sufficient, better educated, and more involved in self-improvement efforts, including participation in the flourishing black women's club movement, they would have had more access to birth control information.[27] As the institutional infrastructure of black women's clubs, sororities, church groups, and charity organizations took hold within black communities, they gave rise to those values and attitudes traditionally associated with the middling classes. To black middle-class aspirants, the social stigma of having many children would have, perhaps, inhibited reproduction. Furthermore, over time, the gradually evolving demographic imbalance in the sex ratio meant that increasing numbers of black women in urban midwestern communities would never marry. Not dating, marrying, or having children may very well have been a decision—a deliberate choice, for whatever reason—that black women made. For instance, on August 23, 1921, Sarah D. Tyree wrote tellingly about her own decision not to date. Tyree had a certificate from the Illinois College of Chiropracty, but was, at the time, taking care of aged parents and her sister's children in Indianapolis. She confided to her sister living in Muskegon, Michigan:

> I have learned to stay at home lots. I firmly believe in a womanly independence. Believe that a woman should be allowed to go and come where and when she pleases alone if she wants to, and so long as she knows who is right, she should not have to worry about what others think. It is not every woman who can turn for herself as I can, and the majority of women who have learned early to depend upon their male factors do not believe that their sister-woman can get on alone. So she becomes dangerously suspicious, and damagingly tongue-wagging. I have become conscious of the fact that because I am not married, I am watched with much interest. So I try to avoid the appearance of evil, for the sake of the weaker fellow. I do not therefore go out unaccompanied at night. There are some young men I would like to go out with occasionally if it could be understood that it was for the occasion and not for life that we go. I don't care to be bothered at any time with a fellow who has been so

cheap and all to himself for 5 or 6 years. I have all patients [sic] to wait for the proper one to play for my hand.[28]

Moreover, social scientists Joseph A. McFalls, Jr., and George S. Masnick persuasively argue that black Americans were much more involved in birth control than previously assumed. They contend, "the three propositions usually advanced to support the view that birth control had little, if any, effect on black fertility from 1880 to 1940—that blacks used 'ineffective' methods, that blacks did not practice birth control 'effectively,' and that blacks used birth control too late in their reproductive careers to have had much of an effect on their fertility— simply have no empirical or even *a priori* foundation. There is no reason now to believe that birth control had little impact on black fertility during this period."[29] Not to be overlooked are the often chronic health problems overworked, undernourished, and inadequately-housed poor black women undoubtedly experienced, especially during the Great Depression. In discussing the morbidity and mortality rates of black Chicagoans, William Tuttle observes that,

> Chicago's medical authorities boasted of the city's low death rate, pointing to statistics which indicated that it was the lowest of any city in the world with a population of over one million. Their statistics told another story as well, however, and it was that Chicago's blacks had a death rate which was twice that of whites. The stillbirth rate was also twice as high; and the death rate from tuberculosis and syphilis was six times as high; and from pneumonia and nephritis it was well over three times as high. . . . The death rate for the entire city was indeed commendable, but the statistics indicated that the death rate for Chicago's blacks was comparable to that of Bombay, India.[30]

One more observation about the declining birth rate among northern black women should be made. Here it is important to note the dichotomy between black women who worked in middle-class occupations and those in working-class ones. Middle-class working women, regardless of color, had fewer children than those employed in blue collar jobs. The professional and semi-professional occupations most accessible to black women during the years between the world wars included teaching, nursing, and social work, on the one hand, and hairdressing or dressmaking, on the other. In some of the smaller midwestern communities and towns married women teachers, race not withstanding, lost their jobs, especially if the marriage became public knowledge or the wife became pregnant. At least one black school teacher in Lafayette, Indiana, confided that she never married, though she had been asked, because in the 1930s and 1940s to have done so would have cost her the position. The pressure on the small cadre of professional black women not to have children was considerable. The more educated they were, the greater the sense of being responsible, somehow, for the advance of the race and the uplift of black womanhood. They held these expectations of themselves and found them reinforced by the demands of the black community and its institutions. Under conditions and pressure such as these, it would be erroneous to argue that this is the same thing as voluntary celibacy. Nevertheless, the autonomy, so hard earned and enjoyed to varying degrees by both professional women and personal service workers, offered meaningful alternatives to the uncertainties of marriage and the demands of childrearing. The very economic diversity—whether real or imagined—that had attracted black women to the urban Midwest, also held the promise of freedom to fashion socially useful and independent lives beyond family boundaries.

None of this is to be taken as a categorical denial of the existence of rampant prostitution and other criminal activity in urban midwestern ghettos. Too many autobiographies and other testimony document the place and the economic functions of prostitution in urban society to be denied. Indeed, Jane Edna Hunter's major contribution to improving black women's lives in Cleveland—the establishment of the Phillis Wheatley boarding homes—stemmed from her commitment to provide training, refuge, and employment for young migrating women who were frequently enticed or tricked into prostitution as a means of survival. She remarked about her own awakening that

> the few months on Central Avenue made me sharply aware of the great temptations that beset a young woman in a large city. At home on the plantation, I knew that some girls had been seduced. Their families had felt the disgrace keenly. The fallen ones had been wept and prayed over. . . . Until my arrival in Cleveland I was ignorant of the wholesale organized traffic in black flesh.[31]

Young, naive country girls were not the only ones vulnerable to the lure of seduction and prostitution. Middle-aged black women also engaged in sex for pay, but for them it was a rational economic decision. Sara Brooks did not disguise her contempt for women who bartered their bodies. She declared, while commenting on her own struggle to pay the mortgage on her house, "Some women woulda had a man to come and live in the house and had an outside boyfriend too, in order to get the house paid for and the bills." She scornfully added, "They meet a man and if he promises em four or five dollars to go to bed, they'd grab it. That's called sellin your own body, and I wasn't raised like that."[32]

Prostitution was not the only danger awaiting single migrating black women. Police in many midwestern towns seemed quick to investigate not only black men but also black women who appeared suspicious. Historian James E. DeVries records several encounters between black women and the police in Monroe, Michigan. "In January 1903, Gertie Hall was arrested after acting in a very nervous manner on the interurban trip from Toledo. An investigation by Monroe police revealed that Hall was wanted for larceny in Toledo, and she was soon escorted to that city." In another incident four years later involving fifteen-year-old Ahora Ward, also from Toledo, DeVries notes that she was "picked up and taken to jail. . . . As it turned out, she had been whipped by her mother and was running away from home when taken into custody."[33]

There exists a scholarly consensus about the origins and the destinations of the overwhelming majority of black migrants throughout the period between 1915 and 1945. Before turning to a discussion of the economic impetus, or the "pull" factors, for black women's migrations, I would like to interject another rarely explored "push" factor, that is, the desire for freedom from sexual exploitation, especially rape by white men, and to escape from domestic abuse within their own families. A full exploration of this theme requires the use of a plethora of sources including oral testimonials, autobiographies, biographies, novels, and court records. The letters, diaries, and oral histories collected by the Black Women in the Middle West Project and deposited in the Indiana Historical Society contain descriptions of the domestic violence which fed the intraregional movement of black women who had migrated from southern states. Elizabeth Burch explained why she left Ft. Wayne for Detroit, "And my mother—and my stepfather—would have problems. He would hit my mother and so, you know, beat upon my mother . . . but he never did beat up on me. My mother would say—'Well you just don't put your hands on her. You better not, hear.'" To avoid these scenes Burch moved to Detroit but later returned to Ft. Wayne.[34]

Similarly Jane Pauline Fowlkes, sister of the above-mentioned Sarah Tyree, was granted a divorce from husband Jesse Clay Fowlkes in Muskegon, Michigan, in 1923 and returned to her family and sister in Indianapolis. Granted the decree because her husband was found "guilty of several acts of extreme cruelty," Fowlkes retained custody of all three children.[35]

While Sara Brooks' experiences are hardly representative, they are nevertheless suggestive of the internal and personal reasons black women may have had for leaving the South. Brooks vividly described the events that led her to leave her husband for the third and final time. When she ran away from home the last time, she didn't stop running until she reached Cleveland almost a decade later. "When he hit me," she said,

> I jumped outa the bed, and when I jumped outa the bed, I just ran. . . . I didn't have a gown to put on—I had on a slip and had on a short-sleeved sweater. I left the kids right there with him and I went all the way to his father's house that night, barefeeted, with that on, on the twenty-fifth day of December. That was in the dark. It was two miles or more and it was rainin. . . . I walked. And I didn't go back.[36]

For whatever reasons Sara Brooks, Melinda, Jane Edna Hunter, and others wound up in the various midwestern cities, they expected to work and to work hard, for work was part of the definition of what it meant to be a black woman in America, regardless of region. The abundant economic opportunities, or "pull factors," especially in automobile plants and, during the First World War, in the defense industries, had been powerful inducements for black male migrants. The dislocation of black workers in southern agriculture, the ravages of the boll weevil, floods, and the seasonal and marginal nature of the work relegated to them in the South were powerful "push" factors.

Taken together these factors help us to understand why 5 percent of the total southern black population left the South between 1916 and 1921.[37]

Black women shared with black men a desire for economic improvement and security. They too were attracted to midwestern cities, specifically to cities with a greater diversity of women's jobs. The female occupational structure of Chicago, for example, held the promise of more opportunity for black women than did Pittsburgh, which was much more dependent on heavy industry.[38] Black men, however, were not as constrained. To be sure, the majority of men and women expected to secure neither white collar jobs nor managerial positions. None were so naive as to believe that genuine equality of opportunity actually existed in the North or the Midwest, but occasionally black women migrants did anticipate that more awaited them in Cleveland and Chicago than an apron and domestic servitude in the kitchens of white families, segregated hotels, and restaurants. Most were disappointed. Author Mary Helen Washington recalled the disappointment and frustration experienced by her female relatives when they migrated to Cleveland:

> In the 1920s my mother and my five aunts migrated to Cleveland, Ohio, from Indianapolis and, in spite of their many talents, they found every door except the kitchen door closed to them. My youngest aunt was trained as a bookkeeper and was so good at her work that her white employer at Guardian Savings of Indianapolis allowed her to work at the branch in a black area. The Cleveland Trust Company was not so liberal, however, so in Cleveland she went to work in what is known in the black community as "private family."[39]

Scholars concur that, while black women secured employment in low level jobs in light industry, especially during the World War I years when overseas immigration came to a standstill, this window of opportunity quickly closed with the end of hostilities. Florette Henri calculates that "immigration dropped from 1,218,480 in 1914 to 326,700 in 1915, to under 300,000 in 1916 and 1917, and finally to 110,618 in 1918." This drop and the draft made it possible for black women to squeeze into "occupations not heretofore considered within the range of their possible activities," concluded a

Department of Labor survey in 1918. Thus the percentage of black domestics declined between 1910 and 1920, from 78.4 percent to 63.8 percent in Chicago, and from 81.1 percent to 77.8 percent in Cleveland.[40]

The study of migrations from the perspective of black women permits a close examination of the intersection of gender, class, and race dynamics in the development of a stratified work force in midwestern cities. During the war years a greater number of black women migrants found work in midwestern hotels as cooks, waitresses, and maids, as ironers in the new steam laundries, as labelers and stampers in Sears Roebuck and Montgomery Ward mail order houses, as common laborers in garment and lampshade factories, and workers in food processing and meat packing plants. But even in these places, the limited gains were short lived and easily erased. As soon as the war ended and business leveled off, for example, both Sears and Ward immediately fired all the black women.[41] In 1900 black women constituted 4 percent of the labor force in commercial laundries; by 1920 this figure had climbed to 6 percent. As late as 1930 a little over 3,000 black women, or 15 percent of the black female labor force in Chicago were unskilled and semi-skilled factory operatives. Thus over 80 percent of all employed black women continued to work as personal servants and domestics. Historian Allan H. Spear points out that "Negro women were particularly limited in their search for desirable positions. Clerical work was practically closed to them and only a few could qualify as school teachers. Negro domestics often received less than white women for the same work and they could rarely rise to the position of head servant in large households."[42]

In Milwaukee, especially during the depression decades, black women were, as historian Joe Trotter observes, "basically excluded from this narrow industrial footing; 60.4 percent of their numbers labored in domestic service as compared to only 18.6 percent of all females."[43] To be sure, this was down from the 73.0 percent of black women who had worked as domestics in Milwaukee in 1900.[44] A decline of 13 percent over a forty-year period—regardless of from what angle it is viewed—is hardly cause for celebration.

Many reasons account for the limited economic gains of black women as compared to black men in midwestern industries. One of the major barriers impeding a better economic showing was the hostility and racism of white women. The ceiling on black women's job opportunities was secured tightly by the opposition of white women. White females objected to sharing the settings, including hospitals, schools, department stores, and offices. Now 90, Sarah Glover migrated with her family to Grand Rapids, Michigan, from Alabama in 1922, where they had jobs working in the coal mines. Although she would in later years become the first practical nurse in the city, during her first seventeen years as a maid at Blodgett Hospital, she scrubbed the floors. After completing her housekeeping chores she'd voluntarily help the nurses. She reminisced, "The nurses used to call me 'Miss Sunshine' because I would cheer up the patients. I'd come over and say you look good today or crack a joke. That used to get most of them smiling again." In spite of her good work record, excellent human relations skills, and eagerness, hospital officials deemed it a violation of racial rules and thus rejected Glover's appeal to become a nurses' aide.[45]

Historians Susan M. Hartmann and Karen Tucker Anderson convincingly demonstrate that while white women enjoyed expanded employment opportunities, black women continued to be the last hired and first fired throughout the Great Depression and World War II years. Employers seeking to avert threatened walkouts, slow-downs, and violence caved into white women's objections to working beside or, most particularly, sharing restroom and toilet facilities with black women.[46] To be sure, many employers, as was the case with the Blodgett Hospital in Grand Rapids, harbored racist assumptions and beliefs in black inferiority but camouflaged them behind white women's objections.

The black media was not easily fooled by racist subterfuges and remained keenly attuned to all excuses that rationalized the denial of job opportunities to black women. In the National Urban League's *Opportunity*, officials catalogued the thinly-veiled justifications that white employers offered when discriminating against women:

> "There must be some mistake"; "No applications have heretofore been made by colored"; "You are smart for taking the courses, but we do not employ coloreds"; We have not yet installed separate but equal toilet facilities"; "A sufficient num-

ber of colored women have not been trained to start a separate shift"; "The training center from which you come does not satisfy plant requirements"; "Your qualifications are too high for the kind of job offered"; "We cannot put a Negro in our front office"; "We will write you . . . but my wife needs a maid"; "We have our percentage of Negroes."[47]

Trotter did, however, discover instances when the interests of white women occasionally promoted industrial opportunities for black women. "The white women of the United Steelworkers of America Local 1527, at the Chain Belt Company, resisted the firm's proposal for a ten-hour day and a six-day week by encouraging the employment of black women."[48] In a classic understatement, historian William Harris hesitantly asserts, "Black women apparently experienced more discrimination than black men in breaking into nonservice jobs."[49]

In their study of labor unions in Detroit, August Meier and Elliott Rudwick conclude that government inaction, as well as white women's hostility, encouraged the employment discrimination and job segregation that black women encountered in the automobile industries. Throughout the World War II era, the Ford Motor Company hired only a token number of black women. According to Meier and Rudwick, "Black civic leaders and trade unionists fought a sustained and energetic battle to open Detroit war production to black women, but because government manpower officials gave discrimination against Negro females low priority, the gains were negligible when compared with those achieved by the city's black male workers." By March 1943, for example, the Willow Run Ford Plant employed 25,000 women, but less than 200 were black. Apparently, Ford was not alone or atypical in these anti-black women hiring practices. Packard and Hudson each employed a mere six black women at this time. Most of those employed in the plants, as was to be expected, worked in various service capacities—matrons, janitors, and stock handlers. Meier and Rudwick point out that "as late as the summer of 1943 a government report termed the pool of 25,000 available black women the city's 'largest neglected source of labor.' "[50]

Through research on industrial workers and urbanization in the Midwest, we can begin to piece together a picture of the lives of black women migrants in the years between 1915 and 1945. But, until the differences force a rethinking and a rewriting of all black urban history no comprehensive synthesis or portrait of the migrants is possible. In addition to the good studies of political and cultural developments in Chicago, for example, more work needs to be done on the relation between migration and the development of black social, political, economic, and religious institutions in other midwestern cities. Although historians Peter Gottlieb and James Borchert have stressed the continuity between black life in the South and in northern cities, we do not yet understand fully the mechanisms by which this continuity was achieved, or its meaning.[51]

There is good reason to think that black women played a critical role in the establishment of an array of black institutions, especially the churches and mutual aid organizations that gave life in the northern cities a southern flavor. Historian Elizabeth Clark-Lewis, addressing the history of Washington, D.C., argues, "The growth of African-American churches in Washington, then, was a direct consequence of the steady influx of these working-class (former live-in) women. They strongly supported church expansion because their participation in the church activities further separated them from the stigma of servitude."[52]

Still in need of refinement is our understanding of the connection between migration and black social-class formation and between migration and the rise of protest ideologies which shaped the consciousness of the "New Negro," not only in Harlem, but also in midwestern cities. We need studies of the relation between migration and family reorganization, and between migration and sex-role differentiation in the black communities, especially in terms of religious activity; and of the development of new types of community-based social welfare programs. Moreover, we need micro-studies into individual lives, of neighborhoods, families, churches, and fraternal lodges in various cities. Examination of these themes makes imperative an even deeper penetration into the internal world of African-Americans. Perhaps even more dauntingly, to answer fully these questions requires that the black woman's voice and experience be researched and interpreted with the same intensity and seriousness accorded that of the black man.

Information derived from statistical and demographic data on black midwestern migration and urbanization must be combined with the knowledge drawn from the small, but growing, numbers of oral histories, autobiographies, and biographies of twentieth-century migrating women. Court records of legal encounters, church histories, black women's club minutes, scrapbooks, photographs, diaries, and histories of institutions ranging from old folks' homes, orphanages, businesses, and Phillis Wheatley Homes to local Young Women's Christian Associations yield considerable information about the lives of black women migrants to and within the middle western region. Actually these sources, properly "squeezed and teased" promise to light up that inner world so long shrouded behind a veil of neglect, silence, and stereotype.

It is reason enough to study black women simply because they are neglected and historically invisible. Yet, it is incumbent upon us that we examine and interpret their experiences, for this new information may very well facilitate the re-construction of an inclusive and thus far more accurate rendering of all of American history from colonial times to the present.

"We Specialize in the
Wholly Impossible"
The Philanthropic Work of Black Women

The philanthropic work of nineteenth- and early-twentieth-century African American women ensured the survival of many of the most vulnerable members of the black population. To date, this important dimension of the black self-help tradition has received scant scholarly attention. In part, to correct the historical oversight, but also to probe the ways in which black women's perceptions of and involvement in philanthropy changed over time this essay will examine the life and philanthropic work of Jane Edna Hunter, founder of the Phillis Wheatley Association in Cleveland, Ohio. Hunter's life is best understood when examined as interrelated sequences: migration to the urban Midwest, establishment of an institution to serve and to save black girls from poverty and prostitution, and the sharing of her private life with a significant female friend, Nannie H. Burroughs.

For centuries, black women, during slavery and in freedom, played a significant role in the creation of social, cultural, educational, religious, and economic institutions designed to improve the material conditions and to raise the self-esteem of African Americans. The records detailing black women's involvement in mutual aid societies, literary and social clubs, churches, antislavery and temperance organizations, as founders of primary schools, orphanages, clinics, and old folks' homes are only now being discovered and interpreted.[1]

To comprehend fully the origins and nature of the modern institutional infrastructure of Black America requires a sustained analysis of the motives and deeds of the generations of black women active between the collapse of Reconstruction and the outbreak of World War II. The rich history of this turbulent period encompasses the domestic feminism of the Progressive era and the economic crises of the Great Depression. Through it all, the vulnerable black community—especially its aged and sick, its orphaned children, and abandoned wives and mothers, its unskilled and illiterate workers—suffered a plethora of social ills. In many communities black women proved especially resourceful, either through the agency of their clubs or as the bedrock of the black church, to redress the harsh consequence of economic discrimination, political subordination and white supremacy.[2]

At the turn of the century Midwestern urban black women had become much more professional in providing assistance to people in need. Spurred by the exigencies of the massive migration of black Southerners and their concentration in key cities such as Chicago, Cleveland, Detroit, Milwaukee, and Indianapolis, black club women embarked upon a veritable crusade of philanthropic or beneficent work. By 1920 determined black women had established in every representative community, homes for the aged, hospitals and sanitariums, nursing schools and colleges, orphanages, libraries, gymnasiums, and shelters for young migrants, especially those who were, as historian Joanne J. Meyerowitz contends, "women adrift."[3]

The black leaders of the women's clubs and organizations, who initiated so much institution building and race-reclamation work never possessed the resources distributed by white philanthropists such as John D. Rockefeller, Julius Rosenwald, or Andrew Carnegie. Yet in many ways their giving of time and effort and commitment to racial uplift work—including providing protection for young black women—and their endless struggle to create living space for segregated, often illiterate, unskilled, and impoverished black Americans were as valuable as were the two-room Rosenwald schools built throughout the South, the libraries funded by Carnegie, and the Rockefeller-supported black medical schools—Meharry Medical College in Nashville, Tennessee, and Howard University Medical School in Washington, D.C.[4]

Unlike the impersonal corporate forms promoted by wealthy whites, such as the General Education Board or the Rosenwald Fund, black philanthropy and charitable giving usually assumed the form of small-scale, personal assistance and involvement. In most cases the women knew well the individuals, families, or groups whom they assisted. They emphasized the importance of volunteer service as preferable to simply making financial donations to worthy causes. Black women's philanthropy, in short, attempted to help black Americans to survive and improve their lot by developing themselves. The goal was social change and individual improvement not social control.[5]

The life and work of educator Ada Harris of Indianapolis, Indiana, illustrates one of the special forms of individual giving and self-help leadership provided in a local community. A 1909 *Indianapolis Star* article heralded Harris as the leader of the reclamation of Norwood, a small impoverished, all-black settlement situated on the outskirts of Indianapolis. According to the *Star,* Norwood was "a moral blot on the map of Marion County." The settlement acquired its bad reputation from the crap games and the prostitution rings that allegedly flourished in the area. Harris, well aware of Norwood's shortcomings, nevertheless moved into the community. She had taught school in the area since the late 1880s. By 1909 Harris was not only a resident of Norwood but principal of the local school. She insisted that her "greatest ambition" was to serve her race: "I want to see my people succeed. I want them to have an equal chance."[6]

To ensure that her students would have that "equal chance," Harris gave a great deal of herself, foregoing a private life in service to her race. At one point she reasoned that hunger, illness, fear, and hopelessness impaired her students' academic performance. Drawing upon the people's desire to improve their own lives and surroundings, especially the women in the community, Harris launched a drive to raise funds for the development of a Boys' Club which she proclaimed would allow the adults to "teach right living in addition to the 3R's," to the young boys. The initial fund-raising campaign for the establishment of a Boys' Gymnasium and Clubhouse netted only $35.00, which Harris used as down payment on property valued at $1,500. In defending her decision to place so much emphasis on erecting a gymnasium, Harris declared, "if it only teaches the colored boy to fight with his fists, and not to pull a knife or a gun on the slightest provocation it will have been worthwhile." She insisted that a gymnasium would allow the young boys to master important work skills and develop appropriate habits. Moreover, she asserted that "the class-work and the drills will strengthen our boys up and give them lungs that fight the tuberculosis that reaps such a harvest in the race."[7]

Although the *Star* article only hinted at the problems of prostitution in the Norwood area, no mention was made of the uninvestigated assaults on black women. Harris' focus on establishing a boys' gymnasium may well have reflected her concern with the ill-treatment and low status of black women in the community. She, as did other women, deplored the molestations of black females in the area and, for that matter, in other parts of the state. Harris, however, believed that to protect black women effectively from criminal abuse and sexual assaults, it was necessary to eradicate the negative stereotypes of their sexuality. Protecting black women also depended upon the success of efforts to teach black boys and men to respect black women more. Developing pride, providing creative outlets for juvenile exuberance, and challenging negative assessments of the moral fiber of black women were the driving motivations of many black women who engaged in social service and reform work during the opening decades of the twentieth century. In assessing her life work, Harris declared, "My field has been small in Norwood, but it has been plenty large enough for my abilities. At least I shall have spent my life for my race."[8]

The schools and colleges they founded, the old folks' homes, orphanages, sanitariums, settlement houses, and clinics—built to ameliorate the disorder of emancipation followed by the trauma of Southern violence, migration, and urbanization—became monuments representing black women's racial uplift and philanthropic work.[9] Yet there is another dimension to black women's philanthropic work, one that is not reflected in structures of brick and mortar. It is what they gave in order to reclaim black women's pride, dignity, and self-esteem. Only black women had the responsibility to fight the larger society's best efforts to define them as inferior, immoral, and therefore as undeserving of respect and equal educational and employment opportunities. Before black women could move into the larger arena of civic reform work, they had to first establish that their sexual natures were above reproach. Only when the larger society accepted them as virtuous women would it be possible to press their broad demands for social reform.[10]

One of the more revealing and successful sets of institutions created by early-twentieth-century black club and community women was the training schools and industrial institutes. Often these vocational high schools were reserved for black girls, but on occasion they were coeducational. The founders of the most noteworthy and long-lived industrial-vocational training schools and institutes were indomitable black women who deserve considerably more scholarly attention than they have heretofore received. Among the most significant activist founders were Mary McLeod Bethune (1875-1955), Charlotte Hawkins Brown (1883-1961), Jane Edna Harris Hunter (1882-1959), and Nannie H. Burroughs (1879-1961).

Mary McLeod Bethune was born on July 10, 1875, near Mayesville, South Carolina, the fifteenth child of former slaves, Samuel and Patsy McLeod. Following completion of her education at Scotia Seminary (now Barber-Scotia College) in Concord, North Carolina, she attended Dwight Moody's Institute for Home and Foreign Missions in Chicago and graduated in 1895. Bethune founded at Daytona, Florida, on October 3, 1904, the Daytona Educational and Industrial Institute for black girls. In 1923 the school merged with an all-boys school named Cookman Institute to become Bethune-Cookman College. Asked why she founded the training school and its significance, Bethune remarked, "Many homeless girls have been sheltered there and trained physically, mentally, and spiritually. They have been helped and sent out to serve, to pass their blessings on to other needy children." Bethune served a two-term stint as president of the National Association of Colored Women's Clubs (1924-1928).[11]

Charlotte Hawkins Brown was born in Henderson, North Carolina, on June 11, 1883, and was educated at the Cambridge English High School in Cambridge, Massachusetts. She attended the State Normal School at Salem, but left there in 1901. In 1902, Brown founded the Palmer Memorial Institute at Sedalia, North Carolina, and served as the principal until 1952. In the intervening years she launched a fund-raising drive to establish a home for delinquent black girls. Brown once lamented, "Until somebody can express confidence enough in a Negro woman to give her the chance to do something big for her people, she will always be looked upon as a maid or as a servant."[12] In 1909 Brown helped to organize the North Carolina State Federation of Negro Women's Clubs. She became the president of the federation in 1915 and occupied that position until 1936. Under her guidance the federation purchased and maintained the Efland Home for Wayward Girls located in Orange County, North Carolina. She was also instrumental in founding the Colored Orphanage at Oxford, North Carolina.[13]

It is ironic that Nannie H. Burroughs and Jane Edna Hunter established institutions precisely to make available to black women training that would enable them to be better maids. Burroughs was born in Orange, Virginia on May 2, 1879, to John and Jennie (Poindexter) Burroughs. She graduated from the Washington High School in Washington, D.C., and secured a post as bookkeeper and associate editor of the *Christian Banner* in Philadelphia. Her interest in the affairs of the Baptist Church brought her into contact with the officers of the National Baptist Convention. Upon moving to Louisville, Kentucky, she worked for several years as the private secretary for Dr. L. G. Jordan, Secretary of the Foreign Mission Board of the National Baptist Convention. She also lectured and wrote denominational papers. In one year, 1908, Burroughs raised more than $13,000 from black women alone to finance the missionary and educational work for the Women's Convention Auxiliary.[14]

Burroughs' talents and passion for religious and missionary work soon catapulted her into the higher echelons of the convention's bureaucracy. She served as the corresponding secretary of the Women's Auxiliary of the National Baptist Convention from 1900 to 1948 and as its president from 1948 until 1961. An anonymously written description of Burroughs exulted:

> She lives a simple life, and is free from vanity and affectation. She has a head full of common sense, and that head is well pinned on. Success does not turn it. Women in all walks of life admire her. She is not affected by praise. Here is a story of a young woman who is just beyond thirty and has come from the bottom of the round to the position of President of the only school of national character over which a Negro woman presides.[15]

Burroughs acquired national renown for establishing the National Training School for Women and Girls in Washington, D.C., which she opened on October 19, 1909, with 35 pupils. The building that housed the school was a dilapidated eight-room farmhouse located in a community called Lincolnville, of less than a dozen houses and without streets, water, telephone or electric lights. Welcoming women and girls of all denominations, Burroughs commented on the purpose of the combination boarding school and training school. "Two thirds of the colored women must work with their hands for a living, and it is indeed an oversight not to prepare this army of breadwinners to do their work well." In 1934 the school was renamed the National Trades and Professional School for Women.

Burroughs raised almost all of the money for the maintenance of the school from black supporters. Indeed, the black woman banker of Richmond, Virginia, Maggie L. Walker, donated $500 to the school while it was still in the planning stage. Burroughs sometimes referred to the institution as the school of the three "B's"—the Bible, the Bath, and the Broom. As one writer described it, "The Institution, then, started as a school, Christian in its teaching, character building in its ideals, cultural in its atmosphere, standardized in its academic work, practical in its vocational courses." The school provided instruction at the secondary and teacher-training levels, and offered vocational courses in "housekeeping, domestic science and art, household administration, management for matrons and directors of school dining rooms and dormitories, interior decorating, laundering, home nursing, and printing."[16]

Although the early circumstances of their lives differed greatly, Jane Edna Hunter's work on behalf of black women can be viewed as the midwestern counterpart to that of the eastern-based Nannie H. Burroughs. Jane Edna Harris Hunter was born on December 13, 1882, in a two-room tenant house on Woodburn Plantation, near Pendleton, Anderson County, South Carolina. Her sharecropping parents, Harriet and Edward Harris, moved four times before she was ten, and with each move their standard of living deteriorated. The death of her father in 1892 left her mother no alternative but to place each of her four children into the employ of white families as domestic servants. Throughout this turbulent period poor, rural black women had virtually no hope of securing employment outside of domestic service or agriculture. Although many sex-segregated jobs in offices and department stores were opening for women, racism blocked black women's advance even in the cities.[17] The most accessible profession for black women of Hunter's working-poor background was nursing.

While still a teenager Jane was compelled to marry a man forty years her senior. Her mother deemed it the best protection for her daughter. The marriage, however, was a disaster, lasting only fifteen months. At the age of seventeen Jane went to Charleston, South Carolina, to work as a domestic servant and child nurse for a prominent white family. While there she learned from Ella Hunt, chairwoman of the Ladies' Auxiliary of the recently opened black hospital, of the opportunity to pursue nursing training.[18]

The Charleston Hospital and Training School for nurses was founded in 1896 by a group of black physicians led by Alonzo McClennan. Rigid adherence to racial exclusion and the denial of attending privileges at the white hospitals had motivated black physicians across the country to found a network of hospitals and nursing schools in the last decade of the nineteenth century. Hunter entered the hospital's nursing program and after completing the eighteen-month course, worked as a private duty nurse in Charleston. In 1904, feeling the need for more training, she entered the Dixie Hospital and Training School at Hampton Institute in Hampton, Virginia. Immediately upon the completion of this second nurse training program, Hunter, like so many others, joined the great migration north in search of better employment opportunities.[19]

Hunter arrived in Cleveland, Ohio, on May 10, 1905, with $1.75 in her pocket. During the first frustrating week of job search, she met with contempt, slammed doors, and outright hostility. One white physician allegedly admonished her "Go back South; white doctors don't employ nigger nurses." Fortunately, with only twenty-five cents left, Hunter persuaded the white county coroner, L. E. Seigelstein, to give her a job. Through his intercession she subsequently secured work providing massages to well-to-do white women. She eventually established a good reputation and became a highly desired bedside nurse. Nursing among Cleveland's prominent white elites allowed

Hunter to make important contacts and to win the confidence of people who controlled sizeable resources.[20]

Up to 1905, Hunter's life was characterized by the same trials and tribulations experienced by most poor, barely educated, young, single black women who grew up in the impoverished South and who believed that nursing or domestic service, coupled with migration, was the key to a better life in the North. The details of Hunter's migration experience, her struggles to find a job and a decent, affordable place to live, and the process through which she became part of a community of women mirrored the processes of migration, immigration, and adaptation of ethnic European and American native-born farm women.[21] The powerful impact of racism, however, severely restricted Hunter's chance for economic advance. Unlike the white farm girls who went to the cities, or the European immigrants who crossed the ocean, Hunter could not aspire to jobs in most factories, department stores, offices, or industrial plants. In describing the conditions of black women workers in Chicago, historian Meyerowitz observed, "Almost no black women held jobs in offices and stores in Chicago in the late nineteenth and early twentieth centuries. . . . Employers also excluded black women from many manufacturing jobs. The growing number of black women who found work in industry frequently found themselves with the work that white women refused to accept."[22]

The vast majority of black women worked only in agriculture or in domestic service while others performed only the meanest, lowest paid, undesirable jobs—and were always the last hired and first fired. For most black women, dreams of acquiring higher education and better jobs were little more than delusions. After World War I, urban black women tended to form a servant and laundress class. In three major Midwestern cities, Chicago, Cleveland, and Detroit, "black women were 4 percent of all women, yet comprised from 23 to 30 percent of servants and from 43 to 54 percent of laundresses." Similarly, historian Alice Kessler-Harris points out that "agricultural labor, domestic service, and laundry work accounted for 75 percent of all black women who worked in 1920." In some cities, she noted, "the proportion of wage-earning black women in domestic service rose to 84 percent."[23]

Hunter's early childhood and young adult encounters with hardships could have induced bitterness and a sense of resignation to a life of poverty and despair. Instead, drawing upon the values instilled in her youth, and a deep religious faith, Hunter eschewed thoughts of giving up or returning to the South. Fully cognizant of the even more restricted opportunities and the sexual dangers inherent in being an unattached and therefore vulnerable black woman in that region, Hunter realized that going home was simply out of the question.

After years of observing the underside of black life in Cleveland, Hunter took action. She mused in her autobiography, "Sometimes I feel I've just been living my life for the moment when I can start things moving toward a home for poor Negro working girls in the city." She resolved to consolidate the negligible resources of the other similarly excluded and oppressed black women with whom she interacted and labored to create an agency to assist young black females in their adjustment to urban life. On November 11, 1911 she called a meeting of a group of young black servant girls whom she had met while nursing in private white homes. She persuaded the girls to pool their resources and—with funds contributed by white women connected to the segregated YWCA—in 1912 they established the Phillis Wheatley Association, opening a boarding house a year later.[24]

At the initial planning meeting for the Phillis Wheatley Association, one young woman exclaimed, "Poor people like us can't do anything." Undaunted, Hunter rejoined, "It's only poor people like you and me who can do anything." She allayed their doubts and misgivings, declaring, "We've all of us been poor motherless children, and the Lord is going to help us build a home for all the other poor daughters of our race."[25] This agency thus became both a "home for friendless negro [sic] girls," and a "training-school for the industrious" and ambitious. As one writer put it:

> Her aim was to rescue and to assist young negro [sic] girls alone and friendless in a great city, without employment, reduced to squalor in disreputable tenements, and well-nigh helpless against mental, physical and moral degradation; and to lift the standards of negro-working women by adequate training for efficient and self-respecting service.[26]

"Moral degradation" was an oblique reference to the prostitution trap awaiting so many naive, impoverished, black country women who, like Hunter, had migrated to Northern cities in search of better lives. Of course, some had fled not only poverty, but domestic violence and sexual abuse. Historian Ruth Rosen argues that poverty directly affected women's choice to enter prostitution. She maintains that "the low wages paid to women workers, the sudden changes in family income status, and the desire for upward mobility were some of the most important economic factors influencing women's decision to practice prostitution. For black girls and women, the effects of racism and poverty made for a powerful push towards prostitution."[27]

It did not take Hunter long to observe the process whereby country girls found themselves trapped in prostitution. She observed:

> The few months on Central Avenue made me sharply aware of the great temptations that beset a young woman in a large city. At home on the plantation, I knew that some girls had been seduced. Their families had felt the disgrace keenly. The fallen ones had been wept and prayed over. In Charleston I was sent by the hospital to give emergency treatment to prostitutes, but they were white women. Until my arrival in Cleveland I was ignorant of the wholesale organized traffic in black flesh.[28]

Hunter's home, named after the eighteenth-century black poetess, Phillis Wheatley, eventually became a pivotal center around which Cleveland's working-class black women residents mobilized and directed their charitable work for girls and young women, many of whom could very well have been their own sisters and daughters. These community women raised funds and those who had no money to give rolled up their sleeves and "washed the dirty windows, scrubbed the dirty floors, and scraped off twenty layers of old paper from the walls." Through well-orchestrated annual fund-raising drives and an exhausting speaking schedule, Hunter developed and honed her public relations skills; and as the decades wore on, she secured substantial contributions from prominent whites in Cleveland, some of whom she had met while practicing private duty nursing in their homes. Undoubtedly, many whites were motivated to donate money in order to preserve the racial exclusiveness of the local Young Women's Christian Association. Other whites, especially middle-class women who frequently bemoaned the inadequacies of their hired help, supported the association out of a desire to promote the production of better trained domestic servants.[29]

Indisputably, the volunteer services and donations of working-class black community women sustained the institution, especially throughout the early years. To be sure, not all black Americans in Cleveland supported the home. Some, on ideological grounds, objected to it because, as they argued, the home represented an accommodation to, and indeed fostered, racial segregation. Hunter appeased this group of dissenters by inviting a number of the most distinguished white men and women in the city to serve on the association's board of directors. It was a wise tactical move, but one done with some ambivalence, for the result was that the management and control of the institution had to be shared with, as historian Kenneth Kusmer put it, "a group of upper-class white women who knew little about the needs and interests of recent southern migrants."[30]

By the start of the Great Depression, the Phillis Wheatley Home had amply demonstrated its value and had become a model and inspiration to other communities throughout the Middle West. An average of 150 girls were being housed yearly in the home, and many more were using its facilities. As word of Hunter's work spread she was soon elected to a prominent position within the National Association of Colored Women (NACW), and oversaw the development of Phillis Wheatley Homes across the country. By 1934 the following cities had homes patterned after Hunter's Phillis Wheatley Home: Denver, Atlanta, Seattle, Boston, Detroit, Chicago, Greenville, Winston-Salem, Toledo, and Minneapolis.[31] It was in the NACW that the lives of most of the first generation of prominent black women institution-builders intersected. As a highly visible member of the organization, Hunter became well acquainted with the work of Mary McLeod Bethune, Charlotte Hawkins Brown, and Nannie H. Burroughs.

The National Association of Colored Women represents the institutionalization of black women's voluntarism and philanthropy. Founded in 1896 by a cadre of well-educated, financially secure black women among whom were Josephine St. Pierre Ruffin (1842-1924), Mary Church Terrell (1863-1954), Fannie Barrier Williams (1855-

1944), Ida Wells-Barnett (1866-1931), Mary B. Talbert (1866-1923), Janie Porter Barrett (1865-1948), and Margaret Murray Washington (1865-1925), the NACW became a powerful advocate of self-improvement and racial uplift. The broad inclusive vision of these indomitable club women mandated an end to all racial and gender discrimination. Black feminist educator and former slave Anna Julia Cooper (1858-1964) best "crystalize[d] the sentiment" and articulated the ideology of these pioneer black voluntarists when she declared in 1893:

> The colored woman feels that woman's cause is one and universal; . . . is sacred and inviolable; [and] not till race, color, sex, and condition are seen as the accidents, and not the substance of life, not till the universal title of humanity of life, liberty, and the pursuit of happiness is conceded to be inalienable to all; not till then is woman's lesson taught and woman's cause won—not the white woman's, not the black woman's, not the red woman's, but the cause of every man and of every woman who has writhed silently under a mighty wrong. Woman's wrongs are thus indissolubly linked with all undefended woe, and the acquirement of her "rights" will mean the final triumph of all right over might, the supremacy of the moral forces of reason, and justice, and love in the government of the nations of earth.[32]

The initial orientation and objectives of the early black women's clubs focused on raising the cultural, intellectual, and educational status of black women and on creating a positive image of their sexuality. The founders of such pioneering clubs as the Woman's Era Club (Boston, 1892), the Colored Women's League (Washington, D.C., 1892), and the Woman's Loyal Union (Brooklyn, 1892) employed identical strategies and rhetoric to achieve their objectives. They asked, usually to no avail, local white employers to hire black women. They raised funds for scholarships and established kindergartens and other childcare facilities, organized clinics and demonstrations for mothers and housewives. Moreover, they sponsored musicals, literary events, and artistic exhibitions. By the early 1920s the black club women were working assiduously to encourage black women to register to vote and become politically aware.[33]

Hunter's philanthropic activities, like those of the first generation of nationally organized black club women, were well grounded in a tradition of what may appear to be contradictory impulses. On the one hand, they were fighting to reclaim the bodies and souls of thousands of black men, women, and children adrift in the Northern urban wilderness. On the other hand, they also made pragmatic accommodations to the racial segregation that jeopardized the same people in the first place. Yet Hunter, with the aid of white beneficence, proved quite adept at inverting and taking advantage of white racial attitudes and customs. She successfully developed an important social service agency, and carved out a sizeable private physical space as well, for black working girls and women without appearing to challenge the racial status quo in Cleveland. She dissembled well.

In terms of approach, values, and objectives, Hunter differed little from Booker T. Washington, "the wizard of Tuskegee," at one end of the spectrum and the ardent nationalist, Marcus Garvey of Harlem at the other end of the continuum. Hunter's leadership style suggests that whenever black women entered the public arena and engaged in the process of institution building they employed the same strategies as did black male leaders. In this context, a racist and oppressive social order, as had been the case in slavery, transformed all black efforts to survive and advance into acts of passive resistance.

Beginning in 1929, Hunter and Nannie Burroughs launched what would become, especially for Hunter, a long life-affirming friendship. Their interests, personalities, ages, backgrounds, and work converged to form a bond from which they each drew inspiration and increased determination to persevere, even when chronically strapped with unending fund-raising drives to sustain their respective enterprises. A half continent separated them. Their letters, however, spanned the decades and reflected the deepening relationship. Hunter idolized Burroughs. The mere act of writing letters (frequently unanswered) provided Hunter an important outlet through which she could share her fears, anxiety, successes, and plans for the future. In public Hunter maintained an imperturbable image of a strong, competent, fearless, resourceful black woman. Perhaps she was able to sustain this public image because she knew that in the privacy of her study or propped up in bed at night, she could write about and share her inner self with a woman whom she trusted to understand.

The Hunter-Burroughs correspondence is a rare mirror onto some of the personal costs exacted when black women devoted entire lives to social reform and to voluntary and philanthropic work to mitigate the impact of racism and sexism in their communities. After sharing a visit with Burroughs, Hunter returned to Cleveland and wrote in 1929:

> It was so nice to see you and to know your real sweet self. Surely we will continue to cultivate a lasting friendship. I want to be your devoted sister in kindred thought and love. You are so deserving and so capable. Your work is unique and remarkable; to me it fulfills a need that is not even attempted by other educators. I shall not be happy until I have made a definite contribution in a tangible way to your school.[34]

For Hunter, perhaps more so than for Burroughs, the friendship provided an emotional anchor and became an important vehicle for the release of pent-up frustration and depression. Alone during the 1937 Christmas holidays, Hunter wrote, "Somehow, I just felt that you were going to surprise me with a visit. This, more than any other Christmas I have felt so lonely. With all I have to do, yet I am positively blue for the want of a friend to open my heart to—I have so much buried within that the valves are about to burst." She ended resolutely, "I suppose this is the price we pay for leadership. Somehow, those who dream alike must dwell so far apart in the physical world." A few months later in March of 1938, a happier Hunter wrote, "You don't know how much you mean to me. I am certainly fortunate to have you for my friend." Each woman annually gave private contributions to, and willingly lectured on behalf of, the other's institution. Following a visit in 1946, Hunter confessed to Burroughs, "I've been re-inspired and lifted high as a result of my only too brief visit with you. If I had a million dollars I would want to give it to you. Old girl the job you are doing is masterful and unique." In the same letter Hunter mused, "Just think of the girls you have saved from miserable wretched lives to become useful fine citizens. I love you for the high and noble example you have given to all of us. I sincerely hope to always number you as my first and genuine friend."[35]

Hunter and Burroughs not only respected and cared for each other but also they were concerned about their sister-founders of schools for black women, Mary McLeod Bethune and Charlotte Hawkins Brown. This respect was born of the understanding of the degree to which they frequently sacrificed themselves, putting the needs of black girls and women before their own. In December of 1942, in a moment of exhaustion, Hunter confided to her friend, "Somehow I wish that you, Mary Bethune and myself could give up raising money and could devote all of our strengths and spiritual life to the building of God's kingdom. This money getting business destroys so much of one's real self, that we cannot do our best, feeling that we need money all of the time." Fortunately Hunter's exhaustion and depression seldom lasted, but the incessant demands on her time and pocketbook continued. She rhetorically queried Burroughs, "I wonder if people call on you as often as they call on me. Last year [1944] by receipts for income tax— I gave away over $800." She hastened to add that she was "Thankful that I had it to give," and concluded, "I will not forget the great work you are doing there for our girls. I speak of you every time I talk in public."[36]

At the thirty-fifth anniversary of the Phillis Wheatley Association, Hunter presided over a triumphant celebration. She informed Burroughs that "when it was all over I was just about ready to give up the ghost. Was so tired and exhausted." She thanked her friend for her "fine cooperation and generous gift," and reported, "The party was a great success. Two hundred thirty odd persons in attendance and to date $13,546.93 in cash.[37]

By the 1950s, Burroughs, Hunter, and Bethune were winding down their public careers. Soon sickness and death would deplete their ranks. Bethune was the first to succumb. Suffering from bronchial pneumonia, Hunter wrote Burroughs, in the wake of Bethune's death, "Somehow I really loved Mary McLeod Bethune but my deepest admiration has always been centered on Nannie H. Burroughs. You have always impressed me as a true leader with understanding of the human problems of life."[38] Earlier, in fact, the indomitable Burroughs had chided her friend to forego such despair:

> I hope you will not allow yourself to feel as your letter seems to indicate. I urge you to be of good cheer and deepest gratitude

to God because He has permitted you to accomplish miracles in the field of Social Science and Human Welfare. . . .You have built a colossal monument that will stand as long as America stands. I know that you are not well but I urge you to be of good cheer. You are no old race horse and cut out that pity stuff—if you do not I shall put you down as an ingrate—what more can God do for you or for any of us for that matter.[39]

The reassuring words must have been what she needed to hear, for a few months later, in August 1955, the now retired but still active Hunter announced a final victory, "We reached the goal of $50,000 and sent two girls to college this fall." On her seventy-fourth birthday she reflected on the meaning of their lives, "Of course, you will realize that both you and me have worked too hard and entirely too long. The wonder of it all; we have made a contribution to America that no one else would for the type of young women we've tried to serve."[40]

It is noteworthy that although these women engaged in essentially the same kind of mission—creating institutions to save young black girls—a spirit of mutual cooperation and support pervades these letters. Surely there exists similar correspondence between black male institution builders during this period.

At the time of her death, at the age of seventy-seven, the woman who had come to Cleveland with $1.75 in her pockets, and who entitled her 1940 autobiography *A Nickel and a Prayer*, left an estate of $409,711.72. In attempting to explain Hunter's holdings, certainly a substantial sum for any person to have accumulated at that time, her attorney declared, "Miss Hunter was a stickler for savings. She held onto every penny and did some shrewd investing. Her salary was only $3,000 for many years (like all other Welfare Federation Workers). But she received excellent free advice on investing from a bank official at Cleveland Trust Co."[41]

Future research may well uncover the specific details of how Hunter accumulated this remarkable sum. This is no simple "rags to riches" story, nor is Hunter a Horatio Alger in blackface and petticoat. The social construction of racism and gender roles in America lends to Hunter's life a more troubling complexity. Although I have not examined the estate records of Nannie H. Burroughs, Charlotte

Hawkins Brown, or of Mary McLeod Bethune, it is reasonable to speculate that none of them died poverty-stricken. However, it is not their relative wealth or capital accumulation that needs explanation. After all, they were daughters of former slaves, they each possessed strong religious convictions, and each had reached maturity in a climate in which the conservative economic ideologies of Booker T. Washington held sway, especially among the ambitious and educated black elite. Moreover, their own desires to save money was undoubtedly fired by living through the Great Depression.

More germane to our concerns are the reasons why they were so wedded to the work of helping poor black girls and women. These women made it a first priority in their lives to challenge the larger society's negative views and stereotypes of black women. At a time when black men were deprived of a meaningful public voice and presence, and few of them could find adequate permanent employment owing to structural inequalities and white violence, the sexual exploitation and economic oppression of black women continued. In an 1895 speech delivered before the first national conference of African American women, Josephine St. Pierre Ruffin declared, "if an estimate of the colored women of America is called for, the inevitable reply glibly given is, 'For the most part ignorant and immoral,' some exceptions of course, but these don't count."[42]

Negative images, racial stereotypes, and biased perceptions serve specific functions in a capitalistic patriarchal society. There existed a direct correlation between the low status African Americans occupied in American society and the derogatory images held of them in the white mind. Pejorative images not only highlight real or imagined differences between ethnic groups, races, and sexes, they also serve as critical indices of social worth, political significance, and economic power. The first post-slavery generation of black women activists and club organizers well understood the power of images to determine the treatment of black girls and women by the larger society.

Fannie Barrier Williams of Chicago commented on the apparent obsession some black women exhibited over the allegations of moral laxity. In an 1893 speech, she proclaimed that "because the morality of our home life has been commented upon so disparagingly and meanly . . . we are placed in the unfortunate position of being defenders of our name."[43] One of the most objectionable stereotypes was the label of prostitute. As Williams and Ruffin intimated, accusations of immorality and the labeling of all black women as prostitutes impeded the development of positive identities and both reflected and perpetuated racist and sexist social conditions. Such accusations and labels, of course, obscured and diverted attention from the economic discrimination and lack of good jobs that made some women's lives so wretched that they were forced into prostitution in order to survive. Furthermore, negative images and stereotypes camouflaged the repeated sexual abuse of black women in all regions of the country. As a consequence, rape of black women, when reported, was seldom investigated by police officials, who found it more convenient to attribute blame for such attacks to the victim's "inherent wantonness." Moreover, as historian Ruth Rosen has demonstrated, correctional facilities across the country reported an overrepresentation of black women, proving that they were more often arrested for alleged prostitution than were white women.[44]

As long as the larger society viewed black women as whores and prostitutes, they remained vulnerable and powerless. Derogatory images hampered even the work of elite black women who struggled to improve the overall status of black Americans. In the minds of elite black women, true racial advancement depended upon the extent to which black women themselves could demolish and erase these negative images. Williams' remarks are illustrative of the deep determination of black women to reclaim themselves and to defend their reputations. She declared, "This moral regeneration of a whole race of women is no idle sentiment—it is a serious business; and everywhere there is witnessed a feverish anxiety to be free from the mean suspicions that have so long underestimated the character strength of our women."[45]

Thus Hunter, Burroughs, Bethune, and Brown—as major representatives of a generation of postslavery black women philanthropists, charitable organizers, and institution builders—carried onward the mission of self-reclamation. These descendants of slaves were active agents for social change throughout the first half of the twentieth century. In their speeches, writings, and fund-raising drives, these leaders rallied thousands of community women and engaged them in the battle to reclaim and save their defenseless and impoverished black sisters. It matters not a little that several of these schools and homes prepared black girls and young women for skilled service in the domestic sector. Hunter was quite correct when she observed as late as 1957 that no one else would or had paid much, if indeed any, attention to the needs of the thousands of "young women we've tried to serve." Burroughs echoed these sentiments but with a slightly different focus. "We make our girls believe in themselves and in their power to do anything that anybody can do, be it ever so difficult. . . . 'We specialize in the wholly impossible.' "[46]

The philanthropic work of black women contains a palpable undertone of muted defiance of the racial and gender inequalities pervading virtually every aspect of American society. Reflecting a sense of entitlement but couched in the rhetoric of religious piousness their efforts to do good deeds on behalf of black people, to save black women from lives of poverty and induced prostitution, appear on the surface to amount to a conservative embrace of American moral values and of the status quo. Yet each black girl and boy saved from the streets, educated to be a productive and self-respecting citizen, restored to good health, and trained for a skilled job, represented a resounding blow to the edifice of Jim Crow, patriarchy, and white privilege. Those so reclaimed were able to return to the black community and become additional agents in the struggle for social change and liberation.

The Housewives' League
of Detroit
Black Women and Economic Nationalism

The Great Depression of the 1930s was one of the most catastrophic periods in American history. All Americans suffered massive economic dislocation, but none more than African Americans. For those who had always occupied a subordinate position in the American economy, the tenuous economic gains of the World War I era rapidly evaporated. Indeed the deterioration of economic opportunity for black Americans had commenced shortly after the cessation of hostilities and the return of white servicemen from European fronts. Employers lost little time firing black workers and replacing them with white veterans. As their economic status plummeted, black Americans in cities across the Middle West and Northeast encountered increased incidences of violence, blatant job discrimination, and housing segregation. The thousands of black men and women who had quit the Jim Crow, lynching, and rape-infested South for northern urban areas in search of a better future, jobs, and housing found themselves (as early as the mid-twenties) embroiled in a fierce and sometimes deadly struggle for survival.

Some scholars have argued that the Depression affected black Americans less severely than it did their white counterparts simply because for black Americans economic conditions had deteriorated long before 1929. Such arguments, however, fail to take into consideration the experience of postwar gains and the hopes and heightened expectations of improvement that had motivated thousands of black migrants in the first place. In short, few of the southern migrants were strangers to poverty, political powerlessness, segregation, or discrimination, but the promises of access to relatively well-paying jobs in northern industries and the (albeit limited but real) success some had achieved during World War I made the depression conditions even more unbearable.

It was during these dire times that black women in Detroit founded an ingenious united action organization based upon principles of economic nationalism. Established in 1930, the Housewives' League of Detroit had as one of its mottos "Stabilize the economic status of the Negro through directed spending." For the next thirty years, members of the league adhered to five basic tenets, all intended to retain material resources within their own communities. They pledged to patronize all organized Negro businesses; to patronize "stores that employ Negroes in varied capacities and that do not discriminate in types of work offered"; to support and encourage institutions training Negro youth for trades and commercial activities; to teach "Negro youth that no work done well is menial"; and finally to conduct "education campaigns to teach the Negro the value of his spending."[1]

The Housewives' League of Detroit is best understood as part of a cluster of nationwide grass-roots movements that cut across racial and gender lines to help workers, black Americans, and women survive the massive economic dislocation brought on by the Great Depression. Throughout this era, black Americans in key urban centers including Chicago, Baltimore, Washington, D.C., Detroit, and Harlem launched a series of "Don't buy from where you can't work" boycotts and picketing movements against white-owned businesses.

Throughout the 1920s, in a similar vein, white workers and unions in various parts of the country organized consumer movements that articulated an independent, working-class political perspective on consumption. These consumer cooperatives and boycotts united workers across lines of gender, skill, and trade, and they helped bridge the gap between paid and unpaid labor. Union leaders across the North, but especially in Seattle, Washington, put considerable pressure on housewives to "shop union" labels. Many women needed little encouragement to consume in accordance with their families' best interests.[2]

In many communities women's auxiliaries to male-dominated unions initiated and sustained consumer protests. Those groups embraced immigrant and native-born white women as well as black women, though in separate campaigns. In assessing women's involvement in public activism, the historian Nancy Cott suggests three dimensions of consciousness: feminism, female consciousness, and communal consciousness. It is her third form of consciousness that best describes black and white women's involvement in consumer activism and "directed spending" campaigns during the 1920s and 1930s. According to Cott, "Women's communal consciousness ought to be explicitly recognized for its role in women's self-assertions, even while those self-assertions are on behalf of the community that women inhabit with their men and children." For black women in the Housewives' League, such communal consciousness was reinforced by "womanist" consciousness. The historian Elsa Barkley Brown states the point well: many black women at various points in history had a clear understanding that race issues and women's issues were inextricably linked in struggles for equality.[3] To be a womanist required holding together many constituencies and multiple purposes all at once. Those in the Housewives' League seem to have developed a communal womanist consciousness that enabled them to fight one struggle on many different fronts, using strategies according to their effectiveness in a given space and time.

The economic program, the communal womanist consciousness, and the organizing activities of the Housewives' League of Detroit were logical outgrowths of the national black women's club movement that flourished throughout the opening decades of the twentieth century. That movement, along with its white counterpart, has received considerable attention in recent years.[4] In July, 1895, Josephine St. Pierre Ruffin of Boston presided over the first National Conference of Colored Women in America. Out of this meeting emerged the National Association of Colored Women's Clubs (NACW) in 1896. Its constitution conveyed the purpose of the organization: "We, the Colored Women of America, feeling the need of united and systematic effort, and hoping to furnish evidence of moral, mental, and material progress made by the people of color through the efforts of our women, do hereby unite in a national association of colored women." As the historian Anne Firor Scott has demonstrated, the heretofore invisible but significant work of black club women contributed to the survival of regional black communities in myriad ways. The schools, hospitals, clinics, orphanages, homes for the elderly, employment agencies, day-care centers, libraries, playgrounds, and settlement houses they founded addressed the needs of diverse black constituencies.[5]

Ida Wells-Barnett of Chicago, Jane Edna Hunter of Cleveland, Sallie Wyatt Stewart of Evansville, Indiana, and Rosa L. Slade Gragg of Detroit are but four examples of midwestern black women who established settlement or community houses and opened training schools during the Progressive Era. For instance, the Young Women's Christian Association (YWCA) practiced widespread discrimination in this period. Typically, single black women could not secure living accommodations and did not have access to the social facilities and employment bureaus in existing YWCAs. Throughout the twenties black women in communities above and below the Mason-Dixon line mobilized support for the establishment of black branches of the YWCA.

These institution-building activities mirrored the same spirit of voluntarism seen among white women in American society during the Progressive Era. Entrenched racism in the society as a whole and among white women in particular, however, gave black women additional incentives to create both parallel and distinctively new social welfare structures. No social history of twentieth-century America is complete without analysis of the role these women played in erecting an infrastructure of social welfare agencies, community institutions such as penny saving banks and credit unions, protest organizations, and cultural programs. Although largely ignored in earlier histories of black civil rights organizations, the work of the club women, along with that of the National Association for the Advancement of Colored People (NAACP) and the National Urban League, helped ease the transition and accelerated the adaptation of rural black migrants to their urban environments.[6]

The black women's clubs were important in at least two major regards. First, they provided a vehicle that black women used to put into actual practice the ideologies of self-help and racial solidarity advocated by national leaders such as Booker T. Washington of Tuskegee Institute; Marcus Garvey, founder of the Universal Negro

Improvement Association; and W.E.B. Du Bois, editor of the NAACP's *Crisis* magazine. Second, the clubs provided the chief vehicle for implementing black women's determination to serve and uplift their race. Simultaneously, the clubs provided black women the space and means whereby they could nurture positive images of themselves as women and thereby challenge the prevalent negative stereotypes of their virtue.[7]

In 1900 attorney D. Augustus Straker, the political leader of black Detroit, addressed the first convention of the Michigan State Association of Colored Women's Clubs organized by Lucy Smith Thurman. Voicing approval of the political implications of black women's organizing, Straker challenged the group to "Agitate! Agitate! Agitate!" He declared, "I hope before you close your labors you will establish a committee in every city of the State to get employment for our young women and thus protect them against the evil results of idle hands."[8] Straker's emphasis on the need for protection against the evil of idle hands was a thinly veiled reference to the prevailing negative stereotypes of black women's morality. Straker advised the women, "What you need to do is to create American sentiment for equal opportunity for [black] women in the development of true womanhood." He exhorted them to "open the stores and the factories, and the millineries, and the school houses, and the counting houses for our young women, as well as the kitchen, the washtub, the nursery and the scrub room.[9] Of course, Straker's remarks simply echoed what Michigan's black women knew had to be done.

Although several exemplary studies have outlined the larger history of the club women's movement, one theme in need of further exploration is the intersection between the work of black urban club women and the development of what I call strategies for "economic housekeeping." Throughout the Great Depression and World War II the Housewives' League of Detroit and the leagues that sprouted in other cities directed the spending of black families into businesses owned and operated by black men and women. The Housewives' League of Detroit was the sister organization to the Booker T. Washington Trade Association, an affiliate of the National Negro Business League. So successful was the Detroit League that in 1933 it became the model for the newly formed National Housewives' League of

America. The organization flourished in the thirties and forties but finally folded in the late sixties.

Two decades after the founding of the Michigan State Association of Colored Women's Clubs, a strong club women's movement flourished in Detroit. Although black women's clubs with various social and cultural purposes had existed in the city since the antebellum period, the influx of large numbers of migrants and the expansion of Detroit's black middle class stimulated greater club formation and collaboration. By 1920 black women leaders in the city deemed it wise to gather all of the disparate clubs under the umbrella of one large organization, the Detroit Association of Colored Women's Clubs. Under the strong leadership of president Rosa Gragg, the Detroit Association peaked in 1945 with a membership of seventy-three clubs and approximately three thousand individual members. In recognition of her indomitable spirit, untiring effort, and commitment to club work on the local level, Gragg was elected president of the National Association of Colored Women's Clubs in 1958.[10]

A brief survey of the severe employment discrimination black women endured in seeking work other than in domestic service underscores the economic and political significance of the clubs they created. The majority of black women, regardless of regional location, worked in domestic service throughout the opening decades of the twentieth century. Census studies for 1920 reveal that from one-third to one-half of all black women worked in domestic service jobs. In the South, where the number employed was greater than in any other region, their backbreaking work brought low pay and low status. Given the often marginal and seasonal employment of so many southern black men along with the ravages of the Great Depression, black women's meager earnings often proved critical to the survival of their families. Many white women worked to attain middle-class status and then "retired" once they achieved it, but black women tended to remain in the labor force even after marrying or starting a family.[11] Like their male counterparts, many black women had quit the South during World War I with hopes that in cities such as Detroit, Chicago, Milwaukee, and Cleveland they would find jobs in the factories and shops that were providing new employment opportunities for increasing numbers of white women.[12] The reminiscences of author Mary

Helen Washington provide poignant testimony to the dashed hopes of many female migrants:

> In the 1920s my mother and my five aunts migrated to Cleveland, Ohio, from Indianapolis and, in spite of their many talents, they found every door except the kitchen door closed to them. My youngest aunt was trained as a bookkeeper and was so good at her work that her white employer at Guardian Savings of Indianapolis allowed her to work at the branch in a black area. The Cleveland Trust Company was not so liberal, however, so in Cleveland she went to work in what is known in the black community as "private family."[13]

Employment discrimination and racial exclusion of black women from certain occupations was widespread, but in particular in Detroit black women encountered virtually insurmountable barriers to employment in the automobile industries. The Ford Motor Company remained one of the nation's largest employers of black men, even during the depression, yet it was adamant in its refusal to hire black women. The incipient defense orders in 1940 suggested that the tide might turn, but, as the historians August Meier and Elliott Rudwick point out, "when turning to female labor to staff the assembly lines at their new Willow Run bomber plant, they [Ford managers] fought hard to keep the work force there lily-white." Ford's policy towards black women was not an aberration. Other corporations in the Detroit defense industries also refused to hire black women. According to Meier and Rudwick, "Black civic leaders and trade unionists fought a sustained and energetic battle to open Detroit war production to black women, but because government manpower officials gave discrimination against Negro females low priority, the gains were negligible when compared with those achieved by the city's black male workers." Actually, by the end of World War II, black men and women comprised a mere 3.5 percent, or 735, of the work force at Willow Run.[14] In other words, neither group fared particularly well.

One of the major challenges to black women during the economic crises of the 1930s and World War II was finding adequate and respectable jobs for themselves and for their sons and daughters. The destructiveness of underemployment, forced firings, and sexual stratification in the labor force spurred many black women to embrace the idea that economic progress was impossible without concomitant change in their political consciousness. The powerful combination of racial discrimination and the sexual stratification of labor imprisoned them at the bottom of the economic ladder. All traditional patterns of protest and the objections of black rights organizations seemed powerless to alter their exclusion or continued exploitation. The convergence of racial, sexual, and class oppression made it difficult indeed for black women to advance through traditional economic channels. The very complexity of their oppression dictated the need to develop a new political consciousness. Black women in the 1930s and 1940s, like their nineteenth-century forebears, had to depend on their own resources in the ongoing fight for equality of opportunity and social change.

The greatest weapon Detroit black club women had at their disposal during the height of the Great Depression was the leadership and organizing skill they had cultivated during decades of involvement in club work. If there was *one* thing these women knew well, it was how to mobilize their members, how to develop persuasive arguments, how to conceptualize issues, and how to fight for their families and communities. Although it may be tempting to view black women as powerless to combat overwhelming and seemingly intractable racial and sexual discrimination, they were somewhat better prepared to do battle than one might expect. Well grounded in a tradition of social welfare and club work, Detroit's communally conscious black women appreciated the necessity for collective action. When called upon, they were even prepared to blur class lines and transcend color stratification in order to overcome economic and educational barriers to black advancement.

The Detroit Study Club was but one of many organizations that reflected the transition from a strictly cultural orientation to one focused on racial uplift work. This club had been organized on March 2, 1898, as the Browning Study Club. Within a decade the club had shifted from "just a self culture club and branched out into the broader field of Philanthropy and civil social work," according to one of its earliest members, Lillian E. Johnson. "The club was established as a purely literary club; however, the members soon realized the need of sharing in the social welfare work in the city, so a 'department of philanthropy' was established sometime during the first ten years." She elaborated, "the Club contributes liberally to the many charities, civic organizations and education movements in the city, and cooperates with the National, State and City Association of Colored Women."[15]

As black women in Detroit experimented with new strategies to serve their people and to enhance their status as women, they seized upon the idea of harnessing and targeting their economic power, perhaps influenced by the ideas advanced by consumer activism movements and by such black leaders as W.E.B. Du Bois. As the woes of the depression deepened, Du Bois urged that the NAACP adopt a program of "systematic 'voluntary segregation' in the form of a separate black cooperative economy."[16] He advocated that black Americans pool their resources and develop businesses and engage in other self-help endeavors while continuing their pressure for full integration and equality within the larger society. In response to growing national black unemployment and welfare dependency, the NAACP *Crisis* editor advised that the "2,800,000 families in the United States must systematically organize their $106,000,000 a month, consumer purchases," so that black Americans could become an economic power capable of demanding and protecting their own interests.[17] To a great extent throughout the 1930s, Du Bois echoed the ideas that had been espoused in the early 1920s by Marcus Garvey, perhaps the most renowned black nationalist of the twentieth century.[18] Black women in Detroit, however, put an altogether different spin on these ideas.

On June 10, 1930, a group of fifty black women responded to a call issued by Fannie B. Peck, wife of Reverend William H. Peck (1878-1944) who was pastor of the two-thousand-member Bethel A.M.E. Church and president and founder of the local branch of the Booker T. Washington Trade Association. Fannie B. Peck was born August 15, 1879, in Huntsville, Missouri, to Thomas and Leanna Campbell. She married William H. Peck in 1899, and the couple moved to Detroit in June 1928. Out of the initial meeting called by Fannie Peck and held in the gymnasium of Bethel Church emerged the Detroit Housewives' League. Fannie Peck had conceived the idea of creating an organization of housewives following a lecture by Albon L. Holsey, Secretary of the National Negro Business League.

Holsey had described the successful efforts of black housewives in Harlem, who consolidated and concentrated their considerable economic power in support of Colored Merchants Association stores. Peck, like many ministers' wives, exercised considerable influence within her community, and she was convinced that if an organization "to support Negroes in business and professions" worked in New York it was worth replicating in Detroit. According to one handwritten account of the first meeting, Peck "explained to those present the purpose and need of such an organization. She stated that it would be a pioneering organization in its field as there [was] not in existence a pattern by which to plan and govern its activities. Therefore members would learn by doing."[19] The first group of elected officers included Peck as president, Ethel L. Hemsley as first vice president, Mamie C. Boone as second vice president, Wilma Walker as recording secretary, Christina Fuqua as assistant secretary, and Hattie Toodle as treasurer. In 1933 the Detroit Housewives' League would send two delegates to a major meeting convened in Durham, North Carolina, to form the National Housewives' League.

The leaders of individual leagues sought to empower black women across the economic spectrum. Peck lectured to large numbers of black women in Detroit declaring they were not without real economic power. In her opinion, their power simply had to be exercised with coordination.[20] At one point Peck recounted some of the early thinking that underlay the founding of the Housewives' League. "It has been in the minds of our women that they, their husbands and children were the victims of a vicious economic system," she wrote. "They were denied employment in many places where they spent their money, and that even when employed no opportunities for advancement was given." As her successor extolled, "Peck had focused the attention of women on the most essential, yet most unfamiliar factor in the building of homes, communities, and nations, namely—The Spending Power of Women."[21]

Detroit's Housewives' League grew with phenomenal speed. From the fifty members who attended the first meeting, its membership increased to ten thousand by 1935, embracing all segments of the black community. In explaining the "marvelous growth," Peck maintained that it was due to the realization on the part of "the Negro woman" of the fact "that she has been travelling through a blind alley, making sacrifices to educate her children with no thought as to their obtaining employment after leaving school." Mary L. Beasley subsequently organized the first junior unit of the league as a "definite step in helping youth develop a greater appreciation for business owned and controlled by Negroes." Laura Dounveor as chair of the league's Dramatic Committee, inspired members "to write plays, and skits depicting the struggles and progress of business and professional people."[22]

Essentially, the Housewives' League combined communal womanist consciousness and economic nationalism to help black families and black businesses survive the depression. In Detroit at the outset of the depression, black Americans operated 51 of the 147 grocery stores, 18 of the 31 drug stores, and 5 of the 27 haberdasheries in their neighborhoods. By 1932, however, over 48,000 black families in Detroit depended on the city's welfare system. The league helped in ways the city could not.[23]

The only requirement for league membership was a pledge to support black businesses, buy black products, patronize black professionals and keep one's money in the community. As one leader of the Housewives' League argued, black women were the group positioned most strategically to preserve and expand the black internal economy. The members heard frequent exhortations along the lines that, "it is our duty as women controlling 85 percent of the family budget to unlock through concentrated spending closed doors that Negro youth may have the opportunity to develop and establish businesses in the fields closest to them." The league officers promised members that in exchange for their support and work they would instruct and inform them on "prices of merchandise, family budget, food values, and all things pertaining to the management of the home."[24]

Actually, members of the Housewives' League sometimes received material rewards for their work as well as advice on home management. When Lincoln Gordon, a manufacturer of Quality Cleanser, contacted the Housewives' League in 1939, he made it clear that he was willing to share profits: "I shall be very pleased to have this body of business makers select or recommend to me one or more of your group to sell Quality Cleanser. I formally state and announce openly as the business increases, each person will be paid as his or her ability merits." Gordon promised to return to the "agent" one-fifth, or five cents, out of every twenty-five cents earned in the selling of the cleanser. Gordon pledged, "I shall function for the mutual benefit of business for the race and trust that the reciprocity of the race will be the same as far as it is possible to influence the activity of your exemplary body."[25]

League members took great pains defining their objectives and assuring potential critics and competitors that they intended to restrict their activity to matters relating to the home, family, and community. "We see the great need of our social education, religious and economic improvement, and we have selected the economical as our field of endeavor. The great loss of employment upon the part of our people has reduced us to the place where we have not the sustenance for our bodies, clothes to wear, homes to live in, books to read, and none of the many things which are not any longer luxuries, but are prime necessities to the home life of modern standards." The Housewives' League adopted the slogan, "Find a job, or Make one and make your dollar do Triple duty." A dollar doing triple duty would "get *you* what *you* need. Give the Race what it needs—*Employment*, and Bring what all investments should bring—*Dividends*."[26]

The Housewives' League's constitution contained several artfully crafted declarations of independence that emphasized how it differed from traditional advancement agencies and existing institutions in the black community. League members' promises to confine their work to carefully defined "female spheres" reflected an awareness of the broad-ranging needs of the race. These somewhat muted statements also hint at a deeper understanding of the politics of gender roles in the black community. Women seldom occupied visible leadership roles in the churches, nor did any hold or run for elective office in this period. The world of public politics and religious leadership belonged to the men of the community. The one exception in Detroit was Rosa Gragg. In 1941 President Franklin D. Roosevelt appointed her to the volunteers' participation committee in the Office of Civil Defense. In 1948 Mayor Eugene I. Van Antwerp appointed her president of the Detroit Welfare Commission with 1,947 employees and an operating budget of $20 million. Still, Gragg adhered to convention in that she did not hold or seek an elective political position.[27]

In Section 7 of the Housewives' League's constitution the women inserted yet another qualification: "We recognize the place of the church and allied organizations among us for the advancement of our group. We are in full sympathy with their purposes, but are not a religious organization and shall not permit any discrimination for or against to in any way enter our thought or determine our action on any question of policy in our organization." Moreover, in Section 8 they declared, "We are mindful of achieving political solidarity among us, increasing our opportunity of representation in bodies that control the activities in our city, state, and nation—but we are not a political organization."[28] By disclaiming religious and political involvement, the women disarmed potential male critics who may have felt their authority threatened.

Essentially, the women cleverly let it be known that they were not in competition with other organized black advancement groups. This did not, however, prevent Gertrude J. West, secretary of the Housewives' League, from appropriating the rhetoric of black male leaders like Booker T. Washington. She proclaimed, "This is a challenge to Negro women, who control largely the finance that comes into the home. It offers an opportunity to make Christianity a reality by letting down your bucket where you are, knowing that you must first set your house in order before going out to help your neighbor."[29]

The Housewives' League's attempt to eliminate a sense of competition with other black organizations and institutions was apparently effective, for, I was unable to locate evidence that proved male hostility to the goals and strategies employed by the women. The statements that disarmed and avoided antagonizing male leaders in politics and the churches are, perhaps, one facet of successful communal womanism. League leaders effectively practiced a politics of reassuring that they had taken to heart the entire community's interests, a reassurance that was reflected in the league's structure as well as in its statements.

Each neighborhood had its own Housewives' League unit. The different units all belonged to the Central Committee. This organizational structure permitted maximum participation on neighborhood levels. The neighborhood officers attended meetings of the executive board, usually held on the second Tuesday of each month. Any woman who pledged to "help build bigger and better Negro businesses and to create and increase opportunities for employment" was welcomed to membership in her neighborhood unit. One card declared, "A belief in the future of Negro business and a desire to assist in every way by patronizing and encouraging the same is all that is necessary to become a member."[30] The organization took pains to make sure that all interested women had the opportunity to join and participate in the league's work.

Becoming a member was the easy part; keeping up with league activities required considerable effort and commitment. Members of each unit canvassed their neighborhood merchants demanding that they sell black products and employ black children as clerks or stockboys. Unit leaders also organized campaigns to persuade their neighbors to patronize specific black-owned businesses or white businesses that employed black Americans. In 1946 the Housewives' League launched a bulletin and solicited paid advertisements from local businesses. They charged twelve dollars for half-pages and twenty dollars for whole pages. In 1950 the bulletin was enlarged to include "a new feature . . . which will better call to the attention of the reader, the kind of businesses owned by you." Potential advertisers were urged to "take the buying public to your business through pictures."[31] Throughout the city league officers organized lectures, planned exhibits at the annual state fair, discussed picketing and boycott strategies, and disseminated information concerning the economic self-help struggles of black Americans across the country. Accurate, timely communication was imperative for the smooth operation of the league. The head of the Research Committee gathered data and made recommendations about the types of businesses needed in various communities and neighborhoods and then she reported on the results of "directed spending" tactics.[32]

By 1946 the members of the Housewives' League of Detroit no longer had to maintain the fiction of being apolitical. In the post-World War II years, both male and female leaders boldly informed their people that it was wise to employ the ballot in the war for racial advancement. One letter by a league officer observed that, "it has become necessary for other racial groups to become more and more concerned about entering politics as candidates for public office, and as organized groups, to see that the masses are educated to their responsibility as voters."[33] The heightened political consciousness of black Americans undoubtedly reflected their frustration with the federal government's hypocritical denunciation of German nazism and Italian fascism while maintaining rigid adherence to stateside segregation policies.

As late as 1963 the Housewives' League was still going strong. In a letter to the Detroit mayor, Jerome P. Cavanagh, league president Naomi Jefferies declared "we recognize the economic power which the housewife possesses, and we believe that through these constructive efforts, we hold the key to the doors of opportunity that will make it possible to 'Stabilize our economic status and be instrumental in placing us in a position where, by virtue of efficiency the Negro Race will be within and not without this great American Business World.' "[34] By the late 1960s the Housewives' League would run its course. The success of the civil rights movement, expanding employment opportunities made possible through affirmative action legislation, and the failure to find women to take the places of the aging founding leadership perhaps contributed to the league's demise.

While the Housewives' League was a force for black nationalism, the leaders also deserve recognition for their early appeals to women's solidarity. The leaders concluded that "certainly the Negro woman whose home must suffer most, ought become concerned and join hands with other women who realize what happens in party politics affects homes as directly as what happens in her block. . . . Housing, economic equality, education opportunity for children and security are all affected by government." Black women's activism and womanism remained securely attached to concern for home, family, and community uplift, although in one revealing speech Peck urged black women to participate in the Housewives' League's programs in order to win the respect of white women, asserting that "if we are to be respected by other women, if we are to walk side by side with them, we cannot continue to spend thoughtlessly and buy the things we want and beg for the things we need."[35] By the dawn of the modern civil rights movement, then, black women in Detroit consciously perceived their advancement along both sexual and racial lines as being inextricably connected to and grounded in the tripartite base of home, family, and community.

It is impossible to calculate the full impact of the Housewives' League of Detroit on the city's economic life. The historian Jacqueline Jones does, however, venture an assessment of the overall impact of the leagues:

> The struggles in Chicago, Baltimore, Washington, Detroit, Harlem, and Cleveland relied on boycotts sponsored by neighborhood 'Housewives' Leagues,' whose members took their grocery and clothes shopping elsewhere, or did without, rather than patronize all-white stores. These campaigns captured an estimated 75,000 new jobs for blacks during the depression decade, and together they had an economic impact comparable to that of the CIO in its organizing efforts, and second only to government jobs as a new source of openings. In the process women's energies at the grassroots level were harnessed and given explicit political expression.[36]

Certainly the Housewives' League of Detroit made a significant difference in the political consciousness of the women who attended the meetings. They could scarcely avoid becoming more confident and aggressive in their confrontations with neighborhood businessmen and more insistent in demands for jobs and opportunities for their children. In assessing the performance of the Housewives' League, one member wrote, "The League feels that its greatest accomplishments have been the vision of self-help it has given the Negro woman; the confidence it has inspired in Negro business and professional men and women, the courage it has imparted to our young people to continue their education."[37]

This brief sketch of the Housewives' League of Detroit raises many questions about power and the intersection of race, gender, and ideology in the black community. Black women extended into the public arena their collective concerns for social reform and the problems confronted by poor, uneducated, infirm, aged, and unemployed black people. Most studies ignore the importance that women, particularly black women, place on economic self-determination. Clearly, scholarly investigation of the history of black women workers in

America is sorely needed. Moreover, our understanding of the participation of black women in labor unions remains incomplete. Other questions come to mind. Were there costs to economic nationalism? Were working poor black women torn between buying black and buying cheaper from white-owned businesses with higher inventories and volume—a conflict that would have been less severe for the better-off league members? The connection between the club women's movement and the fashioning of economic and political strategies based on the subordinate position that black women occupied by virtue of their race and sex promises to increase our understanding of the dynamic processes of black institutional development throughout the nation. Although they were excluded, discriminated against, and received little respect from the larger society, these women never gave up the struggle. The story of the Housewives' League of Detroit teaches us that even those at the bottom of the social, political, and economic ladder often have resources with which to effect change.

PART 3

Co-Laborers in the Work of the Lord

Nineteenth-Century Black Women Physicians

The Afro-American woman physician of the late nineteenth and early twentieth centuries remains an enigma. Today only scattered bits and pieces of evidence—an occasional biographical sketch, a random name in an old medical school catalogue—attest to the existence of this first generation of black women doctors. In spite of this negligible evidence, we know that in the quarter century after the demise of slavery and during the height of racial segregation and discrimination, 115 black women had become physicians in the United States.[1]

An examination of their lives and experiences will illuminate the conditions in and the transformations of the American medical profession in the last half of the nineteenth and the first quarter of the twentieth century. If white women, black men, and poor whites, as many scholars argue, were outsiders in medicine, then black women, belonging as they did to two subordinate groups, surely inhabited the most distant perimeters of the profession.[2] Yet it is precisely because of this dual—sexual and racial—marginality that any examination of their lives and careers bears the possibility of shedding new light on many conventional interpretations in American medical history.

To be sure, the history of black women physicians is one worthy of study in its own right. From an analysis of factors ranging from family background, to medical education, to medical practice, to social status, to marriage, to Victorian sex-role definitions, a portrait of one of the earliest and most significant groups of black professional women emerges. Insights gleaned from looking at the early black women doctors will further the re-construction of a more inclusive and, perhaps, more accurate picture of the opportunities and restrictions that all women and black male physicians encountered in pursuit of medical careers.

In 1864, one year before the Civil War ended and fifteen years after Elizabeth Blackwell became the first American woman medical school graduate, the first black woman graduate, Rebecca Lee, received an M.D. degree from the New England Female Medical College in Boston. Three years later, one year before the ratification of the Fourteenth Amendment to the United States Constitution, the second black American woman physician, Rebecca J. Cole (1846-1922), was graduated from the Woman's Medical College of Pennsylvania. They were followed by Susan Smith McKinney Steward (1847-1918), who completed her studies at New York Medical College for Women in 1870.[3] Lee, Cole, and Steward signaled the emergence of black women in the medical profession.

During this era, white women, like black men and women in general, challenged traditional subservient roles and demanded improved educational opportunities and greater individual autonomy. Medical school matriculation statistics reflect the efforts and desires of many middle-class white and black women to expand restrictive private spheres to encompass areas outside of the home. The late nineteenth century witnessed a dramatic increase of women doctors in America. Their numbers rose from a mere 200 or fewer in 1860 to 2,423 in 1880 and to more than 7,000 by 1900. During this period nineteen medical schools for women were founded, although by 1895 eleven had disbanded.[4] By the 1920s the United States census listed only 65 black women as actually practicing physicians. Not surprisingly, black male physicians far outnumbered their female counterparts. In 1890 there were 909 black physicians; by 1920 the number had jumped to 3,885.[5]

The increase in the numbers of black physicians was due largely to the existence of several medical schools founded for black students in the post-Reconstruction South. At one time seven such institutions flourished. Four of the seven schools were considered by black and white observers to be adequate. According to one contemporary black male physician, M. Vandehurst Lynk, the big four—Howard University School of Medicine in Washington, D.C.; Meharry Medical School in Nashville, Tennessee; Leonard Medical School of Shaw University in Raleigh, North Carolina; and Flint Medical College (originally known as the Medical Department of New Orleans University) in New Orleans, Louisiana—labored to keep up with quickly evolving medical standards. They "not only extended the instruction over four years, but have increased the number of subjects to be taught and have better equipped facilities," Lynk wrote in 1893.[6] By 1914, however, of the approved medical schools only Howard and Meharry remained open. These two institutions played the most significant role in the education of black women physicians.

The Howard University medical school, chartered in 1868 and supported by the United States government as an institution to train black medical professionals, actually had more white students than black ones during the early years. The founders of the Howard medical school had all been officers in the Union Army, including Dr. Alexander T. Augusta, the only black member of the original faculty. The first woman faculty member was Isabel C. Barrows, who was graduated from the Woman's Medical College in New York City and who studied ophthalmology in Vienna. She lectured on this subject at Howard in 1872 and 1873.[7]

By 1900 Howard University had graduated 552 physicians, 35 of whom (or 5 percent of the total) were women. Only 25 of the 35 women, however, were black. The first two women to be graduated from the medical school, Mary D. Spackman (1872) and Mary A. Parsons (1874), were white.[8]

Howard's gender-blind policy sparked outright hostility and retaliation from some medical colleges. In 1873, the school's Medical Alumni Association denounced discrimination against women "as being unmanly and unworthy of the [medical] profession," and declared, "we accord to all persons the same rights and immunities that we demand for ourselves."[9] Four years later, however, the Association of American Medical Colleges, spurred by objections of the Jefferson Medical College of Philadelphia faculty, refused to seat the Howard delegation at its annual convention, in part because the Howard School of Medicine permitted men and women to be taught in the same classes.[10]

Meharry Medical College in Nashville, Tennessee, actually graduated the largest number of black women physicians (39 by 1920). Beginning in 1876 as the medical department of Central Tennessee College, Meharry was the first medical school in the South to provide for the education of black physicians. In light of the fact that the majority of black Americans still resided in the eleven southern states of the old Confederacy, where racial segregation and exclusionism prevailed, Meharry's location made it the logical place for the majority of black women to pursue a medical education. In 1893, seventeen years after its opening, Meharry graduated its first black women physicians, Annie D. Gregg and Georgia Esther Lee Patton. Three black women had reached junior class status in 1882 but for reasons unknown they were never graduated.[11]

Meharry had a penchant for hiring its own graduates. The first woman to teach at Meharry and the first to attain a position of leadership there was Josie E. Wells, a member of the class of 1904. Wells had received prior training as a nurse. Specializing in diseases of women and children, Wells gave freely of her time and resources. She dispensed free medicine and treatment to poor black patients in Nashville two afternoons a week. As superintendent of Hubbard Hospital, the teaching facility associated with Meharry, Wells executed her duties with skill. A black male colleague wrote that "she was really a remarkable woman, and under a more favorable environment might have risen to fame."[12]

By the turn of the century the Woman's Medical College of Pennsylvania, established in 1850 as the first regular medical school for females (now the Medical College of Pennsylvania), had graduated approximately a dozen black women physicians. The Woman's Medical College blazed a new trail of providing medical training to women of every race, creed, and national origin. Indeed, all of the women's medical colleges, which in most instances were founded as temporary expediences, enabled women to escape social ostracism, subtle discrimination, and overt hostility throughout their training in a male-dominated profession. Still, integration with male medical schools remained the guiding aspiration of most women in the medical profession. Unfortunately, the trend toward coeducation in the 1870s did not signal much change in the percentage of black female physicians.

Few of them actually attended the integrated coeducational institutions.[13]

Among the early black women graduates of the Woman's Medical College were Rebecca J. Cole (1867), Caroline Still Wiley Anderson (1878), Verina Morton Jones (1888), Halle Tanner Dillon Johnson (1891), Lucy Hughes Brown (1894), Alice Woodby McKane (1894), Matilda Arabella Evans (1897), and Eliza Anna Grier (1897). Of this group a large proportion became pioneers in establishing, simultaneously, a female and a black presence in the medical profession in several southern states. Three of the early black women graduates from the Woman's Medical College—Johnson, Jones, and Brown—became the first of their sex to practice medicine in Alabama, Mississippi, and South Carolina, respectively.[14] It is open to speculation whether the successes achieved by the Woman's Medical College's black graduates attest to a high quality of education or simply underscore the advantage of a more nurturing and supportive, sex-segregated environment, in which students learned from female faculty role models. Closer scrutiny suggests other factors, including family background, prior education, and social status, may have influenced their securing a medical education in the first place and subsequently their success.

That family background and prior education were important determinants of success in acquiring a medical education is reflected in the lives of a few of the early black women physicians, such as Caroline Still Wiley Anderson and Halle Tanner Dillon Johnson. The majority of the early black women physicians were the daughters of socially privileged or "representative" black families who, perhaps to protect them from menial labor or domestic servitude, encouraged their daughters to educate themselves. Of the few career options open to black women, teaching was the most accessible profession. Indeed, outside of the professions of teaching, medicine, and nursing, black women possessed scant opportunity for white- or pink-collar jobs as sales clerks, elevator operators, or typists. Ironically, they either entered the professions at the outset or remained mired in service occupations; there was little in between.[15]

Caroline Still Wiley Anderson (1848-1919) was the daughter of William and Letitia Still of Philadelphia. Her father had achieved widespread fame as a founder of the Underground Railroad and Vigilance Committee in antebellum Philadelphia and as the author of *The Underground Railroad*, which chronicled the means and patterns of escape for runaway slaves. Anderson received her primary and secondary education at Mrs. Henry Gordon's Private School, The Friends Raspberry Alley School, and the Institute for Colored Youth. She entered Oberlin College, in 1874, the only black woman in a class of forty-six. Upon graduation she married a black classmate; after his premature death she moved to Washington, D.C., where she taught music and gave instruction in drawing and elocution at Howard University. She completed one term at the Howard University School of Medicine before entering, in 1876, the Woman's Medical College in Philadelphia. In 1880 she married a prominent minister and educator, Matthew Anderson.[16]

Halle Tanner Dillon Johnson, born in 1864 in Pittsburgh, was also a member of an outstanding family. She was the daughter of Bishop B. T. Tanner of the African Methodist Episcopal Church in Philadelphia.[17] Sarah Logan Fraser, a New York native, was the daughter of Bishop Logan of the Zion Methodist Episcopal Church. Like William Still, Bishop Logan had aided and harbored escaping slaves in his home, in Syracuse, New York.[18] Unlike Caroline Still Wiley Anderson and Halle Tanner Dillon Johnson, Fraser received her medical degree from the Medical School of Syracuse University. Another New Yorker, Susan Smith McKinney Steward, the seventh of ten children born to Sylvanus and Anne Springsteel Smith, was the daughter of a prosperous Brooklyn port merchant. One of her sisters was married to the noted antislavery leader Reverend Henry Highland Garnett.[19] Among southern black women doctors, Sarah G. Boyd Jones is a good example of a daughter of a representative black family who enjoyed a highly successful medical career. Her father, George W. Boyd, was reputed to be the wealthiest black man in Richmond. A native of Albemarle County, Virginia, Sarah attended the Richmond Normal School before completing medical training in 1893 at Howard University's medical school. After graduation she returned to Richmond, where she became the first woman to pass the Virginia medical board examinations. She later founded the Richmond Hospital and Training School of Nurses, which in 1902 was renamed the Sarah G. Jones Memorial Hospital.[20]

To be sure, not all of the first generation of black women physicians belonged to illustrious and socially prominent families. They had, however, received the best undergraduate preparations then available to black Americans. Some, such as Eliza Anna Grier, were former slaves who worked their way through college and medical school, occasionally receiving minimal financial assistance from parents and siblings.

It took Eliza Anna Grier seven years to work and study her way through Fisk University in Nashville, Tennessee. In 1890 she wrote to the Woman's Medical College concerning her financial straits, "I have no money and no source from which to get it only as I work for every dollar." She continued, "What I want to know from you is this. How much does it take to put one through a year in your school? Is there any possible chance to do any work that would not interfere with one's studies?" Grier apparently completed the medical program by working every other year, for it took her seven years to earn the degree. She was graduated in 1897.[21]

Even those black families who for various reasons could not afford to assist their daughters financially did, nevertheless, provide much-needed moral support and encouragement. May E. Chinn, who in 1892 became the first black woman graduate of the University of Bellevue Medical Center, noted the importance of her mother's support. Interviewed at the age of eighty-one, she recalled that her father, who had been a slave, opposed her even going to college, but her mother, who "scrubbed floors and hired out as a cook," became the driving force behind her educational effort.[22]

Black women who were fortunate enough to secure medical education, in spite of limited access to training and segregation and gender discrimination in the schools, did so only to encounter additional obstacles. For most black women the establishment of a financially and professionally rewarding medical practice proved a most formidable challenge. Racial customs and negative attitudes toward women dictated that black women physicians practice almost exclusively among black patients, and primarily with black women, for many of whom the payment of medical fees was a great hardship. Poverty usually was accompanied by superstition and fear.

The newly minted black woman doctor frequently had to expend considerable effort persuading, cajoling, and winning confidence before being allowed to treat physical illness. May E. Chinn's experiences are again illustrative of the problems encountered. She observed that one of the peculiar problems she had to overcome as late as the 1920s was the negative attitude of some black women toward her. In one instance a black woman patient wept as Chinn approached because "she felt she had been denied the privilege of having a white doctor wait on her." Not surprisingly, few black women doctors enjoyed the support of or were consulted by their white male colleagues in the communities in which they practiced. They were, however, frequently taken aback by the actions of some of their black male colleagues. According to Chinn, black male doctors could be divided into three groups, "those who acted as if I wasn't there; another who took the attitude 'what does she think she can do that I can't do?'; and the group that called themselves supporting me by sending me their night calls after midnight."[23]

It is significant that many black women who were able to establish private practices also had to found hospitals, nursing training schools, and social service agencies. These institutions became adjuncts to their medical practices and simultaneously addressed the needs of the black communities. By custom, black professionals and patients were prohibited from using or were segregated within local health care facilities. As late as 1944 one black physician remarked, "Within the past five years, I have seen colored patients quartered in a sub-basement separated from the coal-fire furnace, of a white denominational hospital, by a thick plaster board partition not extending to the ceiling." He added, "There is much credence to be placed in the constantly repeated charge that even this concession was made only because Negro patients furnished material for the training of the white surgical staff."[24]

Several black graduates of the Woman's Medical College, most notably Lucy Hughes Brown (1863-1911) and Matilda Arabella Evans (1869-1935), journeyed south to launch medical careers. Brown, a North Carolinian by birth, moved after her 1894 graduation to Charleston, South Carolina, becoming the first black woman physician in that state. In 1896 she joined a small group of eight black male physicians led by Alonzo C. McClellan and established the Hospital and Nursing Training School.

Matilda Arabella Evans returned after graduation to her native South Carolina, where she practiced medicine for twenty years in Columbia. Inasmuch as there were no hospital facilities open to black patients in the city, Evans initially cared for patients in her own home. Eventually, as the number of clients grew, she was able to rent a separate building with a bed capacity for thirty patients and to establish a full-scale hospital and nurses' training school. During her tenure in Columbia, she also founded the Negro Health Association of South Carolina.[25]

Black women physicians such as Rebecca J. Cole and Caroline Still Wiley Anderson skillfully combined private medical practice with community service work among white and black women. Cole worked for a time with Elizabeth and Emily Blackwell at the New York Infirmary for Women and Children as a "sanitary visitor." The Blackwell's Tenement House Service, begun in 1866, was the earliest practical program of medical social service in the country. As a sanitary visitor or "tenement physician," Cole made house calls in slum neighborhoods, teaching indigent mothers the basics of hygiene and "the preservation of health of their families." Elizabeth Blackwell described Cole as "an intelligent young coloured physician," who conducted her work "with tact and care," and thus demonstrated that the establishment of a social service department "would be a valuable addition to every hospital."[26]

After a stint in Columbia, South Carolina, during the Reconstruction, Cole returned to Philadelphia. There, with the aid of physician Charlotte Abbey, she launched a new effort on behalf of destitute women and children. In 1893 Cole and Abbey founded the Woman's Directory, a medical and legal aid center. The purpose of the Woman's Directory was, according to its charter, "the prevention of feticide and infanticide and the evils connected with baby farming by rendering assistance to women in cases of approaching maternity and of desertion or abandonment of mothers and by aiding magistrates and others entrusted with police powers in preventing or punishing [such] crimes." During the later part of her fifty-year career,

Cole served as superintendent of the Government House, for children and old women, in Washington, D.C.[27]

A sister Philadelphian, Caroline Still Wiley Anderson, combined her private medical practice with the dispensary and clinic operated in conjunction with the Berean Presbyterian Church, of which her husband was the pastor. For forty years, Anderson managed the church clinic, or Berean Dispensary, as it was called, "for the benefit of women and children within the immediate neighborhood of the Church." A community activist, Anderson played a major role in establishing the first black Young Women's Christian Association (YWCA) in Philadelphia, served as treasurer of the Woman's Medical College Alumnae Association, was a member of the Women's Medical Society, and for several years occupied the position of president of the Berean Women's Christian Temperance Union. Anderson performed all of these services while maintaining her position of assistant principal and instructor in elocution, physiology, and hygiene at the Berean Manual Training and Industrial School. In 1888 she read a paper entitled "Popliteal Aneurism," which was published in the alumnae journal of the Woman's Medical College.[28]

Given the uncertainty, costs, and emotional strain of establishing a successful private practice, it is understandable that several black women physicians initially accepted appointments as resident physicians in segregated black colleges and universities established in the South during Reconstruction. Such appointments provided small but steady stipends and much-needed experience at working in an institutional setting. Moreover, these appointments assured a degree of professional autonomy, status, and visibility and enabled the development of greater confidence.

During the 1890s and early 1900s, black women physicians Halle Tanner Dillon Johnson, Ionia R. Whipper, Verina Morton Jones, and Susan Smith McKinney Steward became resident physicians at black colleges. Not only did they minister to the health care needs of the college students and faculties, but they often taught courses and lectured on health subjects. Johnson served as a resident physician at Tuskegee Institute from 1891 to 1894. During her tenure she was responsible for the medical care of 450 students as well as for 30 officers and teachers and their families. Johnson was expected to make her own medicines, while teaching one or two classes each term. For her efforts she was paid $600 per year plus room and board; she was allowed one one-month vacation per year.[29]

In 1903, Ionia R. Whipper, a member of the 1903 graduating class of Howard's medical school, succeeded Johnson and became the second black woman resident physician at Tuskegee Institute. Reflecting social change, however, Whipper was restricted to the care of female students at the Institute. After leaving Tuskegee, Whipper returned to Washington, D.C., where she established a home to care for unwed, pregnant, school-age black girls. Aided by a group of seven friends, Whipper commenced this work in her home. In 1931 she purchased some property and opened the Ionia R. Whipper Home Inc. for Unwed Mothers, which had a policy of nondiscrimination as to race, religion, or residence.[30]

After completing her education at the Woman's Medical College, Verina Morton Jones accepted an appointment as a resident physician of Rust College in Holly Springs, Mississippi. Like Johnson and Whipper, Morton doubled as a teacher, giving classes to the students enrolled in the industrial school connected with the university.[31] Jones and Dillon shared another characteristic in that they both were the first women to pass their states' medical board examinations, in Alabama and Mississippi respectively.

To be sure, acquiring a medical education and establishing a practice before the turn of the century was difficult, but later generations of black women physicians were further encumbered in their pursuit of medical careers. Entrance into the medical profession became more difficult as the requirements for certification were raised. Medical graduates were increasingly expected to secure internships and residencies for specialization and to pass state medical board examinations for certification. Only a small number of the highly rated hospitals in the country accepted black or women applicants for internships and residencies. Consequently, black women faced fierce competition for available slots. Most of the all-black hospitals preferred to grant internships and residencies to black men, while the few women's hospitals usually selected white women. The confluence of sexual and racial segregation strengthened the barriers blocking the aspirations and careers of black woman physicians.[32]

The experiences of Isabella Vandervall, who studied at the Woman's Medical College, reveal the difficulties involved in securing internships. Vandervall wrote in an article detailing her frustrations:

> I had almost given up hope of securing an internship when one day, I saw a notice on the college bulletin board saying the Hospital for Women and Children in Syracuse, New York wanted an interne. Here I thought was another chance. So I wrote, sent in my application, and was accepted without parley. . . . So to Syracuse I went with bag and baggage enough to last me for a year. I found the hospital; I found the superintendent. She asked me what I wanted. I told her I was Dr. Vandervall, the new interne. She simply stared and said not a word. Finally, when she came to her senses, she said to me: "You can't come here; we can't have you here! You are colored! You will have to go back."[33]

As the professionalization of medicine progressed, so too increased the exclusionary practices and privileging strategies of the white male power elite. For example, black women physicians, like their black male counterparts, chafed under the denial of membership in the leading professional organization, the American Medical Association. In response to this exclusion, black physicians met in 1895 in Atlanta, Georgia, to create the National Medical Association (NMA). From the outset, black women participated in the NMA. Although few were elected or appointed to prominent positions, they nevertheless, on occasion, held offices, attended the annual conventions, and periodically published papers in the *Journal of the National Medical Association*. For example, Georgia R. Dwelle, a graduate of Meharry who began her practice in Atlanta, Georgia, in 1906, was a vice-president of the NMA during the 1920s.[34]

In addition to their struggles with race-related problems within the medical profession, black women physicians had also to be concerned with gender-related issues. Like their white women counterparts, black women physicians remained sensitive to the prevailing social attitude that higher education and professional training threatened a woman's femininity. To be sure, black Americans, more so than white Americans, tended to tolerate women working outside the home. Economic necessity and racism so circumscribed the opportunities of black males that black women, regardless of marital status, had to contribute to the well-being of the family. Indeed, the black woman physician was frequently a much sought-after marriage partner. Many black women physicians married black ministers, fellow black physicians, or educators. Susan Smith McKinney Steward, commenting on the marriageability of black women physicians, observed, "Fortunate are the men who marry these women from an economic standpoint at least. They are blessed in a three-fold measure, in that they take unto themselves a wife, a trained nurse, and a doctor." She went on, however, to point out the necessity for the black woman physician to avoid becoming "unevenly yoked." She cautioned that "such a companion [would] prove to be a millstone hanged around her neck." Steward concluded on an optimistic note, asserting that "the medically educated women are generally good diagnosticians in this direction also."[35]

Actually, nineteenth-century medical practice permitted the best of both worlds. Offices were frequently located in the home. Thus, marriage and career could be conducted in the same location. Aspiring black middle-class women, especially those associated with the black women's club movement and authors of the inspirational biographies of the time, saw both as important in their praise of professional black women. They celebrated the accomplishments of the black women physicians and at the same time applauded the fact that these professional role models successfully fulfilled their obligations as wives and mothers. Of Steward, for example, the author of one black women's club publication declared, "She had fairly outdone her white sisters in proving that a married woman can successfully follow more than one profession without neglecting her family." In the same publication Caroline Still Wiley Anderson was hailed as a wife, mother, physician, teacher, clubwoman, and "co-laborer in the work of the Lord."[36]

Susan Smith McKinney Steward married another minister after her first husband, Reverend William C. McKinney, died. Her second husband, Reverend Theophilus G. Steward, was a former chaplain of the United States Army. An extremely successful physician, she had offices in Brooklyn and Manhattan and served on the staffs of the New York Hospital for Women, the Brooklyn Women's Homeopathic Hospital, and the Brooklyn Home for Aged Colored People.

She was also a church organist and choirmaster and founded the Woman's Local Union, which was black New York's leading women's club, and the Equal Suffrage League of Brooklyn.[37]

Verina Morton Jones was also held up for commendation. She married W. A. Morton in 1890 and, after she resigned from her position as resident physician at Rust College, she and her husband established a practice in Brooklyn together, although they specialized in different areas.[38] The Brooklyn *Times* noted in 1891, "they do not interfere with each other in the least. They are a handsome young couple, intelligent and refined looking."[39] Alice Woodby McKane and her husband, Cornelius McKane, also practiced medicine as a team. In 1895 they traveled to Monrovia, Liberia, where they opened and operated the first hospital in that republic. In 1896 they returned to Savannah, Georgia, and together established the McKane Hospital for Women and Children, which was renamed Charity Hospital in the 1920s.[40]

This brief examination of black women physicians under-scores the fact that much more research and discovery of additional primary source materials needs to be done before definite conclusions can be drawn concerning the impact of their work and experiences on the larger medical profession. The lives of the few women discussed reveal the depth and breadth of their struggle to overcome the gender and race barriers thwarting their access to medical schools, intern-ships, and residencies and impeding subsequent professional development. It is fair to say that in an age in which the standards of medical practice were low and the backgrounds of most physicians were wanting, these black women doctors defied, for the most part, traditional stereotypes and characterizations. This dedicated, albeit small, group of professionals was drawn, with few exceptions, from the upper echelons of black society.

Several points distinguish black women physicians, the most obvious one being that they were an integral part of the black commu-nities in which they practiced. Moreover, these women not only administered to the health care needs of black patients but also founded an array of related health care institutions. They established hospitals and clinics, trained nurses, taught elementary health rules to students and patients, and founded homes and service agencies for poor women and unwed girls of both races. They were self-reliant, committed, and talented women who successfully combined a multiplicity of roles as physicians, wives, mothers, daughters, and community leaders. Although they were, by any standard, elite black women, each of them employed her education and skills to the advantage of her people. It is reasonable to conclude that the convergence of the triple forces of racism, sexism, and professionalization resulted in a significant reduction in the number of black women physicians in the 1920s. It is also likely, however, that instead of entering the medical profession as physicians, many aspiring, career-oriented, black women began focusing on nursing as the more viable alternative for a professionally rewarding place in the American health care system. Thus, these early black professional women played an undeniably significant role in the overall survival struggle of all black people. For their contributions, sacrifices, and services, all black Americans owe to them a great debt of gratitude, one that is only beginning to be acknowledged.

"They Shall Mount Up
with Wings as Eagles"

Historical Images of Black Nurses,
1890-1950

Although diverse and often contradictory images of nurses permeate American society, few writers have investigated or dissected the particular images of black nurses. Two general images of the professional black nurse prevailed during the first half of twentieth-century America. The black nurse was viewed, on the one hand, as an essential and competent provider of health care in black communities. She, more than most other health care personnel, was viewed as being completely responsive to the needs of black people. Within the largely segregated communities, the black nurse represented an uncompromising voice for the best interests of black Americans. On the other hand, the black nurse was perceived as an inferior member of the nursing profession when compared to her white counterparts. The image of black nurses as inferior professionals was created and reinforced by discriminatory treatment. Accordingly they were subjected to employment discrimination, educational segregation, economic exploitation, professional exclusion, and social abuse. The real-life experiences of four black nurses, Mary Elizabeth Lancaster Carnegie, Frances Elliott Davis, Mabel Keaton Staupers, and Eunice Rivers (Laurie), enhance our understanding of the dual processes of image formation and transformation.

On an eventful day in 1942, Mary Elizabeth Lancaster Carnegie reported for duty as a clinical instructor at the St. Philip Hospital, the separate black wing of the white-controlled Medical College of Virginia. Carnegie had earned her diploma in 1937 from the segregated Lincoln School of Nurses in New York City. After graduation, she worked for several years as a general-duty nurse at the black Veterans Administration Hospital in Tuskegee, Alabama, before receiving a Bachelor of Arts degree in 1942 from West Virginia State College. In spite of her previous nursing experience and unique academic preparation, Carnegie, recalling that unforgettable day at St. Philip, wrote: "Here began my first in-training lessons in what it means to be a Negro nurse in the South."[1]

In keeping with long-established patterns of racial etiquette, all of the white administrators, physicians, and nurses at St. Philip addressed white nurses as "Miss" and black nurses as "Nurse." This practice underscored the inferior status of black nurses and the low esteem in which they were held by white co-workers. Yet, as Carnegie noted, being called, "Nurse so-and-so" was "a step up from being addressed by first name."[2] As if to compound their subordination, however, Carnegie observed: "Not only were Negro nurses addressed this way by the white nurses and doctors, they were instructed to address each other and refer to themselves in this manner."[3] Refusing to acquiesce to this social affront and professional slight, Carnegie declared to her black co-workers, "You can't control what someone else does, but you can control what you do."[4] Unconcerned with the consequences and perhaps suspecting that her tenure at St. Philip would be brief, Carnegie admonished the black student nurses to "address themselves and each other as 'Miss.' "[5] She insisted that the black students extend this courtesy and manifest respect by addressing all of their black patients as "Miss, Mrs., or Mr.," in spite of the fact that white nurses and doctors also addressed the black patients by their first names.

Carnegie's head-on collision with the symbolic racism of denying appropriate titles to black women nurses was one small skirmish in a decades-long war for professional recognition and acceptance. Between 1893, when the first group of professionally trained black nurses appeared, and 1951, the year of the dissolution of the National Association of Colored Graduate Nurses (NACGN, founded in 1908), black nurse leaders had struggled on every conceivable front to win equal pay, access to better quality training institutions, admission into advanced educational programs, broader employment opportunities, and individual membership in the American Nurses' Association. Progress toward these objectives and the eradication of the image of professional inferiority were slow, as deeply entrenched negative white perceptions, attitudes, and actions toward black nurses halted advance.[6]

Actually, the many discriminatory practices of key American institutions, such as the United States military establishment and organized nursing bodies, contributed to the growth of negative images of black nurses and reinforced the already low esteem in which whites held them. The American Red Cross' treatment of Frances Elliott Davis, a 1912 graduate of the black Freedmen's Hospital training school in Washington, D.C., is but one illustration of this point. Davis was the first black nurse to secure enrollment in the American Red Cross. At the end of World War I all nurses, with one exception, received identical pins indicating their enrollment and service in the Red Cross. However, the pin given to Davis was marked "1A," indicating that she was the first black nurse to be enrolled in the Red Cross. Thereafter, beginning with Frances Elliott Davis, from 1918 to 1949, all Negro nurses enrolled in the American Red Cross received special pins with the letter "A" inscribed.[7]

To be sure, Davis could have refused to accept the Red Cross pin with its discriminatory inscription. She had protested against segregation and other humiliating practices throughout her career. On her first Red Cross assignment in Jackson, Tennessee, Davis had pointedly objected to her white supervisor's introducing her to patients and co-workers as "Fannie." Moreover, she had successfully challenged the local custom requiring black patients and black health care personnel to enter the local hospital through the back door. Yet, when presented with the choice of accepting or rejecting the differently marked pin, Davis acquiesced. She swallowed her pride, accepted the pin, and consoled herself with the knowledge that she had, at least, opened a previously closed door through which other black nurses would enter. In short, to advance the professional interests of black nurses she chose to put aside personal considerations. As her biographer maintains, Davis ultimately could not "turn her back . . . simply because she had to face a certain amount of humiliation from white people who thought themselves superior."[8]

While Davis endured silently, World War II created a fortuitous array of circumstances that enabled some black nurses under the leadership of Mabel Keaton Staupers to loudly protest historical patterns of institutional racism and discrimination. Staupers, a 1917 graduate of the Freedmen's Hospital School of Nursing and executive secretary of the NACGN, took advantage of the war emergency and the increased demand for nurses to improve the status and image of black nurses as competent and valuable health care givers. Early on, War Department officials had declared that black nurses would not be called to serve in the Armed Forces Nurse Corps. As a result of pressures and protests from organized nursing groups skillfully orchestrated by Staupers, the army soon modified this policy and, in January 1941, announced that a quota of fifty-six black nurses would be recruited and assigned to the black military installations at Camp Livingston in Louisiana and Fort Bragg in North Carolina. Navy officials remained intransigent, and the Navy Nurse Corps continued to exclude black nurses throughout the war years.[9]

Staupers readily conceded that the army's quota of fifty-six represented an advance over World War I practices of total exclusion. Yet she remained determined to continue the assault on all such barriers. From 1941 to 1945 Staupers met repeatedly with white nursing groups, top military officials, First Lady Eleanor Roosevelt, and leaders of black civil rights organizations. She cultivated relations with editors of black newspapers, women's clubs, and white philanthropists, urging them to protest the imposition of quotas for black nurses.[10] Her strategic maneuvering eventually bore fruit.

The personal appeals of Eleanor Roosevelt and the protests of the National Nursing Council for War Service, combined with the acute nurse shortage toward the end of the war, eventually forced the army to increase the numbers of black nurses. By 1945, approximately 330 black nurses were serving in the Army Nurse Corps. Had black nurses been accepted in proportion to their numbers, as were white nurses, there would have been 1,520 of them in the Army and Navy Nurse Corps. There were at the time approximately eight thousand black graduate nurses active in nursing.[11] Unable to withstand the unrelenting pressure, the surgeon general of the navy declared on

January 31, 1945: "There is no policy in the Navy which discriminates against the utilization of Negro Nurses."[12]

Although the American Red Cross, the United States Army and Navy, and some white nurses and doctors discriminated against black nurses, viewing them as inferior professionals, the black community's general reactions to and perceptions of black nurses were strikingly different. In part, this divergence is explained by the insufficient health care available to large portions of the black population. The small numbers of black physicians, coupled with a growing trend to concentrate in urban areas, and the frequently insulting treatment meted out by white physicians often meant that only a black nurse was available in most rural communities.[13] In many such areas, rural black nurses, similar to Eunice Rivers (Laurie), a 1922 graduate of Tuskegee Institute's nursing program in Tuskegee, Alabama, played a pivotal role in the black health-care delivery hierarchy in rural Alabama.

Rivers attributed the higher esteem that the black nurses found among black patients to the position they occupied as mediators between patients and physicians. Historian James H. Jones, in his provocative study of the Tuskegee syphilis experiment conducted by the United States Public Health Service (1932-1972), underscored the significant role played by Rivers. Her immense interpersonal skills won the trust and respect of hundreds of the male patients involved in the experiment. Jones describes Rivers as "a facilitator, bridging the many barriers that stemmed from the educational and cultural gap between the physicians and the subjects."[14] In one interview, Rivers elaborated on her image of the role the black nurse played:

> The doctor saw the patient and he was gone and it was up to you to help that patient carry out his orders, do whatever the doctor suggested. The doctor said you do so and so. . . . First thing, the patient doesn't know how to do it. He doesn't know what his reaction is going to be. He doesn't want to be stuck. . . . So the nurse plays an important part there. She's closer to the patient. Patients would get to the point where if they're not sure, they're going to ask you. They get you in the middle.[15]

Rivers recalled, "A lot of my patients would not call a doctor until I had come to see them, to see how they were doing and see if they needed a doctor." She added, "I had an awful time training them to go ahead and get their own doctor."[16]

These capsule glimpses into the experiences of Carnegie, Davis, Staupers, and Rivers provoke more questions than answers concerning both the images of black women and the reality of their struggles as professional nurses. Why were black nurses denied the usual appellations denoting respect? Why were they given Red Cross pins inscribed with the letter "A"? Why did the United States Army and Navy first exclude black nurses altogether, as in World War I, and then, in World War II, establish quotas for recruiting them into the Armed Forces Nurse Corps? In light of the demeaning treatment accorded them in the larger society, why were black nurses held in such high esteem within the black community? What did the black community expect and receive from black nurses? Finally, how did discrimination, racism, and negative stereotypes spur or impede the personal and professional development of the black nurse?

Traditional histories of nursing pay scant attention to the accomplishments of and peculiar difficulties encountered by black nurses. Yet the struggle of black nurses for respect, recognition, acceptance, and status parallels and, in many ways, exemplifies the historical quest of all professional nurses. It is the difference that racism made, giving rise to a store of derogatory images, which separates and distinguishes the black nurses' story from the larger history. Examining some of the historical images of black nurses and contrasting them with the objective reality provide deeper insights into the process of professionalization in nursing. Such an investigation enhances our understanding of the old images that American pioneer nursing leaders desired to destroy and the new ones that they substituted. In the years of the early professionalization, concerned nursing leaders initiated actions designed to limit the number of nurses, halt the proliferation of training schools, and recruit "women of the better classes" into the profession. From the outset, the quest for image control and exclusiveness in nursing were essential components and characteristics of the overall professionalization process.[17]

Unfortunately, black women, and lower-class white women to some extent, were most affected by exclusionary tendencies and hence were sacrificed on the altar of nursing advancement. As nursing increasingly acquired the trappings of a profession, the restrictions and impediments placed in the paths of black women mushroomed. They were denied admittance into training schools, barred from membership in professional associations, refused listing in employment registries, and discouraged from aspiring to meet the higher requirements of nurse registration and licensing laws. Black women, because of their racial identity and slavery heritage, were seen as a permanently alien and inferior group that could not be assimilated. In the white mind the slavery-born images of the black woman as a defeminized beast of burden, a sexually promiscuous wanton, or a domineering mammy held sway long after the demise of the "peculiar institution." These negative images, mixed with entrenched racism, probably motivated those of the white nursing establishment seeking greater status and esteem to eschew association with or recognition of black women as professional peers.[18] Before I proceed, it will be useful to place these images of black women and nurses within the appropriate historical context.

In the latter part of the nineteenth century, the social conventions and normative attitudes of an industrialized society consigned women to the private sphere of the home. The ideology of "virtuous womanhood" sharply and oppressively defined their proper actions and behavior in very narrow and restricted terms. Women were considered to be repositories of moral sensibility, purity, refinement, and maternal affection in a male-dominated society. Thus, woman's highest calling consistent with her biological destiny was deigned to be that of mother and nurturer. For many women, growing adherence to the ideology of separate spheres occurred in tandem with constricting career opportunities in the public sphere of business and politics. Actually, the tension between theory and reality created a paradox, for as certain doors closed, other new female-stereotyped occupations and professions reserved for women opened.[19]

Of all such sex-segregated occupations, nursing was preeminent. The movement for formalized nursing training and practice provided an attractive alternative to middle-class, sphere-restricted women. Before the Civil War, nursing, as historian Janet Wilson James has pointed out, was a "low-paid, low-status job for laboring class women, who, over a twelve-hour day, attended to the physical needs of the patients while doing the heavy domestic work on the wards."[20] The opening of the first nursing schools, in 1873, launched the movement to upgrade nursing, to distance it from identification with domestic service, and to attract a "higher-class woman" into the profession. Considered a woman's job, nursing neither threatened nor challenged society's views of her traditional domestic functions. Rather, the substance of nursing and settings in which training was provided actually reinforced the image of the subordinate woman. Deemed less exacting and autonomous than being a physician, nursing existed always under the control of the male-dominated medical and hospital professions.[21]

The late nineteenth- and early twentieth-century struggle to professionalize and upgrade the image of nursing concentrated, in part, on recruiting middle-class students while purging and excluding from the occupation the uneducated and untrained women of the lower socioeconomic classes. These efforts also coincided with the hardening of the color line in American society. As segregation pervaded the country, all southern and most northern nursing schools barred black women. Even in the most liberal northern institutions enrollments of black women were subjected to restrictive quotas. The charter for the New England Hospital for Women and Children, for example, expressly stipulated that only *one* Negro and *one* Jewish student each year would be accepted. The first black trained nurse, Mary E. Mahoney, was graduated from the New England Hospital in 1879.[22]

If black women were to have access to professional nursing training, then it was incumbent on black leaders, in the name of racial self-help, to establish the corresponding institutions. Beginning in the early 1890s, black physician Daniel Hale Williams of Chicago and educator Booker T. Washington, founder of Tuskegee Institute, spearheaded a movement to found hospital nursing schools for black women. They solicited operating funds for these new institutions from their respective black communities and from private philanthropies. The rhetoric of the founders of the early black nursing schools reveals much about their own and the larger society's images of nurses.

Washington and Williams espoused the new romantic and idealized image of the Florence Nightingale-type nurse. They merged this image with their views of what constituted the "proper" woman's role. Uppermost in their minds, however, was the belief that black women bore a large part of the responsibility for proving the humanity of black people to a skeptical white public. Accordingly, they portrayed the black nurse as a self-sacrificing, warm, and devoted mother figure, and downplayed her as the efficient, autonomous, and assertive professional. Fund-raising campaigns for the hospitals and training schools employing this romantic image of the black nurse-mother proved most successful. Evoking this romantic image had other practical implications as well. Clearly, the black nurses trained in these black community-based and supported institutions would forever owe primary allegiance to that community and be responsible participants in the climb up the racial and social ladder.[23]

Williams, as founder of two black nursing schools, Provident Hospital and Training School in Chicago in 1891 and the Freedmen's Hospital nursing school in Washington, D.C., in 1894, frequently informed potential black supporters of nursing schools: "The servant class no longer furnishes the nurse."[24] Ironically, Williams was prone to invoke the ubiquitous "mammy" image to illustrate his claim that the black woman was a "natural" nurse possessed of a long heritage, in slavery and freedom, of caring for the sick of both races. He was, perhaps, unmindful that this continued association of black nurses with the mammy image would retard their advancement within the nursing profession. Williams insisted: "The young colored woman who chooses this calling enters the training school richly endowed by inheritance with woman's noblest attributes—fidelity, tenderness, sympathy."[25] After extolling all the nurturing qualities of black women, Williams declared the black nurse an object lesson, who "teaches the people cleanliness, thrift, habits of industry, sanitary housekeeping, the proper care of themselves, and of their children. She teaches them how to prepare food, the selection of proper clothing for the sick and the well, and how to meet emergencies."[26] As Rivers would do thirty years later, Williams predicted that the trained black nurse would soon become a major force serving the black community in racial uplift work.[27]

Booker T. Washington, when launching the nursing program at Tuskegee Institute in 1892, linked it with the school's industrial education emphasis. He justified the new program on the grounds that nursing training would enable a black woman to have a career prior to marriage, one, however, that would also make her a better wife, mother, and homemaker. Moreover, he argued that should hard times befall the family, the trained nurse would always be able to help earn money. In describing the philosophical foundation on which the school was based, Washington reiterated tenets of the Victorian belief concerning women's role and function: "A man can build the house but the woman must, for the most part furnish the sort of culture and refinement that makes it a home," he said.[28] Washington wedded nursing training firmly to vocational work: "The course in child nurture and nursing has been established to complete the training in home building which is carried on as part of the industrial training of young women at Tuskegee."[29]

Williams' and Washington's images of the black nurse were shared for many years by most of the black hospital administrators and physicians responsible for their training. In a 1918 article, John A. Kenney, a black physician named superintendent of the new and enlarged John A. Andrew Memorial Hospital and Nurse Training School of Tuskegee Institute, echoed Williams' and Washington's conviction that the black nurse was equal, if not superior, to white nurses. In an effort to persuade more black women to enter into the backbreaking, endless toil euphemistically referred to as nursing training, he unabashedly lauded the black nurses' many womanly virtues of "devotion, endurance, sympathy, tactile delicacy, unselfishness, tact, resourcefulness, [and] willingness to undergo hardships."[30] The fact that he played an important role in training black women did not challenge Kenney to view the trained nurse as a serious professional rather than a mother-nurturer. Even when commenting on the good deeds performed by the black graduate nurses of Tuskegee Institute, Kenney interjected remembrances of his mother's unpaid nurturing activities. He wrote: "Regardless of the demands made upon her by the exacting duties of her own household, if there was a case of serious illness among her friends, white or colored, even miles away, she thought it her duty to go and care for them night after night, if necessary.[31]

Black nurses were entrapped in the vortex of the sexual and racial currents dominating black and white thought in late nineteenth-century America. To be sure, at this juncture much of the language describing black nurses and the "advantages" to be reaped by pursuing a nursing career were used with white women as well. Although reality and image frequently diverged, the ideology of separate spheres nevertheless severely reduced a woman's chances of securing challenging and remunerative work. Because of racial prejudice, most of the sex-segregated jobs were beyond black women's reach. The transformation of nursing into a skilled profession requiring formal training in a structured institutional setting further encumbered black women. With black women barred from the white nursing schools, black leaders, in order to provide access to the profession, proceeded to combine the ideology of woman's separate sphere with the doctrine of racial uplift. Thus, because black communities contributed so much to the start-up funds creating and sustaining black nursing schools, early generations of graduates were expected to repay the communities' investments. Hence, in addition to seeking professional acceptance and recognition, black nurses bore the extra burden of providing health care for, and lifting from the bottom of the American social scale, the entire black race. All future images of black nurses would be inextricably connected to their role within, and responsibility to, the black community.

By the 1920s, the separate black training schools had produced approximately three thousand nurses. The burgeoning numbers caused white nurses, especially those engaged in private-duty work, to fear increased economic competition, which only exacerbated the tenuous relations between the two groups. Meanwhile, economic exigencies and racism compelled many black nurses to act in ways that reinforced existing negative images of them in the minds of their white colleagues. For example, many black nurses worked for lower wages and longer hours than white nurses. Often, black nurses performed household and child-care chores in addition to tending sick members of the family. The fact that many white physicians spoke in glowing terms of the submissive and accommodating black nurse who adapted "well to the needs to the household" did not help matters.[32] Equally damaging were their expressions of delight with black private-duty nurses, whom they perceived as being more "willing to render the small personal services only grudgingly performed by white nurses."[33] In a depressed job market, characterized by an oversupply of nurses, whites imagined black nurses to be the group least committed to advancing the profession and more willing to compromise on salary and working conditions.[34]

The scarcity of data precludes the development of a definitive analysis of white nurses' images of black nurses during the 1920s. Available, however, are a limited number of surveys and reports commissioned by philanthropic and nursing organizations, which canvassed white nurses, physicians, and hospital and public health officials for their personal evaluations and perceptions of black nurses. In 1925, Ethel Johns, an Englishwoman trained in a Canadian hospital, conducted one of the most illuminating surveys and reports. Under the aegis of the Rockefeller Foundation, Johns queried hundreds of white administrators and nurse superintendents in more than two dozen hospitals and she included scores of visiting nursing associations and municipal boards of health.

Johns' report, though frozen in time, does record the attitudes of the black nurses' professional colleagues while shedding light on the black nurses' social and economic status. The images white nurses and other health care personnel had of black nurses were informed by the widely held assumption of the poor quality of all black training schools. Moreover, the fact that black Americans as a group occupied a subordinate position influenced the negative assessments of their leadership abilities. Most of the white superintendents of the twenty-three black hospitals Johns visited frankly admitted their displeasure with black nurses. They contended that black nurses exhibited "a marked tendency to concealment of what is going on in their respective wards. They will not report mistakes or accidents."[35] These claims, while perhaps accurate, did not take into consideration the forces that may have encouraged black nurses to cover for each other when they had a white supervisor. Few black nurses held supervisory positions in hospitals or sanitariums. Without dissecting the underlying reasons for the absence of black administrators, Johns simply concluded that they were inherently lacking in leadership qualities: "My observations lead me to believe that the negro woman is temperamentally unsuited for the constant unremitting grind of a hospital superintendent's life. She finds it difficult to discipline her staff and yet to remain on friendly terms with them."[36]

Though opportunities to become a supervisor were scarce, the black nurses' chances for employment in the public health field during the 1920s were even bleaker. Visiting nursing association officials rationalized their aversion to hiring black public health nurses, insisting that they were of limited usefulness. Most agency leaders maintained that black nurses could work only with black patients, but white public health nurses could deal with both races. After all, these officials contended, black nurses were educationally deficient and ill-prepared to assume the heavy responsibility of being a public health nurse. Supervisors of the nursing services for the municipal boards of health in New York, Chicago, and Philadelphia acknowledged that, as much as possible, they hired only white nurses because the employment of black women "complicates the service and creates social friction."[37] Municipal boards of health supervisors in Birmingham, Baltimore, Atlanta, and Nashville regarded black public health nurses as "admittedly inferior in intelligence to the white group."[38] They let it be known that, where employed, the black nurse was "paid substantially less than the white nurse . . . , excluded from supervisory rank and . . . treated as a social inferior.[39]

Several directors of visiting nursing services did comment positively on the role of black nurses in public health nursing. Lillian Wald, founder of the Henry Street Settlement and a staunch friend of black nurses, employed 25 black and 150 white nurses, paid them equal salaries, and accorded them identical professional courtesies and recognition. Even here, however, black and white nurses were viewed and treated differently in two respects: black nurses were never sent to white homes, nor were they promoted to supervisory rank. Johns discovered similar conditions prevailing in Philadelphia, Chicago, and St. Louis. Southern-based visiting nursing services employed black nurses; nevertheless, when they were hired they always received much lower salaries and were treated as social inferiors.[40]

Among the whites interviewed, Johns discerned nearly unanimous agreement that black nurses were professional inferiors. According to most white nurses, supervisors, and administrators, the lower wages paid black nurses were entirely justified and simply confirmed their alleged shortcomings. The fact that black nurses were rarely promoted to or held supervisory and administrative positions reinforced white beliefs that black nurses were incapable of leading. Only when she dealt with black patients did a black nurse stand a chance of being referred to as a competent and adept professional. Apparently, only as long as she remained in the black community, caring only for black patients, would a black nurse earn praise from her white counterparts and enjoy a better image. Johns captured these mixed messages when she observed:

> It is quite apparent that the negro nurse cannot be utilized successfully in public health work except among her own people. Even among them she has not the same authority as the white nurse although she has a better psychological approach. She has been very successful in overcoming their superstitious fears regarding immunization, vaccination and other preventive measures. The social and economic problems involved in case work are commonly too much for her but she can ferret out information and interpret domestic complications which would baffle a white nurse who lacks her intuitive understanding of racial characteristics.[41]

Contrary to Jones' observations and white nurses' resentment and racism, black nurses were highly regarded within black urban and rural communities. For thousands of black poor the nurse often meant the difference between living and dying. The black nurse allayed the fears and quelled the hostilities of those superstitious rural black patients who refused to seek medical care in hospitals and usually resorted to folk cures and questionable remedies. Frequently, black nurses became the bridge connecting the rural black impoverished—mired in nineteenth-century notions of sickness—with the twentieth-century reality of hospitals, physicians, scientific advances, and the germ theory of disease.[42]

Actually, the image of the race-serving, strong, and resourceful black nurse laboring amongst the poor and downtrodden is too one-dimensional. Eunice Rivers, to be specific, was described by her family, friends, colleagues, and black patients as a "born nurse." She had entered nursing out of a desire "to get closer to people who needed" her. Rivers attributed her success as a nurse to an innate ability to accept people on their own terms. She stated in an interview, "I go there and visit awhile until I know when to make some suggestions. . . . I don't ever go into any person's house, fussing with him about how he keeps his house, first." Rivers insisted, "I accepted them as they were and they accepted me."[43]

Rivers was more than a good country nurse. Her more than forty years' involvement in the Tuskegee syphilis experiment, in which treatment was deliberately withheld from patients, raises questions concerning relationships between the black nurses and the black community and between black nurses and white health care professionals. Indeed, it is fair to say that without her the white "government doctors" would not have been successful in engaging so many black males in such a detrimental and ethically bankrupt experiment. It was their unquestioning faith in Rivers as someone selflessly looking out for and protecting them that led the men to continue in the experiment for so many unrewarding years. Though they remained fundamentally suspicious of the "government doctors'" motives, they always tended to do what Rivers told them. According to historian James H. Jones, "more than any other person [Rivers] made them believe that they were receiving medical care that was helping them."[44] They were not.

Rivers' motives for collaborating in this experiment and deliberately manipulating these black men are complex. It is possible that Rivers viewed the experiment as a way of ensuring for at least some black patients an unparalleled amount of medical attention. Jones offers several compelling explanations for Rivers' complicity. He argues that, as a nurse, Rivers had been trained to follow orders and so probably it simply did not occur to her to question a, or for that matter any, doctor's judgment. Moreover, she was incapable of judging the scientific merits of the study. For Rivers, a female in a male-dominated world, deference to male authority figures reinforced her ethical passivity. Finally, and perhaps most significantly, Rivers was black and the physicians who controlled the experiment were white. Jones points out that years of conditioning and living in the South made it virtually impossible for Rivers to have rebelled against a white government doctor, the ultimate authority figure in her world.[45] In this case the needs and interests of the black community of Tuskegee were not addressed and protected by a black nurse.

The image of the black nurse as self-sacrificing mother-nurturer, servant, and leader of the black community persisted with slight modifications. In the urban northern black communities, the white uniform-clad black nurse with satchel at her side cut an imposing and impressive figure. One black nurse, Elizabeth Jones, recounted ways in which the black community viewed the black nurse as someone special. She describes, for example, her own approach one day to two children playing on a Harlem street. One child, as she walked toward them, ordered his playmates, " 'Get up, and let the lady pass.' While making a passage, all eyes were turned upon [her] with great intent. Suddenly, as if having solved a problem, one little voice chimed in, and said with much glee, 'Aw! She ain't a lady, she's a nurse!' "[46] Jones, musing about this reflection on the status of the black nurse in the black community, declared: "Not only is she a teacher, but she is looked upon by most of those with whom she comes in contact, as an example of the higher life."[47] For many the black nurse became a symbol of white middle-class virtues and respectability. Residents of the black communities where the nurse visited, worked, and sometimes resided looked upon her with pride tinged with awe. The fact that she was there to tend to their needs and to help them solve their problems engendered feelings of possessiveness while intensifying the desire to obey.

Throughout the brief history of professional nursing, black nurses struggled to create and sustain positive self-images while simultaneously pursuing an often frustrating quest for acceptance and recognition within their chosen occupation. Accommodation to their "place" and resistance to white efforts to devalue them developed as two forms of a single process by which black nurses accepted circumstances they could not change and vigorously fought individually and collectively for professional equality.

Throughout her long nursing career, Red Cross nurse Davis demonstrated pride and a positive self-image. Her deep spiritual convictions and unyielding sense of responsibility to her race, combined with the support and love of her husband, sustained her quest for professional equality. These internal and external forces helped to deflect the psychological and moral aggression of a racist society. When gloom threatened to immobilize and depress her, she invariably reached for her Bible and reread her favorite passage from the Book of Isaiah: "But they that wait upon the Lord shall renew their strength; they shall mount up with wings as eagles; they shall run, and not be weary; and they shall walk, and not faint" (40:31).[48]

Mabel Keaton Staupers was thirteen years old when her family moved from Barbados, West Indies, in 1903, to the Harlem community of New York City. She spent the early years of her nursing career in New York City and Washington, D.C.; in 1920, in cooperation with a couple of prominent black physicians, she organized the Booker T. Washington Sanatorium, the first facility in the Harlem area where black physicians could treat their patients. In 1921 she was awarded a working fellowship in Philadelphia and was later assigned to the chest department of the Jefferson Hospital Medical College in Philadelphia. The following year Staupers returned to New York, and under the auspices of the New York Tuberculosis and Health Association, she made a survey of the health needs of the community. This work eventually resulted in the organization of the Harlem Committee of the New York Tuberculosis and Health Association and her twelve-year stint as executive secretary of this body.[49]

In 1934 Staupers was appointed as the first nurse executive of the National Association of Colored Graduate Nurses (NACGN). Founded in 1908 by a group of black nurses in New York, the organization was virtually moribund by the time Staupers assumed the helm. Throughout the 1940s Staupers combined her struggle for the integration of black nurses into the Armed Forces Nurse Corps with the fight for full integration of black nurses into American nursing. In 1948 the American Nurses' Association (ANA) House of Delegates opened its doors to black members on an individual basis, appointed a black woman nurse as assistant executive secretary in its national headquarters, and witnessed the election of black nurse Estelle Massey Riddle to the Board of Directors. In 1950 the NACGN membership elected Staupers president. The NACGN's Board of Directors charged Staupers with overseeing the dissolution of the organization. Her book, *No Time for Prejudice* (1961), details the history of the black nurses' victorious struggle to integrate into the American Nurses' Association.[50]

The fight for integration into state nurses' associations in the South continued even after the ANA openly accepted black members. Mary Elizabeth Lancaster Carnegie led the attack against the Florida

State Nurses Association. After leaving St. Philip, Carnegie worked as assistant director of the Division of Nurse Education at Hampton Institute in Virginia. In 1945 she was named Dean of the Division of Nursing Education at Florida A & M College. In 1951 Carnegie received a fellowship to earn a master's degree from Syracuse University in New York. She was assistant editor of the *American Journal of Nursing* from 1953 to 1956, then became associate editor and, in 1970, editor of *Nursing Outlook*. While pursuing her editorial career, Carnegie was a part-time student at New York University, where she received a doctoral degree in 1972. The next year she assumed the editorship of *Nursing Research*.[51]

Carnegie's somewhat exceptional career was unlike that of most black nurses; yet even her advancement was profoundly impeded by racist attitudes and discrimination. A clearly hostile larger social environment littered her path with innumerable reminders of her status as a "Negro nurse." Carnegie, however, deliberately chose to resist those practices that assaulted her self-image. Carnegie's description of the black nurses' struggle for the right to participate in the meetings of the Florida State Nurses Association illuminates the strength of their determination to win professional recognition and acceptance and the ludicrous nature of the efforts of some white nurses to preserve segregation and subordination: "For many months, we played a game of 'musical chairs.' The white nurses would wait on the outside of the buildings for us to arrive and be seated; then they would proceed to sit on the opposite side of the meeting room. If we sat in the back, they would sit in the front, and vice versa."[52] Carnegie devised a clever scheme to end "the game." She and her fellow black nurses simply waited for the white nurses to arrive and would scatter throughout the room in order to ensure, at least, integration in the seating arrangements. When, in 1950, she was elected to the association's board for a three-year term, she continued to press quietly for integration. After the 1950 meeting Carnegie observed that "for the first time, all Negro nurses attended all business and program meetings, but [they were still] barred from the luncheon."[53] By the 1952 convention in Daytona Beach, Florida, she reported modest improvements: "There was integration in every respect but housing and the events that were strictly social."[54] (The luncheon meetings at the hotel included all members on an equal basis.)

By the 1950s it was evident that the self-image of black nurses was formed in part by the twin realities of racism and sexism in American society. Black nurses recognized that their struggle for recognition, acceptance, and equality of opportunity within nursing was inextricably linked to overcoming this double-edged prejudice. Carnegie captured the relationship between the development of a positive self-image and struggle for unfettered access to professional opportunities when she asserted:

> In the length and breadth of the United States of America, Negro nurses, many unknown to each other, have always fought for a common cause. . . .They were fighting on the same front in schools of nursing and in professional organizations in other states, and on other fronts—in the military, public health, hospital nursing service, industry, private duty, and the national organizations—throughout the country.[55]

Actually, the dual processes of accommodation and resistance enabled black nurses to develop a collective self-consciousness and pride that allowed them to retain a viable sense of self-worth in the face of the oppression they endured. Central to their identity, however, was a strong conviction that, in the words of black nurse educator-administrator Gloria R. Smith, "black nurses were accountable to black people in a special way."[56] As late as 1971, Smith observed that black nurses would always serve as "spokesmen who could articulate the needs of the black community for compatible care delivery systems as well as the dreams of black people for equal access to and mobility within the health care system."[57]

In 1971 black nurses found it desirable again to organize in a separate body to continue the fight for full participation and equal access to opportunities in the profession. The new National Black Nurses' Association reminds us of the resiliency of negative images, racism, discrimination, and the will to overcome injustices of all kinds.

Mabel K. Staupers and the Integration of Black Nurses into the Armed Forces during World War II

The social and economic changes associated with the New Deal and the fairer hearing that race advancement organizations were receiving in the courts and federal executive offices in the 1930s brought a rising black militance that escalated with the coming of World War II. The achievements of this wartime militance included A. Philip Randolph's March on Washington, the creation of the Fair Employment Practices Committee, and Mabel Keaton Staupers' crusade for the employment and integration of Negro nurses in the armed services. Staupers' career provides an illuminating case study of the way in which many black leaders have made skillful use of pressure by both black Americans and well-placed white sympathizers to advance the cause of equal opportunity.

World War II was a watershed in black history. Many black men and women resolved to take advantage of the war emergency and to push for the full realization of their rights as American citizens and as human beings. Scholars have justifiably dubbed this period as "the forgotten years of the Negro Revolution." Black leaders such as A. Philip Randolph of the Brotherhood of Sleeping Car Porters and organizer of the March on Washington Movement, Walter White of the National Association for the Advancement of Colored People, Lester Granger of the National Urban League, Claude Barnett of the Associated Negro Press, and James Farmer and Bayard Rustin of the Committee (later Congress) of Racial Equality employed a variety of tactics and struggled to dismantle the entire edifice of white supremacy and racial proscription.

To the dismay of black Americans, the federal government proved slow in responding to their attacks and charges of discrimination. Those already situated on the bottom rung of the socioeconomic ladder had suffered to a remarkable degree during the Great Depression. Much of the New Deal relief legislation designed to ameliorate the deprivation and suffering of impoverished Americans actually preserved Jim Crow practices. To be sure, black Americans received significant amounts of work, housing, and federal relief, but this was certainly not sufficient to solve the basic problems arising from white prejudice and discrimination.

The resurgence of economic activity at the outset of World War II registered only imperceptible changes in the black condition. Private industries with and without government defense contracts continued to discriminate against black workers in hiring, wages, and promotion. While many white unions excluded black Americans, the U.S. Employment Service, a federal agency, continued to fill "white only" requests from employers of defense labor. The Fair Employment Practices Committee (FEPC) appointed by President Franklin Delano Roosevelt to implement Executive Order 8802 banning employment discrimination in government defense industries lacked enforcement powers and proved to be of only limited effectiveness. Yet, stimulated by the limited reforms of the New Deal and the democratic ideology stressed by U.S. anti-Nazi propaganda, black Americans became much more militant in attacks on the racial status quo. Thus the vigilance with which black editors observed and reported accounts of racial segregation, discrimination, and civil inequalities surpassed all previous coverage.

One black leader, Mabel Keaton Staupers, heretofore unheralded and virtually ignored as executive secretary of the National Association of Colored Graduate Nurses (NACGN), successfully challenged the highly racist top echelons of the U.S. Army and Navy and forced them to accept black women nurses into the military nurses corps during World War II. This essay focuses on her leadership in the campaign to win long-denied rights for black women nurses.

Within the federal government, the Army and Navy displayed the strongest adherence to and defense of the ideology and practice of racial discrimination and segregation. Military leaders saw nothing amiss in sending a segregated Army and Navy to obliterate the forces of Fascism and Nazism to make the world safe for democracy. These contradictions were not lost upon black Americans. Walter White wrote at the time, "World War II has immeasurably magnified the Negro's awareness of the disparity between the American profession and practice of democracy."

As the country mobilized for the impending conflict, government authorities informed the major nursing organizations of the increased need for nurses. Staupers and the members of the NACGN heeded the alert. The NACGN had been founded in 1908 to champion the interests and promote the professional development of black women nurses. The leading nurses organizations, the American Nurses' Association (ANA) and the National League of Nursing Education (NLNE), refused to accept individual membership from black nurses residing in seventeen, primarily southern, states. Every southern state association barred black women, thereby making the majority of black women nurses professional outcasts.

Handicapped by lack of a permanent headquarters, low membership, and insufficient funds with which to pay a salaried executive, the NACGN accomplished little during its first two decades. Thus, as late as 1930 black nurses had not obtained membership in the ANA, were excluded from the vast majority of nurse training schools, and suffered employment discrimination. One black nurse succinctly described the NACGN's plight, "There was a great need for a program which would bring into clear focus the fact that Negro nurses not only needed better educational and employment opportunities, but that these needs were aggravated by racial bias."

In 1934 the NACGN secured grants from the Julius Rosenwald Fund and the General Education Board of the Rockefeller Foundation. The money enabled the organization to move into permanent headquarters at Rockefeller Center, where all of the major national nursing organizations resided. More significantly, the grant enabled the NACGN to employ an executive secretary. The time was never more propitious. The reorganization brought together Staupers and Estelle Massey Riddle, two exceptionally talented black nurses who immediately contacted the white nursing leaders of the ANA and the NLNE and who lobbied for the removal of discriminatory policies that denied black nurses membership in state professional organizations. Staupers served as the first executive secretary from 1934 to 1946 and Riddle reigned as president of the NACGN from 1934 to 1938. Riddle, a native of Palestine, Texas, had attended the Homer G. Phillips Hospital and Nurses Training School in St. Louis, Missouri. She moved to New York in 1927 and entered Teachers College, Columbia University, becoming the first black recipient of a Rosenwald Fund Fellowship for nurses and the first black woman nurse to earn a Master's degree.

Staupers, born in Barbados, West Indies, in 1890, had migrated with her parents to New York in 1903. After graduating from Freedmen's Hospital School of Nursing in Washington, D.C., in 1917, Staupers began her professional career as a private duty nurse in New York City. She was instrumental in organizing the Booker T. Washington Sanatorium, the first facility in the Harlem area where black doctors could treat their patients. Later Staupers served for twelve years as the executive secretary of the Harlem Committee of the New York Tuberculosis and Health Association. When the opportunity came, she unhesitatingly embraced the challenge of rebuilding and leading the NACGN. An ardent integrationist and feminist, Staupers set as her prime objective the full integration of black women nurses into the mainstream of American nursing. It would take years before her dream became a reality.

The long and arduous struggle for the professional recognition and integration of black nurses into American nursing acquired new momentum and a heightened sense of urgency with the outbreak of World War II. Between 1934 and 1940 Staupers' efforts to win for black women nurses unfettered membership in the major professional associations, particularly on the state level, had been unsuccessful. Staupers resolved therefore to seize the opportunity created by the war emergency and the increased demand for nurses to project the plight of the black nurse into the national limelight. Fully cognizant of the discrimination and exclusion black nurses suffered in World War I, Staupers vowed that history would not be repeated. In a long letter to

William H. Hastie, the black civilian aide to the secretary of war, Staupers laid bare the strategy of mobilizing supporters (both black and white) that she would pursue in the campaign to force the complete integration of black nurses into the total war effort. Staupers viewed the acceptance of black nurses into the Army and Navy Nurse Corps as critical to the achievement of her major objective, that is, the full integration of black women into American nursing. Fortunately, the NACGN was in a much stronger position to coordinate the struggle for inclusion than it had been during the previous world conflict. She confided to Hastie:

> Although we know that pressure from Negro groups will mean something, nevertheless I am spending all of my time contacting white groups, especially nursing groups. I have a feeling that if enough white nursing organizations can register a protest and enough white organizations of influence other than nurses do the same, it will create in the minds of the people in the War Department the feeling that white people do not need protection in order to save themselves from being cared for by Negro personnel.

Staupers adopted this particular strategy in order to address simultaneously two interrelated concerns. She was fully cognizant that the white American public's appreciation for nurses and the status of the nursing profession as a whole increased sharply whenever the country was involved in a war. This had been especially true during World War I. Therefore, to improve the economic, social, and educational opportunities of black nurses and their relationship with the professional nursing establishment, Staupers had to make sure that the larger white society recognized and valued the contributions of black women nurses in the Army and Navy Corps because these agencies possessed high public visibility. If the white public, especially the armed forces nurse corps, approved of and accepted black women as competent and desirable nurses, then surely the white professional nursing groups would follow suit. Her strategy was further complicated by the fact that any struggle to win public support mandated that she also attract the allegiance of sympathetic white nurses within the nursing profession.

By the time of the Japanese attack on Pearl Harbor in December 1941, Staupers had already developed a sharp sense of political timing and possessed a finely tuned facility for strategic maneuvering. She had skillfully cultivated close interaction with white nursing leaders, and as a consequence the NACGN's interests were well represented by its former president, Riddle, on the National Defense Council (which was renamed in 1942 the National Nursing Council for War Service). Staupers continued to nurture her earlier long-term friendship with Congresswoman Frances Payne Bolton of Ohio, and before long she made contact with First Lady Eleanor Roosevelt to solicit her assistance in the integration campaign. Also, as of 1940 Staupers purposefully had arranged for officers of the major civil rights organizations to be placed on the NACGN National Advisory Committee. Finally, Staupers appreciated the value of the black press and remained in constant communication with several black editors, sending them a constant stream of NACGN press releases.

Grants from various philanthropic foundations provided the money used for her continuous travel and feminist networking activities. Staupers logged thousands of miles, spoke with hundreds of black nurses, and welded the NACGN into a powerful instrument for social change. She urged black nurses in major urban areas to form cells of local citizens, so that they could more effectively implement the programs and strategies designed at NACGN headquarters. The NACGN organized and sponsored regional institutes to which it invited key nursing figures, white and black, to discuss openly plans for further action. They particularly emphasized the need to arouse public support against the discrimination and segregation of black women nurses.

Plans to effect the complete integration of black women into the U.S. armed forces unfolded gradually as the war progressed. During the first years of peace time mobilization, 1940 and 1941, Staupers concentrated on preventing the exclusion of black women from the Army and Navy Nurse Corps; once the war began she fought to have abolished the quotas that had been established by the Army. Throughout 1943 and 1944 she challenged the Army's practice of assigning black nurses only to care for German prisoners of war and not to white American soldiers. In addition Staupers cooperated with other groups to ensure that legislative measures proposed in Congress concerning nurses and hospitals contained anti-discrimination clauses. In spite of the continuous NACGN pressure, the U.S. Navy proved to be unalterably opposed to the induction of black women into the Navy Nurse Corps.

The American Red Cross Nursing Service under the leadership of Mary Beard in 1939 was, as in World War I, designated the official agency for the procurement of nursing personnel for the armed services. In the summer of that year Virginia Dunbar, Beard's assistant director, contacted Staupers to formulate the requirements for black nurses who desired to serve in the armed forces nurse corps. As most black nurses residing in southern states were barred from membership in state nurses associations, Staupers and Dunbar agreed to consider membership in the NACGN an acceptable substitute. Dunbar expressed concern that large numbers of black women would decide not to enroll, the likelihood of which was great, considering the continued hostility many black Americans harbored toward the American Red Cross. For example, Hastie and Granger both questioned the desirability of designating the Red Cross as the chief procurement agency for nursing personnel in the armed forces. They cited the Red Cross' policy of separating the blood of black donors from that of whites as an indication of the organization's racial bias. In spite of these reservations Staupers nevertheless urged Dunbar to send letters and application forms to all black nurses training schools, nurse superintendents, and hospitals. She appealed to Claude Barnett, of the Associated Negro Press, to publicize the fact that black nurses should enroll in the Red Cross in order to enter Army service. She asserted with determination that "we will not be left out" this time.

In addition to membership in a professional nurses association, armed forces nurses were required to be between the ages of eighteen and thirty-five. Nurses were expected to be single, divorced, or widowed. Another set of stipulations required that the potential nurses corps recruit provide references of her good moral character. Nurses in the Army and Navy Corps received a lower initial salary than any other nurse in government employ.

In spite of these deterrents, and the fact that there was so much reluctance about recruiting them, black women responded well to the call. Approximately 350 black women enrolled in the Red

Cross Nursing Service, anticipating appointment in the Army Nursing Corps. As it turned out, only 117 were judged eligible for the First Reserve. Many were eliminated because of marriage and age. Several other black enrollees saw their hopes of being inducted dashed against the wall of racial exclusion. In mid-1940 they received letters informing them that the Army did not have a program that would permit the utilization of the services of black nurses. A few of the black nurses angrily forwarded copies of the rejection letters to Staupers at NACGN headquarters. An incensed Staupers wrote Beard and railed against the hypocrisy of urging black women to join up and serve their country and then callously rejecting their applications. She exploded, "We fail to understand how America can say to the World that in this country we are ready to defend democracy when its Army and Navy is committed to a policy of discrimination." The die was cast. Clearly then, the next move was up to the Army.

On October 25, 1940, on the same day Secretary of War Henry Stimson appointed Hastie, then dean of the Howard University Law School, as his civilian aide on Negro Affairs, James C. Magee, surgeon general of the U.S. Army, announced the War Department's "plan for the use of colored personnel." According to the policy statement, separate black wards were to be designated in station hospitals where the number of black troops was sufficient to warrant separate facilities. In the South and Southwest, where the overwhelming percentage of black troops was located, several exclusively black hospitals were to be established: Camp Livingston in Louisiana, Ft. Bragg in North Carolina, and Fort Huachuca in Arizona. The black wards and hospitals were to be manned entirely by black doctors, dentists, nurses, and attendants. In a later official clarification, Magee stated, "Where only a few of that race are to be hospitalized in any given hospital . . . it would . . . be poor economy to set aside separate wards for the segregation of such cases."

The black press, nursing organizations, and black physicians immediately rallied to protest the War Department's segregation policy. In defense of his position, Magee asserted that he "would not place white soldiers in the position where they would have to accept service from Negro professionals." The War Department from the very beginning disclaimed to be an "appropriate medium for effecting social adjustments." One War Department officer would later explain to Staupers that the racial segregation supported and practiced by the U.S. Army derived from the conviction that "men who are fulfilling the same obligations, suffering the same dislocation of their private lives, and wearing the identical uniform should, within the confines of the military establishment, have the same privileges for rest and relaxation" that they enjoyed at home.

Staupers and a group of black nurses requested a meeting with Julia O. Flikke, head of the Army Nurses Corps. A few weeks following the October announcement black nurses met with Flikke, Major General George F. Lull, the deputy surgeon general for the War Department, and Colonel Love. Both Love and Lull simply reiterated the official policy: black nurses in limited numbers would be called upon to serve black troops in segregated wards and in separate military hospitals. Staupers and the NACGN committee found themselves in a dilemma. They had envisioned a broader use of black women and what had been offered fell far short of their desires. Yet it was better than total rejection. Consequently, the NACGN decided to accept, for the time being, the half-opened door. They reasoned that once a handful of black nurses penetrated, then they could intensify agitation for more complete integration. The group refused, however, to compromise on the second proposal. Love had asked if the NACGN would be willing to assume responsibility for the recruitment of black nurses for the Army Nurse Corps as the need arose. Staupers adamantly rejected the suggestion, reminding the colonel that such tasks were the responsibility of the American Red Cross Nursing Service of which black nurses were members.

Although the meeting resulted in very little change in official Army and War Department policy, the NACGN's militant stance nevertheless initiated later changes. Magee announced in January 1941 the Army's decision to recruit fifty-six black nurses who would be assigned to the black installations at Camp Livingston and Fort Bragg. Staupers, desiring to strengthen the NACGN and to present a semblance of advancement to her followers, quickly sought to capitalize upon the announced quota. She confided to Marion B. Seymour, the chair of the NACGN's National Defense Committee: "I hope this story will get to the newspapers as coming from this organization before [Walter White] gets a chance to claim credit for it after all the work we have done." She quickly sent press releases to the editors of the leading black newspapers: Chicago *Defender*, Amsterdam *News*, New York *Age*, Pittsburgh *Courier*, and the Norfolk *Journal and Guide*.

Although she desired to obtain credit for the NACGN for the announcement of the induction of black women nurses into the Army Nurse Corps, Staupers realized that the quota of fifty-six was a slap in the face. As she pointed out, the quota implied that black nurses were inferior to the other nurses. Quotas were both floors and ceilings. The important question, simply put, now became how could she secure the foundation yet raise the roof. Like many other black leaders, Staupers found herself being pulled in two directions: the first toward the elimination of segregation and discrimination, and the second toward attempting to exploit to the fullest the possibilities for the use of black nurses within a segregated system. However, she found a way to do both and informed a nurse colleague, "Our next job is to see that our nurses are not segregated in those states where segregation is not approved by law."

Opportunity to fight for this objective came a few months later. In March 1941 members of the subcommittee on Negro Health of the Health and Medical Committee of the National Defense Council met with Magee, all of the assistant surgeon generals, Brigadier General Fairbanks, Colonel Love, and civilian aide Hastie. The subcommittee on Negro Health was comprised of the black Chicago physician, M. O. Bousfield, chair and director of Negro Health of the Julius Rosenwald Fund; Russell Dixon, dean of the Howard University School of Dentistry; A. N. Vaughn, president of the black National Medical Association; Albert W. Dent, Dillard University president and superintendent of the black Flint-Goodridge Hospital in New Orleans; and Staupers. The subcommittee at Staupers' insistence strongly urged that the plan for segregated wards for black troops not be extended to areas outside the South. Staupers pointed out that black Americans had made very substantial progress in civilian life in the integration of black patients and professionals into general hospitals. The subcommittee argued that "the extension of the segregated ward plan to many areas of the country would represent an unfortunate reversal of current trends."

The members spent much time discussing the quotas that called for, in addition to the fifty-six nurses, only 120 doctors and forty-four dentists. They unanimously objected to the quotas as being disproportionately small even for the service of black troops stationed in the South. They implored Magee to use his influence in favor of an increase. Magee adamantly supported the official policy of "segregation without discrimination." The black press castigated the obdurate Magee. The Philadelphia *Tribune* editor observed, "It has become apparent to onlookers in Washington, that at least some of the difficulties which have been experienced by black professionals in the medical branches of the armed forces have their origin in the office of one man. He is Major General James C. Magee." Most members of the military bureaucracy staunchly adhered to the quota system. Magee was, of course, reflecting the views of his superiors in the War Department, who proved unyielding in their position. Robert P. Patterson, the undersecretary of war, declared that in establishing separate units the War Department could not be judged guilty of any discrimination against black nurses or physicians. He maintained that "the Medical Department has not discriminated in any sense against the Negro medical professions, nurses, or enlisted men. It has assigned Negro personnel in keeping with War Department policy and provided field and service units in support of Negro troops with Negro Personnel." Patterson continued, smugly noting that for the first time in the history of the Army opportunity had been furnished the black medical profession and ancillary services "to exercise full professional talent through the establishment of separate departments at two of our large cantonment hospitals for the care of Negro soldiers."

Thus, as far as War Department officials were concerned, segregation, implying only separation, was nondiscriminatory if equal facilities were provided. Black Americans, on the other hand, considered the concept of enforced segregation discriminatory. From their perspective separation prevented freedom of movement and produced inequalities of facilities and opportunities. Traditionally, minority groups possessed few means of enforcing equality guarantees. Staupers, arguing from a black perspective, contended, "My position is that, as long as either one of the services reject Negro nurses they are discriminated against and as long as either Services continue to assign them to duty as separate Units they are segregated."

Hastie, in his function as civilian aide to the secretary of war, tried valiantly to convince the War Department of the unfairness of quotas and segregation. He urged that these flaws be rectified or abolished before they became too entrenched. His carefully drafted recommendations for the desegregation of the Army were summarily rejected. According to one student of the era, the general staff took the point of view that Hastie wished the Army "to carry out a complete social revolution against the will of the nation." Days before the Japanese bombed Pearl Harbor, Hastie and the Army's high command had reached an impasse. General George C. Marshall wrote in response to Hastie's desegregation memorandum. "The War Department cannot ignore the social relationships between negroes and whites which have been established by the American people through custom and habit." Marshall added that "either through lack of opportunity or other causes the level of intelligence and occupational skill of the negro population is considerably below that of the white." He predicted that were the Army to engage in social experiments only "danger to efficiency, discipline, and morale" would result. Finally, he observed that the Army had attained maximum strength by properly placing its personnel in accordance with individual capabilities. This racist response coupled with several other examples of blatant disregard for him and his recommendations left Hastie no alternative but to resign as civilian aide to the secretary of war. This he did on January 31, 1943.

However, compared to the position adopted by the U.S. Navy, the Army was a model of racial enlightenment. The Navy found unnecessary the establishment of quotas, for it held black women simply ineligible and undesirable for service in the Navy Nurse Corps. According to Lt. Commander Sue S. Dauser, superintendent of the Navy Nurse Corps, Navy nurses were special nurses. They combined the responsibilities and roles of teacher, counselor, dietician, laboratory technician, X-ray operator, bookkeeper, and confidante of the sick. The Navy nurse was required to instruct hospital corpsmen in modern nursing methods. In turn the men so taught would be responsible for the welfare of the patients in the sickbays of battleships, cruisers, destroyers, and other combat vessels to which members of the Nurse Corps were not assigned. While the Army nurse engaged in some teaching activity, this was considered incidental when compared to ward or bedside duties. In sum, a Navy nurse had to be a "tactful, clearminded administrator and teacher." Presumably black women were devoid of such qualities. Furthermore, there were very few black sailors in the Navy.

Yet midway through the war both the Army and Navy moved hesitatingly toward greater integration. Staupers received notice in 1943 that the Navy had decided, at last, to place the matter of inducting black nurses "under consideration." The Army had raised its quota of black nurses to 160; 30 of them assigned to foreign duty and another 31 were deployed to form a new separate unit at Ft. Clark, Texas. These actions did not appease Staupers.

Frustrated by her inability to persuade the Navy and War Department to abolish quotas completely and to institute plans for immediate and full integration of black nurses, Staupers resolved to present the case of the black nurses to America's First Lady. Shortly after she made contact with Eleanor Roosevelt, the First Lady sent discreet inquiries to Secretary of War Stimson and to Beard. She wrote, "I have several protests lately that due to the shortage of nurses, the colored nurses be allowed to serve where there is not serious objection to it." While Stimson's response was essentially defensive and noncommittal, Beard confessed that the American Red Cross Nursing Service had been "greatly concerned with the unequal treatment of qualified Negro nurses as compared with the white nurses" serving in the armed forces. She reassured the First Lady that the National Nursing Council for War Service was attempting quietly to influence the assignment policy of the Army and Nurse Corps. Elmira B. Wickenden, executive secretary of the National Nursing Council, offered similar reassurances. Indeed, the National Nursing Council in late 1943 had sent the following resolution to the surgeons general of the Army and Navy Medical Corps: "Be it resolved that Negro graduate registered nurses be appointed to the Army (or Navy) Nurse Corps on the same basis as any other American nurses who meet the professional requirements, as was done in the last war."

Staupers' patience had grown thin; she wanted results, not promises or resolutions. Propitiously, 1944 was a presidential election year. Staupers let it be known in the appropriate political circles that she was an avowed Roosevelt supporter and did not wish to make a fuss or "give any publicity to the present situation during this pre-election period." A friend, Anna Arnold Hedgeman, the executive secretary of A. Philip Randolph's National Council for a Permanent Fair Employment Practice Committee, interceded and suggested to Eleanor Roosevelt that she invite Staupers to meet with her.

Staupers and Roosevelt met in November 1944, whereupon the NACGN executive secretary described in detail the black nurses' relationship with the armed forces. She informed the First Lady that 82 black nurses were serving 150 patients at the Station Hospital at Ft. Huachuca at a time when the Army was complaining of a dire nursing shortage. Staupers expounded at length on the practice of using black women to take care of German prisoners of war. She asked, rhetorically, if this was to be the special role of the black nurse in the war. Staupers elaborated. "When our women hear of the great need for nurses in the Army and when they enter the Service it is with the high hopes that they will be used to nurse sick and wounded soldiers who are fighting our country's enemies and not primarily to care for these enemies." Roosevelt, apparently moved by the discussion, applied her own subtle pressure to Norman T. Kirk, surgeon general of the U.S. Army, Secretary Stimson, and the Navy's Rear Admiral W. J. C. Agnew.

As 1944 faded into 1945, events on the black nursing front took a sudden upswing. In early January 1945, Kirk announced to a crowd of 300 nurses, politicians, and private citizens assembled at the Hotel Pierre in New York City that in order for the Army to be adequately supplied with nurses it might be advisable to institute a draft. Staupers immediately rose to her feet and pointedly asked the surgeon general, "If nurses are needed so desperately, why isn't the Army using colored nurses?" She continued, "Of 9,000 registered Negro nurses the Army has taken 247, the Navy takes none." Kirk, visibly uncomfortable according to press reports, replied, "There are 7,000 Negro nurses in comparison to a 200,000 total in the United States. I believe that the average share of colored nurses in the army is equal to the total number of Negro troops." News of the exchange received nationwide coverage and made the headlines of virtually every black newspaper in the country. The Boston *Guardian* declared, "It is difficult to find calm words to describe the folly which color prejudice assumes in the desperate shortage of nurses." The editor anticipated the kind of future action that occurred when he predicted that "the Commander-in-Chief will be backed up in this instance by the great majority of the people if he orders a cessation of the outrageous ban on nurses because of skin color and thus helps to modernize the armed forces by ridding them of the fogyism which is the greatest barrier to national growth."

Compounding the tension surrounding the Kirk-Staupers incident, on January 6, 1945, in a radio transmitted address to the U.S. Congress, President Roosevelt announced his strong desire for the enactment of legislation amending the Selective Service Act of 1940 to provide for the induction of nurses into the Army. He justified the need for such legislation on the grounds that volunteering had not produced the number of nurses required. Roosevelt adopted this position over the objections of Chief of Staff Marshall and Major General Stephen G. Henry, both of whom advised that the proposed legislation would be "most discriminatory in that it singles out a small group of especially trained women for induction under the Selective Service Act." As if on cue, however, Representative Andrew J. May (Democrat, Kentucky) introduced the Draft Nurse Bill, H. R. 1284 79th Congress, on January 9, 1945, and it was immediately referred to the Committee on Military Affairs.

The ensuing public outcry was quickly forthcoming and totally unexpected and it jarred the military brass. Roosevelt apparently had not the slightest appreciation for the depth of public dissatisfaction with the restrictive quotas for black nurses. Staupers with alacrity sought to harness, direct, and channel the wave of public anger and sympathy. She urged black nurses, women's groups, and sympathetic white allies across the country to send telegrams directly to Roosevelt and May, protesting the exclusion, discrimination, and segregation of black nurses. Staupers in numerous press releases pleaded, "We stress again for the Negro nurses all over the country that they rally now as never before to the support of the NACGN." And rally they did. The sheer hypocrisy of calling for a draft of nurses while excluding large numbers of black nurses willing to serve was too much for many Americans to swallow. Telegrams poured into the White House from the National Association for the Advancement of Colored People (NAACP), the Catholic Interracial Council, National Nursing Council for War Services, Congress of Industrial Organizations, American Federation of Labor, National Board of the Young Women's Christian Association (YWCA), Alpha Kappa Alpha Sorority, Philadelphia Fellowship Commission, New York Citizens' Committee of the Upper West Side, National Negro Congress, National Council of Negro Women, United Council of Church Women, and the American Civil Liberties Union. From Cleveland, Jane Edna Hunter, president of the Ohio State Federation of Colored Women's Club and former nurse, in a telegram to the President declared: "If the proposal to draft nurses must be resorted to, then we urge that all inductees be given consideration on bases of training and fitness and allowed to serve in all branches of the Army and Navy and not restricted to Negro soldiers alone."

Buried beneath the avalanche of telegrams and seared by the heat of an inflamed public, Kirk, Agnew, and the War Department declared an end to quotas and exclusion. On January 20, 1945, Kirk stated that nurses would be accepted into the Army Nurse Corps without regard to race. On January 25, 1945, Admiral Agnew announced that the Navy Nurse Corps was now open to black women, and a few weeks later Phyllis Dailey became the first black woman to break the color barrier and receive induction into the Navy Nurse Corps. There was no outcry against accepting of black nurses into the armed forces nurse corps.

Eventually the War Department decided to stop the entire scheme to enact a draft of nurses. Staupers' carefully orchestrated telegram campaign and tedious years of continuous effort had culminated in the breaking of at least this one link in the chain that oppressed, excluded, and prohibited black women from the full realization of their civil rights. This was by no means the end of their war. It was, however, a welcome victory in what had been a long struggle overwhelmingly characterized by defeat, setbacks, humiliation, and frustration. The proposal to draft nurses and the ensuing congressional debate had been the catalytic component to which Staupers and black nurses had joined their struggle for full integration into the armed forces and from which they gained support and sympathy from both white and black Americans. Presidential and congressional speeches bemoaning the shortage of nurses had only fed the fire that Staupers' public protests had generated. While Staupers and black nurses may have supported in principle the nurse-draft legislation, they nevertheless used it to draw attention to the fact that they had been excluded, segregated, and subjected to discrimination. She displayed a flawless sense of timing and political maneuvering.

The battle to integrate black women nurses into the Army and Navy Nurse Corps had been an exhaustive and draining one. In 1946 Staupers relinquished her position as executive secretary to take a much needed and well-earned rest. This was to be of short duration, however, for Staupers considered her work incomplete. She had not accomplished her major objective, the integration of black women into the ANA. Beginning in 1934, Staupers and Riddle had appeared before the House of Delegates at the biennial meeting of the ANA. After ten years of fruitless persistence, Staupers wrote Congresswoman Bolton, "Each year although we have not gained our ultimate objective we have gained friends and are in a stronger position than ever before." After the 1944 meeting Staupers confided to Bolton her hope that "integration may be an accomplished fact before 1945."

General integration into the ANA did not come in 1945. It came three years later. In 1948 the ANA House of Delegates opened the gates to black membership, appointed a black woman nurse as assistant executive secretary in its national headquarters, and witnessed the election of Riddle to the board of directors.

For Staupers, the breakdown of the exclusionary barriers was a triumphant vindication of her leadership role. In 1950 Staupers, now president of the NACGN, convinced black nurses that the purpose for which the organization had been established had been achieved and that it was time to dissolve the NACGN. Staupers wrote in a press release dated January 26, 1951, that as far as it was known the NACGN was the first major black national organization to terminate its work "because it feels that its program of activities is not longer necessary." She continued, "The doors have been opened," and the black nurse "has been given a seat in the top councils." Staupers later exulted, "We are now a part of the great organization of nurses, the American Nurses' Association."

Staupers received many accolades for her leadership in the integration fight and in the dissolution of the NACGN. By far, the crowning acknowledgement and recognition of Staupers' role and contribution in the quest of black nurses for civil rights and human dignity came from a rather unexpected source. The Spingarn Award Committee of the NACGN chose Staupers to be the recipient of the Spingarn Medal for 1951. Channing H. Tobias, director of the Phelps-Stokes Fund, confided to Staupers, "I know the committee was especially appreciative of the fact that you were willing to sacrifice organization to ideals when you advocated and succeeded in realizing the full integration of Negro nurses into the organized ranks of the nursing profession of this country."

Mabel Keaton Staupers was one of the truly outstanding black women leaders in this century. The key identifying characteristic of her leadership style was the establishment of close working relationships with leading white women, black male heads of organizations, and fellow black women nurses. She secured her base first, that is the NACGN, by maintaining continuous communication and contact with the membership. Staupers furthermore manipulated the press extremely well by releasing statements at the most strategic moment. Her public remarks unfailingly emphasized the cause for which she was fighting. In so doing, she constantly reminded the country of the plight of black women nurses, of the racism and sexism that robbed them of the opportunities to develop their full human potential. Small of frame, energetic, and fast-talking, Staupers knew when to accept a half-loaf of advancement and when to press on for total victory. It is unlikely that the successful integration of black women into American nursing on all levels could have been accomplished during the 1940s without Staupers at the helm of the NACGN.

Sources

UNPUBLISHED SOURCES

American Red Cross Manuscript Collection. National Archives, Washington, D.C.

Claude Barnett Papers. Chicago Historical Society, Chicago, Ill.

Frances Payne Bolton Papers. Western Reserve Historical Society, Cleveland, Ohio.

National Association of Colored Graduate Nurses Collection. New York City Public Library, Schomburg Afro-American History Collection, New York, N.Y.

Eleanor Roosevelt Papers. Franklin Delano Roosevelt Library, Hyde Park, N.Y.

Rosenwald Fund Papers. Fisk University Library, Nashville, Tenn.

Mabel Keaton Staupers Papers. Amistad Research Center, New Orleans, La.

Mabel Keaton Staupers Papers. Moorland-Spingarn Research Center, Howard University, Washington, D.C.

Records of the Surgeon General's Office of the U.S. Army. National Archives Research Center, Suitland, Md.

Records of the War Department, General and Special Staff. National Archives Research Center, Suitland, Md.

PUBLISHED SOURCES

Carnegie, Mary Elizabeth. *The Path We Tread: Blacks in Nursing, 1854–1984.* Philadelphia: Lippincott, 1986.

Hine, Darlene Clark. *Black Women in White: Racial Conflict and Cooperation in the Nursing Profession, 1890-1950.* Bloomington: Indiana University Press, 1989.

Staupers, Mabel Keaton. *No Time for Prejudice: A Story of the Integration of Negroes in Nursing in the United States.* New York: Macmillan Co., 1961.

Thoms, Adah B. *Pathfinders: A History of Progress of Colored Graduate Nurses.* New York: McKay, 1929.

PART 4

Carter G. Woodson

White Philanthropy and
Negro Historiography

Today Afro-American history is a legitimate and recognized area of study. Indeed, the recent proliferation of excellent, prize-winning books attests to the vitality and excitement abounding in this field of American history. In October 1983, the American Historical Association (AHA) sponsored a major state-of-the-art conference on the Study and Teaching of Afro-American History, providing even further testimony to the maturation of this sub-specialty within American history. This was not always the case. Around the turn of the century few American historians acknowledged that Afro-Americans had a history, or at least one worth investigating. Much of the credit for the rise of what was then called "Negro history" belongs to one man.

Carter Goodwin Woodson was born in 1875 in New Canton, Virginia. He earned a B.A. degree (1907) and an M.A. degree (1908) from the University of Chicago and subsequently received a Ph.D. degree in American history (1912) from Harvard University, under the direction of Edward Channing, McLean Professor of Ancient and Modern History. Whereas Woodson's academic credentials ostensibly qualified him for "inside" status, racial discrimination relegated him to the "outside" or periphery of the historical profession. Unable to secure an appointment at any of the leading American institutions, Woodson taught French, Spanish, English, and history, and eventually became principal of the all-black Armstrong Manual Training High School in Washington, D.C. Between 1919 and 1922, Woodson served brief tenures as Dean of the School of Liberal Arts both at

Howard University and at the West Virginia State College. By 1922 frequent contentions, especially with white administrators of black schools, soured Woodson on academic teaching and led him to aver that he would never again work within the confines of a university or college.

Embittered and disillusioned by the fierce academic politics in black educational institutions, Woodson was further alienated by the insensitivity of the American Historical Association to the peculiar constraints which proscribed the professional development of historians of African descent. Woodson chafed under the exclusion of black scholars from active participation in the affairs of the American Historical Association. To be sure, Woodson and other black historians could join and pay membership dues to the AHA, but racial customs and practices frustrated all their attempts to attend conferences held in southern and some northern cities.[1]

As Woodson surveyed his meager options for a career as a professional historian he concluded that the only path open to him and others similarly encumbered was to create a separate, alternative institutional structure which would facilitate the researching, writing, and publishing of the history of the Negro in America. To accomplish his objectives Woodson needed money. Thus, Woodson's efforts to launch the scientific study of Negro history brought him into close association with major white philanthropists and officers of the Carnegie Foundation, Julius Rosenwald Foundation, and the three Rockefeller trusts—the Rockefeller Foundation, the Laura Spelman Rockefeller Memorial, and the General Education Board. These relationships and interactions were never harmonious and were attenuated by intermittent ideological battles. While the philanthropists provided much of the early support for Woodson's activities, he steadfastly refused to accommodate to their wishes and suggestions. Woodson's paradoxical and, at times, peculiar relationship with other outstanding white and black historians during the 1920s and 1930s illuminates his views of what should comprise the substance and structure of Negro history.

As a first step in the process of establishing an independent organization through which he could research, write, and publish the history of the Negro, Woodson, in the fall of 1915, met with a small group of black professionals at the Wabash Avenue Young Men's

Christian Association (YMCA) building in Chicago and founded the Association for the Study of Negro Life and History (ASNLH). A month later, he incorporated ASNLH in Washington, D.C., with George Cleveland Hall, a black physician in Chicago, installed as chairman of the executive council, and Jesse E. Moorland, head of the black component of the YMCA, as secretary-treasurer, and himself as executive director. As dominant spokesman and chief architect of the ASNLH, Woodson described its purpose to be the "scientific" study of "neglected aspects of the Negro life and history," a plan which included the training of a cadre of young black men in the canons of historical research. Woodson made it clear from the outset that he would conduct the affairs of the young organization with an iron fist and would tolerate little opposition from council members or from the young scholars brought into the fold. In 1916, acting without the advice and consent of the executive council, Woodson borrowed $400 to produce the first issue of the *Journal of Negro History*. Appalled by his failure to consult with them, one member of the executive council resigned immediately and another threatened to do so.[2]

Woodson early envisioned that ASNLH would rest on a broad public foundation and represent more than an elite cadre of black scholars simply communicating among themselves. The ASNLH therefore quickly became more than an intellectual association of historians, evolving into an institution which appealed to the larger black community. Within a few years Woodson had deftly engineered a national constituency for the ASNLH comprised of local civil officials, primary and secondary school teachers, church leaders, women's groups, and fraternal organizations. The process involved several steps: organizing a series of local Negro history clubs that soon became branches of the ASNLH; inaugurating in 1926 the annual celebration of Negro History Week and developing history kits outlining and highlighting significant themes and personalities in the Negro past; holding annual conventions in which scores of branch members arrived at designated cities for intellectual as well as social stimulation; and finally, in 1937, issuing the *Negro History Bulletin* designed specifically for secondary school teachers and interested lay people who desired more popular versions of Negro history than those found in the *Journal*.[3] Thus Woodson's Negro history movement was a three-tiered operation. At the base were the ASNLH branch members who paid nominal dues, organized the special annual celebrations for Negro History Week, and attended the ASNLH conventions. The middle tier was comprised of the small group of professionally trained historians who conducted much of the research, wrote the articles, books, and reports that were then published in the ASNLH's *Journal, Bulletin*, or by its affiliate, Associated Publishers, founded in 1920. Woodson headed the ASNLH pyramid, serving simultaneously as the executive director, and editor of the *Journal*, the *Bulletin*, and of Associated Publishers.

In the face of the disillusionment of the post-World War I years, Woodson continued his endeavors to fashion a usable, more satisfying historical anchor upon which black Americans could fasten their dreams and visions of a better future. Of those years he wrote, "I have made every sacrifice for this movement. I have spent all my time doing this one thing and trying to do it efficiently."[4] As historian Lawrence Levine has observed, the 1920s was a decade of black revitalization epitomized in the Harlem Renaissance and the rise of Marcus Garvey. Both Garvey and the Renaissance reflected the mood of black Americans who yearned for a greater appreciation of black culture and liberation from alien influences. While Garvey and his Universal Negro Improvement Association enjoined black Americans to "canonize our own saints, create our own martyrs, and elevate to positions of fame and honor black men and women who have made their distinct contributions to our racial history,"[5] Woodson, through the ASNLH, attempted to do precisely that.

Although Woodson responded to the mood and needs of black Americans, he was no less influenced by his generation of prominent white historians, men like Herbert Baxter Adams at The Johns Hopkins University, Albert Bushnell Hart and Edward Channing at Harvard University, and Charles Kendall Adams at the University of Michigan; Adams, Hart, and Channing were all pioneers of "scientific history" in the United States and organizers of the historical profession. Woodson shared with these historians a conviction that "truth" about the past lay in the vast, unexplored territory of original and specific data that historians must gather and interpret. Yet Woodson was also attracted to the "New History" and its progressive era advocates like James Harvey Robinson, Charles A. Beard, and Carl L.

Becker. The historians of the "New History" called for a history that spoke of contemporary problems and drew upon the social sciences.[6]

Although Woodson identified with both the "scientific history" and "New History" proponents, there were significant ideological departures in his thought. He argued that Negro history should serve a dual purpose. It should help to shape the character and morality of black Americans and at the same time serve as a means with which to establish a rightful black presence on both the historical and contemporary landscapes. He wrote that Negro history must ensure that "the world see the Negro as a participant rather than as a lay figure in history." Woodson insisted, moreover, that the racial background of the historian not only determined the ability to gather data but also affected or influenced the resultant interpretations. Early on he declared that "while the Association welcomes the cooperation of white scholars in certain projects . . . it proceeds also on the basis that its important objectives can be attained through Negro investigators who are in a position to develop certain aspects of the life and history of the race which cannot be otherwise treated." He concluded, "In the final analysis, this work must be done by Negroes. . . . The point here is rather that Negroes have the advantage of being able to think black." In so positing, Woodson anticipated by several decades the heated debates between black and white scholars during the 1960s which provoked C. Vann Woodward to declare, "Negro history is too important to be left entirely to Negro historians."[7]

An examination of Woodson's leadership of ASNLH and his editorship of the *Journal* further illuminates the strategies he devised and employed in order to achieve his objective of creating a body of scholarship about Negroes produced by Negro historians. As a first step in his quest for intellectual acceptance and professional autonomy, Woodson appointed to the ASNLH executive council not only historians and educators but also a number of wealthy and socially prominent whites. Woodson had once remarked to Joel E. Spingarn, then chairman of the National Association for the Advancement of Colored People's executive council, that "millionaires cannot be reached through letters." Occasionally there were exceptions. At least three white philanthropists—Julius Rosenwald, George Foster Peabody, and James Hardy Dillard—responded favorably to Woodson's written appeal and consented to serve on the ASNLH executive council. Rosenwald, who had amassed a considerable fortune as head of Sears, Roebuck and Company and was a longtime benefactor of Booker T. Washington, added only one reservation. He wrote, "I am entirely willing to have my name included with such committee provided it is understood that I am not obligated to take part in the organization."[8]

Carefully selected and assiduously courted, these men conferred upon the ASNLH an aura of respectability and thus legitimacy, while their personal and business connections immeasurably enhanced fund-raising potential. As cautious as Woodson was to select the "right" kind of whites—that is, those who like Julius Rosenwald preferred not to be directly involved in ASNLH affairs—he miscalculated in two cases. Not only were white historian Albert Bushnell Hart and white educator Thomas Jesse Jones unwilling to play the passive and mute role desired, they soon would question and eventually denounce Woodson's rigid, somewhat autocratic control of the organization.

Woodson knew that a secure and adequate financial base was critical to a systematic study of Negro history. He therefore devised and launched a two-pronged fund-raising effort. His initial mailing of one copy of the first issue of the *Journal of Negro History* to approximately 200 philanthropists and prospective donors netted the Association a mere $14.[9] A second mailing garnered a financial commitment from Julius Rosenwald who personally pledged $100 toward every issue of the *Journal* produced. Woodson also sought subscribers and by the end of 1917 these numbered approximately 1,300 with 995 actually paying the $1.00 subscription fee. An additional 300 copies of the *Journal* were sold at newsstands each quarter. In spite of this numerical success, Woodson still had to use personal funds to defray *Journal* expenses.[10]

In response to appeals for donations, a few of Woodson's white supporters suggested that the subscription fees were too modest. Channing, for example, chided Woodson for not charging enough for the *Journal*, even though he understood that higher prices would place the publication beyond the reach of most African Americans.[11] Another $100 a year contributor, Harold H. Swift of the Union Stock Yard, cautioned against publishing such a high quality quarterly. He reminded Woodson that "pioneer work usually has to be done in a relatively cheap fashion."[12] Woodson, defending the low fees, argued that he would not publish the *Journal* at all if some other publication would agree to serve the same purpose. More to the point he insisted it was "merely a means to an end." That is, the *Journal* was essential to popularizing the study of Negro life and history and "for this reason it is being sold far below cost to bring it within reach of all."[13]

Woodson continued to publish and sell the *Journal* below cost. His 1918 appeal to George Foster Peabody repeated his lament that he had reached his "extremity" and that the *Journal* would die if nothing happened to alleviate his financial distress.[14] This request for funds included an appeal for money to pay for the employment of a special business and fund-raising agent. To impress upon the philanthropist the urgency of his fiscal requirements, Woodson even implored R. R. Moton, successor to Booker T. Washington as head of Tuskegee Institute and a longtime beneficiary of Peabody largess, to contact the philanthropist and to urge him to influence or "interest some friends of friends" to donate "a thousand dollars" each to save the *Journal of Negro History*.[15] Apparently moved by the entreaties, Peabody did in fact contact several millionaire friends, explaining why they should support the *Journal*. He wrote, "I believe it would be a great misfortune at this particular stage of the Negro's development . . . to have this *Journal* suspended."[16] Wallace Buttrick at the Rockefeller Foundation showed the letter to John D. Rockefeller who quickly refused to contribute.[17] Rosenwald likewise declined to increase his annual $100 pledge, explaining that he was in fact not much interested in "the printer's ink method" of helping the Negro.[18]

Unable to raise large sums to save the *Journal*, Woodson changed his fund-raising appeal. In 1920 he focused more on securing money to support a massive research program under the aegis of the ASNLH. The new emphasis proved successful. When James R. Angell assumed the presidency of the Carnegie Corporation, Woodson submitted a grant proposal and implored a fellow historian, J. Franklin Jameson, the director of the Department of Historical Research in the Carnegie Institution in Washington, D.C. and former editor of the *American Historical Review*, to support it. Jameson in turn persuaded Angell that the Carnegie Corporation should contribute to Woodson's program. Jameson pointed out that "neither Congress nor the states [the southern states] most concerned, nor the southern historical societies, nor even the southern universities are likely to spend money in the field of such history, yet it is the history of something like ten percent of our population, and a history which cast a light upon important problems of the present and future." Echoing Woodson, Jameson moreover asserted, "There are important portions of it [Negro History] which cannot be so well elaborated by a white man as by a colored man—fields in which a colored man can get by 'field work' facts and documents which a white man could not readily obtain." Of primary importance, Jameson concluded, was the "unusual opportunity that is presented, when a colored man competently qualified, and who has the confidence of his race, is ready to embark upon this line of investigation."[19] Shortly thereafter Angell approved an appropriation of $25,000 to be paid in annual $5,000 installments to the Association, stipulating that the money be used to pay the organization's accumulated debts, operating expenses, and the salaries of researchers in Negro history.[20] The Carnegie grant spurred Woodson to continue to pursue additional funds.

Cloaked now with the increased legitimacy which the Carnegie grant conferred, Woodson again approached other key philanthropists. He petitioned the Laura Spelman Rockefeller Memorial (LSRM) for additional funds to support more extensive research, suggesting that more money would permit him time to pursue the study of Negroes prior to 1861, a topic which he described as "the most difficult aspect of Negro history." He outlined his research agenda and attempted to distinguish it from other works in the field. "What I have in mind is not to follow the well-beaten path of the usual studies of the Free Negro in the various states. These are mainly based on Southern laws defining the social, economic, and political status of this class." He alleged, "I can write a work of this sort every ninety days," adding, "Inasmuch as many of these laws were never enforced because every southern aristocrat was a law unto himself, such studies are not worth publishing. It will mean more to learn the real attitude of the white man toward the Negro as it is reflected in letters, diaries, plantation documents, and public records."

Woodson emphasized that he was not "primarily concerned with what was being done to and for the Negro but with what the Negro was thinking, feeling, attempting, and doing himself." Moreover, Woodson proposed that A. A. Taylor, a young black historian working on a Ph.D. degree at Harvard University, should be employed to complete research on a history of the social and economic conditions of the black population during Reconstruction in Virginia and South Carolina. (Later, other investigators were added to the Association staff. H. B. Campbell was charged with the task of collecting social and economic data on the black population in Florida from 1865 to 1880. George Francis Dow, the secretary of Essex Institute, was paid to gather data on the free Negroes in colonial New England, a subject that Lorenzo Greene would subsequently undertake.)[21]

It is clear that the generous Carnegie Corporation grant favorably impressed the LSRM officials. Although W. S. Richardson, secretary of the LSRM, pointed out that in 1918 Rockefeller had declined to contribute to ASNLH because "the undertaking was a small one and did not promise much success," Richardson now recommended that the LSRM alter its former position. He recommended to John D. Rockefeller that "on the basis of his [Woodson's] fact it is easy to see that much good may result where now there is misunderstanding from lack of authoritative information."[22] A few months later, a jubilant Woodson acknowledged receipt of a second $25,000 grant. The LSRM agreed to pay annual installments of $5,000, provided the sums be expended solely "for investigation including the Negro's part in the Reconstruction and the activities of the free Negroes before the Civil War." In a subsequent inter-office memorandum one LSRM official made it clear that the Memorial was interested primarily in the matter of continuous and methodical research on the problems of Negro life rather than in supporting the general ASNLH budget. The fund officers noted, however, that by providing enough money to cover the salaries of the research assistants, Woodson would have more time to direct the affairs of the Association and to edit and publish the *Journal*.[23] By 1922 Woodson had apparently resolved his financial woes. At this juncture, however, his problems with prominent white members of the ASNLH executive council threatened to destroy all that he had accomplished.

Disquiet between Hart, Jones, and Woodson erupted into a full-blown controversy shortly after Woodson had secured the $25,000 grants from the Carnegie Corporation and the Laura Spelman Rockefeller Memorial Fund. A long letter of resignation from Albert Bushnell Hart detailing Woodson's many faults shocked his philanthropic patrons. Hart castigated not only Woodson's dictatorial manner but his plans for spending the grant money. Hart declared, "I beg hereby to lodge my protest against management which enables one man, however able, trained and capable, to lay out a plan greatly to his personal advantage." Elaborating, he objected specifically to Woodson's hiring of two investigators at "high salaries" to research topics of interest only to the director. Apparently Woodson had dismissed Hart's suggestions as to how funds should be spent, to wit, that "a group of from five to ten young colored students, men and women, . . . be sent to different universities to receive a year's intensive instruction in research and then engage in the work of the Society."[24]

When a man of Hart's reputation and stature resigned from an executive council of a black organization, white benefactors became concerned. Fellow ASNLH executive council member and investment banker George Foster Peabody quickly reassured Hart that he would investigate Woodson's program.[25] Similarly Rosenwald, who had previously professed disinterest in the operation of the organization, now ordered his secretary, William Graves, to reassess Woodson. In discreet letters to black associates and former friends of Woodson, namely Jesse Moorland of New York and Emmett J. Scott at Howard University, Graves confided that Rosenwald "naturally wants information in view of Dr. Hart's contentions and other reports." Actually, Rosenwald had grown increasingly suspicious of Woodson as rumors reached him to the effect that Woodson was inclined "toward the radical side."[26]

As the charges of mismanagement, alienation, and radicalism circulated, Woodson moved with alacrity. As far as Hart's resignation was concerned, Woodson wrote that while he did not consider the professor "a dishonest man" he described him as "very much advanced in years" and "rather quick on the trigger." In short, Woodson first dismissed Hart as one whose "main trouble" stemmed from Hart's mistaken assumption that he knew more about the affairs of the Association than he actually did. Perhaps sensing that Rosenwald, for one, would not be easily convinced that Hart was simply a meddlesome old fool, Woodson, following an elaborate delineation of his plans for the

Carnegie and LSRM money, decided that Hart's suggestion possessed some merit. Woodson thereupon assured Rosenwald that he would indeed seek additional funds with which to train young black scholars.[27]

As Woodson grappled with the problems created by the Hart resignation, he was confronted with the even more damaging allegations of executive council member Thomas Jesse Jones. Unlike Hart, Jones, a native of Wales, had taught at Hampton Institute prior to publishing the widely acclaimed *Report on Negro Education in the U.S.A.* in 1916. The report, financed by the Phelps-Stokes Fund, catapulted him into the national limelight and resulted in his appointment as educational director of the fund.[28] In order to improve his chances of securing more contributions from the Phelps-Stokes Fund, Woodson had placed Jones on the Association's executive council. Years later Woodson, still angry, recalled, "for five years, beginning in 1916, the Phelps-Stokes Fund gave our work annually $200, the usual amount they give agencies, not adequate to provide substantial aid, but sufficient to justify meddling."[29] Jones protested his ouster from the executive council, publicly accusing Woodson of reorganizing the body so as "to place radicals in charge." Furthermore, Jones contended that the new council was aimed "to stir up prejudice rather than promote scientific study."[30]

Woodson's response to Hart was mild compared to his treatment of Jones. Woodson declared heatedly that "an investigation will show that Dr. Jones is detested by ninety-five percent of all Negroes who are seriously concerned with the uplift of their race." Furthermore, he asserted that black people hated Jones because Jones was "the self-made white leader of the Negroes, exercising the exclusive privilege of informing white people as to who is a good Negro and who is a bad one, what school is worthy of support and what not, and how the Negroes should be helped and how not." Woodson justified the removal of Jones from the executive council as an act of political expedience, claiming "it had become unpopular to retain him in that position."[31]

In an effort to retain Rosenwald's support and to defend himself against allegations of radicalism, Woodson attempted to discredit Jones. He mused, "I am surprised indeed that Dr. Jones, by his propaganda, could make anyone think of me as radical or even socialistically inclined." Woodson added, "I have never believed, however, and have never tried to leave the impression that capitalism is a danger to society." To the contrary Woodson opined that "every man with common sense realized that the development of the modern world through capital has laid the foundation for the present progress of mankind."[32] Actually, Woodson's self-defense was unsuccessful; only the calm reassurances of Emmett Scott salvaged the relationship with Rosenwald. Scott, a longtime Woodson advocate, persuaded Rosenwald that he was not a radical unless a radical was one who "unsparingly denounced injustice and hypocrisy." Scott conceded that though Woodson was often difficult to deal with he was not "a follower of the cult which seeks the overthrow of the established order." Scott deplored the general tendency to label as "radical" any black man who fought for the rights of black people.[33]

Aftershocks of the executive council shake-down reverberated throughout the white philanthropic community. The Hart and Jones affairs eventually passed although not without considerable damage to Woodson's relationship with the philanthropists. While Rosenwald continued to support ASNLH, George Foster Peabody resigned and demanded that his name be removed from the Association's letterhead. The Phelps-Stokes Fund abruptly ceased all contributions and the Carnegie Corporation refused to renew the earlier grant once it had expired.[34]

During the mid-1920s the Association and Woodson nevertheless flourished as he and his associates used the Carnegie and LSRM monies to research and publish numerous articles and books on the Negro. These were the golden years of the ASNLH and the *Journal.* During this period Woodson completed *Free Negro Owners of Slaves in the United States in 1830,* a compilation of approximately 50,000 names of black men, women, and children extracted from the 1830 manuscript census schedules. His second volume, *Absentee Ownership of Slaves in the United States in 1830,* was based, in part, on the same body of research. *The Negro in South Carolina during the Reconstruction* was A. A. Taylor's major effort.[35] Each of these studies first appeared as a monograph length article in the *Journal of Negro History* and then was published in book form. By 1925, the Association had published ten different monographs through its affiliate, Associated Publishers, and the *Journal* had printed 6,000 pages of articles and documents concerning various aspects of black history and culture.

Unlike the Carnegie Corporation the officers of the LSRM renewed Woodson's grant in June 1926, thereby providing him with $22,800 payable in three $7,600 installments. Furthermore, the LSRM board appropriated an extra $15,000 to assist the Association in establishing a permanent publication endowment.[36] With this rather substantial increase in foundation support, Woodson immediately awarded stipends to several young black researchers: Abraham L. Harris began a study of the failure of black banks; Zora Neale Hurston started collecting black folklore in Florida; I. R. Marshall studied the development of black workers in occupations since the Civil War; and Charles H. Wesley, who later became chairman of the Department of History at Howard University, commenced to work on a study of black industrial development after the Civil War. Woodson used a portion of the money to publish a volume by a white scholar, Frank J. Klingberg, later professor of history at the University of California at Los Angeles, entitled *A Side-Light on Anglo-American Relations, 1839-1861, The Tappan Papers.*[37] In total, between February 1922 and December 1928 the LSRM contributed approximately $62,000 to Woodson and ASNLH.

This massive infusion of the Rockefeller money did not ease the worsening relationship between Woodson and the LSRM officers. As early as 1925 LSRM officials had suggested to Woodson that he should consider affiliating ASNLH with one of the black universities then receiving Rockefeller support. Woodson's position at that time had been decidedly negative. He had argued that the Negro colleges were a generation behind the Association and that the organization's work was the first and only systematic effort ever made by scholars of both races to treat the records of the Negro scientifically. He expressed the opinion that Negro institutions were not yet capable of doing advanced work in Negro history or in any other subject on the graduate level.[38]

Woodson's refusal to consider an affiliation with a black college or university frustrated his white benefactors. In 1929 his request for a renewal of the LSRM grant met with a cool reception.[39] LSRM officials decided to review the whole of their relationship with Woodson and most important to assess the scholarly merit of the books and the *Journal*. As part of this reevaluation officials invited several leading white historians who had written on slavery and reconstruction to give candid, confidential opinions of the Association, the *Journal of Negro History*, and the various historical monographs published by Woodson and his research associates. Among those responding were Ulrich B. Phillips—then of the University of Michigan, Walter L. Fleming of Vanderbilt University, William E. Dodd of the University of Chicago, and J. G. de Roulhac Hamilton of the University of North Carolina.

Considering the fact that Woodson had consistently and with considerable justification attacked all of the major works of these scholars on the grounds of racial bias,[40] it is not surprising that their evaluations of his writings were condescending and paternalistic. The fact remains that regardless of their assessments Woodson was doing work that no one else was undertaking at that time. Phillips assessed the work of the Association as "worthy in purpose and prospect rather than in present accomplishment." He argued that "Woodson and Taylor, who seem to be the chief performers, produce books too hastily. They don't take pains to save the reader pains, therefore, they don't get many readers." Phillips cited as an example Woodson's *Mind of the Negro*, which was a 700-page compilation of letters written by black men and women prior to the Civil War. He dismissed it as "a haystack in which needles may be found by perseverance," adding that it would have been more cogent if Woodson had left aside three-quarters of its "trivial or irrelevant" contents. Phillips noted that "at the present stage, amateurishness is to be expected" before urging the foundation to continue to support Woodson, his associates, and ASNLH. He declared, "the manifest enthusiasm merits encouragement along with a precept, perhaps, of more digestion and less volume of output."[41]

Conceding their initial pessimism over the value of Woodson's undertaking. Dodd and Fleming confessed that they had lately become, for different reasons, more favorably disposed. Dodd wrote, "The money which has been appropriated to this purpose has been better spent than any other money I know." He "heartily" endorsed continued support and ended by professing his wish that "they might have a great deal more."[42] Fleming admitted that he had read some issues of the *Journal* and while he did not consider "the history in it very sound," he believed that the standards of the *American Historical Review* should not be applied to the *Journal of Negro History*. Condescendingly, Fleming described the *Journal* as "an outlet for the rather intelligent group of Negroes," adding that "the psychological effect of these various subjects upon the better class of Negroes is very wholesome even if the views contained in the publications are frequently, in my opinion, wrong or inaccurate." Fleming asserted on the one hand that there was "enough scholarship, enough science, enough economic value, enough historical value" in the publication to justify support. On the other hand, he insisted, "Of course you can't expect exact scientific unbiased history or economics from these Negroes." Fleming objected to the fact that "every book is distinctly from the Negro point of view" and alleged that Woodson frequently disregarded "unfavorable sources of information." In spite of the alleged deficiencies, Fleming thought that white historians would one day find the works "very useful as sources."[43] Like Fleming, Hamilton confided that he had only briefly examined Taylor's book on black history during Reconstruction and Woodson's *Heads of Negro Families* and considered them to be "potentially useful to the student of Negro History." He observed that "they are rather biased, naturally, and have a touch of propaganda, and I imagine that is unavoidable under the present circumstances."[44]

Aware of the Foundation's confidential solicitation of evaluations, Woodson attempted to counter what he imagined would be forthcoming from the historians whose biased interpretations he had consistently challenged.[45] Again he appealed to J. Franklin Jameson and to Arthur M. Schlesinger. Schlesinger freely acknowledged his "great confidence in Woodson's accurate Scholarship," emphasizing that, after all, Woodson had received "careful training" at Harvard. Schlesinger placed Woodson's efforts within a broader context of the historical profession and assessed its significance. He pointed out that Woodson had broken much new ground and was "by all odds the most important Negro historian in the United States. At the same time his work ranks high in comparison with the work produced by the better white historians."[46] Later Schlesinger would reiterate his view that "the *Journal of Negro History* compares favorably with the best scholarly periodicals in the historical field," elaborating that "the separate publications are of a research character and in no sense 'niggerish.' "[47]

Jameson underscored his unwavering support of Woodson: "Whatever work in Negro History may be done by white men, Negro investigators if properly qualified have some distinct advantages in the pursuit." He continued, "Such work not only increases the knowledge of the negro race possessed by us white people, but it is also an important consideration that the pursuit of these investigators is a distinct source of interest, encouragement, and inspiration to a large contingent among the intelligent negroes, of whom Dr. Woodson spares no pains through the *Journal of Negro History* to enlist their support of his work."[48]

With some trepidation, on June 14, 1929, George E. Vincent of the Rockefeller trusts informed Woodson of the "good news" that the executive committee had voted to give the Association a one-year $10,000 grant for research studies and publications. The officers summarized for Woodson the evaluation preferred by his historical peers. They noted that practically every colleague commended the work of the Association but criticized it repeatedly for undertaking too many studies in too short a time. They pointed out that most of the white historians judged the editing of the studies inadequate, citing repetition and unnecessary detail in certain instances as chief weaknesses. Thereupon the Foundation officers informed Woodson that this would be the final grant awarded him unless he seriously considered affiliating with a black college or university.[49]

At the suggestion of an affiliation with a Negro university Woodson exploded, "To link up the work of the Association with one of the undeveloped institutions in which there is no atmosphere for the work which the Association is doing is out of the question." He repeated his critique of Negro universities, claiming that "there is no such thing as a Negro university in the sense of a circle of teachers addressing themselves to the advanced phases of their work in which young men whom they instruct develop the power of original treatment and independent research." He argued that Negro educational institutions were merely called universities. He did concede that the "inferiority" of the Negro institutions was not entirely their fault. He explained that much of the money given to Negro institutions by philanthropic foundations went to construct buildings and purchase equipment and not toward the development of a competent teaching staff. Woodson maintained that the educational policies of southern state-school administrators prevented Negro universities from progressing above the high school level and predicted that it would take at least a generation more to develop them into first rate colleges. More specifically, he pointed out that most of the general operating funds for ASNLH came from secondary teachers. He remained convinced that if the Association attached itself to one particular institution "practically all of this income would be cut off; and the work of the Association, which is now national, would be reduced to an unattractive performance sidetracked at a way station."[50]

Undaunted by the cessation of the LSRM support, Woodson sought assistance from two other Rockefeller trusts, the Rockefeller Foundation and the General Education Board, hinting that he would, in time, work out an affiliation with a Negro college. Apparently persuaded that Woodson was about to do as they wished, the Rockefeller Foundation managers voted to grant him $22,500, payable in three installments between July 1, 1930 and June 30, 1933. The award came with the stipulation that Woodson secure matching funds. Woodson successfully raised the required amount primarily from gifts and donations from black churches, schools, and dozens of private individuals. His longtime patron Julius Rosenwald made the largest single private donation of $1,000, while the Rosenwald Fund contributed an additional $2,500.[51]

Actually Woodson quickly forgot his "hints" and during the course of the new grant made little progress toward securing an affiliation. The Rockefeller Foundation officers, soon realizing that they had been manipulated, invited Woodson to New York to discuss the issue of affiliation. To be sure, Jackson Davis conceded that Woodson and the Association had completed "fine pioneer work in creating a wide-spread interest in historical subjects and in preserving historical records dealing with Negro life." Davis then pressed his major concern, informing Woodson that the officers of all the Rockefeller trusts agreed that now was the time for him to shift the Association's work to a black educational institution and to "let the association play the part of the coordinating agency." Davis subsequently reported to his colleagues that he had taken a firm stand: "I made it clear to Dr. Woodson that the Board had invested large sums of money in these institutions and that it seemed to the officers that the opportunity and responsibility of the Board was in helping them to become centers of study and research rather than to build up independent agencies without institutional connections."[52]

Again Woodson hedged, leaving Davis with the impression that he would cooperate. Eager to facilitate the development of an affiliation, Davis approached John Hope of Atlanta University, confiding that continued philanthropic support of ASNLH was contingent upon Woodson's removal of the *Journal* to a Negro university. He wrote, "If some plan can be worked out by which the *Journal of Negro History* may be brought under the aegis of the Negro universities I think the Board would be willing to consider aid over a temporary period of reorganization and adjustment."[53] Hope's subsequent suggestion to Woodson that Atlanta University assume publication of the *Journal* met with outright rebuke. Indeed, Woodson took umbrage at the proposal just as he had done to similar offers from Tuskegee Institute in 1920 and Howard University in 1930. He argued that for a black university to assume publishing responsibility for the *Journal* would amount to a "disestablishment of the Association." He again reiterated his claim that the black universities lacked research libraries and appropriate sophistication to produce the *Journal*. Moreover, he asserted that "Professors Carlton J. H. Hayes, Evarts B. Greene, A. M. Schlesinger, and W. E. Dodd would hardly favor attaching the *American Historical Review* to the History Department of Harvard or Chicago." Woodson stubbornly declared, "We may have to pass through another 'starvation' period, and if we reach the time when we cannot further write the history of the Negro we shall drop a period at that point and call the task finished." He concluded, "We may die at our post, but we shall not desert it."[54] Foundation officers were prepared for this intransigence. Davis wrote Woodson simply, "We regret your decision and wish you well in your continued efforts."[55]

Woodson's intransigence toward affiliation eventually affected his relationship with the Rosenwald Fund. Actually Edwin Embree, the director of the Rosenwald Fund, had previously been a key officer at the General Education Board and had upon assuming his post questioned Rosenwald's involvement with Woodson. In 1936, Embree seized upon the opportunity afforded by the loss of Rockefeller support to cease Rosenwald aid. He informed one of Rosenwald's heirs, "It is interesting and important work but he continues to refuse to have it affiliated with any established university or institution. I do not see how he can expect continued support as a free lance worker."[56]

By the close of the decade, Woodson depended almost exclusively on black subscriptions and contributions to keep the Association afloat. Of the $13,000 raised by the Association in 1939, at least 75 percent of it came from black supporters. Woodson observed, "Few whites now help us because we are too independent."[57] Throughout the 1940s Woodson persisted in a by now futile quest for adequate funds. In the 1945 Annual Report he announced the closing of the ASNLH's research program. The year before he died he borrowed $2,000 to meet ASNLH obligations. The *Journal* held its own but the *Negro History Bulletin* lost 3,000 subscribers.[58] Woodson died in 1950.

There are several aspects of this discussion of Woodson's work with the Association and the *Journal of Negro History* which warrant further comment. Woodson clearly saw any affiliation with a black college, such as Fisk, Howard or Atlanta, as a threat to his personal independence and autonomy, since, contrary to his claims, such an affiliation would not have prevented the production of scholarship on Negro life and history. By the 1930s and certainly in the 1940s these black educational centers had witnessed considerable development. The student rebellions of the 1920s had resulted in the transference of administrative leadership of these schools from white to black professionals.[59] After all, John Hope was president of Atlanta University, Mordecai Johnson headed Howard University, and Charles S. Johnson would soon assume leadership of Fisk University. Indeed, one of the most positive consequences of Woodson's aid to black scholars was the training and eventual placement of many excellent black historians on the history and social science faculties of the major black institutions. Charles H. Wesley was head of the history department at Howard University, where Ralph Bunche and Rayford Logan were doing good work. A. A. Taylor assumed the chairmanship of the Department of

History at Fisk University, where Lorenzo Dow Turner would work for a number of years. Luther P. Jackson taught at Virginia State College, while Lorenzo Greene found employment at Lincoln University in Jefferson City, Missouri. Benjamin Quarles taught at Dillard University in New Orleans, Louisiana, and then served a long tenure at Morgan State University in Baltimore, Maryland. Clearly, then, these universities were not as intellectually backward or as white-dominated as Woodson argued. Thus, Woodson's struggle to establish the legitimacy and relevancy of Negro history bore exquisite fruit. The ASNLH and the *Journal of Negro History*, his creations, proved to be key institutions paving the way for future generations of black historians to enter into the mainstream of the historical profession.

Black Studies

An Overview for the Ford Foundation

During the late 1960s and early 1970s, unique historical circumstances propelled the development of Afro-American and Africana studies in colleges and universities. Few of these early endeavors were the result of careful and deliberate planning and analysis. Typically, they were established in response to political exigencies rather than intellectual and academic imperatives. These and other factors contributed to ongoing structural and organizational diversity. Today it seems that no two black studies programs are alike. Their diversity is evidenced in faculty size and composition, relations with university administrators and more traditional departments, curriculum, degrees offered, budgets, spatial resources, range of special programs, and the nature of their community outreach.

An important objective of this investigation was to examine the present status of these programs: How well have they been supported by their institutions? To what degree have they been able to secure productive faculty? Have they provided their faculties with the requisite resources and nurturing that encourage the quality teaching, research, and service required for success in the academy?

The ongoing debate over nomenclature is a graphic illustration of residual problems growing out of the turbulent times in which these programs burst upon the academic scene. The term "black studies" has become a generic designation, vociferously opposed by some who view the phrase as less than illuminating. Critics argue that this designation suggests that only black students and black faculty should be interested in this area of intellectual inquiry. Most institutions appear to prefer the titles "Afro-American," "African and Afro-American," or "Africana" studies. On the one hand, those who insist on the term "Africana studies" maintain that "Afro-American studies" implies that the primary focus of teaching and research is the historical, cultural, and political development of Afro-Americans living within the boundaries of North America. Moreover, "African and Afro-American studies" neglect the Caribbean and other parts of the Americas. On the other hand, "Africana studies" encompasses a broader geographical, and disciplinary, reach, spanning both North and South America, the Caribbean, and the African continent—in short, the African Diaspora. Of course, few of the current programs possess the requisite institutional resources, faculty positions, or budget lines to be truly "Africana." But the intent points in the right direction and therefore is certainly praiseworthy.

The attempt to identify and assess black studies endeavors accurately is further complicated by the differences in structure and mission between "departments," "programs," "centers," and "institutes." Black studies "departments" are best characterized as separate, autonomous units possessing an exclusive right and privilege to hire and grant tenure to their faculty, certify students, confer degrees, and administer a budget. Black studies "programs" may offer majors and minors but rarely confer degrees. And perhaps more important, all faculty appointments in programs are of the "joint," "adjunct," or "associate" variety. These professors are in the unenviable position of having to please two masters to secure appointment and tenure.

"Centers" and "institutes" defy easy categorization. As a rule, they tend to be administrative units more concerned with the production and dissemination of scholarship and with the professional development of teachers and scholars in the field than with undergraduate teaching. Unfortunately, considerable confusion surrounds the name "center." Many people view centers as merely cultural or social facilities designed to ease the adjustment of black students to predominantly white campus life. Thus, centers are often denigrated and dismissed as having little or no relevance to black studies, which is imagined to be purely an academic or intellectual endeavor, albeit with political-advocacy overtones. However, the good work being done at centers like those at the University of California at Los Angeles (UCLA) and the University of Michigan certainly should correct these misconceptions.

University Administrators

It was encouraging and refreshing to encounter so many white university administrators who sang the praises of their black studies departments, programs, centers, and institutes. In fact, there was scarcely a discordant note. From the perspectives of the more positively inclined administrators on predominantly white campuses, it appears that black studies not only has come of age but also has been making important contributions to the academy. Although it is heartening to witness this attitudinal transformation, given the initial vehement objections to the creation of black studies units, it is nonetheless necessary to probe beyond the surface to assess fully the contemporary status of black studies.

Twenty years ago, when black students first demanded the establishment of black studies departments, programs, and centers, few of the beleaguered white administrators would have predicted a long life for the enterprises. Many undoubtedly wished that black studies would go away; others tried to thwart growth and development. Most of those who opposed the creation of black studies units claimed that these units would lower academic standards because they believed such endeavors lacked intellectual substance.

It is not surprising that at some institutions black studies units offered little intellectual challenge. Undertrained people were brought in to head programs hastily contrived to preserve campus peace. Unfortunately, the early development and subsequent evolution of black studies were further tainted by the media's sensationalized coverage of the armed black students at Cornell University and the 1969 shoot-out at UCLA, which left two students dead. In the minds of many, black studies would forever remain nothing more than a new kind of academic ghetto. University administrators who valued "peace" and "campus rest" had little inclination, courage, or will to insist on quality. Thus, black studies units seldom were held to the traditional modes of evaluation and scrutiny observed elsewhere in the academy.

By 1987, however, the tide had turned. There has been a discernible shift among college administrators from amused contempt or indifference to enthusiastic support of black studies. Now administrators are eager to improve the quality of their programs and departments. One potent factor has been the availability of a larger pool of productive, well-trained black scholars willing, indeed anxious, to head and/or work in black studies. No longer do administrators have to rely on the local minister or community activist to oversee and teach black studies. If they are willing to put up the money, administrators can recruit productive black scholars.

Another motivation fueling the change in attitude toward black studies is institutional expediency. Faced with the specter of declining black student enrollments, university administrators are increasingly using strong black studies departments, programs, centers, and institutes as recruitment devices. Moreover, as is often the case, the only critical mass of black faculty working at many of these institutions is housed in black studies divisions. It is sad but true that without black studies, Chicano studies, women's studies, or Native American studies departments or programs, few colleges and universities could boast of having an integrated or pluralistic faculty.

Institutional expediency and a larger pool of black scholars notwithstanding, one fact deserves underscoring. Black studies departments and their faculties have proven to be a continuing source of intellectual stimulation on many American campuses. Black studies has opened up vast and exciting new areas of scholarship, especially in American history and literature, and has spurred intellectual inquiry into diverse social problems affecting the lives of significant portions of the total population. Lectures, seminars, and conferences sponsored by black studies units provide a threefold benefit: Students introduced to authorities from outside of the academy are impressed with the fact that there are many ways of expressing and knowing. Faculty, black and white, have the opportunity to share their expertise, test assumptions, and receive immediate feedback on work in progress. Finally, black community residents are encouraged to perceive universities as more accessible and less foreign. As members of these communities begin to identify with universities, they develop a greater appreciation for learning, and a respect for the scholarship of black professors.

Black Studies Curriculum

Despite its contributions and successes over the past twenty years, black studies still has to contend with and resolve rampant confusion, conflict, and creative tensions. The issues being debated include nomenclature; curriculum; identity, mission, and structure; graduate programs; faculty recruitment, retention, and development; accreditation; and professionalization. There is an ongoing debate, with no signs of immediate resolution, over whether black studies is a field or a discipline. The problems surrounding curriculum are worthy of special attention. Even within the same departments, faculties often find it impossible to agree upon a standard or core for all sections of the same introductory course in Afro-American studies. It is regrettable that there is no special summer institute or training program where black studies administrators and faculty could discuss and perhaps map an appropriate and effective curriculum.

The curriculum—whether it is called black studies, Africana studies, or Afro-American and African studies—should reflect an ordered arrangement of courses progressing from the introductory through the intermediate to advanced levels. In terms of content, a sound black studies curriculum must include courses in Afro-American history and in Afro-American literature and literary criticism. There should be a complement of courses in sociology, political science, psychology, and economics. A cluster of courses in art, music, and language and/or linguistics should also be made available to students. Finally, depending on resources and the number of faculty, a well-rounded black studies effort should offer courses on other geographical areas of the black Diaspora—the Caribbean and/or Africa. African and Afro-American and Africana studies programs and departments should, as their names imply, offer a variety of courses on black societies in the New World as well as in Africa.

Although deciding what to name a unit and developing a sound and coherent curriculum are challenging, a more daunting task is acquiring resources to recruit and retain an appropriate faculty, one that includes assistant, associate, and full professors. In the late 1960s and early 1970s, black studies units simply drew into their domain whoever happened to be available and willing to join them. Thus, little uniformity in curriculum could be achieved across the country.

With the economic difficulties and retrenchment of the late 1970s, many black studies faculties declined in size, producing an even more fragmented curriculum. To ensure that existing courses were offered on a reasonable and routine basis, black studies administrators had to rely heavily on part-time, visiting, or temporary appointees. Most often those available to accept such positions were in the creative arts—musicians, dancers, poets, and fiction writers.

More recently, black studies departments have increasingly relied on cross-listing courses to augment curriculum. The cross-listing of courses is both reasonable and advantageous because it builds bridges between black studies and the more traditional departments within the university, thus decreasing somewhat any tendencies toward isolation and marginality. To be sure, there are pitfalls, and cautious administrators must be ever vigilant. Adaptive "survival" measures may encourage some university administrators to reduce further the resources allocated to black studies. After all, if black studies is consistently able to "make do" with less, one could logically conclude that it needed fewer resources in the first place. This is a special concern for departments and programs with small numbers of majors and minors and with low course enrollments.

All of these factors—lack of a critical mass of well-trained faculty, excessive reliance on temporary hires, absence of a coherent curriculum and of content consensus for even introductory courses—bespeak the difficulties confronting and perhaps threatening the autonomy of many black studies departments. These are certainly among the concerns of the leadership of the National Council for Black Studies (NCBS). I suspect that the officers of NCBS will experience considerable frustration as the organization attempts to design a standardized curriculum. Although it is perhaps perverse to see anything positive in this disarray, the major strength of the black studies enterprise may well be its ever-changing and evolving nature. The rapid proliferation of knowledge in the field is a strong argument in support of institutional flexibility. Faculty in this area need to be free to develop new courses, to experiment with different methodologies, and to adopt nontraditional texts, just as quickly as new knowledge is produced.

Undergraduate and Graduate Degree Programs in Black Studies

One of the characteristics of a viable discipline is the authority to confer degrees and certificates to students who have mastered a particular body of knowledge. Black studies faculty and administrators have been quite concerned with this issue. The majority of the more autonomous departments of black studies do, in fact, award bachelor of arts degrees. Programs in black studies vary. Some offer majors while most offer at least minors to students receiving a degree from the more traditional academic disciplines. In other words, the student may receive a bachelor's degree in history, sociology, political science, or biology, chemistry, business administration, or education—with a concentration in Afro-American studies.

Few black studies units offer master's degrees. Of the half dozen or so that do, the departments at Cornell and UCLA and the program at Yale are the most visible and are highly respected. Most of the master's degree students at Cornell and Yale go on to pursue doctoral degrees in traditional disciplines. Others enter the labor force, working in social service agencies, businesses, or state and local governments. Cornell's Master of Professional Studies degree is specially designed to prepare students to work in community settings.

As with many other issues in black studies, there is no consensus about the wisdom of developing graduate degree programs in African American studies. Certainly, at this stage in the evolution of black studies, there is a need for a creditable doctoral degree program. As I traveled around the country, black studies scholars expressed enthusiasm about the prospects of making a doctoral program available to students. In 1988 Temple University established the first Ph.D. program in African-American studies.

Black Scholars and the Modern Black Studies Movement

At present, there are a number of top-flight black scholars, more than at any time in history. They are producing first-rate, indeed award-winning, books and articles in areas of black studies. By far the most exhilarating part of my consideration of black studies has been meeting these scholars and becoming familiar with their work. No assessment of the overall status and impact of black studies would be complete without noting the research activities of this latest generation of black professors and administrators. Because the absolute numbers of black professors is small and declining, it is easy to lose sight of the quality and breadth of their research and to minimize the impact that they have had on scholarship in all branches of knowledge.

The collective scholarship of black professors provides a sound foundation for the future development of black studies as a discipline. To a great extent, this scholarship will ensure the eventual institutionalization of black studies within the academy. As long as black scholars remain productive and competitive, and devote considerable attention to recruiting and training the next generation of scholars, black studies will enjoy a presence on America's campuses. It is, however, precisely the need to recruit, retain, and educate young black men and women in the humanistic and social science disciplines that casts a cloud over the joy and exuberance accompanying any serious examination of the quality of black scholarship in the last two decades. For a variety of reasons, fewer black students are entering graduate school with plans for academic careers. At every stop on my tour of black studies units, faculty members and administrators, black and white, broached the topic and admitted that this problem was of critical importance to the future of black studies.

The numerous monographs, articles, and manuscript editing projects produced by black scholars have fueled the movement to reclaim the forgotten or obscured dimensions of the black past. Their new interpretations of past and present conditions affecting all aspects of black life have wrought a veritable revolution, albeit a still largely unheralded one, in the ways in which even traditional historians, literature theorists, sociologists, anthropologists, philosophers, psychologists, and political scientists approach their work whenever it touches upon the experience of black people.

There is reason to be excited and pleased with the record of intellectual accomplishment evident in scattered institutions around the country. Regrettably, few of these black scholars have more than a little contact with each other. Nevertheless, because there are so many recognizably productive and accomplished scholars, the future of black studies appears bright in spite of all of the structural complexities and creative tensions. In the remainder of this paper, I will address several factors concerning black scholars: the role of philanthropic foundations in their development, the perspectives reflected in some of their works, and the relationship between their scholarship and black studies as an organized unit within universities and colleges.

Any perusal of the acknowledgements and prefaces of some of the refreshingly original recent works of black scholars demonstrates the critical importance of the scholarships and fellowships made available by foundations and other organizations, including those specifically set aside for minority group scholars. Without these special fellowships, I dare say the record of productivity in black studies would not be so impressive.

To illustrate this point, I shall discuss three recently published and widely praised (within black studies circles, that is) volumes authored by black women scholars, the most recent group to establish a viable presence in the academy. Gloria T. Hull, co-editor of *All the Women Are White, All the Blacks Are Men, But Some of Us Are Brave: Black Women's Studies* (Old Westbury, N.Y.: Feminist Press, 1982) and editor of *Give Us Each Day: The Diary of Alice Dunbar-Nelson* (New York: Norton, 1984), published a provocative and icon-shattering book, *Color, Sex, and Poetry: Three Women Writers of the Harlem Renaissance* (Bloomington: Indiana University Press, 1987). No one who reads it will ever again be able to think of the Harlem Renaissance in quite the same way. Hull effectively unveils the rampant sexism and chauvinism of the black male leaders of the Renaissance. In her preface, Hull wrote that in addition to a faculty research grant from the University of Delaware and a summer stipend from the National Endowment for the Humanities, a Rockefeller Foundation Fellowship enabled her "to do the requisite, remaining travel and research" (ix).

E. Frances White, author of *Sierra Leone's Settler Women Traders: Women on the Afro-European Frontier* (Ann Arbor: University of Michigan Press, 1987), observed in her preface: "I received funding from the African American Scholars Council, the Danforth Foundation (Kent Fellowship) and the Roothbert Fund to aid me in my initial research. An A. W. Mellon Faculty Development Grant and a

Fulbright Senior Research Scholar Fellowship helped me to return to Sierra Leone to collect further material" (x). White's brilliant study contributes a feminist perspective to the continuing debate over the impact of colonial rule on women in Africa.

I first learned of Sylvia Ardyn Boone's *Radiance from the Waters: Concepts of Feminine Beauty in Mende Art* (New Haven, Conn.: Yale University Press, 1986) from black historian Nell Irvin Painter who commented, "It's a *wonderful* book that takes real black beauty, African beauty, seriously, in an academic not a commercial way."* The volume is indeed dazzling. Boone noted in her acknowledgements, "The Foreign Area Fellowship Program of the Social Science Research Council funded the first part of my work in England and later in Sierra Leone. A Dissertation Year Fellowship from the American Association of University Women and a grant from the Ford Foundation National Fellowship Fund financed additional research and then the write-up" (ix).

I have highlighted these outstanding examples of black scholarship because the study of black women is the current frontier in black studies. Combined with the historical studies of professors Jacqueline Jones (*Labor of Love, Labor of Sorrow: Black Women, Work and the Family From Slavery to the Present* [New York: Basic Books, 1985]) and Deborah G. White (*Ar'n't I a Woman: Female Slaves in the Plantation South* [New York: Norton, 1985]), the novels of Toni Morrison, Alice Walker, and Paule Marshall, the literary criticism of Professor Barbara Christian (*Black Women Novelists: The Development of a Tradition* [Westport, Conn.: Greenwood, 1980]), and the black feminist theory of Professor bell hooks, the three examples of black scholarship mentioned above would make for a dynamic course. Because the curriculum in black studies is so flexible and fluid, unfettered by disciplinary constraints, such a course would be introduced and taught with élan. Moreover, it should be noted that quite a few of the directors and chairs of black studies—for example, at Cornell and at the University of Mississippi—have established working ties with women's studies.

In addition to fellowship support, foundations have provided major funding for a host of black editing projects. A few of the no-

---

*Personal communication, June 22, 1987.

table projects are: the Frederick Douglass Papers, John Blassingame, editor; the Booker T. Washington Papers, Louis Harlan, editor; and the Freedmen and Southern Society Project, Ira Berlin, editor. These projects have made accessible to scholars invaluable documents and important primary sources. Their significance to black studies scholarship cannot be exaggerated.

The massive Black Periodical Literature Project edited by Professor Henry Louis Gates, Jr., author of *Figures in Black: Words, Signs, and the "Racial" Self* (New York: Oxford University Press, 1987), is a particularly important venture. His monographs, on the one hand, continue to break new ground in literary theory and are indeed changing the way theorists evaluate and interpret black literature. The fiction project, on the other hand, reclaims the literary efforts of past generations of black writers. Gates' efforts are well-funded and deservedly so.

An especially encouraging sign of the vitality of black studies is the rising number of black scholars who are contemplating and/or engaging in collaborative research projects. This progression from individual research to collaborative efforts involving many people from different disciplines is a natural one. A typical first book or major publication is usually a revised dissertation. Now that many black scholars are working on second and third books and, most important, have acquired tenure, they are eager to develop collaborative studies. This impulse should be encouraged, as it bodes well for the development of black studies as a discipline.

In the early years, black studies units justified their intellectual existence on the grounds that they shattered the confining and restrictive boundaries of traditional disciplines. Actually, as far as I have been able to discern, most of the individual scholars in these programs and departments have published works that are very much in keeping with the methodological canons of the disciplines in which they were formally trained. It was naive and unrealistic to expect the young historian or sociologist of the Afro-American experience to retool, then master a new, still inadequately defined Afrocentric methodology, and then prepare publishable manuscripts and win tenure—all within a six-year period.

In sum, I am optimistic about the future of black studies because of the energy, creativity, industry, and achievements of black scholars. The dream that black studies can be in the forefront of interdisciplinary research and writing deserves all available nourishment. The contemporary black studies movement will be considerably enhanced and sustained by serious professional scholars engaged in research and writing of the black experience. The creative potential of black studies, however, will become a reality only to the extent that foundations and universities provide full support.

The Black Studies Movement

Afrocentric-Traditionalist-Feminist Paradigms for the Next Stage

In 1987 the Ford Foundation asked me to visit a select number of Black Studies programs, departments, centers, and institutes and to prepare a report that would help to determine and direct the nature and extent of foundation involvement over the next few years. After I completed the project the Foundation decided to publish in essay format the report's introduction, and summaries of similar investigations conducted by Robert L. Harris of Cornell University, and by Nellie McKay of the University of Wisconsin-Madison. The document was appropriately edited to protect the identities of those interviewed. Although the report became a basis for the subsequent distribution of over $3 million in grant monies not all Black Studies scholars and administrators were pleased.

Most critical of my specific involvement in the Ford Foundation examination of Black Studies was Selase W. Williams, chair of National Council for Black Studies (NCBS). Williams maintained in the fall 1990 NCBS *Newsletter*, "While Hine is a reputable historian, her minimal contact with the Black Studies Movement and lack of understanding of the real issues in this developing discipline become readily apparent to the initiated reader." He elaborated, "After reading Hine's essay, it appears that Hine does not view the mission of Black Studies as fundamentally different from that of traditional academic disciplines." It was this latter comment that started me on a course of systematic review of just about everything that I could find concerning the evolution of Black Studies over the past two decades.

Williams was correct on one score, I had assumed that as an academic endeavor the purpose or mission of Black Studies was to create and disseminate new knowledge about the social, political, cultural, and historical experiences of Black people of African descent in Diaspora. Yet, his criticism struck more than a defensive chord. I wondered indeed if I had missed something, and therefore determined to discover what it was that made Black Studies, as Williams asserts "fundamentally different from that of traditional academic disciplines."

Inasmuch as sufficient time has passed since the modern incarnation of Black Studies as an intellectual movement, what are we to make of its accomplishments, contributions, and shortcomings?[1] This essay is at heart an exercise in black intellectual history of both the movement of Black Studies and the idea of Black Studies.

In their text, *Introduction to Afro-American Studies,* Adbul Alkalimat and Associates define Black Studies by contrasting it with traditional or "mainstream" disciplines. They hold that "in general, the mainstream disciplines have focused on the Black experience by emphasizing race relations from the point of view of the interests of white people. They have lacked a theoretical perspective that is dynamic and is focused on the politics of social change. The mainstream disciplines thus were unprepared to deal with both the intellectual concerns of black people and the political actions of the masses of black people."[2] Though this contrast is useful, it does not acount for the fact that many black scholars working within mainstream disciplines have offered brilliant critiques and have successfully transformed the work being done in key disciplines. Does their work count as Black Studies?

In 1969, the chair of the Black Studies Department at the University of Pittsburgh, Jack L. Daniel, maintained in another definition:

> Black Studies constitutes an attempt to understand the human experience using Black experience as both a focal point and a platform from which to view. . . . Black studies is not a matter of empirical versus descriptive, historical, and intuitive, nor is Black Studies a matter of politics and economics versus culture and consciousness. Black Studies in this sense is not a matter of "versus," and at a minimum Black Studies is concerned with the integration of these "approaches." Similarly, Black Studies is

concerned with the integration of the objective and the subjective, the material and the spiritual, or the visible and the invisible. . . . Black Studies is for all human beings.[3]

In 1969, Nathan Hare and Jimmy Garret at San Francisco State organized the first Black Studies program in the country. Hare offered the following assurances as to the purpose of Black Studies: "The main motivation of Black Studies is to entice black students (conditioned to exclusion) to greater involvement in the educational process. Black Studies is, above all, a pedagogical device."[4] His view was consistent with those of the students whose demands were intended to make Black Studies a pedagogical instrument. The twin pillars of student demands called for the teaching of black history and the hiring of black faculty. Out of this oppositional student consciousness emerged a two-decades-long critique of institutional racism in higher education.

It is important to underscore that members of other excluded or distorted minority, or emerging majority groups, and women took cues from the Black Studies movement and made their own demands for curriculum revision and faculty diversification. Thus, on the heels of, or in some instances, contemporaneously with Black Studies, Ethnic Studies and Women Studies appeared on college and university campuses.

Most Black Studies scholars agree that the field is distinguished from other academic endeavors because of the tension between theory and practice and that they must always respond to the needs of two masters, the academy on the one hand, and the black community on the other. Due to the political underpinnings surrounding the birth of the field and a persistent, though often muted and intangible academic racism, however, some Black Studies scholars nurture an oppositional consciousness to the very mainstream institutions that employ them, and from the more established disciplines in which they received their graduate training. Their "outsider within" posture arose, in part, out of the radical protests and demands of the first generation of black college students on predominantly white college and university campuses during the late 1960s. As one scholar has described the impetus:

Black college students recognized the urgent necessity for Black Studies in the nation's higher education institutions as one way to make schools more understanding of diversity. These students had marched in Mississippi, been spat upon in Alabama, survived attacks in the inner cities of Chicago, Detroit and Newark, and they were ready to revamp higher education and rid it of its racist policies. One way to do this was to insist on intellectual treatment of the Black American experience.[5]

Recently, Molefi Asante, the author and architect of "Afrocentricity,"[6] has argued that there were problems with the initial formulation of Black Studies. He declared that,

> The field of Black Studies or African-American Studies was not born from a clear ideological position in the 1960s. Our analyses as students were correct, but our solutions were often fragmentary, ideologically immature, and philosophically ill-defined. The absence of a comprehensive philosophical position, with attendant possibilities for a new logic, science, and rhetoric condemned us to experimentation with an Islamic base, a Marxist base, a civil service base, a reactionary nationalist base, a social service base, a systematic nationalist base, or a historical-cultural base.[7]

Asante further maintains that systematic nationalists tended to be grouped with the historical-cultural school because they, at least, understood that Black Studies implied a different perspective although they could never thoroughly articulate that perspective. Asante, however, names the Afrocentric perspective, and highlights the crucial distinction that just because a professor is black, it does not mean that the professor is Afrocentric. He argues that "Afrocentricity as that perspective becomes indispensable to our understanding of Black Studies; otherwise, we have a series of intellectual adventures in Eurocentric perspectives about Africans and African Americans." That is why the students of the sixties, in an underappreciated but perhaps incomplete reaction to Eurocentricity, railed against white instructors of Black Studies. Asante continues "As we now know the mistake was not in their intention: to have a black perspective (they did not refer to it as Afrocentricity) but it was in their misunderstanding that *Afrocentricity* meant *black professors.*"[8]

The tortured birth of Black Studies has long affected how this newest of the academic disciplines has been perceived and evaluated. But this is not the only difficulty impeding a judicious assessment of its institutional and intellectual evolution. Race remains a substantial barrier that blocks and distorts our view. In one regard, Asante is on target. All African American academicians who work on subject matter pertaining to peoples of African descent are, as a rule, lumped together and categorized as Black Studies scholars, regardless of their individual perspectives and orientations. It would appear that their racial identity outweighs other differences. I have experimented with ways of ordering and distinguishing differences between Black Studies scholars, and analyzing the Afrocentric impulse. Risking oversimplification, and the ire of those mentioned and unnamed, I have devised a model of ideal types within the Black Studies community of scholars, writers, and thinkers. It is important to emphasize that these are ideal types and that there is considerable movement between them.

The three groups of scholarly practitioners fueling the Black Studies mission of creating and disseminating new knowledge that illuminates the past and present social, economic, political, and educational conditions of African Americans and of all peoples of African descent throughout the Diaspora can be separated into "Traditionalists," "Authentists" and/or "Originists," and "Black Feminists."

When I prepared the Ford Foundation report I focused on the scholarship produced by the "Traditionalists," consisting of both black and white academicians in sociology, history, and in literary theory. Based upon an assessment of their work, I concluded that Black Studies was alive and well and indeed flourishing at institutions fortunate enough to boast a critical representation of academically respected, highly visible scholars. It was easy for me to "roll call" the names and titles and the books authored by James D. Anderson, John Blassingame, Clayborne Carson, Barbara Fields, Thomas Holt, Earl Lewis, Nell Irvin Painter, Leslie Owens, Albert Raboteau, Joe Trotter, and the late Nathan I. Huggins, to name only a few historians. Among the scholars of African American literature the stellar roster included Michael Awkward, Houston Baker, Hazel Carby, Barbara Christian, Henry Louis Gates, Jr., Deborah McDowell, Nellie McKay, Arnold Rampersad, Valerie Smith, and Mary Helen Washington. Similarly, among the acknowledged black sociologists are Walter Allen, Elijah Anderson, Bart Landry, Aldon D. Morris, and William Julius Wilson. Neither time nor space permits the listing of all the traditional scholars of African descent who have enriched intellectual discourse, challenging through their works old paradigms that diminished, distorted, and dismissed the meaning and essence of black thought, culture, and history. Virtually every established social science and humanities discipline, including art history, music, psychology, political science, and economics has had to contend with the fresh interpretations and perspectives, innovative methodologies, new sources, and probing questions that characterize the best of traditional Black Studies scholarship.

The scholarly monographs collectively gave notice to and unveiled the myriad accomplishments and experiences of black men and women from every strata, segment, and territory in the African World. The previously muted voices and actions of slaves, agricultural workers, urban migrants, industrial laborers, writers, artists, musicians, reformers, accommodationists, and nationalists demonstrate a relentless critical reflection on the fundamental principles, and the as yet largely unrealized ideals, that undergird our total society.

Let us take the history of slavery as a case in point. The pioneering generation of Black Studies scholars who entered the academy in the post-Civil Rights Movement era amassed clearly impressive records. We now know a great deal more about slavery as an institution and about the inner lives of slaves. The innovative and imaginative scholarship on slave communities, slave religion, slave resistance, slave health, and slave families not only provided more factual data but deepened our appreciation of non-traditional sources. We know, thanks to the new social history methodologies and to the reclamation of black history, that even the most oppressed and downtrodden people who did not leave manuscript collections, write diaries, or build monuments, nevertheless created and sustained significant institutions and fashioned a remarkably resilient and progressive culture reflected in song, folktales, dance, and in quilts. Their essential humanistic values and belief in the sanctity of life and black worldviews grounded largely upon a theology of hope ensured the survival of African Americans in slavery and in freedom.

In spite of the dazzling achievements of historians of slavery, a sober assessment revealed a special lacuna. The voices and experiences of black women remained mute, unexamined. In most of the studies both the slaves and the masters were male. Beginning in the late 1970s an emergent group of black feminist scholars raised disturbing and challenging questions about the androcentric bias in black history. Were not black women captured and enslaved on the coasts of Africa? Did not black women suffer the middle passage and participate in the often futile rebellions on board the slave ships? Did not black women bear the responsibility of reproducing the entire slave labor force after the 1808 close of the African slave trade? To be sure, Angela Davis, writing from prison in the early 1970s, suggested that black women had a unique slavery experience worth exploring on its own merits, but few heeded her call.[9]

The appearance of Deborah Gray White's study of slave women in the plantation South significantly altered our understanding of the "peculiar institution" and its gender relations.[10] Her critique of the stereotypes of black women as Jezebels, mammies, and Sapphires revealed the myriad ways in which American society attempted to devalue and dehumanize black women. Raped with impunity both in and out of slavery, exploited as producers and reproducers, black women developed a culture of dissemblance and self-reliance in order to survive.[11] They had no choice but to become creative agents for change and to embark upon the heroic task of re-imagining themselves and their sex. Moreover, the study of women's experiences under slavery revealed the layered depth of white women's complicity in the exploitation and oppression of black women and the extent to which white women were privileged on the backs of black bondwomen in slavery and black women domestic servants in freedom. When black women occupy the center of the intersection, then slavery studies and all labor studies of the late nineteenth and twentieth centuries will examine new, more complex questions of gender as well as of racial power relations.

I am much encouraged by the number of scholarly works that have appeared in the past decade chronicling the historical and literary experiences and contributions of black women. The monographs by historians Cynthia Neverdon-Morton, Jacqueline Rouse, Adrienne Lash

Jones and Marilyn Richardson to name only a few have legitimized the study of black women's history. The textbook history written by Paula Giddings, the collected essays of Angela Davis, the important anthologies edited by Rosalyn Terborg-Penn, Sharon Harley, and Filomina Chioma Steady attest to the vibrancy of this field. Of course, the numerous works in progress, including Gwendolyn Keita Robinson's study of the black cosmetic industry, Elsa Barkley Brown's examination of Maggie Lena Walker and the Independent Order of St. Luke, Evelyn Brooks Higginbotham's research on black women and the black Baptist church, along with Wilma King's, Brenda Stevenson's and Stephanie Shaw's work on black women and children in slavery bode well for a provocative future in black women's history.

Armed with impressive scholarship in black women's studies, we are able to speak with greater confidence and accuracy about the external and inner lives of black women in the United States. We now know that black women played essential roles in ensuring survival and progress of families, institutions, and communities. We know that even oppressed black women were able to develop, as in the case of Maria Stewart, a political agenda for black liberation that pivoted on the emancipation of black women. We now know that black women's angle of vision enabled them collectively and individually to fashion an autonomous worldview and oppositional consciousness.

Black feminist scholars have been especially critical in the development of theories of intersectional analyses of race, class, and gender. In describing the existence of sexism among black men, and by documenting "the ways in which racism empowers white women to act as exploiters and oppressors" black feminists have opened a Pandora's box. In short, as bell hooks declares, "By calling attention to interlocking systems of domination—sex, race, and class—black women and many other groups of women acknowledge the diversity and complexity of female experience, or our relationship to power and domination."[12] Patricia Hill Collins, writing along the same line in her book, *Black Feminist Thought*, argues that race, class, and gender may not be the most fundamental or important systems of oppression, but they have most profoundly affected African American women. She adds that one significant dimension of black feminist thought is its potential to reveal insights about the social relations of domination organized along other axes such as religion, ethnicity, sexual orientation, and age. Collins and hooks agree that "investigating black women's particular experiences thus promises to reveal much about the more universal process of domination."[13] Clearly black feminists are working within the prescribed definition of Black Studies scholarship while at the same time challenging androcentric biases. Arguably, it may well be the case that the "Traditionalists" and "Black Feminists" make up one camp in the Black Studies debate. Both groups critically interrogate reigning intellectual systems, but with the positive intention of somehow reforming the academy, or making it live up to its potential.

"Authentist" Black Studies scholars and writers have likewise engaged in and produced important intellectual work. Most prominent among this group are Wade Nobles, Maulana Karenga, James Turner, Molefi Asante, Nathan and Julia Hare, Robert Staples, Ronald Bailey, Cedric Robinson, Haki Madhubuti, James Stewart, Asa Hilliard, Ak'im Akbar, and a host of others too numerous to mention. Among black women "Authentists," I would include the following: Vivian Gordon, Kariana Welsh-Asante, Carol Barnes, Rosalind Jeffries, and Frances Cress Welsing.

Although I list these names together I am not unmindful or unaware of the critical perspective and ideological differences among these scholars and thinkers. "Authentists" can be cultural nationalists, pan-Africanists, Afrocentrists, and/or Marxists. Their works can be descriptive, prescriptive, or proscriptive. At the outset, I must underscore that I do not wish to suggest that the scientific merit of the work of the "Traditionalists" is more important than that of the "Authentists." Nevertheless, the acceptance accorded the work of the "Traditionalists" in the larger academy suggests what white and some black academic gatekeepers deem meritorious. Suffice it to say that there are many leading edges and many streams in multidimensional academic intellectual space.

The theme unifying the work of "Authentists" is an intellectual and often overt political commitment to black liberation from European, or more crassly white, categories of thought and analysis. "Authentists" are determined to create a new African methodology that allows Africans to control knowledge about themselves. Their rejection of European categories often means a rejection of "Traditionalist" and even "Black Feminist" approaches that remain rooted in European tenets of research, evidence, and argument even as they transform those tenets in use.

Of the earlier generation of Black Studies scholars and liberation activists who most inform the work of contemporary "Authentists" are Carter G. Woodson, W.E.B. Du Bois, E. Franklin Frazier, Booker T. Washington, Marcus Garvey, Elijah Muhammad, Malcolm X, Langston Hughes, C.L.R. James, Frantz Fanon, Kwame Nkrumah, Cheikh Anta Diop, and Eric Williams.

Until quite recently neither the writings nor the identities of the "Authentist" Black Studies academicians penetrated mainstream awareness. Recent magazine and newspaper articles have effectively captured the excitement, controversy, and tension surrounding the concept of Afrocentricity and the growing prominence of a contingent of speakers, writers, adjunct or retired professors variously referred to as Nile Valley scholars, Egyptologists, or African World scholars. I refer to this important subset of "Authentists" as "Originists." Among the most prominent "Originists" are Yosef ben-Jochannan, John Henrik Clarke, John Jackson, Drusilla Dunjee Houston, St. Clair Drake, Ivan Van Sertima, and Cheikh Anta Diop. Originists, as the titles of their many books attest, argue that Africa is the cradle, or origin of civilization (High Culture) and that most significantly Egyptians were African. In sum, the "Originists" provide African Americans with our own origin stories that lay claim to the credit for much of the knowledge that allegedly has been erroneously attributed to Greeks and Romans. Asante defines Afrocentricity as "the belief in the centrality of Africans in post-modern history. It is our history, our mythology, our creative motif, and our ethos exemplifying our collective will."[14]

Although "Originists" have been teaching, writing, and privately publishing their own books and pamphlets for decades, they went into eclipse for a period of years, but now they are experiencing a resurgence. The degree to which this resurgence is related to the problems growing out of modern manifestations of racism is unclear. A brief survey of the arguments and titles of some of the "Originists'" books is suggestive. Martin Bernal, author of the controversial *Black Athena*, declared that "the political purpose . . . is, of course, to lessen European cultural arrogance."[15]

John G. Jackson in his *Introduction to African Civilizations* declares on the dedication page, "This book is dedicated to everybody with an African ancestry—the whole human race!" Jackson's main point is that "Civilization did not start in European countries, and the rest of the world did not wait in darkness for the Europeans to bring the light." Then there is the trilogy of Yosef ben-Jochannan *African Origins of the Major Western Religions* (1970), *Black Man of the Nile and His Family* (1978), and *Africa: Mother of Western Civilization* (1971).[16] Ben-Jochannan declares that the purpose of his *Black Man of the Nile* is to help African peoples' "re-identification with their great ancestral heritage."

> For the Black Peoples have maintained that: If the European Jews can fight for an arid piece of desert; the Irish for a small emerald island; the British for a barren island of misery; protestant Anglo-Saxon Americans for their stolen "Indian" empire; why should the black man (the African, African-Caribbean, and African American) not fight for the richest piece of real estate on the planet earth—His original homeland—Mother Africa.[17]

Linking the African past to the discovery of the New World Ivan Van Sertima declared in 1976, in *They Came before Columbus: The African Presence in Ancient America,* that by design and by accident "in several historical periods long before the coming of Columbus, Africans traveled to America."[18] Van Sertima writes, "We now know, without a shadow of a doubt, through the most modern methods of dating, that some of the Negroid stone heads found among the Olmecs and in other parts of Mexico and Central America are from as early as 800 to 700 B.C."[19]

The father of the scholarly project to reclaim and re-construct the African basis of Western civilization, beginning with a reidentification of Egypt as African, was Cheikh Anta Diop, author of *The African Origin of Civilization: Myth or Reality*. Diop espoused the theory of the cultural unity between Egypt and Africa in order that a revision of the curriculum of African history would teach the young their own history "rather than that of the colonizer." The most recent additions to this literature are the two volumes of St. Clair Drake, *Black Folk Here and There* (1987).[20]

Traditional Black Studies scholars have generally remained aloof from the passion engulfing Nile Valley Civilization scholarship and Afrocentricity. But as these topics capture the imagination of students, it becomes important to take a closer look, not to dismiss but to explain what is happening. All groups and societies need origin stories. Taken collectively the works of Diop, Jackson, and ben-Jochannan provide a sense of beginning and belonging. The late Nathan Huggins observed that "tradition is a legitimizing phenomenon. All peoples and all nations want to tie themselves to an ancient past (ideally, preliterate and mythic)." He continued, "The Founding Fathers were conscious that the actual history could not be the rationale on which their new nation could rest. They wanted to found their roots in a classical and honored past, while they were deliberately severing themselves from the one tradition that gave them place and reason." But then Huggins departs sharply from "Originist" claims of how African Americans came to be. He declared,

> Afro-Americans, too, are new, a new people brought into being as a consequence of American history, a new people for whom after several generations in America, it was impossible to trace back to any tradition beyond the American experience itself. This newness of people and nation has caused in both a problematic relationship with tradition.[21]

As may be imagined, assertions or descriptions of African Americans as new people are guaranteed to raise the ire of any "Originist." The important question remains unresolved. Is there a problem or intrinsic threat to the intellectual integrity of Black Studies, and the larger field of historical studies, from the thought-control implicit in the writings of "Originists" and "Authentists"?

In other words, the development and dissemination of origin stories must not comprise the final objective of Black Studies. The battlefield remains the minds of students and the goal is control or liberation, depending on one's perspective, through the development of an oppositional consciousness. A recent issue of *Black Issues in Higher Education* featured the current debate over Egypt's and Africa's place in the ancient world. As the article pointed out, the real challenge was how to move school systems toward Afrocentric education.[22] John Henrik Clarke in an article excerpted from his book, *The Afrikan*

World at the Crossroads: Notes for an Afrikan World Revolution (1991) summed it up boldly. He announced:

> What I've been pointing to is that if there's going to be a world revolution among Afrikan people we have to locate Afrikan people and connect with Afrikan people. No matter what we call ourselves and what island we came from or what part of Georgia or Alabama, we can still identify with these regions. But overall identification is with Afrika and with Afrikan people wherever they are on the face of this Earth.[23]

Black Studies is heterogenous and complex. No single category of analysis should be allowed immunity from criticism. In order that the intellectual domain remain healthy each group of Black Studies scholars must engage in continuous critique, not in a quest for academic dominance, but to keep the ongoing movement free from dogma or absolutes. We must continually ask questions in order to keep the discipline vital. For example, is the Nile Valley view a fundamental acceptance of the old-racist-imperialist European view that nothing of note was accomplished in sub-Saharan Africa, and certainly not after, say 1000 B.C.? Or, is it that true "civilizations" are literate (versus oral), politically, economically and socially centralized (versus decentralized), and architecturally monumental, and that all less complex cultures are "backward" and unimportant?

Black Studies is now poised at the most propitious moment in its evolution. I suspect that the long-range consequences of the contemporary phase of the struggle will pivot on the theoretical coherence of the field, the extent to which Afrocentrism wins converts and gains currency, and the response of the entire Black Studies movement to "Black Feminists'" call for attention to gender. In conclusion, we must remember that there is much Black Studies work that remains to be done. There is room for innumerable contributions. Above all, dignity across categories must be maintained.

Stop the Global
Holocaust

It's happening in Chicago, Detroit, Los Angeles, Miami, Rio de Janeiro, Johannesburg, Berlin, London.

In every region of the globe the killing of black women's children, most notably their sons, is escalating.

On the west side of Chicago, alienated and dispossessed black youths and gang members pull triggers on each other. Merchants in Rio de Janeiro hire others to kill homeless black children whose constant begging drives away tourists and customers. In South Africa, white policeman kill young demonstrators against apartheid, and in European countries white extremist groups murder people with dark skins.

The causes of this global holocaust against black male children are complex and interconnected. Understanding the problem in all of its complexity amounts to little more than an intellectual exercise unless we break out of our paralysis and act purposefully to end the killing.

I suggest that the American people in general, and black Americans in particular, call a time out and begin the process of national and international mobilization to stop the killing and to renew our commitment to the doctrine that everyone is entitled to life, liberty, and the pursuit of happiness.

The killing of young black males became an in-my-face issue on September 19, 1992, when my 15- and 17-year-old nephews were shot in the side and in the knee respectively while standing in the doorway of a friend's house across the street from their own home on the south side of Chicago. They had refused to join the local neighborhood gang.

The family decided that to save them and to avoid further bloodshed the nephews had to be relocated, thus irrevocably transforming the lives of the family members.

As a university professor I understand intellectually the crisis, but I considered myself far removed from the killing fields. Silence and inaction I can no longer afford. The killing, shooting, maiming and destruction of black children across this globe must stop. Tomorrow the war zone may be in-your-face.

Notes

Introduction

I am grateful to friends and colleagues William C. Hine, Anne Boylan, Susan Reverby, David Barry Gaspar, Wilma King, William B. Hixson, Rudolph Byrd, David Bailey, Earl Lewis and Linda Werbish for their invaluable support and critical readings of drafts of this essay. I also owe a special intellectual debt to James D. Anderson for a decades-long conversation about how to reconstruct American history.

1 Evelyn Brooks Higginbotham, "African American Women's History and the Metalanguage of Race," *Signs: Journal of Women in Culture and Society* 17, no. 2 (Spring 1992): 251-74.

2 Even though the project ended in 1983, both institutions have continued to develop their Black manuscript collections. The Indiana Historical Bureau published the *Comprehensive Black Women in the Middle West Project Resource Guide* (Indianapolis: Indiana Historical Bureau, 1983) that describes the project, lists the 300 collections amassed, and contains biographical profiles of the hundreds of volunteers who made it a success. All of the essays in part two of this collection draw heavily upon the materials collected by the BWMW project.

3 Gerda Lerner, ed., *Black Women in White America: A Documentary History* (1972); Sharon Harley and Rosalyn Terborg-Penn, eds., *The Afro-American Woman: Struggles and Images* (1978); Gloria T. Hull, Patricia Bell Scott, and Barbara Smith, eds., *All the Women Are White, All the Blacks Are Men, But Some of Us Are Brave* (1982).

4 Eugene Genovese, *Roll, Jordan, Roll: The World the Slaves Made* (1974).

5 John Blassingame, *The Slave Commu-*

nity: Plantation Life in the Antebellum South (1972); Leslie Owens, *This Species of Property: Slave Life and Culture in the Old South* (1976); Herbert Gutman, *The Black Family in Slavery and Freedom, 1750-1925* (1976).

6 Deborah Gray White, *Ar'n't I a Woman: Female Slaves in the Plantation South* (1985). The collection of fifteen original essays that historian David Barry Gaspar and I are editing on Black women and slavery in the Americas promises further advance.

7 Brenda Stevenson, "Slavery," in *Black Women in America: An Historical Encyclopedia* (1993), 1045-70; Paula Giddings, *When and Where I Enter: The Impact of Black Women on Race and Sex in America* (1984); Jacqueline Jones, *Labor of Love, Labor of Sorrow: Black Women, Work, and the Family from Slavery to the Present* (1985); Wilma King, ed., *Tryphena Blanche Holder Fox* (1993).

8 Susan Reverby's unpublished work on Nurse Eunice Rivers, "Creating Nurse Rivers: History, Memory, and Representations in the Tuskegee Syphilis Experiment," is a significant example of "crossover history." Copy of essay is in my possession.

9 Elsa Barkley Brown, "Womanist Consciousness: Maggie Lena Walker and the Independent Order of St. Luke," *Signs* 14, no. 3 (Spring 1989): 610-33, quote on 631.

Lifting the Veil, Shattering the Silence: Black Women's History in Slavery and Freedom

1 Herbert G. Gutman, *The Black Family in Slavery and Freedom, 1750-1925* (New York, 1976); John W. Blassingame, *The*

Slave Community: Plantation Life in the Antebellum South (New York, 1972); Eugene D. Genovese, *Roll, Jordan, Roll: The World the Slaves Made* (New York, 1974); Robert William Fogel and Stanley Engerman, *Time on the Cross: The Economics of American Negro Slavery* (Boston, 1974); Suzanne Lebsock, "Free Black Women and the Question of Matriarchy: Petersburg, Virginia, 1784-1820," *Feminist Studies* 7 (Summer 1982), 271-92, and *The Free Women of Petersburg: Status and Culture in a Southern Town, 1784-1860* (New York, 1984); Shepard Krech, III, "Black Family Organizations in the Nineteenth Century: An Ethnological Perspective," *Journal of Interdisciplinary History* 19 (1982): 429-52.

2 Rennie Simson, "The Afro-American Female: The Historical Context of the Construction of Sexual Identity," in Ann Snitow, Sharon Thompson, and Christine Stansell, eds., *The Powers of Desire: The Politics of Sexuality* (New York, 1983), 229-35; Harriet Jacobs, *Incidents in the Life of a Slave Girl* (Boston, 1861); Elizabeth Keckley, *Behind the Scenes: Thirty Years a Slave and Four Years in the White House* ([1868] reprint ed. New York, 1968); Genovese, *Roll, Jordan, Roll,* 485, 501; Gerda Lerner, ed., *Black Women in White America: A Documentary History* (New York, 1973); Catherine Clinton, *The Plantation Mistress: Woman's World in the Old South* (New York, 1982), 188.

3 Angela Davis, "Reflections on the Black Woman's Role in the Community of Slaves," *Black Scholar* 3 (1971): 2-15; Deborah G. White, "Ar'n't I a Woman? Female Slaves, Sex Roles, and Status in the Antebellum Plantation South," Ph.D. diss., University of Illinois, Chicago, 1979; Jacqueline Jones, " 'My Mother Was Much of a Woman': Black Women, Work, and Family under Slavery, 1830-1860," *Feminist Studies* 7 (Summer 1982): 235-69; Jacqueline Jones, *Labor of Love, Labor of Sorrow: Black Women, Work, and the Family from Slavery to the Present* (New York, 1985); Debra Newman, "Black Women in the Era of the American Revolution in Pennsylvania," *Journal of Negro History* 61 (July 1976): 276-89.

4 Deborah G. White, "Female Slaves: Sex Roles and Status in the Antebellum Plantation South," *Journal of Family History* 7 (Fall 1983): 248-61; Darlene Clark Hine and Kate Wittenstein, "Female Slave Resistance: The Economics of Sex," *Western Journal of Black Studies* 3 (Summer 1979): 123-27; Jessie Parkhurst, "The Role of the Black Mammy in the Plantation Household," *Journal of Negro History* 23 (July 1938): 349-69.

5 Quoted in Irene V. Jackson, "Black Women and Music: From Africa to the New World," in Filomina Chimoa Steady, ed., *The Black Woman Cross-Culturally* (Cambridge, Mass., 1981), 393.

6 John Michael Vlach, *The Afro-American Tradition in Decorative Design* (Cleveland, 1978), 67; Gladys-Marie Fry, "Harriet Powers: Portrait of a Black Quilter," in *Missing Pieces: Georgia Folk Art, 1770-1976* (Atlanta, 1976), 16-23; Robert Farris Thompson, "African Influence on the Art of the United States," *Journal of African Civilization* 3 (November 1978): 44; Gladys-Marie Fry, "Slave Quilting on Ante-Bellum Plantations," in *Something to Keep You Warm* (Roland Freeman Collection of Black American Quilts from the Mississippi Heartland Exhibit Catalog), 4-5.

7 Gloria T. Hull, "Black Women Poets from Wheatley to Walker," in Roseann P. Bell, Bettye J. Parker, and Beverly Guy-Sheftall, eds., *Sturdy Black Bridges: Visions of Black Women in Literature* (New York, 1979); Arna Alexander Bontemps, ed., *Forever Free: Art by African American Women, 1862-1980* (Alexandria, Va., 1980); Eileen Southern, *The Music of Black Americans: A History* (New York, 1971); Lawrence W. Levine, *Black Culture and Black Consciousness: Afro-American Folk Thought from Slavery to Freedom* (New York, 1977).

8 Ellen N. Lawson, "Sarah Woodson Early: Nineteenth-Century Black Nationalist 'Sister,' " *Umoja: A Scholarly Journal of Black Studies* 5 (Summer 1981): 21; Jacquelyn Grant, "Black Women and the Church," in Gloria T. Hull, Patricia Bell Scott, and Barbara Smith, eds., *All the Women Are White, All the Blacks Are Men, But Some of Us Are Brave* (New York, 1982), 141-52.

9 "The Life and Religious Experiences of Jarena Lee: A Colored Lady Giving an Account of Her Call to Preach the Gospel," in Dorothy Porter, ed., *Early Negro Writings 1760-1837* (Boston, 1971), 494-514; Bert James Loewenberg and Ruth Bogin, eds., *Black Women in Nineteenth-Century American Life: Their Words, Their Thoughts, Their Feelings* (University Park, Penn., 1976), 135.

10 Loewenberg and Bogin, *Black Women in Nineteenth-Century American Life*, 236. See also Arthur Huff Fauset, *Sojourner Truth: God's Faithful Pilgrim* (Durham, N.C., 1938); Olivia Gilbert, *Narrative of Sojourner Truth, a Northern Slave* ([1850] reprint ed. Boston, 1884); Hertha Pauli, *Her Name Was Sojourner Truth* (New York, 1962).

11 Jean McMahon Humez, *The Gifts of Power: The Writings of Rebecca Jackson, Black Visionary, Shaker Eldress* (Boston, 1981). Also see "Gifts of Power: The Writings of Rebecca Jackson," in Alice Walker's *In Search of Our Mothers' Gardens* (New York, 1983), 71-82.

12 Amanda Berry Smith, "An Autobiography of Mrs. Amanda Smith, the Colored Evangelist," in Loewenberg and Bogin, *Black Women in Nineteenth-Century American Life*, 171; Marshall W. Taylor, *Amanda Smith, or the Life and Mission of a Slave Girl* (Cincinnati, Ohio, 1886).

13 Maria Stewart's speech is included in Loewenberg and Bogin, eds., *Black Women in Nineteenth-Century American Life*, 192; Maria W. Stewart, *Meditations from the Pen of Mrs. Maria W. Stewart, Negro* (Washington, D.C., 1879); Maria W. Stewart, "What If I Am a Woman?" in Lerner, ed., *Black Women in White America*, 562-66. Also see Rosalyn Cleagle, "The Colored Temperance Movement: 1830-1860," M.A. thesis, Howard University, 1969.

14 Ira V. Brown, "Cradle of Feminism: The Philadelphia Female Anti-Slavery Society, 1833-1840," *Pennsylvania Magazine of History and Biography* 102 (April 1978): 143-66; Janice Sumler-Lewis, "The Forten-Purvis Women of Philadelphia and the American Anti-Slavery Crusade," *Journal of Negro History* 66 (Winter 1981-1982): 281-88. Also see Janice Sumler-Lewis, "The Fortens of Philadelphia: An Afro-American Family and Nineteenth-Century Reform," Ph.D. diss., Georgetown University, 1976; Willie Mae Coleman, "Keeping the Faith and Disturbing the Peace: Black Women, From Anti-Slavery to Women's Suffrage," Ph.D. diss., University of California at Irvine, 1982.

15 Katharine DuPre Lumpkin, *The Emancipation of Angelina Grimké* (Chapel Hill, 1974), 104-5.

16 Ruth Gogin, "Sarah Parker Remond: Black Abolitionist from Salem," *Essex Institute Historical Collections* 100 (April 1974): 120-50; Dorothy Porter, "Sarah Parker Remond, Abolitionist and Physician," *Journal of Negro History* 20 (July 1935): 287-93; Coleman, "Keeping the Faith," 15-16.

17 Pauli, *Her Name Was Sojourner Truth*, 176-77; Loewenberg and Bogin, eds., *Black Women in Nineteenth-Century American Life*, 235; bell hooks, *Ain't I a Woman: Black Women and Feminism* (Boston, 1981), 160; Rosalyn Terborg-Penn, "Discrimination against Afro-American Women in the Women's Movement, 1830-1920," in Rosalyn Terborg-Penn and Sharon Harley, eds., *The Afro-American Woman: Struggles and Images* (New York, 1978), 17-27. Also see Rosalyn Terborg-Penn, "Afro-Americans in the Struggle for Woman Suffrage," Ph.D. diss., Howard University, 1976, and her "Discontented Black Feminists: Prelude and Postscript to the Passage of the 19th Amendment," in Lois Schraf and Joan M. Jensen, eds., *Decades of Discontent: The Woman's Movement, 1920-1940* (Westport, Conn., 1983), 261-78; Adele Logan Alexander, "How I Discovered My Grandmother . . . and the Truth about Black Women and the Suffrage Movement," *MS* (November 1983): 29-37.

18 Lerner, ed., *Black Women in White America*, 569-70.

19 Keckley, *Behind the Scenes*, 113-16; Coleman, "Keeping the Faith," 59-61.

20 "Fannie Barrier Williams," in Loewenberg and Bogin, eds., *Black Women in Nineteenth-Century American Life*, 236-79; "A Northern Negro's Auto-biography," in Lerner, ed., *Black Women in White America*, 164-66.

21 Loewenberg and Bogin, eds., *Black Women in Nineteenth-Century American Life*, 263-79. Also see Anna J. Cooper, *A Voice from the South by a Black Woman of the South* (Xenia, Ohio, 1892).

22 Linda Perkins, "Black Women and Racial 'Uplift' Prior to Emancipation," in Steady, ed., *The Black Woman Cross-Culturally*, 317-34; Sylvia Lyons Render, "Afro-American Women: The Outstanding and the Obscure," *Quarterly Journal of the Library of Congress* 32 (October 1975): 306-21.

23 Bettye C. Thomas, *Twenty Nineteenth-Century Black Women* (Washington, D.C., 1979), 31; Hallie Quinn Brown, *Homespun Heroines and Other Women of Distinction* (Xenia, Ohio, 1926); Sadie Iola Daniels, *Women Builders* (Washington, D.C., 1970); Sylvia G. L. Dannett, *Profiles of Negro Womanhood*, Vol. 1, 1619-1900 (Chicago, 1964); Mary Church Terrell, *A Colored Woman in a White World* (Washington, D.C., 1940).

24 Josephine St. Pierre Ruffin's speech is included in Elizabeth Lindsay Davis, *Lifting as They Climb* (Washington, D.C., 1933), 13-15. Also see Gerda Lerner, "From Benevolent Societies to National Club Movements," in Lerner, ed., *Black Women in White America*, 435-36.

25 Howard Rabinowitz, *Race Relations in the Urban South, 1865-1890* (New York, 1978), 46; Bettina Aptheker, *Woman's Legacy: Essays on Race, Sex, and Class in American History* (Amherst, 1982), 62-63.

26 Mary Church Terrell, "First Presidential Address to the National Association of Colored Women," Nashville, Tennessee, September 15, 1897, in Mary Church Terrell Papers, box 102-5, folder 127, Library of Congress; Gloria M. White, "The Early Mary Church Terrell, 1863-1910," *Integrateducation* 12 (November-December 1975): 40ff; Dorothy Sterling, *Black Foremothers: Three Lives* (Old Westbury, N.Y., 1979), 118-58; Beverly Jones, "Mary Church Terrell and the National Association of Colored Women, 1896-1901," *Journal of Negro History* 67 (Spring 1982): 20-33. Also see Ruby M. Kendrick, "They Also Serve: The National Association of Women, Inc., 1895-1954," *Negro History Bulletin* 17 (March 1954): 171-75; Gerda Lerner, "Early Community of Black Club Women," *Journal of Negro History* 59 (April 1974): 158-67; Cynthia Neverdon-Morton, "The Black Woman's Struggle for Equality in the South," in Terborg-Penn and Harley, eds., *The Afro-American Woman*, 43-57; Lawrence B. de Graff, "Race, Sex, and Region: Black Women in the American West, 1850-1920," *Pacific Historical Review* 49 (May 1980): 285-313; Linda Faye Dickson, "The Early Club Movement among Black Women in Denver, 1890-1925," Ph.D. diss., University of Colorado, 1982.

27 For a case study in one state, see Darlene Clark Hine, *When the Truth Is Told: A History of Black Women's Culture and Community in Indiana, 1875-1950* (Indianapolis, 1981); Coleman, "Keeping the Faith," 77-88; Thomas C. Holt, "The Lonely Warrior: Ida B. Wells-Barnett and the Struggle for Black Leadership," in John Hope Franklin and August Meier, eds., *Black Leaders of the Twentieth Century* (Urbana, 1982), 39-62; Alfreda M. Duster, ed., *Crusade for Justice: The Autobiography of Ida B. Wells* (Chicago, 1970); Sterling, *Black Foremothers*, 60-117.

28 B. Joyce Ross, "Mary McLeod Bethune and the National Youth Administration: A Case Study of Power Relationships in the Black Cabinet of Franklin D. Roosevelt," in Franklin and Meier, eds., *Black Leaders of the Twentieth Century*, 191-219; Florence Johnson Hicks, ed., *Mary McLeod Bethune: Her Own Words of Inspiration* (Washington,

D.C., 1975); Mary McLeod Bethune, "Faith That Moved a Dump Heap," *Who, the Magazine About People* (June 1941): 31-35, 54; John B. Kirby, *Black Americans in the Roosevelt Era: Liberalism and Race* (Knoxville, 1980), 111-21. For a good discussion of other black women educators, see: Daniels, *Women Builders*, 137-67; Charlotte H. Brown, *The Correct Thing to Do* (Boston, 1940); Lessie Lois Fowle, "Willa A. Strong: An Historical Study of Black Education in Southeastern Oklahoma," Ph.D. diss., University of Oklahoma, 1982; Evelyn Brooks Barnett, "Nannie Burroughs and the Education of Black Women," in Terborg-Penn and Harley, eds., *The Afro-American Woman*, 97-108. Burroughs founded the National Training School for Women and Girls in Washington, D.C., on October 19, 1909. See Linda M. Perkins, "The Black Female American Missionary Association Teacher in the South, 1861-1870," in Jeffrey J. Crow and Flora J. Hatley, eds., *Black Americans in North Carolina and the South* (Chapel Hill, 1984), 122-36.

29 Paula Giddings, *When and Where I Enter: The Impact of Black Women on Race and Sex in America* (New York, 1984), 19-31; Thomas C. Holt, "The Lonely Warrior: Ida B. Wells-Barnett and the Struggle for Black Leadership," in Franklin and Meier, eds., *Black Leaders of the Twentieth Century*, 39-62; Duster, *Crusade for Justice*; David M. Tucker, "Miss Ida B. Wells and Memphis Lynching," *Phylon* 32 (Summer 1971): 112-22.

30 Rosalyn Terborg-Penn, "Discontented Black Feminists: Prelude and Postscript to the Passage of the Nineteenth Amendment," in Schraf and Jensen, eds., *Decades of Discontent*, 272-73.

31 Alice Kessler-Harris, *Out to Work: A History of Wage-Earning Women in the United States* (New York, 1982), 237; William H. Harris, *The Harder We Run: Black Workers since the Civil War* (New York, 1928), 51-76. Also see Florette Henri, *Black Migration: Movement North, 1900-1920* (New York, 1976); Delores Elizabeth Janiewski, "From Field to Factory: Race, Class, Sex, and the Woman Worker in Durham, 1880-1940," Ph.D. diss., Duke University, 1979; Sharon Harley, "Black Women in a Southern City, 1890-1920," in Joanne V. Hawks and Sheila L. Skemp, eds., *Sex, Race, and the Role of Women in the South* (Jackson, Miss., 1983), 59-74.

32 Karen Tucker Anderson, "Last Hired, First Fired: Black Women Workers during World War II," *Journal of American History* 69 (June 1982): 96-97; Lois Rita Helmbold, "Making Choices, Making Do: Black and White Working Class Women's Lives during the Great Depression," Ph.D. diss., Stanford University, 1982; Claudia Golden, "Female Labor Force Participation: The Origins of Black and White Differences," *Journal of Economic History* 37 (March 1977): 87-112. Also see Phyllis A. Wallace, *Black Women in the Labor Force* (Cambridge, Mass., 1980).

33 Terborg-Penn, "Discontented Black Feminists," in Schraf and Jensen, eds., *Decades of Discontent*, 269; Mark D. Matthews, " 'Our Women and What They Think': Amy Jacques Garvey and The Negro World," *Black Scholar* 10 (May-June 1979): 2-13.

34 Susan M. Hartman, "Women's Organizations during World War II: The Interaction of Class, Race, and Feminism," in Mary Kelley, ed., *Woman's Being, Woman's Place: Female Identity and Vocation in American History* (Boston, 1979), 317; Darlene Clark Hine, "Mabel K. Staupers and the Integration of Black Nurses into the Armed Forces Nurses Corps," in Franklin and Meier, eds., *Black Leaders in the Twentieth Century*, 241-57.

35 "Purposes of NCNW—1935," Press Release, November 11, 1948, Mary Church Terrell Papers, container 23, Library of Congress, Washington, D.C. Also see Mary Church Terrell, *A Colored Woman in a White World*.

36 "Purpose of NCNW—1935," Press Release, November 11, 1948, Terrell Papers.

37 Anne Moody, *Coming of Age in Mississippi* (New York, 1968). Also see Sara

Evans, *Personal Politics: The Roots of Women's Liberation in the Civil Rights Movement and New Left* (New York, 1980).

38 Aldon D. Morris, *Origins of the Civil Rights Movement* (New York, 1984).

39 Ibid., 51, 52, 53.

40 Ibid.

41 Ibid., 102-4, 114.

42 Ibid.

43 Giddings, *When and Where I Enter*, 287-90, 293-94.

44 Barbara Christian, *Black Women Novelists: The Development of a Tradition, 1892-1976* (Westport, Conn., 1980), 41-54; Carol Watson, "The Novels of Afro-American Women: Concerns and Themes, 1891-1965," Ph.D. diss., George Washington University, 1978; David Levering Lewis, *When Harlem Was in Vogue* (New York, 1982), 120-25, 140ff; Erlene Stetson, ed., *Black Sisters: Poetry by Black American Women, 1746-1980* (Bloomington, 1981); Roseann P. Bell, Bettye J. Parker, and Beverly Guy-Sheftall, eds., *Sturdy Black Bridges: Visions of Black Women in Literature*; Deborah E. McDowell, "The Neglected Dimension of Jessie Redmond Fauset," *Afro-Americans in New York Life and History* 5 (July 1981): 33-49.

45 Darlene Clark Hine, "To Be Gifted, Female, and Black," *Southwest Review* 67 (Autumn 1982): 357-69.

46 Sandra R. Lieb, *Mother of the Blues: A Story of Ma Rainey* (Amherst, 1981); Robert Hemenway, *Zora Neale Hurston: A Literary Biography* (Urbana, 1978). The Elizabeth Catlett Papers are available at the Amistad Research Center in New Orleans, Louisiana. See also Gloria T. Hull, ed., *Give Us Each Day: The Diary of Alice Dunbar-Nelson* (New York, 1984); Mamie Garvin Fields with Karen Fields, *Lemon Swamp and Other Places: A Carolina Memoir* (New York, 1983).

Female Slave Resistance: The Economics of Sex

1 See, for example, Herbert Aptheker, *American Negro Slave Revolts* (New York:

International Publishers, 1963); Eugene Genovese, *Roll, Jordan, Roll: The World the Slaves Made* (New York: Random House, 1974); Herbert Gutman, *The Black Family in Slavery and Freedom, 1750-1925* (New York: Pantheon, 1976); Gerald Mullin, *Flight and Rebellion* (New York: Oxford University Press, 1972); and Peter Wood, *Black Majority* (New York: W. W. Norton, 1974).

2 Genovese, 360-61.

3 Winthrop Jordan, *White Over Black: American Attitudes toward the Negro, 1550-1812* (Baltimore: Penguin Books, 1969), 151.

4 Linda Brent, *Incidents in the Life of a Slave Girl* (New York: Harcourt Brace Jovanovich, 1973), 27.

5 Frederic Bancroft, "New Orleans: The Mistress of the Slave Trade," in Irwin Unger and David Reimers, eds., *The Slavery Experience in the United States* (New York: Holt, Rinehart and Winston, 1970), 77.

6 Quoted in Bancroft, 77.

7 Elizabeth Keckley, *Behind the Scenes: Thirty Years a Slave and Four Years in the White House* ([1868] New York: Arno Press and the New York Times, 1968), 38-39.

8 Ibid., 39.

9 Brent, 28.

10 William Craft and Ellen Craft, "Running a Thousand Miles for Freedom," in Arna Bontemps, ed., *Great Slave Narratives* (New York: Beacon Press, 1969), 285.

11 Gutman, 80-81.

12 Ibid., 81.

13 Ibid., 81-82.

14 Raymond Bauer and Alice Bauer, "Day to Day Resistance to Slavery," in Unger and Reimers, 186.

15 Ibid., 186.

16 Genovese, 497.

17 Bauer, 190.

18 Genovese, 497.

19 Ibid.

20 Quoted in Gerda Lerner, ed., *Black Women in White America* (New York: Vintage Books, 1973), 38.

21 Genovese, 6.

22 Stanley Feldstein, *Once a Slave: The*

Slaves' View of Slavery (New York: William Morrow, 1970), 90.

23 Quoted ibid., 90.

Rape and the Inner Lives of Black Women: Thoughts on the Culture of Dissemblance

1 Hazel V. Carby, *Reconstructing Womanhood: The Emergence of the Afro-American Woman Novelist* (New York and Oxford: Oxford University Press, 1987), 39. For a discussion of the relationships among suffrage, rape, and lynching see Bettina Aptheker, *Woman's Legacy: Essays on Race, Sex, and Class in American History* (Amherst: University of Massachusetts Press, 1982), 53-76. It is interesting to note as Neil R. McMillen points out in his study of black Mississippians that of the 476 recorded lynchings in the state between 1889 and 1945 at least fourteen were black women, two of whom were well advanced in pregnancy (*Dark Journey: Black Mississippians in the Age of Jim Crow* [Urbana: University of Illinois Press, 1989], 229). Joel Williamson offers a rather problematic assertion about sexual relations between the races that begs credibility: "The myth arose that Negro women were especially lusty creatures, perhaps precisely because white men needed to think of them in that way. With emancipation, however, white men's access to black women virtually ended. Miscegenation, contemporary observers agreed, practically stopped." Ignoring the fact that black women continued to work as domestic servants in white households, Williamson asserts that "Mulatto women and black men went with their husbands, and dark Victoria was no longer easily available in either body or imagination to upper-class white men" (*The Crucible of Race: Black-White Relations in the American South since Emancipation* [New York and Oxford: Oxford University Press, 1984], 307).

2 Susan Tucker, *Telling Memories among Southern Women: Domestic Workers and Their Employers in the Segregated South* (Baton Rouge and London: Louisiana State University Press, 1988), 248.

3 Ibid., 18.

4 See Terry McMillan, *Mama* (Boston: Houghton Mifflin Company, 1987); Grace Edwards-Yearwood, *In the Shadow of the Peacock* (New York: McGraw-Hill, 1988); Alice Walker, *The Color Purple: A Novel* (New York: Washington Square Press, 1982); Toni Morrison, *The Bluest Eye* (New York: Holt, Rinehart and Winston, 1970); Gloria Naylor, *The Women of Brewster Place* (New York: The Viking Press, 1982); Maya Angelou, *I Know Why the Caged Bird Sings* (New York: Random House, 1969). Descriptions of interracial rape of black women abound in non-fiction writings. In his autobiography, Robert Parker, maitre d' of the Senate Dining Room from 1964 to 1975, recalls a white planter's rape of his sister in Montgomery County, Texas, and his own futile efforts at revenge. He wrote, "Robbie was never the same again. The white man had stolen her dignity and dirtied a precious corner of her self when he had taken her, at dusk, on the leaves in the woods" (Robert Parker, *Capitol Hill in Black and White* [New York: Dodd, Mead and Company, 1986], 6). For a painful and poignant account by a black woman of the rape of her mother, see Daisy Bates, *The Long Shadow of Little Rock: A Memoir* (New York: David McKay, 1962), 14-15: Bates wrote, "Daddy, who killed my mother? Why did they kill her?" Her father replied, "Your mother was not the kind to submit, so they took her. They say that three white men did it. There was some talk about who they were, but no one knew for sure, and the sheriff's office did little to find out."

5 Rennie Simson, "The Afro-American Female: The Historical Context of the Construction of Sexual Identity," in *Powers of Desire: The Politics of Sexuality*, ed. Ann Snitow, Christine Stansell, and Sharon Thompson (New York: Monthly Review Press, 1983), 229-35. For a fascinating discussion of Harriet Jacobs'

Incidents in the Life of a Slave Girl ([1861] New York: Oxford University Press, 1988) see Elizabeth Fox-Genovese, *Within the Plantation Household: Black and White Women of the Old South* (Chapel Hill: University of North Carolina Press, 1988). See also David Katzman, *Seven Days a Week: Women and Domestic Service in Industrializing America* ([1978] reprint ed. Urbana: University of Illinois Press, 1981), 203-4; Aptheker, *Woman's Legacy*, 111-28.

6 Allan H. Spear, *Black Chicago: The Making of a Negro Ghetto, 1890-1920* (Chicago and London: University of Chicago Press, 1967), 34.

7 Kathryn L. Morgan, *Children of Strangers: The Stories of a Black Family* (Philadelphia: Temple University Press, 1980), 18; Audrey Olsen Faulkner et al., *When I Was Comin' Up: An Oral History of Aged Blacks* (Hamden, Conn.: Archon Books, 1982), 58.

8 Lawrence W. Levine, *Black Culture and Black Consciousness: Afro-American Folk Thought from Slavery to Freedom* (New York: Oxford University Press, 1977), 274; Morgan, *Children of Strangers*, 11.

9 Bob Blaunder, *Black Lives, White Lives: Three Decades of Race Relations in America* (Berkeley: University of California Press, 1989), 24-25; See also John Dollard, *Caste and Class in a Southern Town* (New Haven, Conn.: Yale University Press, 1937), 142.

10 Deborah Gray White, "Mining the Forgotten: Manuscript Sources for Black Women's History," *Journal of American History* 74 (June 1987): 237-42.

11 Robin S. Peebles, "Detroit's Black Women's Clubs," *Michigan History* 70 (January/February 1986): 48; Cynthia Neverdon-Morton, *Afro-American Women of the South and the Advancement of the Race, 1895-1925* (Knoxville: University of Tennessee Press, 1989), 191-201.

12 Mary Church Terrell, "First Presidential Address to the National Association of Colored Women," Nashville, Tennessee, September 15, 1897 in Mary Church Terrell Papers, box 102-5, folder 127, Library of Congress.

13 Evelyn Brooks Barnett, "Nannie Burroughs and the Education of Black Women," in *The Afro-American Woman: Struggles and Images*, ed. Rosalyn Terborg-Penn and Sharon Harley (Port Washington, N.Y.: Kennikat Press, 1978), 97-108; Rosalyn Terborg-Penn, "Woman Suffrage: 'First because We Are Women and Second because We Are Colored Women,'" *Truth: Newsletter of the Association of Black Women Historians* (April 1985), 9.

14 Sara Brooks, in Thordis Simonsen, ed., *You May Plow Here: The Narrative of Sara Brooks* (New York and London: Simon and Schuster, 1987), 218, 219.

Black Women's History, White Women's History: The Juncture of Race and Class

1 Thomas S. Kuhn, *The Structure of Scientific Revolutions* (Chicago: University of Chicago Press, 1970), 110.

2 Melton A. McLaurin, *Celia, A Slave* (Athens: University of Georgia Press, 1991).

3 Katharine Du Pre Lumpkin, *The Making of a Southerner* ([1947] Athens: University of Georgia Press, 1991).

4 Katharine Du Pre Lumpkin, *The Emancipation of Angelina Grimké* (Chapel Hill: University of North Carolina Press, 1974); Katharine Du Pre Lumpkin and Dorothy W. Douglas, *Child Workers in America* (New York: International Publishers, 1937), and *The South in Progress* (New York: International Publishers, 1940).

5 Lumpkin, *Making of a Southerner*, 228.

6 Ibid., 87.

7 Ibid., 128.

8 Ibid., 132.

9 Ibid., 133.

10 Lumpkin and Douglas, *The South in Progress*, 13.

11 Lumpkin, *Making of a Southerner*, 182.

12 Ibid., 222.

13 Ibid.

Black Women in the Middle West:
The Michigan Experience

The author wishes to express her deep appreciation for the research assistance provided by Pamela Smoot, a graduate student in the Department of History at Michigan State University, and to her colleague Professor William B. Hixson, Jr. for his provocative comments, critical reading of several drafts of this manuscript and helpful source suggestions. DeWitt Dykes at Oakland University provided valuable editorial review.

I David M. Katzman, *Before the Ghetto: Black Detroit in the Nineteenth Century* (Urbana: University of Illinois Press, 1975), 135-74.
2 Gerda Lerner, "Early Community Work of Black Club Women," *Journal of Negro History,* 59 (April 1974): 158-67; Karen J. Blair, *The Clubwoman as Feminist: True Womanhood Redefined, 1868-1914* (New York: Holmes and Meier Publishers, 1980), 117-19. Blair discusses "domestic feminism" as it existed among middle-class white women during the latter half of the nineteenth century to the beginning of World War I. In the chronology of black women's historical experiences, the era of nationally organized black "domestic feminism" begins in the 1890s and extends to the Great Depression. Daniel Scott Smith coined the term in "Family Limitation, Sexual Control, and Domestic Feminism in Victorian America," in *Clio's Consciousness Raised,* ed. Mary Hartman and Lois W. Banner (New York: Harper and Row, 1974), 119-36. Also see Fannie Barrier Williams, "Club Movement among Negro Women," in *Progress of a Race,* ed. John W. Gibson and William H. Crogman ([1902] reprint ed. Miami, Florida: Mnemosyne Publishers, 1969), 197-281; Maude T. Jenkins, "The History of the Black Woman's Club Movement in America," Ph.D. diss., Columbia University, 1984, 79-104, 124-35; Lynda Faye Dickson, "The Early Club Movement among Black Women in Denver: 1890-1925," Ph.D.

diss., University of Colorado, 1982; Nancy F. Cott, *The Grounding of Modern Feminism* (New Haven, Conn.: Yale University Press, 1987).
3 *Michigan: A Guide to the Wolverine State,* compiled by Writer's Program of the Work Projects Administration in the State of Michigan (New York: Oxford University Press, 1941), 103.
4 Benjamin C. Wilson, *The Rural Black Heritage between Chicago and Detroit, 1850-1929* (Kalamazoo: Western Michigan University Press, 1985), 13. Only the adoption of the state's first constitution, in 1837, abolished the last remnants of slavery in Michigan. David M. Katzman, "Black Slavery in Michigan," *Midcontinent American Studies Journal* 11 (Fall 1970): 56-66; Blanche Coggan, "The Underground Railroad in Michigan," *Negro History Bulletin* 27 (February 1964): 123-24, and "Ex-slave's Dream Builds White Church: Freed woman contributed first thousand dollars toward exclusive Detroit Church," *Ebony* 14 (May 1959), 81-84.
   The Denison family sued for the freedom of the four Denison children (Elizabeth, James, Scipio and Peter, Jr.) from slavery to Catherine Tucker, widow of William Tucker. The case was heard in September 1807. When assigned "slavery for life" by *Denison v. Tucker,* Lisette and Scipio escaped to Canada, eventually returning to the United States between 1813 and 1816. In 1827, Lisette married Scipio Forth, becoming Elizabeth Denison Forth.
5 John Kern, *A Short History of Michigan* (Lansing: Michigan History Division, Michigan Department of State, 1977), 33. In this regard Michigan whites shared anti-black sentiments identical to those of Wisconsin whites. In 1857, Wisconsin whites also voted down a constitutional amendment to give black men suffrage.
6 Katzman, *Before the Ghetto,* 7; Wilson, *The Rural Black Heritage between Chicago and Detroit, 1850-1929,* 74; Leon Litwack, *North of Slavery: The Negro in the Free States, 1790-1860* (Chicago:

University of Chicago Press, 1961), 70-72; Jacque Voegeli, *Free but Not Equal: The Midwest and the Negro during the Civil War* (Chicago: University of Chicago Press, 1967), 2; Tom L. McLaughlin, "Grass-Roots Attitudes toward Black Rights in Twelve Nonslaveholding States, 1846-1869," *Mid-America* 56 (July 1974): 175-81.

7 Laura S. Haviland, *A Woman's Life and Work: Including Thirty Years' Service on the Underground Railroad and in the War* (Chicago: S.B. Shaw, Memorial Edition, 1888), 117.

8 Harold B. Fields, "Free Negroes in Cass County before the Civil War," *Michigan History* 44 (December 1960): 375-83; Stephen B. Weeks, *Southern Quakers and Slavery: A Study in Institutional History* (Baltimore: Johns Hopkins University Press, 1896), 227-28; W.B. Hartgrove, "The Story of Marie Louise Moore and Fannie M. Richards," *Journal of Negro History* (January 1916): 23-33; James E. DeVries, *Race and Kinship in a Midwestern Town: The Black Experience in Monroe, Michigan, 1900-1915* (Urbana: University of Illinois Press, 1984), 8-9; Haviland, *A Woman's Life and Work*, 116-19.

9 Katzman, *Before the Ghetto*, 13.

10 For an interesting discussion of black family relations and structure in a small Michigan town see DeVries, *Race and Kinship*, 8-12.

11 Beverly Ann Fish, "Sojourner Truth: Crusader for Women's Rights," in *Historic Women of Michigan: A Sesquicentennial Celebration*, ed. Rosalie Riegel Troester (Lansing: Michigan Women's Studies Association, 1978), 15-22; Lerone Bennett, Jr., "Pioneers in Protest: Sojourner Truth," *Negro History Bulletin* 36 (March 1963): 254; Willi May Coleman, "Keeping the Faith and Disturbing the Peace: Black Women from Anti-Slavery to Women's Suffrage," Ph.D. diss., University of California, Irvine, 1982, 9-10, 24-28.

12 William W. Stephenson, Jr., "Integration of the Detroit Public School System during the Period, 1838-1869," *Negro History Bulletin* 26 (October 1962): 23-26; "Pioneer Women of Afro-American Descent in Detroit," typescript, n.d., Federation of Colored Women's Clubs Collection, box 60-14-1, State Archives of Michigan, Lansing.

13 Dorothy B. Porter, "The Organized Educational Activities of Negro Literary Societies, 1828-1846," *Journal of Negro History* 5 (October 1936): 55-57.

14 "Pioneer Women of Afro-American Descent in Detroit," Federation of Colored Women's Clubs Collection, box 60-14A, State Archives of Michigan, Lansing.

15 For an excellent discussion of women's benevolence in a Northeastern community see Nancy A. Hewitt, *Women's Activism and Social Change: Rochester, New York, 1822-1872* (Ithaca, N.Y.: Cornell University Press, 1984), 69-73, 81-91, and Christina Stansell, *City of Women: Sex and Class in New York, 1789-1960* (Urbana: University of Illinois Press, 1987), 30-37, 45-52, 175-80.

16 John M. Green, ed., *Michigan Manual of Freedmen's Progress*, compiled by Frances H. Warren, Secretary of Freedmen's Progress Commission (1968), 72; Blanche Glassman Hersh, *The Slavery of Sex: Feminist-Abolitionist in America* (Urbana: University of Illinois Press, 1978), 167-70.

17 Hallie Q. Brown, "Mrs. Lucy Smith Thurman, 1858-1918," in *Homespun Heroines and Other Women of Distinction* ([1926] reprint ed. Cleveland, Ohio: Aldine, 1971), 176-77; Robin S. Peebles, "Detroit's Black Women's Clubs," *Michigan History* 70 (January/February 1986): 48.

18 W.B. Hartgrove, "The Story of Marie Louise Moore and Fannie M. Richards," 31.

19 Stephenson, "Integration of the Detroit Public School System," 26-28. Also see, June Baber Woodson, "Century with the Negroes of Detroit, 1830-1930," M.A. thesis, Wayne State University, 1949; *Joseph Workman v. The Board of Education of Detroit*, 18 Michigan 400, 402-8. Fragmentary records of the case are in the Michigan Records Center,

Case Files 1222, 1324, 1326, 1327, Lansing, Michigan; J. Morgan Kousser, *Dead End: The Development of Nineteenth-Century Litigation of Racial Discrimination in Schools* (Oxford: Clarendon Press, 1986), 40, 46.

20 Hartgrove, "The Story of Marie Louise Moore and Fannie M. Richards," 31.

21 Robin S. Peebles, "Fannie Richards and the Integration of the Detroit Public Schools," *Michigan History* 64 (January/February 1981): 30-31.

22 "Pioneer Women of Afro-American Descent in Detroit," Federation of Colored Women's Clubs Collection, box 60-14A.

23 *Pathways to Michigan's Black Heritage* (Lansing: Michigan Department of State, 1988), 14.

24 Peebles, "Detroit's Black Women's Clubs," 48; Green, *Michigan Manual of Freedmen's Progress*, 142.

25 Edith V. Alvord, ed., *A History of the Michigan State Federation of Women's Clubs, 1895-1953* (Ann Arbor: Michigan Federation of Women's Clubs, 1953), 5, 21.

26 Jenkins, "The History of the Black Women's Club Movement," 80-83.

27 For an analysis of voluntary associations see Anne Firor Scott, "On Seeing and Not Seeing: A Case of Historical Invisibility," *Journal of American History* 7 (June 1984): 9-18.

28 D. Augustus Straker, "Manhood and Womanhood Development," *Colored American Magazine* (February 1901), 312-13. For a good analysis of black club women and their contributions to the community see Lerner, "Early Community Work of the Black Club Women," 158-67; Susan Lynn Smith, "The Black Women's Club Movement: Self-Improvement and Sisterhood, 1890-1915," M.A. thesis, University of Wisconsin, Madison, 1986.

29 Davis, *Lifting as They Climb*, 316.

30 Kern, *A Short History of Michigan*, 50.

31 Joanne J. Meyerowitz, *Women Adrift: Independent Wage Earners in Chicago, 1880-1930* (Chicago: University of Chicago Press, 1988), xxiii; Davis, *Lifting as They Climb*, 316.

32 Davis, *Lifting as They Climb*, 316.

33 Ibid., 321.

34 Ibid.

35 Biographical profile of Dr. Rosa L. Slade Gragg, Federation of Colored Women's Clubs Collection, box 60-14-AB1, folder 25; Robin S. Peebles, "Detroit's Black Women's Clubs," 48.

36 Davis, *Lifting as They Climb*, 321-24. Additional information on Rosa Slade Gragg is contained in her manuscript collection located in the Burton Historical Collection, Detroit Public Library.

37 Davis, *Lifting as They Climb*, 321-24.

38 Lillian E. Johnson, "The Founding," typescript, March 1938, Detroit Study Club Collection, box 2, Burton Historical Collection, Detroit Public Library.

39 Lillian E. Johnson, "Reminiscences," typescript, March 2, 1928, Detroit Study Club Collection, box 2. Detroit's population in the 1890s was nearer 250,000.

40 Ibid.

41 Lillian E. Johnson, "History of the Detroit Study Club," typescript, May 1949, Detroit Study Club Collection, box 2.

42 The complete records and minute books of the Grand Rapids Study Club are located in the Grand Rapids Public Library, Grand Rapids, Michigan. They are among the most thorough and extensive records of a midwestern black women's club I have examined, spanning the years between 1920 to the early 1980s. Also see, Carol Tanis, "A Study in Self-Improvement," *Grand Rapids Magazine* 42 (January 1987): 41-44.

43 Johnson, "Reminiscences," Detroit Study Club Collection.

44 "The Detroit Study Club," typescript, January 28, 1955, box 2, Detroit Study Club Collection.

45 Tanis, "A Study in Self-Improvement," 42.

46 Ibid.

47 Davis, *Lifting as They Climb*, 329. Davis notes that immediately after the formation of the League, the women forged cooperative agreements with the black merchants of the Booker T. Washington Trade Association. They canvassed the communities informing the residents of, and creating demand for, the products made and sold by black merchants. Simultaneously they asked merchants to place in their stores goods made by black men and women. Also see Fannie B. Peck, "History and Purpose of Housewives' League," May 2, 1934, Housewives' League of Detroit Collection, box 1, Burton Historical Collection, Detroit Public Library; and Richard W. Thomas, "From Peasant to Proletarian: The Formation and Organization of the Black Industrial Working Class in Detroit, 1915-1945," Ph.D. diss., University of Michigan, 1976, 246ff.

48 Christine M. Fuqua, President, National Housewives' League of America, "Declaration of May 18, 1948, as Fannie B. Peck Day," Housewives' League of Detroit Collection, box 4.

49 Fannie B. Peck, "Negro Housewives, What Now?" reprinted from *Service Magazine* (November 1942), Housewives' League of Detroit Collection, box 4.

50 Typed and handwritten undated speeches, Housewives' League of Detroit Collection, box 3, folder "Speeches."

51 Peck, "History and Purpose of Housewives' League."

52 Constitution of Housewives' League of Detroit and Declaration of Principles, box 1.

53 Section 9 of Constitution of Housewives' League, box 1.

54 Typescript, "Slogan" of Housewives' League of Detroit, box 1.

55 Declaration of Purpose, Housewives' League of Detroit, box 1, folder "Constitution and Bylaws."

56 Gertrude J. Tolber, Secretary of the Housewives' League of Detroit, "What Now That the War Is Over?" box 3, folder "Speeches."

57 Section 10 of the Constitution stated, "Any Negro woman interested in promoting the object of this organization may become a member by signing an application for membership and by signifying her willingness to be governed by said constitution and desire for a realization of its object." Box 1.

58 Report and notes of the Research Committee of the Housewives League of Detroit, box 3, folder "Speeches."

59 Ibid.

60 Ibid.

61 See Melvin Banner, *The Black Pioneer in Michigan*, Vol. 1, Flint and Genesse County (Midland: Pendell, 1973).

62 Katzman, *Before the Ghetto*, 8-12.

Black Migration to the Urban Midwest: The Gender Dimension, 1915-1945

1 D. J. Steans, *Backward Glance: A Memoir* (Smithtown, N.Y.: Exposition Press, 1983), 1.

2 Thomas C. Cox, *Blacks in Topeka, Kansas, 1865-1915* (Baton Rouge: Louisiana State University Press, 1982); Nell Irvin Painter, *Exodusters: Black Migration to Kansas after Reconstruction* (New York: W. W. Norton, 1977); Quintard Taylor, "The Emergence of Black Communities in the Pacific Northwest, 1865-1910," *Journal of Negro History* 64 (1979): 342-45; Janice L. Ruff, Michael R. Dahlin, and Daniel Scott Smith, "Rural Push and Urban Pull: Work and Family Experience of Older Black Women in Southern Cities, 1880-1910," *Journal of Social History* 16 (Summer 1983): 39-48; James O. Wheller and Stanley D. Brunn, "Negro Migration into Southwestern Michigan," *Geographical Review* 58 (April 1968): 214-30. For a description of the development of eight all-black towns in northern communities of more than 1,000 population, see Harold M. Rose, "The All-Negro Town: Its Evolution and Function," *Geographical Review* 55 (1965): 362-81; Edwin S. Redkey, *Black Exodus: Black Nationalism and Back-to-Africa Movements, 1890-1969* (New Haven, Conn.: Yale University Press, 1969), 150-94; Wilson Jeremiah Moses, *The Golden Age of Black Nationalism, 1850-1925* (New York: Oxford University Press, 1978), 83-102.

3 Allan H. Spear, *Black Chicago: The Making of a Negro Ghetto, 1890-1920* (Chicago: University of Chicago Press, 1967); Peter Gottlieb, *Making Their Own Way: Southern Blacks' Migration to Pittsburgh, 1916-1930* (Urbana: University of Illinois Press, 1987); Kenneth Kusmer, *A Ghetto Takes Shape: Black Cleveland, 1870-1930* (Urbana: University of Illinois Press, 1976); Joe William Trotter, Jr., *Black Milwaukee: The Making of an Industrial Proletariat, 1915-1945* (Urbana: University of Illinois Press, 1985); Darrel E. Bigham, *We Ask Only a Fair Trial: A History of the Black Community of Evansville, Indiana* (Bloomington: Indiana University Press, 1987); Florette Henri, *Black Migration: Movement North, 1900-1920* (New York: Anchor Press, 1975); Richard Walter Thomas, "From Peasant to Proletarian: The Formation and Organization of the Black Industrial Working Class in Detroit, 1915-1945" (Ph.D. diss., University of Michigan, 1976).

4 Trotter, *Black Milwaukee*, 25; Thomas, "From Peasant to Proletarian," 6-7; Henri, *Black Migration*, 52, 69. For a general overview of the historiography of Black urbanization see, Kenneth Kusmer, "The Black Urban Experience in American History," in *The State of Afro-American History: Past, Present, and Future*, ed. Darlene Clark Hine (Baton Rouge: Louisiana State University Press, 1986), 91-122. In an important study of women in Chicago, historian Joanne J. Meyerowitz comments on the different migratory patterns. "Black women followed different paths of migration to Chicago. In 1880 and in 1910, the largest group of black women adrift in Chicago, almost half, came from the Upper South states of Kentucky, Tennessee, and Missouri. A smaller group of migrants listed birthplaces elsewhere in the South. In 1880, one-fourth of black women adrift came from the states of the Deep and Atlantic Costal South; in 1910, almost one-third. During and after World War I, the stream of migrants from Mississippi, Alabama, Georgia, and other parts of the Deep South swelled to

a flood." Joanne J. Meyerowitz, *Women Adrift: Independent Wage Earners in Chicago, 1880-1930* (Chicago: University of Chicago Press, 1988), 10.

5 Henri, *Black Migration*, 69; August Meier and Elliott Rudwick, *Black Detroit and the Rise of the UAW* (New York: Oxford University Press, 1979), 5-7; Spear, *Black Chicago*, 129-30.

6 Elizabeth Clark-Lewis, " 'This Work Had a End': African-American Domestic Workers in Washington, D.C., 1910-1940," in *"To Toil the Livelong Day": America's Women at Work, 1780-1980*, ed. Carol Groneman and Mary Beth Norton (Ithaca, N.Y.: Cornell University Press, 1987), 198-99; David M. Katzman, *Seven Days a Week: Women and Domestic Service in Industrializing America* (New York: Oxford University Press, 1979), 219-21.

7 Darlene Clark Hine, "Rape and the Inner Lives of Black Women in the Middle West: Preliminary Thoughts on the Culture of Dissemblance," *Signs: Journal of Women in Culture and Society* 14 (Summer 1989): 912-20.

8 H. F. Kletzing and William F. Crogman, *Progress of a Race* ([1917]; reprint ed., New York: Negro University Press, 1969), 193.

9 Lynda F. Dickson, "Toward a Broader Angle of Vision in Uncovering Women's History: Black Women's Clubs Revisited," *Frontiers* 9, no. 2 (1987): 62-68, esp. 67.

10 Ibid., 67.

11 See Moses, *The Golden Age of Black Nationalism*, chapter 5, "Black Bourgeois Feminism versus Peasant Values: Origins and Purposes of the National Federation of Afro-American Women," 103-31; Darlene Clark Hine, *When the Truth Is Told: Black Women's Culture and Community in Indiana, 1875-1950* (Indianapolis: National Council of Negro Women, Indianapolis Section, 1981), 49-78.

12 Lawrence W. Levine, *Black Culture and Black Consciousness: Afro-American Folk Thought from Slavery to Freedom* (New York: Oxford University Press, 1977), 274.

13 Gottlieb, *Making Their Own Way*, 46-49, 52; Jacqueline Jones, *Labor of Love, Labor of Sorrow: Black Women, Work, and Family from Slavery to the Present* (New York: Basic Books, 1985), 159-60.

14 Carol Tanis, "A Study in Self-Improvement," *Grand Rapids Magazine* 42 (January 1987): 41-44 (quote on 43). The complete records and minute books of the Grand Rapids Study Club are located in the Grand Rapids Public Library, Grand Rapids, Michigan. They are among the most thorough and extensive records of a midwestern regional black women's club that I have found, spanning the years between the 1920s to the early 1980s.

15 Sara Brooks, *You May Plow Here: The Narrative of Sara Brooks*, ed. Thordis Simonsen (New York: Touchstone Edition, Simon and Schuster, 1987), 195-96.

16 Steans, *Backward Glance*, 17.

17 Jane Edna Hunter, *A Nickel and a Prayer* (Cleveland, Ohio: Elli Kani, 1940), 65-66. Hunter's papers are located at the Western Reserve Historical Society, Cleveland, Ohio.

18 The Maddy Bruce Story, May 18, 1984, transcript, Deborah Starks Collection, box 1, folder 4, Oral Histories, Black Women in the Middle West (BWMW) Project, Ft. Wayne, Indiana (Indiana Historical Society, Indianapolis). There is considerable confusion surrounding the spelling of the name in the transcript. Sometimes her name is spelled Burch, which is the way she spelled it in the text of the oral history. The listing of the oral history, however, is under Bruce. For the sake of consistency in the narrative, I refer to her as Burch.

19 Brooks, *You May Plow Here*, 211-14, 216-17.

20 Gottlieb, *Making Their Own Way*, 49-50; Jones, *Labor of Love, Labor of Sorrow*, 156-60. Also see Earl Lewis, "Afro-American Adaptive Strategies: The Visiting Habits of Kith and Kin among Black Norfolkians during the First Great Migration," *Journal of Family History* 12 (1987): 407-20.

21 The Maddy Bruce Story, BWMW Project.

22 Brooks, *You May Plow Here*, 195.

23 LeRoi Jones, *Blues People: The Negro Experience in White America and the Music that Developed from It* (New York: William Morrow, 1963), 105-7; Sandra R. Leib, *Mother of the Blues: A Story of Ma Rainey* (Amherst: University of Massachusetts Press, 1981), 21-22, 78-79; Daphne Duval Harrison, *Black Pearls: Blues Queens of the 1920s* (New Brunswick, N.J.: Rutgers University Press, 1988), 18-21.

24 Roger Lane, *The Roots of Violence in Black Philadelphia, 1860-1900* (Cambridge, Mass.: Harvard University Press, 1986), 130, 158-59.

25 Brooks, *You May Plow Here*, 206, 109. For a provocative discussion of earlier black women who practiced abstinence, see Rennie Simson, "The Afro-American Female: The Historical Context of the Construction of Sexual Identity," in *The Powers of Desire: The Politics of Sexuality*, ed. Ann Snitow, Sharon Thompson, and Christine Stansell (New York: Monthly Review Press, 1983), 229-35. Simson's observations warrant quoting at length: "[Harriet] Jacobs's attempt to maintain control over her life is also shown in her pattern of living after her escape to freedom in the North. She mentioned no sexual attachments and relied on herself for financial support. [Elizabeth] Keckley too learned self-reliance. A brief marriage with a Mr. Keckley ended in divorce as she found him 'a burden instead of a helpmate.' No children issued from this marriage as Keckley did not wish to bring any more slaves into the world and thus fulfill her function as a breeder. When her marriage was terminated she said of her husband, 'Let charity draw around him the mantle of silence.' Keckley never mentioned another sexual relationship and, like Jacobs, she remained self-supporting for the rest of her life" (232). For additional insight into incidences of domestic violence in the aftermath of emancipation, see Ira Berlin, Steven F. Miller, and Leslie F. Rowland. "Afro-American Families in the Transition from Slavery to Freedom," *Radical History Review* 42 (November 1988): 89-121, esp. 99-100.

26 Stewart E. Tolnay, "Family Economy and the Black American Fertility Transition," *Journal of Family History* 11, no. 3, (1986): 272-77.

27 The Minute Book of the 1935 meetings of the Grand Rapids Study Club notes that among other issues one topic earmarked for discussion was birth control. On January 10, 1935, the Study Club met to discuss "Public Institutions-Prisons, Asylums, Hospitals, etc." The question that focused the discussion was, "Who belongs in Prison—Habitual drunkard? Prostitutes? Homosexual? Non-supporter?" box 1 (Grand Rapids Public Library, Grand Rapids, Michigan); Gerda Lerner, "Early Community Work of Black Club Women," *Journal of Negro History* 59 (1974): 158-67. For a probing examination of black club women's work and institution building in one midwestern city, see Earline Rae Ferguson, "The Woman's Improvement Club of Indianapolis: Black Women Pioneers in Tuberculosis Work, 1903-1938," *Indiana Magazine of History* 84 (September 1988): 237-61.

28 Sarah Darthulin Tyree to Jennie P. Fowlkes, August 23, 1921, Frances Patterson Papers, box 1, folder 2, BWMW Project (Indiana Historical Society, Indianapolis).

29 Joseph A. McFalls, Jr., and George S. Masnick, "Birth Control and the Fertility of the U.S. Black Population, 1880 to 1980," *Journal of Family History* 6 (Spring 1981): 103.

30 William M. Tuttle, Jr., *Race Riot: Chicago in the Red Summer of 1919* (New York: Atheneum, 1982), 164.

31 Hunter, *A Nickel and a Prayer*, 68. Also see, for a judicious discussion of white and black prostitution, Ruth Rosen, *The Lost Sisterhood: Prostitution in America, 1900-1918* (Baltimore: Johns Hopkins University Press, 1982). See

Thomas Connelly, *The Response to Prostitution in the Progressive Era* (Chapel Hill: University of North Carolina Press, 1980), 48-66, for a discussion of the relations between prostitution and European immigration.

32 Brooks, *You May Plow Here*, 219.

33 James E. DeVries, *Race and Kinship in a Midwestern Town: The Black Experience in Monroe, Michigan, 1900-1915* (Urbana: University of Illinois Press, 1984), 90-91.

34 The Maddy Bruce Story, May 18, 1984, BWMW Project.

35 Divorce Decree: Jesse Clay Fowlkes vs. Jane Pauline Fowlkes, April 12, 1923, Frances Patterson Papers, box 2, folder 3 (Indiana Historical Society, Indianapolis). J. C. Fowlkes was ordered to pay $7.50 per week for the support of the children.

36 Brooks, *You May Plow Here*, 219. For an insightful historical analysis of the meaning of wife-beating and battered women's resistance, see Linda Gordon, *Heroes of Their Own Lives: The Politics and History of Family Violence, Boston 1880-1960* (New York: Vintage Press, 1988), 250-88.

37 Gerda Lerner, *Black Women in White America: A Documentary History* (New York: Vintage Books, 1973), 238-39; Jones, *Labor of Love*, 161-64; Gottlieb, *Making Their Own Way*, 107-9.

38 Spear, *Black Chicago*, 29, 34, 155; Henri, *Black Migration*, 142, 168.

39 Mary Helen Washington, *Invented Lives: Narratives of Black Women, 1860-1960* (New York: Anchor Press, 1987), xxii.

40 Henri, *Black Migrations*, 52.

41 Spear, *Black Chicago*, 151-55, Henri, *Black Migration*, 143-44.

42 Spear, *Black Chicago*, 34.

43 Trotter, *Black Milwaukee*, 14, 47, 81, 171, 203.

44 Ibid., 174.

45 Tanis, "A Study in Self Improvement," 42.

46 Susan M. Hartmann, "Women's Organizations during World War II: The Interaction of Class, Race, and Feminism," in *Woman's Being, Woman's Place:*

Female Identity and Vocation in American History, ed. Mary Kelley (Boston: G. K. Hall, 1979); Karen Tucker Anderson, "Last Hired, First Fired: Black Women Workers during World War II," *Journal of American History* 64 (June 1982): 96-97.

47 George E. DeMar, "Negro Women Are American Workers, Too," *Opportunity* 21 (April 1943): 41-43, 77. For a description of the stratified workforce in Milwaukee, see Trotter, *Black Milwaukee*, 159, 171. Trotter notes that, "Where black females worked in close proximity to whites, the work was stratified along racial lines. At the Schroeder Hotel, for example, black women operated the freight elevator, scrubbed the floors, and generally performed the most disagreeable maid's duties. Conversely, white women worked the passenger elevator, filled all clerical positions, and carried out light maid's duties" (159).

48 Trotter, *Black Milwaukee*, 174.

49 William H. Harris, *The Harder We Run: Black Workers since the Civil War* (New York: Oxford University Press, 1982), 64.

50 Meier and Rudwick, *Black Detroit and the Rise of the UAW*, 136, 153-54. Joe Trotter also notes that in spite of vigorous efforts to extend the benefits of the Fair Employment Practices Committee (FEPC) to black women, the FEPC focused upon traditionally white female-dominated industries. Yet, he notes, the complaints of black women of racial discrimination in heavy industries like Allis Chalmers, Norberg, and Harnishchfeger were "frequently dismissed by the FEPC due to insufficient evidence, although some of their charges were as potently documented as those of black men" (Trotter, *Black Milwaukee*, 171).

51 Gottlieb, *Making Their Own Way*; James Borchert, *Alley Life in Washington: Family, Community, Religion, and Folklife in the City, 1850-1970* (Urbana: University of Illinois Press, 1980), 237. Borchert stresses throughout his study "the strong continuities not only between slave and alley culture, but also between alley culture and both rural and urban black cultures of the third quarter of the twentieth century" (237-78). Also see Kusmer, "The Black Urban Experience," 113; Dianne M. Pinderhughes, *Race and Ethnicity in Chicago Politics: A Reexamination of Pluralist Theory* (Urbana: University of Illinois Press, 1987); St. Clair Drake and Horace R. Cayton, *Black Metropolis: A Study of Negro Life in a Northern City* (New York: Harcourt, Brace and World, 1945; revised ed., 1970).

52 Clark-Lewis, " 'This Work Had a End,' " 196-212, esp. 211.

"We Specialize in the Wholly Impossible": The Philanthropic Work of Black Women

1 Cynthia Neverdon-Morton, *Afro-American Women of the South and the Advancement of the Race, 1895-1925* (Knoxville: University of Tennessee Press, 1988); Darlene Clark Hine and Patrick Biddleman, eds., *Black Women in the Middle West Project, Comprehensive Resource Guide—Illinois and Indiana* (Indianapolis: Indiana Historical Bureau, 1985); Deborah Gray White, "Mining the Forgotten: Manuscript Sources for Black Women's History," *Journal of American History* 74 (1987): 237-42.

2 Darlene Clark Hine, *When the Truth Is Told: A History of Black Women's Culture and Community in Indiana, 1875-1950* (Indianapolis: National Council of Negro Women, Indianapolis Section, 1981).

3 Joanne J. Meyerowitz, *Women Adrift: Independent Wage Earners in Chicago, 1880-1930* (Chicago: University of Chicago Press, 1988), xvii-xxiii; Gerda Lerner, "Community Work of Black Club Women," *Journal of Negro History* 59 (1974): 158-67; Maude T. Jenkins, "The History of the Black Women's Club Movement in America" (Ph.D. diss., Teachers College, Columbia University, 1984); Lynda Faye Dickson, "The Early Club Movement among Black Women in Denver, 1890-1925" (Ph.D. diss., University of Colorado, 1982).

4 Hallie Q. Brown, *Homespun Heroines and Other Women of Distinction* ([1926]; reprint ed. New York: Oxford University Press/The Schomburg Library of Nineteenth-Century Black Women Writers, 1988), introduction by Randall Burkett, xxxii; Mrs. N. F. Mossell, *The Work of the Afro-American Woman* ([1894]; reprint ed. New York: Oxford University Press/The Schomburg Library of Nineteenth-Century Black Women Writers, 1988), introduction by Joanne Braxton, 104-14; Darlene Clark Hine, "The Pursuit of Professional Equality: Meharry Medical College, 1921-1938, A Case Study," in *New Perspectives on Black Educational History*, ed. James D. Anderson and V. P. Franklin (Boston: G. K. Hall, 1978), 173-92.

5 Elizabeth Lindsay Davis, *Lifting as They Climb* (Washington, D.C.: National Association of Colored Women's Clubs, 1933), 315-21; Susan Lynn Smith, "The Black Women's Club Movement: Self-Improvement and Sisterhood, 1890-1915" (M.A. thesis, University of Wisconsin-Madison, 1986).

6 *Indianapolis Star*, August 1, 1909.

7 Ibid.

8 Ibid.; Davis, *Lifting as They Climb*, 13; "Fannie Barrier Williams," in *Black Women in Nineteenth-Century American Life: Their Thoughts, Their Words, Their Feelings*, ed. Bert Loewenberg and Ruth Bogin (University Park: Pennsylvania State University Press, 1976), 263-79.

9 Hine, *When the Truth Is Told*, 49-66.

10 D. Augustus Straker, "Manhood and Womanhood Development," *Colored American Magazine* (1901), 312-13; Paula Giddings, *When and Where I Enter: The Impact of Black Women and Race and Sex in America* (New York: William Morrow, 1984), 135-52; Karen J. Blair, *The Clubwoman as Feminist: True Womanhood Redefined, 1868-1914* (New York: Holmes and Meier, 1980), 117-19.

11 Sadie Iola Daniel, *Women Builders* (Washington, D.C.: Associated Publishers, 1931; revised and enlarged, 1970), 79-110, quote on 86; Bernice Reagon, "Bethune, Mary Jane McLeod," in *Dic-*

tionary of American Negro Biography, ed. Rayford W. Logan and Michael R. Winston (New York: W. W. Norton, 1982), 41-43.

12 Daniel, *Women Builders*, 137-67, quote on 161. See also Elvena Tillman, "Brown, Charlotte Hawkins," in *Dictionary of American Negro Biography*, 65-67.

13 Tillman, "Brown, Charlotte Hawkins," in *Dictionary of American Negro Biography*, 65-67.

14 Daniel, *Women Builders*, 111-36. See also Evelyn Brooks Barnett, "Nannie Burroughs and the Education of Black Women," in *The Afro-American Woman: Struggles and Images*, ed. Rosalyn Terborg-Penn and Sharon Harley (Port Washington, N.Y.: Kennikat Press, 1978), 97-108; and Evelyn Brooks Barnett, "Burroughs, Nannie Helen," in *Dictionary of American Negro Biography*, 81-82.

15 "Nannie H. Burroughs," *National Cyclopedia of the Colored Race* (1919), 89.

16 Ibid.; Daniel, *Women Builders*, 122.

17 Daniel, *Women Builders*, 168-91; John Bennett, "S. C. Negro Woman's Life Is Welfare Drama," *Charleston News and Courier*, November 24, 1940; Jane Edna Hunter, *A Nickel and a Prayer* (Cleveland: Elli Kani, 1940), 63-65, 70-71; Adrienne Lash Jones, "Jane Edna Hunter: A Case Study of Black Leadership, 1910-1950" (Brooklyn, N.Y.: Carlson Publishing, 1990).

18 Jones, "Jane Edna Hunter."

19 Ibid.; Hine, *Black Women in White: Racial Conflict and Cooperation in the Nursing Profession, 1890-1950* (Bloomington: Indiana University Press, 1989), Chapter 3.

20 Biographical information located in the Jane Hunter Papers, box 1, folder 1, Western Reserve Historical Society, Cleveland, Ohio.

21 David M. Katzman, *Seven Days a Week: Women and Domestic Service in Industrializing America* (New York: Oxford University Press, 1978), 77-79; Alice Kessler-Harris, *Out to Work: A History of Wage Earning Women in the United States* (New York: Oxford University Press, 1982), 237-38; Jacqueline Jones, *Labor of*

Love, Labor of Sorrow: Black Women, Work, and the Family from Slavery to the Present (New York: Basic Books, 1985), 128, 153, 164, 168.

22 Meyerowitz, *Women Adrift*, 36.

23 Katzman, *Seven Days a Week*, 78-79; Kessler-Harris, *Out to Work*, 237-38.

24 Hunter, *A Nickel and a Prayer*, 88. See also Daniel, *Women Builders*, 176-77. Hunter, "My Experiences in Race Relations" (1948), Jane Hunter Papers, box 1, folder 9.

25 Hunter, *A Nickel and a Prayer*, 88.

26 *Charleston News and Courier*, November 24, 1940. Initially the home was named the Working Girls Home Association of Cleveland but was changed to the Phillis Wheatley Home on October 31, 1912. Hunter, as the secretary of the Phillis Wheatley Association, described its purpose as "establishing a home of good repute where good honest, upright working girls can have pure and pleasant surroundings where they can be taught the art of housekeeping technics [sic], of hygiene, importance of loyalty, the beauty in neatness and dispatch." Phillis Wheatley Association Manuscript Collection, box 1, bound volume, Minutes of Board of Trustees, 1914-1943, Western Reserve Historical Society, Cleveland, Ohio.

27 Ruth Rosen, *The Lost Sisterhood: Prostitution in America, 1900-1918* (Baltimore: Johns Hopkins University Press, 1982), 147.

28 Hunter, *A Nickel and a Prayer*, 68. See also Rosen, *Lost Sisterhood*, 80-81.

29 Hunter, *A Nickel and a Prayer*, 93-94, 99-100; Kenneth L. Kusmer, *A Ghetto Takes Shape: Black Cleveland, 1870-1930* (Urbana: University of Illinois Press, 1976), 150-51; Phillis Wheatley Association booklet (1918), Lethia C. Fleming Papers (1876-1963), box 1, folder 3, Western Reserve Historical Society, Cleveland, Ohio. The purpose of the home was described in the booklet: "Special attention is given to training in the domestic arts. ... It is intended to lay special emphasis on this feature of the work, thus qualifying the less educated

girl for domestic service for which the more recently arrived southern girls are very much in demand."

30 Kusmer, *A Ghetto Takes Shape*, 49; Hunter, *A Nickel and a Prayer*, 90-91.

31 Jenkins, "History of the Black Women's Club Movement," 80-83; Hunter, *A Nickel and a Prayer*, 101. It is interesting to note that in 1930 Hunter and the Phillis Wheatley Association allegedly rejected an offer of $25,000 from the Rosenwald Fund because of its proviso that the Association had to become a branch of the Young Women's Christian Association. Jane Hunter Papers, box 1, folder 7. In her autobiography, Hunter explained that she rejected any merger with the YWCA because, "only as an independent organization could we win a full measure of justice for colored girls" (*A Nickel and a Prayer*, 110). Of course, by this point, Hunter more likely objected to any diminution of her personal control and autonomy at the helm of the Phillis Wheatley Home.

32 Louise Daniel Hutchinson, *Anna J. Cooper: A Voice from the South* (Washington, D.C.: Smithsonian Institution Press, 1981), 88. See also "Anna Julia Cooper," in *Black Women in Nineteenth-Century American Life*, 317-31.

33 Willie Mae Coleman, "Keeping the Faith and Disturbing the Peace: Black Women, From Anti-Slavery to Women's Suffrage" (Ph.D. diss., University of California-Irvine, 1982); Rosalyn Terborg-Penn, "Afro-Americans in the Struggle for Woman Suffrage" (Ph.D. diss., Howard University, 1977); Davis, *Lifting as They Climb*, 321-24.

34 Jane Edna Hunter to Nannie H. Burroughs, November 2, 1929, Nannie H. Burroughs Manuscript Collection, Container 13, Manuscript Division, Library of Congress, Washington, D.C. Writing in the *Washington Eagle* (March 9, 1928), Burroughs lavished praise on Hunter. "The new Phillis Wheatley home is the greatest social and economic welfare achievement among women of our day. Jane Hunter has given to her women and girls a business and social institution that takes high rank among the best in the world. ... The fact of the matter is that Jane Hunter has given us the biggest and best hotel for Negro women in the whole world." Burroughs Papers, Speeches and Writings File, Container 46.

35 Hunter to Burroughs, December 24, 1937; March 15, 1938; August 6, 1946, Burroughs Papers, Container 13. Again, on December 24, 1940, as she had written on the same date in 1937, Hunter confided, "How much I wish that we could spend this Christmas together in person. Distance cannot make a difference between two sincere friends. ... Between you and me there is no such thing as distance dear. For I am always there and you are always here in my heart." Burroughs Papers, Container 13.

36 Hunter to Burroughs, December 22, 1942, May 11, 1945, Burroughs Papers, Container 13. Hunter was not alone in expressing frustration with the fund-raising work. On December 29, 1934, Mary McLeod Bethune wrote to Burroughs, "I can never tell you how terrible I feel in not being able to comply with your letter of yesterday. I have tried my utmost to secure the money to send to you. My back has been up against a wall for several weeks. I just cant [sic] get a dime from any source. I came into the holidays without money to send cards to my friends and my teachers [went] unpaid for two months. My bills are hanging over me for the daily ruing and everything that would call for money is before me. I went to the bank; I tried personal friends. There is no letting loose at this time. I know just the situation there and how heavy the load is for you but I am helpless at this moment. If any light comes, any development which will enable me to assist, you will hear from me. You know I would not fail you if it was humanly possible for me to do otherwise. Hold on to everything the best that you can. Light MUST come." Burroughs Papers, Container 13. On May 1, 1941, Bethune shared with Burroughs, "I am very happy to inclose [sic] my check for

$25 to help you in your cause. I wish it could be $25,000 so that I might relieve you of your anxiety for real money to carry forward your work." Burroughs Papers, Container 13.

37 Hunter to Burroughs, May 16, 1946, Burroughs Papers, Container 13.

38 Hunter to Burroughs, July 7, 1955, Burroughs Papers, Container 13.

39 Burroughs to Hunter, April 1, 1955, Burroughs Papers, Container 38.

40 Hunter to Burroughs, August 16, 1955, February 3, 1957, Burroughs Papers, Container 13.

41 Folder containing undated newspaper press clipping of Hunter's death, Burroughs Papers, Container 13.

42 Josephine St. Pierre Ruffin, quoted in Davis, *Lifting as They Climb*, 13.

43 "Fannie Barrier Williams," in *Black Women in Nineteenth-Century American Life*, 263-79; quote on 270.

44 Rosen, *Lost Sisterhood*, 80.

45 "Fannie Barrier Williams," in *Black Women in Nineteenth-Century American Life*, 263-79.

46 Hunter to Burroughs, February 3, 1957, Burroughs Papers, Container 13.

The Housewives' League of Detroit: Black Women and Economic Nationalism

1 "Constitution of Housewives' League of Detroit and Declaration of Purpose," n.d., box 1, Housewives' League of Detroit Papers, Burton Collection, Public Library, Detroit, Mich. The league was structured into a central league and units. Twelve distinct committees made up the central league: organizing, membership, program, social, publicity, ways and means, sick, sanitary, research, filing, music and drama, and budget. The president, officers, and chair of all committees from the central league and all individual units constituted the executive board. Each neighborhood unit had eight committees: membership, program, social, publicity, sick, research, sanitary, and budget. According to the constitution, the duties of the Sanitary Committee, for example, were as follows: "to suggest better means of sanitation, to raise the standard in any place where needed, to encourage more artistic and attractive arrangement of merchandise by offering placards of approval or endorsement to those who reach the highest standards proposed and to educate the merchant to appreciate endorsements of the league as other merchants do that of Good Housekeeping." Space does not permit inclusion of more detailed descriptions of the duties and functions of all of the committees. Suffice it to say there was sufficient variety to permit virtually every woman the opportunity to participate on a central or unit committee in a meaningful capacity.

2 Dana Lynn Frank, "At the Point of Consumption: Seattle Labor and the Politics of Consumption, 1919-1927" (Ph.D. diss., Yale University, 1988), 519. See also Maurine Weiner Greenwald, "Working-Class Feminism and the Family Wage Ideal: The Seattle Debate on Married Women's Right to Work, 1914-1920," *Journal of American History* 76 (June 1989): 118-49; Susan Levine, "Workers' Wives: Gender, Class and Consumerism in the 1920s in the United States," *Gender and History* 3 (Spring 1991): 45-64; and Nancy A. Hewitt, "Beyond the Search for Sisterhood: American Women's History in the 1980s," *Social History* 10 (October 1985): 299-321.

3 Nancy F. Cott, "What's in a Name? The Limits of 'Social Feminism': Or, Expanding the Vocabulary of Women's History," *Journal of American History* 76 (December 1989): 827; Elsa Barkley Brown, "Womanist Consciousness: Maggie Lena Walker and the Independent Order of Saint Luke," *Signs* 14 (Spring 1989): 610-33. Brown defines *womanism* as a consciousness that incorporates racial, cultural, sexual, national, economic, and political considerations. My discussion of the multifaceted economic role of black women during the 1930s particularly benefitted from reading Robin D. G. Kelley, *Hammer and*

Hoe: Alabama Communists during the Great Depression (Chapel Hill: University of North Carolina Press, 1990).

4 Gerda Lerner, "Early Community Work of Black Club Women," *Journal of Negro History* 59 (April 1974): 158-67; Karen J. Blair, *The Clubwoman as Feminist: True Womanhood Redefined, 1868-1914* (New York: Holmes and Meier, 1980); Nancy F. Cott, *The Grounding of Modern Feminism* (New Haven, Conn.: Yale University Press, 1987); Cynthia Nerverdon-Morton, *Afro-American Women in the South and the Advancement of the Race* (Knoxville: University of Tennessee Press, 1989); Darlene Clark Hine, *When the Truth Is Told: A History of Black Women's Culture and Community in Indiana, 1875-1950* (Indianapolis: National Council of Negro Women, Indianapolis Section, 1981).

5 Quote from C. H. Wesley, *The History of the National Association of Colored Women's Clubs*, (Washington, D.C.: NACW, 1984), 42; Anne Firor Scott, "Most Invisible of All: Black Women's Voluntary Associations," *Journal of Southern History* 56 (February 1990): 14, 16. See also, Dorothy Salem, *To Better Our World: Black Women in Organized Reform, 1890-1920* (Brooklyn: Carlson, 1990), 103-44; and Susan Lynn Smith, "The Black Women's Club Movement: Self-Improvement and Sisterhood, 1890-1915" (M.A. thesis, University of Wisconsin-Madison, 1986).

6 For an analysis of voluntary associations, see Anne Firor Scott, "On Seeing and Not Seeing: A Case of Historical Invisibility," *Journal of American History* 71 (June 1984): 9-18; and Edith V. Alvord, ed., *A History of the Michigan State Federation of Women's Clubs, 1895-1953* (Ann Arbor, Mich.: Ann Arbor Press, 1953), 5-9.

7 Beverly Guy-Sheftall, *Daughters of Sorrow: Attitudes toward Black Women, 1880-1920* (Brooklyn: Carlson, 1990), 72-75.

8 D. Augustus Straker, "Manhood and Womanhood Development," *Colored American Magazine* (February 1901), 312-13; For discussion of the three black male leaders, see Louis R. Harlan, "Booker T. Washington and the Politics of Accommodation," in *Black Leaders in the Twentieth Century*, ed. John Hope Franklin and August Meier (Urbana: University of Illinois Press, 1982), 1-18. In the same volume, see Elliott Rudwick, "W.E.B. Du Bois: Protagonist of the Afro-American Protest," 63-83, and Lawrence W. Levine, "Marcus Garvey and the Politics of Revitalization," 105-38.

9 Straker, "Manhood and Womanhood Development," 313.

10 Additional information on Rosa Slade Gragg is contained in her manuscript collection located in the Burton Historical Collection, Detroit Public Library, Detroit, Mich.

11 William H. Harris, *The Harder We Run: Black Workers since the Civil War* (New York: Oxford University Press, 1982), 64-65.

12 Florette Henri, *Black Migration: Movement North 1900-1920* (New York: Anchor Press, 1975), 141-43. According to the historian James R. Grossman, Chicago was one of the few cities in which fewer than half (43.9 percent) of all employed black women were classified by the 1920 census as servants or hand laundresses. Over 12 percent, or 2,608 black women, found work in Chicago's factories before World War I. The packing industry, Grossman points out, was probably the greatest single employer of black women during the war. (James R. Grossman, *Land of Hope: Chicago, Black Southerners, and the Great Migration* [Chicago: University of Chicago Press, 1989], 184-85.) In his study of employment trends in Milwaukee during the depression years, the historian Joe Trotter observed that black women were basically excluded from the industrial sector. He found that "60.4 percent of their numbers labored in domestic service as compared to only 18.6 percent of all females." Trotter calculated that following the end of World War II the number of unskilled black females in industry in the city dropped from 620 in 1945 to 249 by 1947. For these women, the readjust-

ment from industrial to domestic service was painful. As Trotter noted, "A mother of eight dependent children was laid off from her defense industry job in mid-August 1945. Unable to find factory work, she finally took a domestic service position at $0.50 per hour compared to the $1.10 per hour she made as a war worker." The woman explained, "I don't see how I can keep my family on such a low income as this domestic job offers. But if I don't take it they might deny my unemployment benefits." (Joe William Trotter, Jr., *Black Milwaukee: The Making of an Industrial Proletariat, 1915-45* [Urbana: University of Illinois Press, 1985], 157, 173.)

13 Mary Helen Washington, *Invented Lives: Narratives of Black Women, 1860-1960* (Garden City, N.Y.: Doubleday, 1987), xxii.

14 August Meier and Elliott Rudwick, *Black Detroit and the Rise of the UAW* (New York: Oxford University Press, 1979), 136, 156.

15 Lillian E. Johnson, "History of the Detroit Study Club," May 1949, typescript, box 2, Detroit Study Club Papers, Burton Historical Collection, Detroit Public Library, Detroit, Mich. Karen J. Blair has written extensively on the literary clubs white women established that eventually became concerned with social action. This process is often contrasted with black women's clubs that were assumed to have always, from inception, focused on social action or political issues. Actually, as the history of the Detroit Study Club illustrates, the pattern was more complex. Only some black women's clubs moved from being literary to involvement with and concern for broader social issues. Blair, *The Clubwoman as Feminist*, 66-67; Lerner, "Early Community Work of Black Club Women," 160-62. For recent examinations of the work of black club women see: Jacqueline Anne Rouse, *Lugenia Burns Hope: Black Southern Reformer* (Athens: University of Georgia Press, 1989); and Stephanie Shaw, "Black Club Women and the Creation of the National Association of Colored Women,"

Journal of Women's History 3 (Fall 1991): 10-25.

16 Quoted in Rudwick, "W.E.B. Du Bois," 81.

17 W.E.B. Du Bois, "N.A.A.C.P. and Segregation," *Crisis* 41 (February 1934): 53.

18 Amy Jacques-Garvey, ed., *Philosophy and Opinions of Marcus Garvey*, 2 vols. (New York: Atheneum, 1969); E. David Cronon, *Black Moses: The Story of Marcus Garvey and the Universal Negro Improvement Association* (Madison: University of Wisconsin Press, 1969 [1955]).

19 Fannie B. Peck, "History and Purpose of Housewives' League," May 1, 1934, box 3, folder "Speeches and Cards," Housewives' League of Detroit Papers; "History of Housewives' League of Detroit," July 27, 1944, box 1, Housewives' League of Detroit Papers. See also Richard Thomas, "From Peasant to Proletarian: The Formation and Organization of the Black Industrial Working Class in Detroit, 1915-1945" (Ph.D. diss., University of Michigan, 1976), 264ff.

In July 1928 Albon Holsey, president of the National Negro Business League, launched the Colored Merchants Association (CMA) in Montgomery, Alabama. It lasted until 1934. The CMA organized local associations to purchase collectively wholesale products at discount prices by forming buyer cooperatives of at least ten black retail stores. The CMA then encouraged the development of housewives' leagues to promote patronage of the stores in particular and black businesses and professionals in general. Gary Jerome Hunter, "Don't Buy from Where You Can't Work: Black Urban Boycott Movements during the Depression, 1929-1941" (Ph.D. diss., University of Michigan, 1977), 53-54. See also Albon Holsey, "The C.M.A. Stores Face the Chains," *Opportunity* 7 (July 1929): 210.

20 Fannie B. Peck, "Negro Housewives, What Now?" reprinted from *Service Magazine* (November 1942), box 4, Housewives' League of Detroit Papers.

21 Christine M. Fuqua, president, National Housewives' Leagues of America, "Declaration of May 18, 1948, as Fannie B. Peck Day," box 4, Housewives' League of Detroit Papers.

22 Typewritten and handwritten undated speeches and fragments of minutes of meetings, box 3, folder "Speeches," Housewives' League of Detroit Papers; "History of Housewives' League of Detroit," July 27, 1944, box 1, Housewives' League of Detroit Papers.

23 Hunter, "Don't Buy From Where You Can't Work," 52, 220.

24 Peck, "History and Purpose of Housewives' League."

25 Lincoln Gordon to Mrs. Christine Fuqua, November 14, 1939, box 1, Housewives' League of Detroit Papers.

26 Peck, "History and Purpose of Housewives' League." This change in strategies to "home sphere" improvements is discussed with considerable sophistication in Earl Lewis, *In Their Own Interests: Race, Class and Power in Twentieth-Century Norfolk, Virginia* (Berkeley: University of California Press, 1990).

27 See: Rosa Slade Gragg collection.

28 "Constitution of Housewives' League of Detroit and Declaration of Purpose," Housewives' League of Detroit Papers.

29 Gertrude J. Tolber, "What Now That the War Is Over?" n.d., box 3, folder "Speeches"; "Constitution and Bylaws," box 1, Housewives' League of Detroit Papers.

30 "Slogan" of Housewives' League of Detroit; Section 10 of "Constitution of Housewives' League," box 1, folder "Constitution and Bylaws," Housewives' League of Detroit Papers.

31 Catherine Pharr to Advertiser, July 31, 1950, box 1, folder "Letters," Housewives' League of Detroit Papers.

32 "Constitution of Housewives' League of Detroit and Declaration of Purpose," Housewives' League of Detroit Papers.

33 "Report and Notes of the Research Committee," n.d.; Tolber, "What Now That the War Is Over?"

34 Naomi Jefferies, Christiana Fuqua

and Dolores Crudup to Jerome P. Cavanagh, May 1, 1963, box 1, folder "Letters," Housewives' League of Detroit Papers.

35 "Report and Notes of the Research Committee"; Tolber, "What Now That the War Is Over?"

36 Jacqueline Jones, *Labor of Love, Labor of Sorrow: Black Women, Work and the Family, from Slavery to the Present* (New York: Basic Books, 1985), 215.

37 Report and notes of the Research Committee of the Housewives' League of Detroit, box 3, Housewives' League of Detroit Papers.

Co-Laborers in the Work of the Lord: Nineteenth-Century Black Women Physicians

1 Dorothy Sterling, ed., *We Are Your Sisters: Black Women in the Nineteenth Century* (New York: W. W. Norton, 1984), 450.

2 Mary Roth Walsh, *"Doctors Wanted: No Women Need Apply": Sexual Barriers in the Medical Profession, 1835-1975* (New Haven, Conn.: Yale University Press, 1977), 194, 225, 236-37; M. O. Bousfield, "An Account of Physicians of Color in the United States," *Bulletin of the History of Medicine* 17 (January 1945): 62, 70, 80; E. Richard Brown, *Rockefeller Medicine Men: Medicine and Capitalism in America* (Berkeley: University of California Press, 1979), 88, 153; Paul Starr, *The Social Transformation of American Medicine: The Rise of a Sovereign Profession and the Making of a Vast Industry* (New York: Basic Books, 1982), 124-25.

3 Bettina Aptheker, "Quest for Dignity: Black Women in the Professions, 1885-1900," in her *Woman's Legacy: Essays on Race, Sex, and Class in American History* (Amherst: University of Massachusetts Press, 1982), 97-98; Sarah W. Brown, "Colored Women Physicians," *Southern Workman* 52 (1923); 586; Sterling, ed., *We Are Your Sisters*, 440-41; Leslie L. Alexander, "Early Medical Heroes: Susan Smith McKinney Steward, M.D.,

1847-1918: First Afro-American Woman Physician in New York State," *Journal of the National Medical Association* 67 (March 1975): 173-75.

4 Walsh, *"Doctors Wanted,"* 186; Cora Bagley Marrett, "On the Evolution of Women's Medical Societies," *Bulletin of the History of Medicine* 53 (1979): 434.

5 Bousfield, "An Account of Physicians of Color," 592; Numa P. G. Adams, "Sources of Supply of Negro Health Personnel: Section A: Physicians," *Journal of Negro Education* 6 (July 1937): 468.

6 *Medical and Surgical Observer* (October 1893): 184. M. Vandehurst Lynk was the editor of this first black medical journal. He also founded the medical department of the University of West Tennessee in Memphis.

7 Rayford W. Logan, *Howard University: The First Hundred Years, 1867-1967* (New York: New York University Press, 1969), 42, 47.

8 Daniel Smith Lamb, *Howard University Medical Department: A Historical Biographical and Statistical Souvenir* (Washington, D.C.: R. Beresford, 1900), 142; Brown, "Colored Women Physicians," 592; Bousfield, "An Account of Physicians of Color," 70; Aptheker, *Woman's Legacy*, 100; *Catalogue of Officers and Students of Howard University, 1871-1872*, 54, 62.

9 Cited in Herbert M. Morais, *The History of the Negro in Medicine* (New York: Association for the Study of Negro Life and History, 1967), 43; *Catalogue of the Officers and Students of Howard University from March 1878 to March 1879*, 12-13. All catalogues found in the Moorland-Spingarn Library of Howard University, Washington, D.C.

10 Morais, *The History of the Negro in Medicine*, 43; Logan, *Howard University*, 47.

11 James Summerville, *Educating Black Doctors: A History of Meharry College* (University: University of Alabama Press, 1983), 31-32; Darlene Clark Hine, "The Pursuit of Professional Equality: Meharry Medical College, 1921-1938, A Case Study," *New Perspectives in Black*

Educational History, ed. Vincent P. Franklin and James D. Anderson (Boston: G. K. Hall, 1978), 173-92.

12 Charles Victor Roman, *Meharry College: A History* (Nashville, Tenn.: Sunday School Publishing Board of the National Baptist Convention, 1934), 64, 76, 107; Summerville, *Educating Black Doctors*, 33.

13 Walsh, *"Doctors Wanted,"* 62, 181, 195.

14 Aptheker, *Woman's Legacy*, 98-99; Sterling, *We Are Your Sisters*, 443-49; Brown, "Colored Women Physicians," 591; Margaret Jerrido, "Black Women Physicians: A Triple Burden," *Alumnae News, The Woman's Medical College of Pennsylvania* (Summer 1979), 4-5; Ruth Abram, "Daughters of Aesculapius," *Alumnae News, The Woman's Medical College of Pennsylvania* (Fall 1983), 10.

15 E. Wilber Block, "Farmer's Daughter Effect: The Case of the Negro Female Professional," *Phylon* 30 (Spring 1969): 17-26; Elizabeth R. Haynes, "Negroes in Domestic Service in the United States," *Journal of Negro History* 8 (1923): 422-28; Lawrence B. de Graff, "Race, Sex and Region: Black Women in the American West," *Pacific Historical Review* 49 (May 1980): 285-313.

16 G. R. Richings, *Evidences of Progress among Colored People* (Philadelphia: George S. Ferguson Co., 1905), 412; L. A. Scruggs, *Women of Distinction: Remarkable in Works and Invincible in Character* (Raleigh, N.C.: L. A. Scruggs, 1982), 177-78; Brown, "Colored Women Physicians," 585; Matthew Anderson, *Presbyterianism: Its Relation to the Negro* (Philadelphia: John McGill, White and Company, 1899), contains sketches of the Berean Church, Caroline Still Wiley Anderson, and the author.

17 Brown, "Colored Women Physicians," 591; Richings, *Evidences of Progress*, 411-12.

18 Richings, *Evidences of Progress*, 411-12; Brown, "Colored Women Physicians," 585-86.

19 Sterling, *We Are Your Sisters*, 441-43; Scruggs, *Women of Distinction*, 100-103.

20 Brown, "Colored Women Physicians," 588; Aptheker, *Woman's Legacy*,

98; Elizabeth L. Davis, *Lifting as They Climb: The National Association of Colored Women* (Washington, D.C.: National Association of Colored Women's Clubs, 1933), 292; Sterling, *We Are Your Sisters*, 443-48.

21 Quoted in Sterling, *We Are Your Sisters*, 445-46; Richings, *Evidences of Progress*, 413; Scruggs, *Women of Distinction*, 364-65; Brown, "Colored Women Physicians," 591.

22 Quoted in Charlayne Hunter-Gault, "Black Women M.D.'s Spirit and Endurance," *New York Times*, November 16, 1977.

23 Ibid.

24 Bousfield, "An Account of Physicians of Color," 72; E. H. Beardsley, "Making Separate Equal: Black Physicians and the Problems of Medical Segregation in the Pre-World War II South," *Bulletin of the History of Medicine* 57 (Fall 1983): 382-86.

25 Sterling, *We Are Your Sisters*, 444-45.

26 Elizabeth Blackwell, *Pioneer Work in Opening the Medical Profession to Women: Autobiographical Sketches* ([1895] New York: Schocken Books, 1977), 228; Jerrido, "Black Women Physicians," 4-5.

27 *Directory of the Philanthropic, Educational and Religious Association of Churches of Philadelphia*, 2d ed. (Lancaster, Pa.: New Era Printing Company, 1903), 158; Philadelphia City Hall, Wills, Inventory and Appraisement, filed, January 11, 1923; Sterling, *We Are Your Sisters*, 440-41; Brown, "Colored Women Physicians," 586.

28 Anderson, *Presbyterianism: Its Relation to the Negro*, 5ff; Margaret Jerrido, "In Recognition of Early Black Women Physicians," *Women and Health* 5 (Fall 1980); 1-3.

29 Aptheker, *Woman's Legacy*, 98, 99, 101; *Atlanta University Bulletin*, November 1891.

30 Logan, *Howard University*, 136; Brown, "Colored Women Physicians," 589-90; Aptheker, *Women's Legacy*, 99.

31 Scruggs, *Women of Distinction*, 267-68.

32 Sister M. Anthony Scally, *Medicine, Motherhood and Mercy: The Story of a*

Black Woman Doctor (Washington, D.C.: Associated Publishers, 1979), 23-27.

33 Isabella Vandervall, "Some Problems of the Colored Woman Physician," *Woman's Medical Journal* 27 (July 1917): 156-58.

34 Aptheker, *Woman's Legacy*. 99.

35 Quoted in Sterling, *We Are Your Sisters*, 440, 441, 443.

36 Scruggs, *Women of Distinction*, 100-103, 177-78; Brown, "Colored Women Physicians," 585.

37 Maritcha Lyons, "Dr. Susan S. McKinney Steward," *Homespun Heroines and Other Women of Distinction*, ed. Hallie Quinn Brown ([1926] reprint ed. Xenia, Ohio: Aldine, 1971), 162; Alexander, "Early Medical Heroes: Susan Smith McKinney Steward," 173-75; Davis, *Lifting as They Climb*, 292; Sterling, *We Are Your Sisters*, 440-43; William Peper, "Boro Had 1st Negro Woman M.D. in 1870s," *Sun*, May 9, 1960; Brooklyn *Times*, June 27, 1891.

38 Scruggs, *Women of Distinction*, 267-68.

39 Brooklyn *Times*, June 27, 1891; Scruggs, *Women of Distinction*, 267-68.

40 Brown, "Colored Women Physicians," 582.

"They Shall Mount Up with Wings as Eagles": Historical Images of Black Nurses, 1890-1950

1 Mary Elizabeth Carnegie, "The Path We Tread," *International Nursing Review* 9 (September-October 1962): 26.

2 Ibid.

3 Ibid.

4 Ibid.

5 Ibid.

6 Joyce Ann Elmore, "Black Nurses: Their Service and Their Struggle," *American Journal of Nursing* 76 (March 1976): 435-37.

7 Jean Maddern Pitrone, *Trailblazer: Negro Nurse in the American Red Cross* (New York: Harcourt, Brace and World, 1969), 88.

8 Ibid., 69.

9 Darlene Clark Hine, "Mable K. Staupers and the Integration of Black Nurses into the Armed Forces."

10 Ibid., 195.

11 Philip A. Kalisch and Beatrice J. Kalisch, *The Advance of American Nursing* (Boston: Little, Brown, 1978), 567-68.

12 Quoted ibid., 568.

13 Carter G. Woodson, *The Negro Professional Man in the Community* ([1934] New York: Negro Universities Press, 1969), 142. See chap. 10; the entire chapter, pp. 133-48, is on black nurses.

14 James H. Jones, *Bad Blood: The Tuskegee Syphilis Experiment* (New York: Free Press, 1981), 6.

15 Interview with Eunice Rivers (Laurie), October 10, 1977, Schlesinger Library Black Women's Oral History Project, Radcliffe College, Cambridge, Massachusetts.

16 Ibid.

17 Janet Wilson James, "Isabel Hampton and the Professionalization of Nursing in the 1890s," in *The Therapeutic Revolution: Essays in the Social History of American Medicine*, ed. Morris J. Vogel and Charles E. Rosenberg (Philadelphia: University of Pennsylvania Press, 1979), 201-44; and Celia Davies, "Professionalizing Strategies as Time- and Culture-Bound: American and British Nursing, Circa 1893," in *Nursing History: New Perspectives, New Possibilities*, ed. Ellen Condliffe Lagemann (New York: Teachers College Press, 1983), 47-63.

18 Darlene Clark Hine, "From Hospital to College: Black Nurse Leaders and the Rise of Collegiate Nursing Schools," *Journal of Negro Education* 51 (Summer 1982): 224; George M. Fredrickson, *The Black Image in the White Mind: The Debate on Afro-American Character and Destiny, 1817-1914*, (New York: Harper Torchbooks, 1971), 1-179ff; and Anna B. Coles, "The Howard University School of Nursing in Historical Perspective," *Journal of the National Medical Association* 61 (March 1969): 105-18.

19 Sheila Rothman, "Women's Special Sphere," in *Women and the Politics of Culture: Studies in the Sexual Economy*, ed.

Michele Wender Zak and Patricia P. Moots (New York: Longman, 1983), 213-23; and Mary Beth Norton, "The Paradox of 'Women's Sphere,'" in *Women of America: A History*, ed. Carol Ruth Berkin and Mary Beth Norton (Boston: Houghton Mifflin, 1979), 139-49.

20 James, "Isabel Hampton," 205.

21 Ibid., 203-5.

22 Hine, "From Hospital to College," 224.

23 Daniel H. Williams, "The Need of Hospitals and Training Schools for the Colored People of the South," *National Hospital Record* 3 (April 1900): 3-7; and Booker T. Washington, "Training Colored Nurses at Tuskegee," *American Journal of Nursing* 2 (December 1910): 167-71.

24 Williams, "The Need of Hospitals," 5.

25 Ibid.

26 Ibid.

27 Ibid., 5-7

28 Washington, "Training Colored Nurses," 171.

29 Ibid.

30 Ethel Johns, "A Study of the Present Status of the Negro Woman in Nursing, 1925," typescript, record group 1.1, series 200, box 122, folder 1507, Rockefeller Foundation Archive, Tarrytown, New York, 27.

31 Ibid.

32 Ibid.

33 Ibid.

34 Estelle Massey Riddle, "Sources of Supply of Negro Health Personnel: Nurses," *Journal of Negro Education* 6 (yearbook issue, 1937): 483-92; Johns, 26-27; Darlene Clark Hine, "The Ethel Johns Report: Black Women in the Nursing Profession, 1925," *Journal of Negro History* 67 (Fall 1982): 212-28; and Donelda Hamlin, "Report on Informal Study of the Educational Facilities for Colored Nurses and Their Use in Hospital, Visiting and Public Health Nursing," Hospital Library and Service Bureau, 1924-25. A copy can be found in Rockefeller Archive Center.

35 Johns, "A Study of the Present Status

of the Negro Woman in Nursing, 1925," 25.

36 Ibid.

37 Ibid., 29.

38 Ibid., 30.

39 Ibid.

40 Ibid.

41 Ibid., 33.

42 Anna DeCosta Banks, "The Work of a Small Hospital and Training School in the South," *Eighth Annual Report of the Hampton Training School for Nurses and Dixie Hospital* (Hampton, Va.: Hampton Training School for Nurses and Dixie Hospital, 1898-1899), 23-28.

43 Interview with Eunice Rivers (Laurie).

44 James H. Jones, *Bad Blood*, 160.

45 Ibid., 164-67.

46 Elizabeth Jones, "The Negro Woman in the Nursing Profession," *Messenger* 5 (July 1923): 764.

47 Ibid.

48 Pitrone, 99-102; and Coles, 111.

49 W. Montague Cobb, "Mabel Keaton Staupers, R.N., 1890-," *Journal of the National Medical Association* 69 (March 1969): 198-99.

50 Mabel Keaton Staupers, "History of the National Association of Colored Graduate Nurses," *American Journal of Nursing* 51 (April 1951): 221-22; and Mabel Keaton Staupers, *No Time for Prejudice* (New York: Macmillan, 1961).

51 Hine, "From Hospital to College," 232.

52 Carnegie, "The Path We Tread," 32.

53 Ibid.

54 Ibid.

55 Ibid., 33.

56 Gloria R. Smith, "From Invisibility to Blackness: The Story of the National Black Nurses' Association," *Nursing Outlook* 23 (April 1975): 226.

57 Ibid.

Carter G. Woodson: White Philanthropy and Negro Historiography

1 Biographical information concerning Carter G. Woodson's early life is available from many sources. The author wishes to thank Dr. W. Montague Cobb, M.D., for sharing his personal recollections of Woodson and a reprint of his essay, "Carter Goodwin Woodson, Ph.D., L.L.D., 1875-1950: The Father of Negro History," *Journal of the National Medical Association* 62 (September 1970): 385-92, 402. Also see D.O.W. Holmes, "A Man with a Purpose: Carter G. Woodson," *Afro-American* (Baltimore, May 1, 1950; July 22, 1950), and Rayford W. Logan, "Carter Goodwin Woodson, 1875-1950," *Journal of Negro History* 35 (October 1950): 344-48. For a discussion of Woodson's refusal to accommodate the demands made of him by the white president of Howard University, J. Stanley Durkee, see Rayford W. Logan's *Howard University: The First Hundred Years, 1867-1967* (New York: New York University Press, 1969), 208. For a detailed treatment of professional exclusion of Afro-American scholars, see Michael Winston, "Through the Back Door: Academic Racism and the Negro Scholar in Historical Perspective," *Daedalus* 100 (1971): 678-719, and Robert L. Harris, Jr., "Segregation and Scholarship: The American Council of Learned Societies; Committee on Negro Studies, 1941-1950," *Journal of Black Studies* 12 (March 1982): 315-31.

2 Carter G. Woodson, "Ten Years of Collecting and Publishing the Records of the Negro," *Journal of Negro History* 10 (October 1925): 598-606.

3 See the Annual Reports of the Director; Proceedings of the Annual Meetings of the ASNLH; and Reports on Negro History Week in the first through thirty-fifth volumes of the *Journal of Negro History*; and Carter G. Woodson, "An Accounting for Twenty-Five Years," *Journal of Negro History* 25 (October 1940): 422-31.

4 Carter G. Woodson to Julius Rosenwald, 3 December 1926, Rosenwald papers (hereafter RP), Box 2, Folder 26, University of Chicago Library, Chicago, Illinois.

5 Lawrence W. Levine, "Marcus Garvey and the Politics of Revitalization," in *Black Leaders of the Twentieth Century*, ed. John Hope Franklin and August Meier (Urbana: University of Illinois Press, 1982), 105-38.

6 The author wishes to thank Deborah L. Hains for the reprint of her Pelzer Award-winning essay, "Scientific History as a Teaching Method: The Formative Years," *Journal of American History* 63 (March 1977): 892-912. The author also wishes to thank Hazel Whitman Hertzberg for sharing her essay, "The Teaching of History," in *The Past before Us: Contemporary Historical Writings in the United States* (Ithaca, N.Y.: Cornell University Press, 1980), 468-98.

7 Woodson to John D. Rockefeller, Jr., 25 March 1927, "Memorandum in Request for an Endowment of $500,000, 1927" by Carter G. Woodson, Laura Spelman Rockefeller Memorial Papers (hereafter LSRM), Box 68, Folder 967, Rockefeller Archive Center, Pocantico Hills, New York; Kelly Miller, "An Estimate of Carter G. Woodson and His Connection with the Association for the Study of Negro Life and History," 1926, LSRM, Box 69, Folder 967; C. Vann Woodward, "Clio with Soul," *Journal of American History* 56 (June 1969): 5-20. Also see Darlene Clark Hine, "The Four Black History Movements: A Case for the Teaching of Black History," *Teaching History: A Journal of Methods* 5 (Fall 1980): 107-17.

8 Woodson to Joel E. Spingarn, 23 May 1916, Joel E. Spingarn Papers, Correspondence with Carter G. Woodson, Moorland-Spingarn Research Center, Howard University, Washington, D.C. The author wishes to thank Esme Bhan of the Center for bringing this letter to her attention. Rosenwald to Woodson, 27 August 1917, Carter G. Woodson Papers (hereafter CGW), Box 56, Manuscript Division, Library of Congress, Washington, D.C.

9 Woodson, "Ten Years of Collecting and Publishing the Records of the Negro," 598-600; Woodson to Abraham Flexner, 23 July 1916, General Education Board Papers (hereafter GEB), Box 205, Folder 1960, Rockefeller Archive Center.

10 Woodson to William C. Graves, 17 December 1917, RP, Box 2, Folder 24.

11 Edward Channing to Woodson, 31 January 1916, CGW, Boxes 5-6.

12 Harold H. Swift to Woodson, 12 January 1918, CGW, Boxes 5-6.

13 Woodson to Flexner, 30 November 1917, GEB, Box 205, Folder 1960.

14 Woodson to Peabody, 11 January 1918, GEB, Box 205, Folder 1960; Peabody to Rosenwald, 25 January 1918, RP, Box 2, Folder 24.

15 R. R. Moton to Peabody, 18 May 1918, CGW, Boxes 5-6.

16 Peabody to Wallace Buttrick, 15 February 1918, GEB, Box 205, Folder 1960.

17 Buttrick to Peabody, 18 February 1918, GEB, Box 205, Folder 1960.

18 Rosenwald to Peabody, 19 February 1918, RP, Box 2, Folder 24; Woodson, "An Accounting for Twenty-Five Years," 424.

19 John Franklin Jameson to James R. Angell, 9 October 1920, LSRM, Box 96, Folder 966. The author wishes to thank Professor Mary Furner of Northern Illinois University for sharing a copy of a similar letter which Jameson wrote to the Commonwealth Fund in support of Woodson's quest for money: James to Max Farrand, Commonwealth Fund, 2 April 1920, J. Franklin Jameson Papers (hereafter JFJ), Manuscript Division, Library of Congress.

20 Woodson, "Ten Years of Collecting and Publishing the Records of the Negro," 598-603.

21 Woodson to W. S. Richardson, 25 April 1922 and Woodson to Trustees of LSRM, 13 January 1923, LSRM, Box 96, Folder 966; Woodson, "An Accounting for Twenty-Five Years," 425-27. In this essay Woodson lists the 27 books published by Associated Publishers, including in addition to those works produced by the paid ASNLH investigators the theses and dissertations of black scholars that focused on black history and culture. Woodson himself was the author or co-author of nine—or one-third—of the books produced; A. A. Taylor wrote two books on reconstruction in South Carolina and Virginia;

Lorenzo J. Greene co-authored two works, *The Employment of the Negro in the District of Columbia* with Myra Colson-Collins, and *The Negro Wage Earner* with Woodson.

22 Inter-office Memorandum written by W. S. Richardson, 14 September 1921; and Richardson, "Outline on the Request of the ASNLH to the LSRM," 26 January 1922, LSRM, Box 96, Folder 966.

23 Woodson to Richardson, 18 February 1922, LSRM, Box 96, Folder 966; Memorandum of interview, Leonard Outhwiate with Woodson, 7 June 1926, LSRM, Box 96, Folder 966.

24 Albert Bushnell Hart to Rosenwald, 12 April 1922, RP, Box 2, Folder 25.

25 George Foster Peabody to Hart, 18 April 1922, RP, Box 2, Folder 25.

26 William C. Graves to Emmett J. Scott, 19 April 1922, RP, Box 2, Folder 25.

27 Woodson to Graves, 18 April 1922 and 4 May 1922, RP, Box 2, Folder 25.

28 Anson Phelps-Stokes, *Negro Status and Race Relations in the United States, 1911-1946: The Thirty-Five Year Report of the Phelps-Stokes Fund* (New York, 1948), 18.

29 Carter G. Woodson, "An Open Letter to the *Afro-American* on the Negro Encyclopedia," 3 June 1936, LSRM, Box 9, Folder 81.

30 Graves to Scott, 19 April 1922 and Woodson to Graves, 4 May 1922, RP, Box 2, Folder 25.

31 Woodson to Graves, 4 May 1922, RP, Box 2, Folder 25.

32 Ibid.

33 Scott to Graves, 22 April 1922, RP, Box 2, Folder 25.

34 Peabody to Hart, 18 April 1922, RP, Box 2, Folder 25; Woodson, "An Open Letter to the *Afro-American* on the Negro Encyclopedia," 3 June 1936, LSRM, Box 9, Folder 81.

35 Woodson to the Trustees of LSRM, 31 December 1924, LSRM Box 96, Folder 966.

36 Ruml to Woodson, 10 June 1926 and Leonard Outwaite to Woodson, 15 January 1927, LSRM, Box 96, Folder 967.

37 Woodson to LSRM, 11 August

1926, LSRM, Box 96, Folder 966; Woodson to LSRM, 1 January 1927, and Woodson to Rockefeller, Jr., 25 March 1927, LSRM, Box 96, Folder 967.

38 Woodson to Guy Stanton Ford, 27 January 1925, LSRM, Box 96, Folder 966.

39 Inter-Office Memorandum, Re: The Association for the Study of Negro Life and History, 13 March 1929, LSRM, Box 96, Folder 967.

40 John David Smith, "A Different View of Slavery: Black Historians Attack the Proslavery Arguments, 1890-1920," *Journal of Negro History* 65 (Fall 1980): 298-311. Also see Woodson's review of U. B. Phillips' "American Negro Slavery" in *Mississippi Valley Historical Review* 5 (March 1919): 480, and in the *Journal of Negro History* 4 (January 1919): 103.

41 Ulrich B. Phillips to Sydnor H. Walker, 9 May 1929, LSRM, Box 96, Folder 967.

42 William E. Dodd to Walker, 9 May 1929, LSRM, Box 96, Folder 967.

43 Walter L. Fleming to Walker, 9 May 1929, LSRM, Box 96, Folder 967.

44 J. G. de Roulhac Hamilton to Walker, 10 May 1929, LSRM, Box 96, Folder 967.

45 Woodson to Walker, 24 June 1929, LSRM, Box 96, Folder 967.

46 Arthur M. Schlesinger to E. E. Day, 16 May 1929, LSRM, Box 96, Folder 967.

47 Schlesinger to Walker, 17 June 1933 and 14 April 1936, RF, Box 9, Folder 81.

48 Jameson to Day, 13 May 1929, LSRM, Box 96, Folder 967.

49 George E. Vincent to Woodson, 14 June 1929 and Walker to Woodson, 19 June 1929, LSRM, Box 96, Folder 967.

50 Woodson to Walker, 24 June 1929, LSRM, Box 96, Folder 967.

51 Woodson to Jackson Davis, 21 April 1932 and Inter-Office Memorandum, 29 November 1933, GEB, Box 205, Folder 1960.

52 Jackson Davis summary of interview with Woodson, 13 May 1932, and Davis to Woodson, 6 November 1933, RF, Box 9, Folder 81.

53 Davis to John Hope, 6 November 1933, GEB, Box 205, Folder 1960; Walker to Schlesinger, 8 June 1933, RF, Box 9, Folder 81.

54 Woodson to Davis, 6 January 1933, GEB, Box 205, Folder 1960.

55 Davis to Woodson, 13 January 1934, GEB, Box 205, Folder 1960; Walker to Davis, 11 January 1934, GEB, Box 205, Folder 1960. The author wishes to thank Professor James D. Anderson of the University of Illinois for sharing a copy of this hand written note.

56 Edwin Embree to N. W. Levin of the Rosenwald Family Association, 4 June 1936, and Levin to Woodson, 9 June 1936, RP, Box 2, Folder 27. Also see Charles S. Johnson, "Phylon Profile, X: Edwin Rogers Embree," *Phylon* 7 (Fall 1946): 317-34.

57 Woodson to Arthur Spingarn, 13 January 1936, Spingarn Papers, Correspondence with Woodson.

58 Woodson, "Annual Report of the Director," *Journal of Negro History* 31 (October 1946): 386, and "Annual Report," *Journal of Negro History* 34 (October 1949): 383-90.

59 For an excellent treatment of the racial changes in the leadership of black colleges, see Raymond Wolters, *The New Negro on Campus: Black College Rebellions of the 1920s* (Princeton, N.J.: Princeton University Press, 1975). Also see James D. Anderson, "Northern Philanthropy and the Training of Black Leadership: Fisk University, A Case Study, 1915-1930," *New Perspectives in Black Educational History*, ed. James D. Anderson and Vincent Franklin (Boston: G. K. Hall, 1979), 97-111. For an in depth treatment of Woodson see Jacqueline Goggin, *Carter G. Woodson* (Baton Rouge: Louisiana State University Press, 1993).

The Black Studies Movement:
Afrocentric-Traditionalist-Feminist Paradigms for the Next Stage

1 Robert L. Harris, Jr. "The Intellectual and Institutional Development of

Africana Studies," *Three Essays: Black Studies in the United States*, by Robert L. Harris, Jr., Darlene Clark Hine, and Nellie McKay (New York: Ford Foundation, 1990), 7-14.

2 Adbul Alkalimat, *Introduction to Afro-American Studies: A Peoples College Primer* (Chicago: Twenty-First Century Books, 1986), 14-15.

3 Quoted in Charles Frye, *The Impact of Black Studies on the Curricula of Three Universities* (Washington, D.C.: University Press of America, 1976), 12-13.

4 Quoted in William E. Sims, *Black Studies: Pitfalls and Potential* (Washington, D.C.: University Press of America, 1978), 9.

5 Ibid., 4.

6 Molefi Asante, *The Afrocentric Idea* (Philadelphia: Temple University Press, 1987).

7 Molefi Asante, *Afrocentricity* (revised ed., Trenton, New Jersey: Africa World Press, 1987), 58.

8 Ibid.

9 Angela Davis, "Reflections on the Black Woman's Role in the Community of Slaves," *The Black Scholar* (December 1971), 3-15.

10 Deborah Gray White, *Ar'n't I a Woman? Female Slaves in the Plantation South* (New York: W.W. Norton, 1985).

11 Patricia Morton, *Disfigured Images: The Historical Assault on Afro-American Women* (New York: Praeger Publishers, 1991).

12 bell hooks, "Feminism: A Transformational Politic," in *Theoretical Perspectives on Sexual Differences*, ed. Deborah L. Rhodes (New Haven, Conn.: Yale University Press, 1990), 187.

13 Patricia Hill Collins, *Black Feminist Thought: Knowledge, Consciousness and the Politics of Empowerment* (Boston: Unwin Hyman, 1990).

14 Asante, *Afrocentricity*, 6.

15 Martin Bernal, *Black Athena: The Afroasiastic Root of Classical Civilization, Vol. I, The Fabrication of Ancient Greece 1785-1985* (New Brunswick, N.J.: Rutgers University Press, 1987), 73.

16 John G. Jackson, *Introduction to African Civilizations* (Secaucus, N.J.: Citadel Press, 1970), 3; Yosef ben-Jochannan, *African Origins of the Major Western Religions* (New York: Alkebu-Lan Books, 1970), *Black Man of the Nile and His Family* (Baltimore: Black Classics Press, 1978), and *Africa: Mother of Western Civilization* (New York: Alkebu-Lan Books, 1971); Drusilla Dunjee Houston, *Wonderful Ethiopians of the Ancient Cushite Empire* ([1926] Baltimore: Black Classics Press, 1985).

17 ben-Jochannan, *Black Man of the Nile,* xiii.

18 Quoted in James D. Anderson, "Secondary School History Textbooks and the Treatment of Black History," in *The State of Afro-American History: Past, Present, and Future,* ed. Darlene Clark Hine (Baton Rouge: Louisiana State University Press, 1986), 262.

19 Ivan Van Sertima, *They Came before Columbus: The African Presence in Ancient America* (New York: Random House, 1976), 24.

20 Cheikh Anta Diop, *The African Origin of Civilization: Myth or Reality,* ed. and trans. Mercer Cook (New York: Lawrence Hill and Company; 1956), 258; St. Clair Drake, *Black Folk Here and There,* 2 vols. (Los Angeles: University of California Press, 1987).

21 Nathan I. Huggins, "Integrating History," in *The State of Afro-American History,* ed. Hine, 160-61.

22 *Black Issues in Higher Education,* February 28, 1991, 1.

23 John Henrik Clarke, *The Black Collegian,* January/February, 1991, 165.

INDEX

Abbey, Charlotte
  See Cole, Rebecca J.
Absentee mothers
  See Great migration
"Agitate! Agitate!" 133
American Historical Association
  conference on Black history (1983), xxv, 203
  The State of Afro-American History: Past Present and Future, xxv
African Methodist Episcopal Church, 7
African studies, 223
Afro-American studies, 223
Afrocentricity
  and Molefi Asante, 238-39
  impact of on Black studies, 246-47
  See also Originists
Alkalimat, Abdul
  Introduction to Afro-American Studies, 236
American Medical Association
  and admission of Black nurses, 179
  exclusionary practices of, 158
  See also Riddle, Estelle Massey; Staupers, Mabel Keaton
American Nurses' Association, 165
  general integration of, 199-200
American Red Cross Nursing Service, 165
  and integration of Army and Navy Nurse Corps, 189-90
  and NACGN, 189-90
  led by Mary Beard, 189
  See also Davis, Frances Elliot
Anderson, Caroline Still Wiley, 151
  and Berean Presbyterian Church, 156
  and early education, 152
  and William Still, 151-52
  See also Black women physicians
Army Nurses Corps
  and quotas used in induction of Black nurses, 191-95
  See also Hastie, William H.; NACGN; Staupers, Mabel Keaton
Asante, Molefi
  See Afrocentricity
Association of American Medical Colleges, 149
Association for the Study of Negro Life and History (ASNLH)
  assessment of by white historians, 215-16
  constituency of, 205-6, 208
  and controversy over grants, 211-12
  early research of, 210-11, 215
  and *Journal of Negro History*, 205, 221-22
  Negro History Bulletin, 205-6
  and ouster of Thomas Jesse Jones, 213-14
  publications of, 214-15
  and resignation of Albert Bushnell Hart, 212-13

and search for funds after loss of grant support, 221
  support from Carnegie grant, 209-10
  and support from LSRM, 210, 211
  support from Phelps-Stokes fund, 214
  under leadership of Carter G. Woodson, 207-22
Augusta, Alexander T., 149
  See also Howard University
Authenticist Black studies scholars
  prominent members of, 243, 244
  unifying theme of work of, 243-44
  See also Afrocentricity; Originists

Baker, Ella
  advocates "group centered leadership," 23
  and Southern Christian Leadership Conference, 22-23
  and Student Nonviolent Coordinating Committee, 23
  and Young Negro Cooperative League, 22-23
Barrows, Isabel C., 149
Bates, Daisy
  The Long Shadow of Little Rock: A Memoir, 21
Beard, Mary, 189
  See also American Red Cross
Beasley, Mary L., 139
ben-Jochannon, Yosef
  and *Black Man of the Nile*, 245
Bennett, Lerone, xviii
Bernal, Martin
  and *Black Athena*, 244
  on resurgence of Originist thought, 244
Bethune, Mary McCleod
  and Bethune-Cookman College, 113
  and Daytona Educational and Industrial Institution for Training Negro Girls, 16-17
  and involvement with Black women's club movement, 17, 113
  See also Hunter, Jane Edna; National Council of Negro Women
Bidelman, Patrick
  See Black Women in the Midwest Project
"Bi-racial dualism," 12-13
Birth rates
  declining among Black women, 45-46, 95-99
Black Arts and Consciousness Movement, xviii
Black churches
  and hierarchy of male leadership, 7
  and itinerant women preachers, 7-9
  women's role in, 9-10
  See also Early, Sarah Woodson
Black Club Women in Michigan
  and allegations of exclusivity, 76-77
  in Detroit, 72

early movement for, 66-69
and needs of Black children, 71-2
and political action, 74-76, 121, 136
and separate needs from white club women,
  69-70
and social consciousness, 70
See also Delaney, Mary; Detroit Study Club
"Black Female Slave Resistance: The
  Economics of Sex," xxvii-iii
Black Issues in Higher Education, 242
Black male physicians
  increase of after Civil War, 148-49
  attitudes of toward Black women physicians,
    154
Black medical schools
  in post-Reconstructionist South, 148
  See also Howard University
Black nationalism
  See Economic nationalism
Black nurses
  admission of to Army and Navy Nurse
    Corps, 198-99
  conflict of with white nurses, xxxiii-iv, 173-
    74, 175
  and creation of positive self images, 178-79,
    181
  and Draft Nurse Bill, 197-98
  training institutions for, 170, 171-72
  images of in Black community, 163, 167-68,
    170-71, 176-78, 181
  and integration of nursing associations, 179-
    81, 199-200
  negative image of held by whites, 165, 174
  and nursing shortage during World War II,
    166-76, 196-97
  and social construction of gender and races,
    xxxiii, 168-70, 172-173
  See also American Nurses Association;
    Carnegie, Mary Elizabeth Lancaster;
    Davis, Frances Elliott; Johns, Ethel;
    NACGN; Rivers (Laurie), Eunice;
    Staupers, Mabel Keaton
Black Periodical Literature Project, 233
  See also Gates, Henry Louis
Black Power Movement, xviii
Black Rage, xviii
Black scholars
  and study of Black women, 232, 242-43
  support of by philanthropic foundations,
    231-33
  of Traditionalist group, 239-41
  See also Authenticists; Boone, Sylvia Arden;
    Collins, Patricia Hill; Gates, Henry Louis;
    hooks, bell; Hull, Gloria T.; White,
    E. Francis
Black Struggle, xix
Black studies, xxxiv,
  and administration of institutions, 224-25
  attracting faculty for, 227-28
  and concerns of NCBS, 226
  controversy over nomenclature, 223-24
  and curriculum, 227, 228

at Cornell, 229
and graduate degree programs, 229
poor image of during 1960s, 225-26
and institutional expediency, 226
and mainstream disciplines, 236-37
and need for intersectional analysis, 247
purpose of, 237-38
and structure of department, 224
at Temple, 229
and white administrators, 225
  See also Afrocentricity; Black Studies
    Movement; Black scholars
Black Studies Movement
  and activities of Black scholars, 229-31
Black women
  institution building by, 16
  literary achievements of, 24-26
  philanthropic work of, 109-11
  and protest movements, 19-21
  providing foundations for national
    organization, 12
  and reform movements of early nineteenth
    century, 9-12
  role of in Civil Rights Movement, 21, 22-24
  See also Black nurses; Black Women's history;
    Black women physicians; Michigan Black
    women; Sexual image of Black women;
    Suffrage
Black Women in America: An Historical
  Encyclopedia, xvii
Black Women's history
  and development of the discipline, 49-50
  dichotomies of, 3
  after Emancipation, 3
  and need for attention to class, 50, 52
  and need for crossover analysis, 50
  and womanist strategies, 51-50
Black Women in the Middle West Project
  (BWMW)
  launching of, xxiv-xxv, 49
  and primary source collection, xxiv-xxv
Black women physicians
  attitudes of Black male physicians toward,
    154
  and appointments to Black colleges, 156-57
  and community service, 155
  difficulties establishing practices, 154
  as enigma of late nineteenth and early
    twentieth century, 147
  and factors determining success of, 151-53
  marriage of, 158-60
  medical training of, 149-51
  and requirements for certification, 157-58
  See also Howard University; Meharry Medical
    College; National Medical Association;
    Woman's Medical College of Pennsylvania
Blackwell, Elizabeth, 148
  and Emily Blackwell, 155
  and Tenement House Service, 155
Blake, Jane
  Memoirs of Jane Blake, 35
Booker T. Washington Trade Association, 133

Boone, Mamie C., 138
Boone, Sylvia Arden
  *Radiance from the Waters: Concepts of Feminine
  Beauty in Mende Art*, 232
Boyd, Sara G., 152
Brooks, Sara, 46
  and contempt for prostitutes, 100
  on northern migration, 92, 94, 94-5, 101
Brown, Charlotte Hawkins
  and North Carolina State Federation of
  Women's Clubs, 113-14
Brown, Elsa Barkley
  and connection of theory and activism, xxxii
  and "womanist" consciousness, 131
Brown, Lucy Hughes, 151
  and Hospital and Nursing Training School,
  154-55
Bumfree, Isabella
  See Truth, Sojourner
Burch, Elizabeth
  and domestic violence, 101
  and separation of families during Great
  Migration, 93-94
  See also Great Migration
Burroughs, Nannie H.
  and Black women's fight for suffrage, 45
  and Jane Edna Hunter, 109, 122-24
  and National Baptist Convention Women's
  Auxiliary, 114
  and National Trades and Professional School
  for Women, 115

Carby, Hazel
  on rape as symbol of oppression, 37
Carnegie, Mary Elizabeth Lancaster
  admitted to Florida State Nurses Association,
  180-81
  and denial of appropriate titles to Black
  nurses, 164
  early nursing career of, 163-64, 179-80
Carnegie Corporation, 209-10
Chicago
  Black Panther Party of, xx
  and Democratic National Convention, xx
  riots of 1968, xix
Chinn, May E., 153, 154
Christian, Barbara, 232
Christian Industrial Club
  and Francis Harper Inn, 72
  and poor Black women, 72
Civil Rights Movement, xviii
  early roots of in club movement, 21-22
  and need for scholarly analysis, 21
  and Rosa Parks, 21-22
  See also Baker, Ella; Hamer, Fannie Lou
Clark, Mark
  murder of, xx
Clarke, John Henrik
  *The African World at the Crossroads: Notes for
  an African World Revolution*, 246-47
Cole, Rebecca J., 148
  and Charlotte Abbey, 155

at New York Infirmary for Women and
  Children, 155
  and Woman's Directory, 155-56
Collins, Patricia Hill
  Black Feminist Thought, 242
  and intersectional analysis, 242-43
Colored Ladies Benevolent Society, 65
"Communal womanist consciousness"
  of the Detroit Housewives' League, xxi-ii,
  79, 130-31, 143-44
  and female slave networks, 5-6
  See also Feminism
Consumer movements
  by white workers and unions during the
  Depression, 130-31
Cooper, Anna Julia
  on early Black volunteerist, 121
Craft, Ellen
  "Running a Thousand Miles for Freedom,"
  30
Crisis, 133
  See also Du Bois, W. E. B.
Crossover analysis
  See Intersectional analysis
"Crossover history"
  need for, xxix, 53-54
  and work of Black women historians, 53
  See also Lumpkin, Katherine Du Pre
Culture of dissemblance
  as analytical framework for historians, 47
  and development of, 37
  in institutionalized form, 44
  See also Dissemblance
Cyrus, Mary Clark
  and Underground Railroad in Detroit, 64

Dailey, Phyllis, 198
Daniel, Jack, 236-37
Dardenella Club
  and needs of Black children, 71
  See also Michigan Black women
Davis, Angela
  and slavery, 241
Davis, Frances Elliot Davis, 163
  and discriminatory treatment by American
  Red Cross, 165-66
  and positive self image, 178-79
Davis, Jackson
  See Rockefeller Foundation
Denison, Elizabeth
  and suit for freedom, 61
Detroit Anti-Slavery Society, 64
Detroit Association of Colored Women's
  Clubs, 73
Detroit Housewives' League, xxi
  and advancement groups, 80-81, 133-34
  and communal womanist consciousness, 79,
  130-31, 143-44
  confinement of activities of, 80, 140, 141
  as consultants to manufacturers, 139
  demise of, 143
  and economic nationalism, 78-80, 81, 141-42

expansion of political activities of, 81, 142-43
growth of, 79, 138-39
membership of, 81, 139, 142-43
origins of, 60, 78
under Fannie Peck, 78-79, 138-39
slogan of, 80, 140
Detroit Study Club
and exclusivity, 76
and growth from literary to social welfare
work, 75, 136-37
See also Johnson, Lillian E.
DeVries, James, E.
on police harassment of urban Blacks, 100
Dickson, Lynda F.
on sexual image of Black women, 90-91
Diop, Cheik Anta
*The African Origin of Civilization: Myth or
Reality,* 245
Dissemblance
and creation of *persona,* 43
definition of, xxviii, 37
as practiced by Black women, xxviii
as practiced by Jane Edna Hunter, 122
as problematic to historians, 43-44
skills perfected by domestic servants, 41-43
See also "Culture of dissemblance"; NACW
Dodd, William E
and assessment of ASNLH, 216-17
Draft Nurse Bill, 197
public outcry to, 197-98
Drake, St. Clair, xviii
and *Black Folk Here and There,* 245
Domestic servants
working conditions of, 39-40
See also Dissemblance; Grier, Elizabeth;
Katzman, David
Domestic violence
as contributor to culture of dissemblance, 37
and migration of Black women, 38-39
Douglass, Frederick
and migration from slavery, 87
Douglass, Sarah Mapps
at Female Anti-Slavery Convention in New
York City, 1837, 10
at Female Anti-Slavery Society of
Philadelphia, 9
and Angelina Grimké, 10
Downey, Virtea, xxiii
Du Bois, W. E. B, xxxvi
editor of *Crisis,* 133
and economic nationalism of NAACP, 137
Dunbar, Virginia, 189
Dunveor, Laura, 139
Dwelle, Georgia R., 158

Early, Sarah Woodson
early church leadership of, 6-7
See also Black churches
Economic nationalism
and white consumer movements, 131
and possible costs to Black women, 144-45
as practiced by Housewives' League, 60, 78-

80, 139
See also Du Bois, W. E. B.; Garvey, Marcus
Embree, Edwin, 220-21
See also Julius Rosenwald Fund
Employment discrimination
See Labor and Black women
Evans, Matilda Arabella
and Negro Health Association of South
Carolina, 155
Executive Order 8802, 184

Fair Employment Practices Committee, 184
Female slave resistance
via abortion, 30-31
by feigned pregnancy, 31-32
found in early slave narratives, 28-29
by infanticide, 32-34
and political and economic implications, 28,
34-36
and role of the "mammy," 27-28
to sexual oppression, 27-28
via sexual abstinence, 29-30
as threat to paternalism, 34
and white master's constructed view of slave
sexuality, 28-29
*Figures in Black: Words, Signs and the "Racial"
Self,* 233
Fleming, Walter E,
and assessment of ASNLH, 216-17
Flicke, Julia O., 191
Flint Medical College, 149
Ford Foundation
and overview of Black studies, 223-24, 235
Ford Motor Company
and discriminatory hiring practices, 105, 135
Forten, Harriet, Margaretta and Sarah
at Female Anti-Slavery Society of
Philadelphia, 9
Fourteenth Amendment, 148
Fowlkes, Jane Pauline
and domestic violence, 101
Franklin, John Hope, xviii
Free Black women
See Black women
Fuqua, Christine, 138

Garvey, Amy Jacques
role of in UNIA, 19
Garvey, Marcus, xxii
and Economic nationalism, 132-33, 137
Gates, Henry Louis
and Black Periodical Literature Project, 233
Genovese, Eugene, xxvii, 27-28
Roll Jordan Roll: The World the Slaves Made, 28
defines paternalism, 34
See also Female slave resistance
Giddings, Paula, xxviii
Glover, Sarah, 104
Gordon, Lincoln
See Detroit Housewives' League
Gottlieb, Peter
on "links in a migration chain," 94

Gragg, Rosa L. Slade
and Detroit Association of Colored Women's
Clubs, 73, 134
and Detroit Welfare Commission, 73, 140-
41
and National Association of Colored
Women, 74, 134
and Office of Civil Defense, 73, 140
and Slade Gragg Academy of Practical Arts,
73-74
Grand Rapids Study Club
exclusivity of, 76-77
and social welfare work during Depression,
76
See also Watson, Amanda Jones
Great Depression
impact of on Black American, 129-30
Great Migration, 18
and Black urbanization in Midwest, 87-88,
95
and Black women as "links in a migration
chain," 94-95
and Black women's search for employment,
39-41, 89, 90
and desire for personal autonomy, 40-41
and economic discrimination, 89
and escape from domestic violence, 100-
101
and escape from threat of rape, 40, 100
and patterns due to gender, 91-93
and "push and pull factors," 100-102
and separation of families, 93
See also Urbanization
Grier, Eliza Ann, 153
Grimké, Angelina
and Douglass, Sarah Mapps, 10
Grier, Florence
and sexual politics of domestic service, 42
Gutman, Herbert
and the Black family, 30-31
See also Female slave resistance

Hamer, Fannie Lou
at Democratic National Convention in
Atlantic City, 24
early life of, 23-24
and Mississippi Freedom Party, 24
Hamilton, Charles H., xviii
Hampton, Fred
murder of, xix
Harper, Francis Ellen Watkins
See Christian Industrial Club
Harris, Abraham L., 215
Harris, Ada
and reclamation of Norwood, 111-12
and upgrading of Black women's sexual
image, 112
Harris, Robert L., 235
Hart, Albert Bushnell, 208
See also ASNLH
Hartman, Susan H.
See Labor and Black women

Hastie, William H.
as civilian aide on Negro Affairs to Secretary
of State, 190, 194
and Mabel Keaton Staupers, 186-87
Haviland, Laura
See Underground Railroad
Hemsley, Ethel, 136
Henri, Florette
on Black women and employment during
World War I, 102
Herd, Shirley, xx-xxi, xxii-iv
See also Black Women in the Midwest
Project
Higginbotham, Evelyn Brooks, xix
hooks, bell, 232
and intersectional analysis, 242
Housewives' League
See Detroit Housewives' League
Hope, John, 220
Howard University
and education of Black women physicians,
149-50
Huggins, Nathan, 246
Hull, Gloria T.
All the Women are White, All the Blacks are
Men, But Some of Us are Brave: Black
Women's Studies, 231
Color, Sex and Poetry: Three Women Writers of
the Harlem Renaissance, 231
Give Us Each Day: The Diary of Alice Dunbar
Nelson, 231
Hunter, Jane Edna, xxxi, 15
and accumulation of wealth, 125-26
and Nannie Burroughs, 122-24
on death of Mary McCleod Bethune, 124-25
early life of, 115-17
early nursing career of, 116-17
and establishment of Phillis Wheatley
homes, 99-100, 118-19
leadership style of, 122
on northern migration to, 92-93
response of to Draft Nurse bill, 198
See also Dissemblance
Hurston, Zora Neale, 215

Institution building
by local Black women, 16
Intersectional analysis
and Black feminist scholars, 242-43
Iona R. Whipper Home Inc. for Unwed
Mothers, 157

Jack, James W.
characterizes Black women as prostitutes, 13-
14
Jackson, Eva Radden
and Women's City Council of Detroit, 73
Jackson, John G.
African Civilization, 245
Jackson, Rebecca Cox
splits with Bethel AME Church, 8
and founding of Black Shaker sisterhood, 8

Jackson State University, xx
Jacobs, Harriet, 51
Jameson, J. Franklin, 209
Jim Crow practices
  in Armed Forces, xxxiv
  in light of New Deal legislation, 184
  in nursing profession, xxxiv
Johns, Ethel, xxxiv
  report of on white nurses' image of Black
    nurses, 174, 175-76
  See also Black nurses
Johnson, Halle Tanner Dillon, 151, 152
  appointed to Tuskegee Institute, 156-57
Johnson, Lillian E. E.
  and Detroit Study Club, 74-75, 136-37
Jones, Elizabeth, 178
Jones, Jacqueline, xxvi, xxviii, 232
  on "links in a migration chain," 94
Jones, James H.
  studies of Tuskegee syphilis experiment,
    167-68
  See also Rivers (Laurie), Eunice
Jones, Thomas Jesse, 208
  and Report on Negro Education in the U.S.A.,
    213
  See also ASNLH
Jones, Verina Morton, 151, 157, 160
Journal of Negro History, 205, 208-9, 221
Julius Rosenwald Fund
  and ASNLH, 212-13
  ends support for ASNLH, 220-21
  supports NACGN, 185-86
  See also Rosenwald, Julius

Katzman, David
  on Great Migration, 38
Keckley, Elizabeth
  and Contraband Relief Foundation, 11-12
  See also Female slave resistance
Kenney, John A., 172
Kent State University, xix
Kessler-Harris, Alice
  on Black women and employment after
    World War I, 117
King, Wilma, xxviii
  See also Crossover history
Kirk, Norman T.
  See Staupers, Mabel Keaton
Klingberg, Frank J., 215
Kuhn, Thomas S.
  The Structure of Scientific Revolutions, 50
Kusmer, Kenneth
  on Phillis Wheatley Homes, 120

Labor and Black women
  after Great Migration, 18, 39-40
  and creation of stratified work force, 103
  exclusion of from industry, 103-4, 117
  and government inaction, 105
  during Progressive Era, 134-35
  and racism of white women, 104
  and white justifications for discrimination,
    104-5

during World War I, 18, 102-3
during World War II, 18-19, 135-36
  See also Black women's history; Washington,
    Mary Ellen
Laura Spelman Rockefeller Memorial
  (LSRM)
  See Woodson, Carter G.
Lee, Jarena
  as itinerant preacher, 7-8
  and Rev. Richard Allen, 7-8
Lee, Rebecca, 148
Leonard Medical School, 149
Lerner, Gerda, xxvi
Levine, Lawrence W.
  on non-economic migratory motivations, 40,
    91
Lincoln, Mary Todd
  See Keckley, Elizabeth
Literary achievements of Black women, 24-26
  See also Black scholars
Lucas, Veronica
  and Detroit Association of Colored Women's
    Clubs, 73
Lull, George F., 191
Lumpkin, Katherine Du Pre
  as example of need for crossover history, 53-
    56, 57
  The Making of a Southerner, 53, 54
  and lives of lower class whites, 56-57
  and rejection of white supremacy ideology,
    54-56
Lynch, Hollis, xvii
Lynching
  as metaphor of oppression, xxvii
  as threat Black men, 17-18
  See also Wells-Barnett, Ida B.
Lynk, M. Vandehurst, 148
  See also Black medical schools

Magee, James C., 190
McClellan, Alonzo C., 155
  See also Brown, Lucy Hughes
McCoy, Mary Delaney
  as "Mother of Clubs," 68
McKane, Alice Woodby, 160
McKay, Nellie, 235
"Making community"
  by Black nurses, xxxiii, xxxiv
  definition of, xxii
  and philanthropic work, 109
  in response to migration and urbanization of
    Blacks, xxx-xi
  See also Michigan Black women
Meharry Medical School, 149
  and hiring of graduates, 150
  See also Wells, Josie
Meier, August, xix
  studies Detroit labor unions, 105
  See also Ford Motor Company
Meyerowitz, Joanne J.
  on Christian Industrial Club, 72
  and "women adrift," 110
  on working conditions for Chicago Black

women, 117
Michigan Black women
and "domestic feminism" of 1900-20, 59-60
and establishment of antebellum clubs, 64-65
and gender roles in antebellum period, 83-84
and making community, 59-60
and Michigan Black codes, 61-62
and pioneer phase, 59
and population growth before Civil War, 62-64
role of in antislavery cause, 63-64
and scarcity of documentation of activities, 82
and self determination phase, 60
See also Black club women; Denison, Elizabeth; Housewives' League of Detroit; Richards, Fannie; Truth, Sojourner
Migration
due to slavery, 87
See also Great Migration
Moody, Ann
Coming of Age in Mississippi, 21
Morgan, Kathryn L.
Children of Strangers, 40
Morris, Aldon D.
on roles of Black women in Civil Rights Movement, 21, 22-24
Morrison, Toni
Tar Baby, 25
Mother's Club of Kalamazoo, 74
Mother's Star of Hope Club, 71-72

National Association for the Advancement of Colored People (NAACP), xxxi
National Association of Colored Graduate Nurses (NACGN), xxxiii, 20
dissolution of, 199-200
during Great Depression, 185-86
Julius Rosenwald Fund supports, 185
networking activities of, 188
and partial integration to Army Nurses Corps, 191-92
Rockefeller Foundation supports, 185-86
and struggle for acceptance, 164-65
See also Staupers, Mabel Keaton
National Association of Colored Women's Clubs (NACW)
creation of, 14, 70, 120-21, 131
and defense of Black women's sexual image, 45
and dissemblance, 44
and Phillis Wheatley Homes, 70
preamble of constitution, 131
National Black Nurses' Association, 181
National Council for Black Studies (NCBS)
See Black studies
National Council of Negro Women, xxiii
founding of, 17, 20
objectives of, 20-21
National Defense Council
See National Nursing Council for War Service

National Housewives' League of America
as modeled after Detroit Housewives' League, 133-34, 138
National Medical Association
and participation of Black women, 158
in response to exclusionary practice of AMA, 158
National Nursing Council for War Service, 188
National Urban League, xxxi
Navy Nurse Corps
excludes Black nurses, 194-95
Naylor, Gloria
The Women of Brewster Place, 25
Negro Revolution, 183
Negro Convention Movement, 64
Negro history
See Black studies; Woodson, Carter G.
Negro World
See Garvey, Amy Jacques
New Deal, 183
and Jim Crow practices, 184
"New History," 206-15
"New Negro"
and need for understanding of consciousness of, 106
Northwest Ordinance (1787)
prohibits slavery in Midwest, 61
No Time for Prejudice
See Staupers, Mabel Keaton

Originists
distancing of Traditionalists from, 246
as subset of Authenticist Black Studies scholars, 244
as threat to Black studies, 246-47
See also Bernal, Martin; Diop, Cheik Anta; Drake, St. Clair; Jackson, John G.; Van Sertima, Ivan

Page, Catherine
See Christian Industrial Club
Painter, Nell
See Crossover history
Paternalism
defined by Eugene Genovese, 34
Paul, Susan
at Boston Female Anti-Slavery Society, 9-10
Peck, Fannie
and Detroit Housewives' League, 78-79, 137
at lecture by M. A. L. Holsey, 78, 137-38
and William H. Peck, 76
See also Detroit Housewives' League
Perkins, Linda
and concept of "racial uplift," 13
Philanthropic work of Black women
difference from white philanthropy, 110-11
self help tradition of, 109
See also Harris, Ada; Hunter, Jane Edna; "Making community"
Phillis Wheatley Association
See Phillis Wheatley Homes

Phillis Wheatley Homes
  as alternative to prostitution, 119
  founding of, 118
  support for by white women, 119-20
Phillis Wheatley Sanitarium and Nursing
    Training School, 16, 45
  as alternative to prostitution, 99-100
Physicians
  See Black male physicians; Black women
    physicians
Political consciousness, 135-36
Powers, Harriet
  and "The Bible Quilts," 6
Preston, Frances E.
  See Temperance movements
Progressive Era
  and Black institution building, 132
Prostitution
  arrest statistics for in Nashville and Atlanta,
    14
  and efforts of Black women's organizations,
    45, 99-100
  economic function of in urban society, 99,
    119
  as synonymous with rape in American
    society, 46
  See also Hunter, Jane; Phillis Wheatley
    Homes; Sexual image of Black women
Protest movements and Black women
  and formation of National Council of Negro
    Women, 20
  in response to economic subordination, 19-21
  in support of A. Philip Randolph's March on
    Washington, 20
  UNIA, 19-20
  See also Civil Rights Movement
"Push" and "Pull" factors of migration
  See Great Migration; Urbanization

Quakers, 62
Quilting
  during slavery, 6

"Racial uplift"
  as linked to racial obligation, 13
  and mobilization movement of Black women
    during 1890s, 13-15
  See also Black club women
Rape
  literary expressions of, 38-39
  as metaphor of oppression, xxvii-ix, 37
  migration as response to, xxix-xx, 38-39, 40
Remond, Sara Parker, 10
Richards, Fannie, 66-67
  and Joseph Workman v. Board of Education of
    Detroit, 67
Riddle, Estelle Massey
  and appointment to American Nurses'
    Association, 179
  and leadership of NACGN, 185-86
  and NCNW, 20
Rivers (Laurie), Eunice, 163

and Tuskegee syphilis experiment, 167-68,
    176-78
  See also Black nurses
Rockefeller Foundation
  and Jackson Davis, 219-20
  supports ASNLH, 219-20
Rosenwald, Julius
  supports ASNLH, 219
  See also Julius Rosenwald Fund
Roosevelt, Eleanor
  See Staupers, Mabel
Rudwick, Elliot
  See Meier, August
Ruffin, Josephine St. Pierre
  response of to James W. Jack, 14
  See also "Racial Uplift"

Sage: A Scholarly Journal on Black Women, 49
Seymour, Marion B., 191-92
Sexual division of labor
  during slavery, 56
Sexual image of Black women
  as impediment to economic and social
    development, 126-27
  and goals of Black women's organizations,
    15, 44-45, 90, 112-13
  as motive propelling Black migration, 90-92
  after slavery, 13-15
  See also Black club women; Female slave
    resistance; Prostitution; Slavery
Slavery
  and construction of sexual self by Black
    women, 4-5, 241
  gender relationships between slaves, 5-6
  familial roles played by women during, 4-5
  and female slave networks, 5-6
  "peculiar institution," xxvii, 4
  and traditional Black scholarship, 240
  and white plantation mistresses, 4
  See also Female slave resistance
Smith, Amanda Berry
  as itinerant preacher and missionary, 8-9
Society of Friends
  and resettlement of ex-slaves in Midwest, 62
"Southern leaves blown north," 40
Spear, Allan W.
  on limited employment for Blacks, 103
Sprague, Rosetta
  address of to Federation of Afro-American
    Women, 90
Staupers, Mabel Keaton, 163
  and Mary Beard, 189-90
  and Frances Payne Bolton, 188
  and Booker T. Washington Sanatorium, 178
  and exchange with Norman T. Kirk over
    nursing draft, 196-97
  as executive secretary of NACGN, 166, 179,
    184, 186
  and integration to American Nurses
    Association, 179
  and integrating Armed Forces Nurse Corps,
    166-67, 179, 186-99

on migration of ancestors, 87
and New York Tuberculosis and Health
 Association, 179
No Time for Prejudice, 179
as recipient of Spingarn Medal of 1951, 200
response of to Draft Nurse Bill, 197-98
and Eleanor Roosevelt, 166-67, 188, 195-96
Stevenson, Brenda, xxviii
Steward, Susan Smith McKinney, 148, 159-60
Stewart, Maria
 address before Afric-American Female
  Intelligence Society of Boston, 9
 agenda of for Black liberation, 50
Stewart, Sallie Wyatt, 15-16
Stimson, Henry, 190
Straker, D. Augustus
 address of to convention of Michigan
  Colored Women's Clubs, 70-71, 133
Suffrage
 and antebellum free Black women's
  involvement, 9-11
 See also Douglass, Sarah Mapps

Taylor, A. A., 210-11
Temperance movements
 in Detroit, 65-66
Tenement House Service, 155
Terrell, Mary Church
 and NACW, 14-15, 44
 See also "Racial Uplift"
Thompson, Sara
 and Women's Republican Research Club,
  74
Thurman, Lucy Smith
 and Black women's club movement, 66
 and Michigan State Association of Colored
  Women's clubs, 70-71, 133
Toodle, Hattie, 138
Trotter, Joe
 on Black women's exclusion from industry in
  Milwaukee, 103
Truth, Sojourner
 "Ain't I a Woman" speech, 11
 as itinerant preacher, 8
 at Women's Rights Convention in Akron,
  Ohio (1851), 11
 at Equal Rights Association convention
  (1867), 11, 63, 64
Tubman, Harriet, 51, 87
Tucker, Susan
 on culture of women in male dominated
  society, 37-38
Turner, Lorenzo Dow, xviii
Tuskegee Institute, 132
Tuskegee syphilis experiment, 167-68
 See also Rivers (Laurie), Eunice
Tyree, Sarah D.
 and deliberate celibacy, 97-98
 See also Birth rates

Urbanization
 and Black employment in Midwest, 102

and need for study of social class formation,
 106-7
and police harassment of Blacks, 100
and prostitution, 99-100
and southernization of Midwest, 95, 106
 See also Birth rates
Underground Railroad, 62
Universal Negro Improvement Association
 (UNIA)
 See Garvey, Amy Jacques; Garvey, Marcus

Van Sertima, Ivan
 *They Came Before Columbus: The African
  Presence in Ancient America*, 245
Voting Rights Act, xviii

Wald, Lillian, 175
Walker, Alice
 The Color Purple, 25
 and womanist consciousness, 25
Walker, Maggie Lena
 on activism, xxxii
Washington, Booker T., xxiii, 170
 and nursing program at Tuskegee Institute,
  171-72
 See also Black nurses
Washington, Mary Ellen
 on Black women and employment in
  Midwest, 102, 134-35
Washington, Mary Margaret
 See "Racial Uplift"
Watson, Amanda Jones, 91
Wells-Barnett, Ida B., 15
 anti lynching activities of, 17-18
 withdraws from NAACP, 18
Wells, Josie, 150
Wesley, Charles H., 215
West, Gertrude J., 141
Western Journal of Black Studies, xxvii
Whipper, Iona R., 157
White, Deborah Gray, xxviii
 See also Dissemblance; Slavery
White, E. Francis
 *Sierra Leone's Settler Women Traders: Women
  on the Afro-European Frontier*, 231-32
White women
 oppose economic opportunity for Black
  women, 103-4
White women's history
 and crossover history, 53
 See also Lumpkin, Katherine Du Pre
Williams, Daniel Hale, 170, 171
 See also Black nurses
Williams, Fannie Barrier
 and Black female militancy after
  Emancipation, 12-13
 on sexual image of Black women, 126-27
Williams, Selase W., 235
Williams, William Appleman, xviii
Willow Run, 135
"Womanist" consciousness
 of Detroit Housewives' League, 131

See also "Communal" consciousness; Walker, Alice
Woman's Directory, 155-56
  See also Cole, Rebecca J.
Woman's Medical College of Pennsylvania, 150-51
Women's City Council of Detroit
  and summer camps for poor children, 73
Women's Political Council
  role of in Montgomery Bus Boycott, 22
  and Jo Ann Robinson, 22
Women's Temperance Union
  See Temperance movements
Woodson, Carter G., xxi
  and Association for the Study of Negro Life and History, 205-22
  and Carnegie Institution, 209-10
  education and early teaching career of, 203-4
  and fundraising for ASNLH, 208-10
  and influence of white historians, 206-7

and *Journal of Negro History,* 205
and LSRM, 210, 211, 215
and pressure to affiliate with Black institution, 215-216, 218-21
and support from Jameson and Schlesinger, 217-18
World War II
  and advances of Black Americans, 183-84
  and economic resurgence, 184
  and increased need for nurses, 185
  and integration of Black personnel, 190
  and segregation of Armed Forces, 185, 190-91
  See also Black nurses
Wright, Mary
  See Quilting

Young Women's Christian Association, 16
  and discrimination against Black women, 132